American Foreign Policy and Yugoslavia, 1939–1941

American Foreign Policy and Yugoslavia, 1939–1941

IVO TASOVAC

Texas A&M University Press
College Station

The paper used in this book meets the minimum requirements
of the American National Standard for Permanence
of Paper for Printed Library Materials, Z39.48-1984.
Binding materials have been chosen for durability.

For a complete list of books in print in this series, see the back of the book.

Library of Congress Cataloging-in-Publication Data

Tasovac, Ivo.
    American foreign policy and Yugoslavia, 1939–1941 / Ivo Tasovac. —
    1st ed.
        p.   cm. — (Eastern European Studies ; no. 11)
    Includes bibliographical references (p.   ) and index.
    ISBN 0-89096-897-7 (cloth : alk. paper)
        1. United States — Foreign relations — Yugoslavia.   2. Yugoslavia —
    Foreign relations — United States.   3. United States — Foreign
    relations — 1933–1945.   4. World War, 1939–1945 — Balkan Peninsula.
    I. Title.   II. Series: Eastern European studies (College Station, Tex.) ; no. 11.
    E183.8.Y8T37   1999
    327.730497'09'043 — dc21   99-25263
                                                                        CIP

Contents

Series Editor's Statement

Whether or not one wants to refer to the era in which we live as one of postmodernism and deconstruction, it is clear that political leaders are no longer treated with the automatic awe and respect that went along with their office in bygone days. Whether dead or alive, political leaders in the United States no longer hold a privileged position. Nowadays, one will read books about Thomas Jefferson's sexual indiscretions, George Washington's hypocrisy on owning slaves, even the social construction of Abraham Lincoln's image as the Great Emancipator, given that many people hated him deeply, in the North and South. The current president, Bill Clinton, is praised for his job performance at the same time that the entire world is privy to intimate details of his sex life, a state of affairs that would have been unimaginable a generation ago. Films have been made about Nixon, Truman, and Kennedy that expose their human and often times darker sides. Similarly, scores of books have been written about Franklin D. Roosevelt, from his sexual affairs to his alleged orchestration of getting the United States involved into World War II. This book by Ivo Tasovac rides the wave of this current deconstructionist attack on U.S. presidents in general and Roosevelt in particular. What is unique about Tasovac's book, however, is the focus on a neglected aspect of U.S. foreign policy toward Yugoslavia.

Thus, Tasovac is filling a black hole in such scholarship, namely, Roosevelt's attitudes and policies toward Eastern Europe in general and Yugoslavia in particular. The recent wars in the former Yugoslavia that began in 1991, and are still smoldering in Kosovo (as of this writing) demonstrate clearly that most people—professional analysts and laypersons alike—do not have a clue as to how Yugoslavia was created, by whom, and for what reasons. It was just assumed by most people that Yugoslavia was a voluntary association of several Slavic ethnic groups, run mostly by Serbs for the good of all, and that it functioned much better than the Soviet Union. After all, the common wisdom went, there was no Iron Curtain surrounding Yugoslavia. After all, scholars would say, Yugoslavia had self-management and other quasi-capitalistic practices. You could buy nylons and chocolates in Yugoslavia when such things could only be dreamed of in Czechoslovakia or Hungary. These are the neat, tidy, and hopelessly superficial images of Yugoslavia that have informed much of American foreign policy in the present century. When Slovenia, Croatia, Macedonia, Kosovo, and Bosnia-Herzegovina, demanded their independence from Belgrade in the 1990s, *most* journalists, diplomats, and persons in general could not understand the reasons why.

Tasovac demonstrates that Roosevelt, along with Churchill and Stalin, made some deals and decisions regarding Yugoslavia that had and continue to have far-reaching consequences for that country in the present century—and will no doubt continue to affect the next century. There was no Yugoslavia prior to 1918. Croatia and Slovenia were part of the Austro-Hungarian Empire and most of the rest of what came to be called Yugoslavia was emerging from the Balkan Wars for independence from the Ottoman Empire. The first Yugoslavia was, in reality, a Serbian dictatorship, and Croatia and Slovenia wanted independence from it in the 1930s. Tasovac makes it clear that Roosevelt wanted to prop up and maintain a synthetic Yugoslavia in order to contain the Nazis. The British were even more deeply implicated in the eventual conceptual morass that persists to this day as to the "liberation" versus "fascist" tendencies of Chetniks, Ustashe, Communists, and other groups they played against each other, all for the sake of slowing down Hitler and making it harder for him to finish off Europe. What Tasovac uncovers is that with these motives and the actions they took, Roosevelt and the British had unwittingly sown the seeds of another Balkan War in the present century, the one that began in 1991 and still has not really ended.

Tasovac makes a compelling case for this interpretation with the use of hitherto unused archival material. The consequences of this new insight are far-reaching. If Roosevelt and the British sold the Croats, Slovenes and others to Belgrade for the sake of a "higher cause," much like they gave away much of Eastern Europe to the Soviet Union, then the general understanding of the Balkans as the alleged pit of ancient tribal hatreds must be reevaluated. The hatreds in the Balkans are neither ancient nor intrinsic to the Balkan people. Had Serbia gone her own cultural way, in the direction of Russia, and the other regions of Yugoslavia in the direction of the West, the history of Europe in this century would have been entirely different. But before Western analysts can begin to conceptualize alternative historical scenarios, and political scientists can thereby begin to imagine alternatives for the future other than continued Serbian domination of Kosovars and others who clearly do not want to be dominated any longer, some of the unpleasant truths found in this book must be confronted first. While some of the facts that Tasovac uncovers in this book might have been shocking a generation ago, and might not have found a publisher willing to question the immense prestige of Roosevelt, humanity has matured, or at least become more cynical about its leaders since then. The time is ripe for a critical assessment of Roosevelt's role in the Yugoslav nightmare that seems to never end.

Stjepan G. Meštrović
Series Editor

American Foreign Policy and Yugoslavia, 1939–1941

Introduction

The twenty-three years of royal Yugoslavia's existence (1918–41) can be described best as a political nightmare. Considering that Yugoslavia was conceived in the minds of non-Serbian intellectuals (mostly Croatians) as a truly democratic and federated state, with all national groups sharing equal power and responsibilities, the reason for such a turn of events is not simple. Yet it is less complicated than believed by many learned scholars sharing a strong belief that Yugoslavia, no matter how badly it turned out, was by virtue of its role in the post-World War I order, virtually irreplaceable.

Given the Serbian state-building practices rooted in the "right of the sword," one therefore could say that Yugoslavia appeared on the stage of history as an act of faith rather than a well-thought-out political system offering a realistic solution to the needs of peoples with diverse traditions and expectations. The Serbian establishment accepted the new state because it offered a convenient protection for the realization of Serbia's expansionist dreams, while the victorious powers saw in it a useful means to an end (i.e., keeping postwar Europe in check).

Before the war ended, von Südland, the nom de plume of the Croatian scholar Ivo Pilar, refuted any illusion about the future southern Slavic state. In his book *Die Südslavische Frage und der Weltkrieg: Ubersichtliche Darstellung des Gesampt-Problems* published in Vienna in 1918, Pilar, by analyzing the socio-historical aspects of the southern Slavic states' development, especially Serbia's state-building pattern and its well-concealed expansionist design, uncovered the pitfalls facing the new state. From reading the book one arrives at the unmistakable conclusion that, given the Serbian tradition, Yugoslavia would eventually become an extension of greater Serbia. Pilar's book, however, instead of helping to elucidate the problems, experienced a strange fate. No sooner had the book come out, the Serbian government destroyed the entire edition. Few copies remained, with one of the remaining copies coming into President Harding's hands.[1] One cannot say with certainty if President Harding or any of his subordinates read it, but the book had no impact on the Versailles peace-makers. As predicted by Pilar, Yugoslavia, supposedly built on the Wilsonian principles of self-determination, became in practice a war acquisition for greater Serbia.

How Yugoslavia was ruled became a grave concern among Yugoslavia's friends abroad, especially after the 1928 assassination of the Croatian leadership in the Belgrade Parliament following King Alexander's dictatorship. The pitfalls could no longer be ignored if Yugoslavia was to survive.

In 1933, a book appeared in Paris, *La Guerre Revient,* written by French publicist Henri Pozzi. The book was translated (with additional material) into English as *Black Hand over Europe* (1935); thirty thousand copies were published in London. Since 1912, Pozzi's intimate knowledge of the inner workings of Balkan politics gave him a clear picture of Yugoslavia's internal and external problems, which he felt threatened peace in the area and within Europe as well. The following passage illustrates quite accurately his assessment of the sociopolitical condition within the nascent state:

> You will notice that I speak of Serbia and not of Yugoslavia. I do it deliberately because the latter is a mere hybrid that exists by and for Serbia. All that is called Yugoslavia is in reality only Serbia, for all who act, all who command, all who count in any way at all in the affairs of the nation are Serbians. The other have no influence at all upon the shaping of the national life. Considering also that the great mass of the Serbian people are illiterate, possessing the mentality of two centuries gone, it would be fair to say that Yugoslavia is not even Serbia—it is Belgrade.[2]

The French government of Doumerque-Barthau, most likely because of Pozzi's criticizing Belgrade, issued him a stern warning to the effect that no one but he would be "responsible for his hide" if he continued to openly criticize the French ally.[3]

Following the publication of Pozzi's book, two other books criticizing the Belgrade regime appeared in Paris in the same year. *La Dictature du Roi Alexandre* was published by Svetozar Pribičević, an overly enthusiastic Serb from Croatia who worked furiously to "unite" Croatia with Serbia at any price, including the obliteration of the Croatian national identity. Having fulfilled the role of a Shakespearean Moor, Pribičević outlived his usefulness to Belgrade and was ousted from the Serbian fold by King Alexander himself. He then joined the Croatians in their struggle for decentralization and democratization of the state. His book, written in exile, expressed strong condemnation of Serbian political practices, including those of the king. Furthermore, having renounced his former role, he realized that only a democracy based on federal principles, as advanced by Croatians, could save Yugoslavia from its ultimate destruction.[4]

Taking into account a general European situation, site of fascism, and gradual decline of the Versailles Order, two other Frenchmen, Ernest Pezet and Henri Simondet, published *La Yugoslavie en Peril* several months after Pribičević's book. Although Pezet was a deputy in the French Parliament and a member of the Foreign Relations Committee and Simondet a professor of political science, neither knew much about Croatian or Serbian history. Despite lacking the expositional brilliance of Pozzi, they nonetheless demonstrated that Yugoslavia was indeed in peril of splitting apart unless changes were made. They also advocated the repudiation of Alexander's dictatorship and promoted parliamentary democracy.

Moved by the same ill foreboding, some of the British intellectuals, too, were worried, especially those who were among the architects of the Yugoslav unification. R. W. Seton-Watson and Wickham Steed shared their concerns and decided to speak up. Unless Alexander shifted his policy toward parliamentary democracy and found some equitable solution for non-Serbian nationalities, they believed that Yugoslavia would go under in blood and destruction. Letters to leading English papers were sent to that effect. One of them was signed by seventeen intellectuals concerned about the future of Yugoslavia.

To avert such a gruesome possibility, R. W. Seton-Watson wrote a lengthy memorandum to Yugoslavia's friends in the Little Entente countries and to the British ambassador to Belgrade, Sir Nevile Henderson, in May 1930.[5] He emphasized that Yugoslavia was drifting toward a police state and if the conditions were not ameliorated, the consequences could be costly for Yugoslavia and Europe as well. He pointed out at the end:

> Those who defended the cause of Serbia before the public opinion of the West during the Great War and who watch her present development in increasing disillusionment have the duty to make abundantly clear that should the misgovernment of Yugoslavia again lead to European complication, her rulers need not again look for moral or material support to Britain, where they have in this eleven years recklessly squandered almost all of the immense moral sympathy and capital which Serbia's role in the war had won for them.[6]

Sir Nevile thanked Seton-Watson for "an immense amount of food for reflection," but in the next letter was very careful not to commit himself in terms of exerting any influence on Alexander with regard to his dictatorial policy. As much as he loved the Yugoslavs, Sir Nevile attributed their existing difficulties to past experiences for which they were not always to blame. Nonetheless, he stressed, reflecting the British government's position, he was not there for Yugoslavia per se, but for the country whose stability and consolidation he regarded as a British interest.[7] Apparently Sir Nevile and the British government believed that stability and consolidation could come about only from within, and not from outside pressure. The same attitude was taken by the governments of other victorious powers including the United States, which had a stake in post–World War I Europe, and especially in maintaining the status quo.

In the United States, an American writer of Slovenian descent, Louis Adamic, published a book in 1934 titled *The Native's Return: An American Immigrant Visits Yugoslavia and Discovers His Old Country*. The book was better than anything previously written on Yugoslavia and was highly praised by the critics, not so much for its political insights as for its style and easy readability that appealed to the American public. What the critics praised most corresponded to the established American image of the Balkans as being colorful, disunited, dangerous, and unpredictable—in short, a quaint place but one having a potential explosion that should be kept under control. Regarding the politics in Yugoslavia, the influential journal *Foreign Affairs* pointed out that Adamic's views were somewhat naive with respect to his political appraisals. True, Americans disliked dictatorships, especially the ones unfriendly to the United States, but Yugoslavia was regarded as a friendly country. Washington therefore adopted the same policy as other victorious powers vis-à-vis Belgrade.

The attitude of noninterference outlived Alexander's assassination in 1935 and survived through 1939. This policy was by no means motivated by respect for Yugoslavia's sovereignty, but was a silence calculated on self-interest. As the client state of the victorious powers, the nascent Yugoslavia was assigned a special role in the region. As a member of the Little Entente, it guarded, together with Czechoslovakia and Rumania, the "revisionists" (i.e., Austria and Hungary); as a member of the Balkan Pact, along with Greece and Turkey, it kept watch over Bulgaria. With the rise of the fascist powers, especially Nazi Germany, the value of Serbian military prowess rose, which in reality amounted to very little. The Yugoslav army remained exclusively under Serbian command. Enchanted by their past glory, they felt no need to restructure the army along multinational lines, or to upgrade it to meet the standards of modern warfare.

A French officer on an official visit to Yugoslavia put it rather succinctly: "If war came about, we would not even be able to communicate with the Yugoslav army."[8] It therefore remained an antiquated institution, badly equipped and corrupt; it was a typical byproduct of the Balkan Wars, given Serbia's war-waging practices of liberation against the waning Ottoman Empire. Such conditions notwithstanding, the Czechoslovak president, Thomas Massaryk, known as a staunch democrat and an influential Little Entente politician, chose to disregard Yugoslavia's internal affairs on the grounds that the Serbian army was too great a threat.[9] Granted, "advice" from the allied government was channeled to Belgrade on occasion to put its internal affairs in order; yet the Serbians never took them very seriously. It therefore amounted to no more than a gentle slap on the Serbian wrist. Guided by their national interests and counting on the alleged Serbian military strength when needed, the victorious powers allowed the Belgrade regime literally to get away with murder.

The events of 1939 (e.g., the destruction of the Czech Republic and the Nazi-Soviet pact), as a prelude to the occupation of Poland, prompted the badly prepared democracies to take closer notice of Yugoslavia's domestic affairs; by then it was too late. The Yugoslav ideology, which was never strong and was meant to operate as a unifying factor, was as good as dead. Because of it, the hostility of Yugoslavia's neighboring states was regarded as a powerful incentive for the oppressed non-Serbian nationalities to look for salvation outside Yugoslavia. On the eve of war, Yugoslavia was left without any inner cohesive power. This prompted the British government, after many years of silence, to advise Prince Paul (who had become regent after Alexander's death in 1934) to strike an equitable agreement with the Croatians.[10] Oddly enough, the same suggestion was extended to Paul by both Hitler and Mussolini.

This anomaly may be explained and understood in terms of Yugoslavia's shaky domestic conditions. Looking for friends abroad, Alexander fixed his gaze on Germany. Sooner than other European monarchs, he perceived the growing importance of Nazi Germany. Friendly relations toward Nazi Germany were beneficial for Alexander's regime in more than one way. They offered a large German market (which Yugoslavia could not find elsewhere) for Yugoslavia's agricultural products, as well as raw materials indispensable for Germany's industrial recovery, in exchange for German industrial products. Furthermore, trade development with Germany relaxed Yugoslavia's dependency upon the British and the French whose policies of national interests were not always in conformity with the interests of their junior partners. More importantly, German commercial interests in the Balkans allowed peaceful incursions into the region, the importance of which, for both Germany and Yugoslavia, became gradually apparent. It furthermore impeded Mussolini,

Alexander's principal rival for domination of the Balkans, from making any significant strides in the area. In turn, under the surface of the Axis unity, it created a strong rivalry between Rome and Berlin, which became a strong ingredient in the making of Yugoslavia's foreign policy.

On the debit side, mutual German-Yugoslav commercial interdependency created the base for a political one as well. Thus the Croato-Serbian Agreement signed in August 1939, hardly ameliorated Yugoslavia's position, but its cosmetic appearance was conveniently taken as a show of unity to be used by the Allies. In fact, it made unity all the more precarious. After the fall of France, Mussolini's invasion of Greece, and the additional German resolve to intervene on Italy's behalf to save it from military disaster, the "traditional" Serbian allies, Britain and the United States, were no longer happy with Yugoslavia's neutral policy. They desired a strict neutrality, but one, they insisted, that was benevolent vis-à-vis Greece and the Allies. In practice, it meant war with Germany. Any change in Yugoslavia's policy that might disturb peace in the Balkans and thereby cut short Germany's supply line necessary for its war effort, would be interpreted in Berlin as a hostile act. Rupture of the relations with Berlin would offer a possibility, the British believed, of creating a unified Balkan front with far reaching consequences, including the defeat of Germany by bringing in the Russians in the absence of American military intervention. This was an idea attractive to Roosevelt whose actions were still restricted by neutrality laws.

To make a stand in the Balkans was therefore a joint Anglo-American show. In this fanciful but clever strategic equation, Yugoslavia was assigned the leading role, provided the new Yugoslav leadership would go along. If they refused the British had a "trump card" of which Americans were thoroughly informed. This consisted of an organized military group backed by pan-Serbian intellectuals, conservative politicians, and the Serbian Orthodox Church, that would carry out a putsch to replace the "appeasers" of the new government. The putsch was accomplished on March 27, 1941, and by April 16, Yugoslavia was no longer in existence.

The shock of the sudden collapse is still debated among historians. Indeed, impressive literature has been written on the events surrounding the putsch and the collapse of Yugoslavia. Most disappointing is the fact that few of these writings ever tackled the larger implications of the Anglo-American Balkan strategy, consequently failing to juxtapose the sudden collapse of Yugoslavia with such a strategy. Because history usually is written from the victor's point of view, an excuse for the collapse was found among Croatian "appeasers." In fact, the most vocal "appeasers" in the government were two Serbian ministers, the foreign minister Aleksandar Cincar Marković and the war minister, General Milan Nedić, who was dismissed from his ministerial post shortly before Yugoslavia's accession to the Tripartite Pact. Not surprisingly, General Nedić became the most ardent quisling in wartime Serbia. Even if this argument were correct, the point is that the British and the Americans knew very well that internally, Yugoslavia was too weak to undertake such a role. After winning the election in 1939, President Roosevelt was bombarded by memoranda from Croatian-Americans warning him about the poisonous condition of Yugoslavia's internal affairs. Like his European counterparts, he too ignored the warnings and gave full support to the British Balkan strategy upon the assumption that the Serbs could do the job alone.

As the above-mentioned books clearly demonstrate, the Allies, including the Americans, cannot be excused by pleading ignorance of Yugoslavia's internal affairs. They based their policy not on facts, but on Serbian fables of invincibility. Here one faces the full impact of the American folk aphorism: "It is much better to know nothing then to know which ain't true." The extent to which these fables of invincibility were pervasive is well illustrated by the American military attaché in Belgrade, Colonel Louis Fortier. Although a realistic man, his reports to Washington were filled with unwarranted optimism regarding the army and unmatched Serbian valor. Contrary to Colonel Fortier's enthusiasm, the Yugoslav army on the eve of war consisted of 25 badly equipped divisions, 35 tanks, and 200 antiaircraft guns with no motorization (according to the war minister, General Pešić). In addition there were 154 bombers, 156 fighters, and 24 reconnaissance aircraft. Surrounded on all sides by its enemies, General Pešić concluded that Yugoslavia was in no position to offer any substantial resistance.[11]

In elucidating the involvement of the United States and its diplomatic contribution to Yugoslavia's collapse, I found it absolutely crucial to examine it in the context of Yugoslavia's internal and external positions. In so doing, my intention is not to condemn, but to seek out the truth.

Chapter 1
The American Perception
of Yugoslavia on the Eve of World War II

Origins of an Illusion

The noted Swiss psychologist Carl Gustav Jung once observed that there were no bad people; there were only bad ideas that take possession of them. People being weak creatures, he argued, often become unwitting slaves of ideas they cannot understand and control.[1] This, however, is of little consolation to a historian, condemned by virtue of the profession to labor with highly elusive materials that reflect human behavior. Historians themselves are creatures of history, and their conscious effort to maintain integrity while seeking the truth notwithstanding, tend to fall victim to their own faulty mores and visions.

To complicate matters still further, history, almost as a rule, is written from the viewpoint of the victor. The British historian Sir Herbert Butterfield has argued convincingly that the historians of victorious nations and causes often write about the events in terms of Christian eschatology. Under the right political climate, such views are often taken for granted and frequently canonized. Repudiating such practices, Butterfield recalled Lord Acton as saying, "the canonization of the historic past [is] more perilous than ignorance, or denial, because it would perpetuate the reign of sin."[2] Preconception, long implanted biases, to use Barbara W. Tuchman's words, frequently determine the course of historical research. In the foreword to Raymond W. Stedman's book, *Shadows of the Indian Stereotypes,* Rennard Strickland compared American images of Indians to the notion of Plato's shadows looked at from the bottom of his cave. He wrote, "In his myth of the cave Plato showed us how shadow images distort reality while creating new and seductive realities of their own."[3] One finds the same phenomenon regarding the perception of southern Slavs in the United States.

Oddly enough, the image of Yugoslavia in the United States was foreshadowed by the caves of the romanticist Talvi, nom de plume of a gifted German writer, Theresa Albertina Luisa von Jakob (1797–1870). The philosophical foundation of Talvi's book[4] was Herder and the Slavic philology; more specifically, Vuk Stefanović Karadžić (1787–1864), a clever Serbian dilettante whose indiscriminate piracy of southern Slavic history and culture secured the preeminent image of Serbs in the eyes of American scholars. Talvi came to Russia from Germany with her family as a young girl. She went to school there and learned Russian and other Slavic languages. As often happens to cultural transplants, she fell in love with her adopted country and everything Russian and Slavic. She knew important men of letters in her time, including Goethe and Karadžić. Through Karadžić, Talvi became familiar with the folk poetry of the southern Slavs; she translated two books into German under the title, *Volkslieder der Serben*. Adhering to the aesthetic canons of the romantic school, Talvi proclaimed this poetry as the greatest achievement among the Slavs, while that of non-Slavic nations could hardly be compared to their counterpart. The principal value of the poetry, according to Talvi, lay in the fact that it was untouched by "pernicious" Latin influences. The lack of a European (Latin) tradition enabled the Slavs to preserve the purity of their national souls. In this sense, the Serbian Orthodox Church was lauded as a veritable preserver and guardian of this purity.

Ideological debates regarding romanticism and its vision of races and peoples were heightened in the United States by the Hungarian and French Revolutions in 1848. American attitudes toward these events were subordinated to the ideological canons of the time. Liberal intellectuals were on the Hungarian side, while the more conservative ones under the influence of the British writers, adopted more realistic views. For the liberal intellectuals, the Hungarian events, as well as their causes, were uncritically equated with the American Revolution. The Hungarian revolutionary drive for freedom and independence was seen as a justified eruption of democratic republicanism that shone like a bright comet under the dark Habsburg sky. Lajos Kossuth, leader of the Hungarian Revolution (in our time regarded as the forerunner of Adolf Hitler), was hailed as the Hungarian George Washington.

Some review articles came out in the *North American Review* against such uncritical views from the pen of its moderately conservative editor, Francis Bowen, under the titles, "The War of Races in Hungary," "Politics in Europe," and "Sir J. Gardner Wilkinson: Dalmatia and Montenegro: with the Journey to Mostar in Herzegovina, and Remark on the Slavic Nations; the History

Dalmatia and Ragusa, the Usccocs, etc." In his review article "Politics in Europe," Bowen analyzed several English and French books by Edward P. Thompson and Paul de Bourgoing, among others, dealing with the revolution in the Habsburg monarchy. These books offered an excellent platform for Bowen to develop his theses against the simplistic liberal views of 1848, the year of the struggle for political republicanism in Europe. He pointed out, however, that the sum of contradictory issues was impossible to judge correctly from any single ideological viewpoint. Bowen concluded that it was embarrassing to look back and see how foolishly we all squandered our honest enthusiasm.

Bowen therefore rejected liberal views of the Slavs as reactionaries in the service of the Habsburg tyrants, and looked upon them as peoples whose time had come to take a place on the stage of the civilized world. In this sense, Bowen had much in common with Talvi, whose book received rave reviews in the United States. What was so dangerous about Talvi's book was that it was based on inaccurate history; no one noticed at the time due to the scarcity of southern Slavic scholarship in the United States. That is why the romantic notion about the Serbs being the preeminent people among the southern Slavs retained a lasting influence in the minds of American scholars.[5]

Thus, on the basis of their aesthetics and rather confused philology of the time, the Serbs were given undisputed primacy while the Croatians with their European (Latin) tradition were to accept the "salvation" of their national souls by submitting to the new canons of this purity. Vuk Stefanović Karadžić saw to it that this transition would be as painless as possible. On the basis of linguistic similarities, namely the "što" dialect used by Serbs and a majority of Croatians, he single-handedly proclaimed Croatians as the Serbians of Catholic faith. To complicate matters, however, the romantic vision of the purity of a national soul went hand in hand with, as yet, a hidden Serbian state-building project. Under the influence of the Polish diplomat Count Adam Czartorysky's (1770–1861) "advice" in the *Conseils sur la conduite à suivre par la Serbie,* we see discussed how Serbia was to conduct its foreign policy vis-à-vis the southern Slavs, with a view of creating a common state as a counterbalance to Austrian and Russian encroachment in the area. Serbia's interior minister, Ilija Garašanin (1812–74), revised it into his *Načartanije,* a blueprint of sorts for the creation of greater Serbia. In short, he turned it into a complete Serbo-centric project that would assure Serbia's preeminence among the southern Slavs. He was unsure of how to implement it, however, whether gradually or by revolutionary means. The cultural propaganda machine, both covert and overt, was applied along the lines of Karadžić's "scholarly" linguistic discoveries through various secret organizations among the Austrian southern Slavs from the start. As most of Talvi's findings were based on "Serbian" epic poetry, pure and unadulterated by "pernicious" foreign influences, in her mind, the Serbians represented the most noble expression of the Slavic soul, predestined to take the lead among the still amorphous southern Slavs.

These views found considerable sympathy in America, which at the time was passing through its own romantic development of Anglo-Saxon racial nationalism. By exalting these fictitious national and racial qualities, Talvi can be placed in the same group of writers whom Reginald Horsman correctly observed let their preconceived notions shape their scholarly research, and whose findings became the theoretical foundation without which no sociopolitical action was possible.[6] The paucity of serious scholarly research in modifying such views kept alive the image of a Serbian as an innately heroic person—natural, undisciplined, and in love with personal freedom. This was truly a picture of a noble savage in revolt against discipline for the sake of instinct and desire.[7] Much of this view was reaffirmed by Serbian participation in the Balkan Wars (1912–13) fought with Greece and Bulgaria for the disposition of the Ottoman Empire and, of course, by World War I, which was precipitated by the Serbian assassination of Austrian Archduke Franz Ferdinand.

A relatively easy victory over the moribund Ottoman Empire reinforced the existing Serbian desire of resurrecting its medieval empire created by Emperor Stephen Dushan. Few people noticed what Herbert Adams Gibbons saw so clearly:

> It is in vain that historical science has demonstrated the purely temporary character of Stephen's conquests. It is in vain that he had been divested of the glamour of the chronicles and songs, and pictured in conformity with fact. To the Serbian peasant he is Saint Stephen, the glorious Czar, who brought the Serbian Empire to its zenith. All the cities in which this adventurer and raider set foot are claimed in the twentieth century as a legitimate part of 'Greater Serbia'. Men have engaged in a bloody war and have died for this fiction.[8]

In the footnote on the same page, Gibbons described how Serbian soldiers, when Serbia turned against its ally Bulgaria in the second Balkan War in July 1913, over the spoils in Macedonia, believed they were fighting for the "sacred soil of the fatherland." The name of the Czar Dushan was invoked before soldiers went into battle.

One may easily excuse the Serbian peasants, but the truth is that such fictitious beliefs were systematically promoted by educated Serbians. A case in point is the book *The Servian People: Their Past Glory and their Destiny*.[9] It was no accident that the book was published two years before the Balkan Wars. Apart from the exaggerated Serbian heroism, the author introduced some new elements; he expanded Serbian territory to a considerable extent. According to the author, the lands populated by the Serb race consisted of "the kingdom of Servia, the principality of Montenegro, the vilayet of Kossovo, parts of the vilayets of Monastir and Scutary (Skodra), in Macedonia (Turkey), Bosnia and Herzegovina, Dalmatia, Istria, Croatia, Slavonia, Banat, and Batchka in Austro-Hungary" (1:6). In short, the entire territory of contemporary Yugoslavia, minus Slovenia, was populated by Serbians. The total number was between ten and eleven million. The author had no hesitation about crossing the borders "populated by Serbs" and claiming Serbian origin of two prominent Renaissance painters, Andrea Schiavone and Vittore Carpaccio, and two Hungarian politicians, Lajos Kossuth and Ferenc Deak (1:19).

The shadows from the Serbian caves were intensified during World War I. Woislav M. Petrovitch [Petrović], the attaché of the Royal Serbian Legation to the Court of St. James, wrote a book titled *Serbia: Her People, History, and Aspiration,* which included the "Yugoslav manifesto to the British nation." Petrović excused Serbia of any responsibility for war, claiming that the assassination of the archduke was in fact in Austro-Hungarian interests, thus suggesting that the assassination was staged by Vienna only to destroy Serbia. The purpose of the book, as Petrović pointed out, was to give a candid and honest exposition of the Serbian people and its history that had been abused by a "superabundance" of information emanating from Vienna and Budapest. His "candid" exposition of Serbian history is bedeviled by the fact that for Petrović, as for most Serbian writers of the period, the southern Slavic unity (Yugoslavia) was synonymous with Serbia and Serbdom. In reality, the Yugoslav idea, a brainchild of Croatian and Slovenian intellectuals, envisioned and propagated a common southern Slavic state, respecting the historical and cultural differences of its constituents.

The idea of a southern Slavic political entity evolved from the Croatian belief in the cultural and racial affinity of Yugoslavism shortly before World War I. Exasperated by the political shortsightedness of the Austro-Hungarian ruling classes regarding the "subject-races," they sought salvation outside of the Austro-Hungarian Empire, which they thought incapable of modernization and reform. The Great War offered them a chance to realize their dream of freedom. At least they believed so. For that purpose, the Yugoslav Committee, composed mostly of Croatians (along with Serbs from Bosnia and some Slovenians), was formed abroad. Many prominent Croats were members of the committee. Among them were Dr. Ante Trumbić, Frano Supilo, and Ivan Meštrović, the renowned artist. By cooperating with the Serbian government, it was hoped that the committee's aims would entail the propagation of its political project among the Allied powers, to build a common southern Slavic state on the ruins of the Austro-Hungarian Empire. Their vision of the new state was a constitutional monarchy respecting the cultural, religious, and historical differences of its members. Thinking that the new state might be patterned after the British model, the idea aroused strong support in Britain. A score of intellectuals, such as H. Wickham Steed and R. W. Seton-Watson, afforded their intellectual support to the committee whose ideas were generously promoted in Lord Northcliffe's press.

The unification process was in trouble from the start. The word "new" state was unacceptable to the Serbian government; it implied a total reorganization of the state and the subsequent loss of Serbia's sovereignty, not to mention its central position, which they intended to maintain. Hence, with a considerable degree of well-calculated flexibility, they insisted that reorganization of the southern Slavic state was unnecessary as long as all southern Slavs were together under the same roof. They justified their position on the grounds that the war situation was not as yet clear, and therefore, such far-fetched ideas were neither feasible nor practical. In essence, they tenaciously adhered to their traditional practice of "liberation" and "attachment" to Serbia. They did change their position eventually (although not their minds) but only when imperial Russia, Serbia's ardent supporter, collapsed. In subsequent negotiations with the Yugoslav Committee, they refused to give in on one crucial point, which would change the nature of the country. The constitution of a new state would be decided by a simple majority, rather than a two-thirds majority as advanced by the Yugoslav Committee. Afraid that the whole Yugoslav agenda (which the committee members believed in with the faith of true zealots) might collapse over this point, they acquiesced in the hope that the Serbian side would see things in a different light once unification was effected.[10] Thus, the idea of political union was in trouble from the start. Adhering faithfully to the vision of the Serbian caves, Petrović concluded that he hoped the book would enable English-speaking readers to understand why Serbia was "predestined" to unify all the Serbs and "other Yugoslavs."[11] In the scheme of the Serbian historical and political vision, "the other Yugoslavs" mattered very little. The Serbian government proclaimed Serbia's war aims strictly in accordance with its "predestination." Its main concern was to bring all Serbians within one state; i.e., greater Serbia to which others, if they so wished, could attach themselves. The point is that Serbians were not disposed toward a multinational federation and could not see why their position would be unacceptable to others.

With the war raging in Europe, a book was published for the American Geographical Society of New York, *The Frontiers of Language and Nationality in Europe* by Leon Dominian.[12] The author sought to demonstrate how the "linguistically ill-adjusted boundary [was] a hatching-oven for war" (vii), and hoped that his findings could serve as a working model for settlement of the European boundary conflict. In chapter 9, "The Balkan Peninsula and its Serbian Inhabitance," Dominian expanded on the romantic notion of linguistic nationalism. The chapter dealt with philology, history, anthropology, geography, etc., based exclusively on Serbian sources. The conclusion was that all Yugoslavs were Serbo-Croatian, namely that they were all Serbians. The differences, if any, were artificially maintained by intrigues directed from Vienna and Budapest. In view of German and Hungarian imperialism, Dominian pleaded for the creation of "Serbia," or rather Serbo-Croatia or "Yugoslavia," as a precondition for peace in Europe.[13] Under the war propaganda, such views were shared by many Yugoslav-oriented Croatians in the United States believing that southern Slavic political unity would usher them into a sociopolitical Garden of Eden. Hence, "scholarly" research about their past simply supplied a theoretical base for pan-Serbian expansion. Some opposing views were expressed, but in a time of intellectual confusion accelerated by war, they were foredoomed to fail. An experienced journalist, C. Townley-Fullam, argued in favor of the Habsburg monarchy and advised Croatian-Americans to seek federation within the monarchy rather than association with Serbia. "Salvation never lay in descend," was his advice.[14] Father Martin Krmpotić, a Croatian priest, attempted in several of his brochures and articles to refute the theoretical base of Serbian territorial claims; but having no support from influential people or institutions, it was a cry in the wilderness.[15]

Two additional volumes appeared from another Serbian, professor of psychology at NYU, Paul R. Radosavljevich.[16] The two volumes were a compilation of his numerous articles and lectures on the Slavic world. They were pan-Slavic and pan-Serbian in outlook and fitted ideally into the anti-German sentiments in the United States. One may say that in praising the Slavs, Professor Radosavljevich, perhaps inadvertently, adopted a somewhat milder response than that of Joseph A. Gobineau and Houston S. Chamberlain. One "learns" that the Slavs had mighty empires since 400 B.C. Even Taurians that guarded the Golden Fleece were Slavs (2:201). The war against Serbia was explicated in terms of the innate democratic spirit and morality of the Slavs, on one hand, and the "cold-blooded barbarism or narrow-minded nationalism advocated by Bernhardi, Treitschke, Hasse," on the other (2:104). To redress the historical injustice wrought against southern Slavs, Radosavljevich pleaded for their unification.

President Wilson's Fourteen Points invoking the principle of self-determination of nations, having come in the wake of the carnage of war, generally was hailed as the hope of the future. It nonetheless inflamed the imagination of the southern Slavs. The process of unification, however, soon eliminated all hope. Suddenly, the mythical being from the mythical cave leaped out. The shadows disappeared and the stark-naked reality glared for everyone to see. With an extensive history, and with over a thousand years of uninterrupted statehood, including an elaborate national ideology, the Croatians, the second largest entity in the nascent Yugoslav state, reacted first. To be sure, they were not necessarily against unification. They objected, however, to the legality of the act, which was applied without the legal consent of the Croatian people.

Taking the unification issue as a means of defending Croatian sovereignty, the leader of the Croatian Peasant Party, Stjepan Radić, became the leader of the entire Croatian nation and the champion of its rights after the war. Even before he became the Croatian leader, his argument was that unification should not be a whim exercised by some irresponsible politicians, but a legal act based on consent of the people. To that end Radić concentrated his remarkable energy.[17] To reverse the process of unification, or as he termed it, the "flight of the geese into the fog," Radić appealed to Wilson and the League of Nations.[18] Wilson's political demise spelled the end to his expectations, but not to his vision. Yugoslavia became a united state patterned after the Serbian shadows, or as the French journalist Henry Pozzi aptly described the people ruling Yugoslavia:

> Born of the dreams of a handful of doctrinaires; exalted by chauvinistic officers, by professors of a hasty and confused science, and by students enlightened by refugees encountered in foreign universities, pan-Serbianism is an affirmation of the Serbian pre-eminence over all Slav lands south of the Danube. Its progress since it first appeared in the second half of the nineteenth century has been rapid, and its influence became immediately very great in all the elements of Serb society.[19]

Pozzi was referring to two Serbians in particular, Ilija Garašanin and Vuk Stefanović Karadžić, both of them instrumental in promoting Serbian national interests in the second half of the nineteenth century. Pozzi did not hate the Serbians as one might surmise from reading the above passages. His anger was tempered by his genuine love for the common Serbian people whom he considered victims of the pan-Serbian fanaticism.

Radić, for a while, attempted to use the dissatisfaction of the Serbian peasants to promote constitutional reforms and create a federation of equal nations, but he ultimately failed. Diplomatically isolated (he was advised in European capitals to work out differences with the Serbians through negotiations and parliamentary methods) and faced with Serbian political intractability, Radić was ultimately assassinated together with his closest associates by a Serbian deputy in the Belgrade parliament in 1928. The assassination of the Croatian leader widened the gap between Zagreb and Belgrade, and led to the creation of the Croatian revolutionary organization "Ustaša," under the leadership of Ante Pavelić. Henceforth, the easily unified Croatian front was split between Pavelić and Dr. Vladimir Maček, Radić's successor who continued to use peaceful means in solving the differences with Belgrade. Under the pretext of defending the state, King Alexander abolished the parties, the Parliament, and the Croatian name, establishing a dictatorship. The violence at home was challenged by Ustaša, which reached its apex during the Croato-Macedonian joint effort against Alexander's life at Marseilles in 1935. By this act, the backbone of the dictatorship was broken but its legacy lingered on.

Diplomatically, however, Yugoslavia was in a better position. As a newly created state, it enjoyed the protection of the League of Nations, especially France, which regarded Yugoslavia as an exponent of its strategic interest in the Balkans and the Danubean basin. As the French watchdog in the area, Yugoslavia was a signatory to the Little Entente designed to police Austria and Hungary, and Germany if necessary. The Balkan Pact, of which Yugoslavia was a member, was designed to keep Bulgaria in check. Both alliances were signed under the auspices of the League of Nations. Due to blood relations with the Russian imperial family, the anti-bolshevik agenda was strong in Yugoslavia's external and internal policies. In short, it fitted ideally into the political pattern of post–World War I Europe. For Mussolini's Italy, however, Yugoslavia would have been fairly secure from the outside. Although a victorious power, Italy turned against the League of Nations and the Versailles peace treaty. The reason was that President Wilson failed to honor a secret deal made by the Allied powers to reward Italy with the Croatian and Slovenian territories on the Adriatic for entering the war against the central powers.[20] At that point, Mussolini became an implacable enemy of Yugoslavia which, as an exponent of the League of Nations, deprived Italy of its "rightful possession" by standing in the way of its Balkan expansion.

Mussolini therefore was determined to destroy Yugoslavia by any means at his disposal. As the implacable enemy of Yugoslavia, Pavelić and his followers found common cause with him and accepted his aid. Italy thus became a safe haven for the revolutionary Croatians whose acts were perpetrated against Alexander's regime, including his assassination.[21] The rise of Nazi Germany added a new element to Yugoslav foreign affairs. To restrain Mussolini from joining Hitler's Germany, the French tended to adopt a more flexible policy toward Italy, which in turn made Belgrade nervous and vulnerable. Belgrade was not altogether happy with France's policy shift toward Mussolini. King

Alexander confided to Meštrović that Yugoslavia indeed owed much to France but that it had no intention of becoming another French Morocco.[22] To keep Mussolini at a safe distance, Belgrade, while Alexander was still alive, reoriented its policy toward Berlin. In fact, he was among the first European rulers to realize the political importance of the future Nazi Germany. Moreover, they had other things in common. Berlin and Belgrade hated Austria and wished to liquidate it. The ghost of Habsburg stood in the way of their internal consolidation.[23] The Weimar policy of peaceful economic penetration (tacitly approved by Britain who disliked French predominance in Europe) into Yugoslavia and the Balkans, was accelerated by the Nazis for economic and military reasons. It served also as a deterrent against Mussolini's aggression in the Balkans.[24] This policy further improved under Prince Paul who succeeded Alexander as regent until the young King Peter came of age. The most remarkable aspect of Belgrade's foreign policy was that on the surface it remained pro-League of Nations in its ideals, but in reality was designed solely to promote and preserve the interests of the Serbian establishment.

In an attempt to draw America's attention to Yugoslavia's internal problems, Croatian immigrants in the United States sent a memorandum to President Roosevelt six months after the inauguration of his first term. The reason why they waited so long was that they had little faith in the Republican administration. The Wilsonian principle of self-determination was still alive among Croatians, and they hoped that the "worthy successor of Woodrow Wilson" would take up and carry on the Wilsonian banner.[25] Their great hopes soon came to nothing. The Croatians miscalculated Roosevelt's immediate concerns; the problems within Yugoslavia were far from his mind. America was in the thick of a depression that threatened to destroy the very fabric of its society. They also underestimated the pervasiveness of the Serbian shadow over the American intellectual landscape. In fact, most Americans believed that a strong hand was necessary to keep that "crazy quilt of ethnic groups" together. The principal commentators of the Yugoslav scene shared such views. Hamilton Fish Armstrong, the very influential editor of *Foreign Affairs,* for instance, praised King Alexander's dictatorial regime as a unifying factor, while the Croatian leaders, in his estimation, were people of "limited knowledge of the world" or small imagination, fit only to be country lawyers.[26] The Yugoslav prime minister, Dr. Milan Stojadinović, an ardent pan-Serb with a strong pro-fascist disposition, was lauded instead as a progressive leader, the true promoter of democracy and national unity.[27] The absurdity becomes only too apparent when contrasted with Roosevelt's remark recorded by Secretary of Interior Harold L. Ickes that "Romania had gone fascist and that Yugoslavia was on its way."[28] Apparently, neither fascism nor Alexander's dictatorship was much of an American concern. It was regarded as a passing stage at best, or a necessary evil at worst, that was helpful in unifying the country. Apart from domestic problems, the United States, as Stephen E. Ambrose pointed out, "was fairly satisfied with the world of 1938. Germany was a threat, especially after Hitler's victory at the Munich Conference of that year, but it seemed possible that Hitler would now be content to consolidate his gains in Austria and Czechoslovakia. Certainly, as long as Britain and France continued to stand against Hitler, the United States had nothing to fear militarily from Germany. Elsewhere, anti-communism was triumphing in Spain; central and eastern European governments hostile to the Soviet Union continued to contain communism."[29]

In *Foreign Affairs,* Armstrong was quite explicit on the point of justifying the royal dictatorship as the necessary response to Croatians, who were the "immature minority" that failed to understand the value of unification and because of it, had to pass through a harsh but maturing process under the dictatorial regime.[30] It was not surprising that Washington never bothered to renegotiate the Treaty of Arbitration and Conciliation originally arranged with the kingdom of Serbia. America adopted the view that no new agreements were necessary, which led Marie S. Good to conclude (and rightly so) that like other victorious powers, the United States as well, "looked upon Croatia as no more than a victorious acquisition for Great Serbia."[31]

Being outside of the parameter of American national interests, Yugoslavia was not Washington's concern. Thus, despite what happened, no one from the administration took note. Even if the American diplomatic representatives assigned to the Yugoslav government were more conscientious, there was no one in Washington, as historian Vladimir Petrov pointed out, capable of evaluating their reports.[32] On a journalistic level, Reuben Markham tried to bring a more realistic picture of Yugoslavia to the American leaders. Markham disliked the political structure of Yugoslavia and, as a sincere admirer of the peasant movements, believed that the still unspoiled Yugoslav peasants could transform Yugoslavia into a true democratic society. For this reason, Markham sympathized with the Croatian political leaders, pointing out that the Croatian natural will would prove stronger than army, police, prison, and staunch absolutism.[33] On the other hand, when the eminent historian Charles A. Beard met with Croatian leader Radić, he had no idea what to make of him and cautiously concluded that only the future would tell.[34]

The picture of Yugoslavia in American minds was further bedeviled and distorted by the official Belgrade propaganda. As Pozzi pointed out, Serbian propaganda spoke pan-Serbian for Yugoslavia. The powerful press bureau in Belgrade was financed from visible and invisible sources. It screened foreign and domestic correspondents. Any news contrary to the official press bureau version was prohibited, and transgressors faced expulsion from the country. It worked in close collaboration with the secret service and state police. To illustrate his point, Pozzi offered the following example. Defending Serbian claims on Macedonia, the press bureau's arguments were that the real Bulgarians were a small percentage of those direct descendants of the Mongols, and the rest, amounting to five million, were of pure Serbian stock. The findings of the Russian Commission before World War I were that in Macedonia, there lived the same people who in the ninth century were called Bulgars. These findings were dismissed with the accusation that the Russians were paid by King Ferdinand of Bulgaria.[35]

No more reliable were Yugoslav diplomatic representatives. Actually, their functions were to enhance Yugoslavia's image as a progressive nation engaged in preserving peace abroad and unity and prosperity at home. The Yugoslav Legation in Washington, for many years after the unification, retained the Serbian name. "Here is the Serbian Legation," was the response on the other end of the line, and no one in Washington thought it unusual.[36] Playing on the American fear of communism, the Yugoslav consul in New York, Pavle Karović, was accusing Croatians and their leaders of being bolsheviks.[37] Later, bolshevism was replaced by fascism; later still, Yugoslavia's benevolent neutrality toward Germany was interpreted in terms of assuaging unreliable Croatians. In light of intense Serbian propaganda, there was little chance that Croatian memorandums might have any influence on Roosevelt; but Croatians were not discouraged. They obstinately believed in Wilson and his ideals. When Wilson died, for instance, a Croatian immigrant, Ivan Krešić, wrote: "Croatia is laying a wreath of flowers upon his tomb thanking him for good will."[38]

In the first memorandum, when Alexander's dictatorship was at its height, the Croatian representative Rev. John Stipanović asked the administration in Washington to furnish him with a quasi-diplomatic passport so he could travel to Switzerland and present Croatian grievances to the League of Nations. He also sought a meeting with President Roosevelt. Because of the "extreme pressure of public business," Stipanović was informed, the administration could not assist him; but he was nonetheless told he could forward his memorandum to the Department of State. In view of Washington's strict policy not to interfere in European affairs in general and Yugoslavia in particular, Stipanović's effort came to a halt. In November 1934, another of the numerous Croatian memorandums reached the White House. Thinking in terms of the federal system as the best solution for a troubled Yugoslavia, the Croatian-Americans asked for help. The "worthy successor to Woodrow Wilson" was asked to put pressure on Serbia to withdraw its troops from Croatian territory.[39] The memorandum was forwarded to U.S. Department of State officials for "consideration" and "acknowledgment."[40] There is no evidence that it was either considered or acknowledged.

The hopes expressed in the memorandums to the White House by Croatian-Americans were beyond reasonable expectations and demonstrated a superficial understanding of the Roosevelt administration's position in world affairs. On December 12, 1934, Special Assistant to Secretary of State James G. Dunn, in an angry letter strongly advised the White House staff not to receive Catholic Archbishop of Sarajevo Ivan Ev. Šarić when the archbishop came to Washington, or to allow him to see the president, unless such a request was cleared with the Yugoslav Legation and the Department of State.[41] There were strong indications, Dunn pointed out in a separate letter, that the archbishop had contacts with the Croatian "terrorist organization" abroad and had no intention of returning to Sarajevo.[42] Although it was true about Šarić's connection to the political emigre groups, the allegation served as a convenient excuse not to meddle in the domestic affairs of a "friendly nation."

As the situation in Europe and in Yugoslavia was becoming more dangerous, Croatian-Americans felt the urgency to send another memorandum to the White House. Twenty-two signatories representing all groups of Croatians from within the United States, requested that in view of the precarious situation in Europe, the president take an active part in promoting peace in southeastern Europe in general and Croatia in particular. Interceding on Croatia's behalf, Illinois Congressman A. J. Sabath urged Edwin M. "Pa" Watson, then secretary to the president, to receive the Croatian delegation at the White House.[43] Watson received the delegation, expressed his appreciation, and promised to forward the memorandum to the president. As evident from the note to Watson, the president read it and asked whether a personal note of thanks would be appropriate.[44] George T. Summerlin, the U.S. Department of State chief of protocol, together with George Messersmith, assistant secretary of state, said no and advised the White House to keep in mind that Croatian activities caused "embarrassment" to the administration.[45]

The memorandum was a rhetorical masterpiece and the most accurate condemnation of the Yugoslav state.[46] It discussed not only a brief history of Yugoslavia, but also the Serbian misuse of power, the political terror of the state within and outside of its borders, and the Croatian response to the cause of freedom. In light of the facts, how was it possible, the memorandum asked, to call only Croatians terrorists when in fact state terrorism was endemic to the Serbian political tradition and practice?

At the same time, the Croatian leader Dr. Vladimir Maček sent a letter to Roosevelt. The letter was dated January 18, 1939, but the President received it in the second half of April.[47] After the fall of Prime Minister Dr. Milan

Stojadinović at the beginning of 1939, Prince Paul ordered his new prime minister, Dragiša Cvetković, to start negotiations with Maček. To make sure that the negotiations would not go on forever, Maček, by soliciting help from European capitals and the United States, apparently wished to exert pressure on Belgrade. In his letter to the president, Maček pointed out that the Wilsonian principle of self-determination was never applied in practice and as a result, the entire area could fall victim to predatory powers. It was not too late, Maček pointed out, to turn this important part of the European continent into a "hearth of genuine and civilized democracy," which ultimately would prove beneficial for all of southeastern Europe.[48] Roosevelt sent the letter to the Department of State for "acknowledgment and consideration." Pierrepont Moffat, chief of the Division of European Affairs, advised the White House that the letter should be "filed," as it was in fact an "appeal for Presidential interest in the fate of a minority movement within a friendly state."[49] The president, of course, never replied. Reading Moffat's advice, the first thought that springs to mind is that Marie S. Good's conclusion was all too correct. The administration regarded Yugoslavia as being a de facto extension of greater Serbia. Except for Secretary of State Cordell Hull, and only because he thought that the agreement between Zagreb and Belgrade might reinforce the status quo in the area, no one else in the administration paid much attention to the events taking place in Yugoslavia.

Realistically speaking, Yugoslavia was still out of the American orbit. When it finally was included shortly before the fall of France, President Roosevelt and his emissaries, however, found no difficulties in relying upon the pan-Serbian elements to bring Yugoslavia into conformity with those American interests designed to help the beleaguered British. The result was war and the destruction of Yugoslavia. While one has no reason to doubt Roosevelt's desire to help Britain and democracy, one questions his judgment in relying upon the Belgrade establishment. A quotation from Barbara Tuchman may shed some light on this: "When information is relayed to policy-makers, they respond in terms of what is already inside their heads and consequently make policy less to fit the facts than to fit the notions and intentions formed out of the mental baggage that has accumulated in their minds since childhood."[50] To what extent this accumulation had an enduring influence on the American mind is best demonstrated by the speech delivered by Undersecretary of State Adolph Berle to the emigre politicians from southeastern Europe after Word War II. With a stick in his hand, Berle pointed to the map of Europe and said that Americans can understand the problems, although not all, of western Europe; however, the moment they cross over into southeastern Europe, they see nothing but jungle. "To engage [Americans] in your problems," Berle said, "you must simplify them, to make them more acceptable. You must never talk about your internal problems, the problems between Bulgarians and Macedonians, Serbs and Croats . . . because it will surprise and disappoint every American politician."[51]

Precisely the same "vision" guided American foreign policy vis-à-vis Yugoslavia on the eve of war. In the meantime, the diplomats from Belgrade were to observe and report to Washington in the hope that the shadows from the mythical caves would spring to life and do the right thing.

Chapter 2
Croato-Serbian Rapprochement in Light of American Diplomacy

From the American point of view, negotiations between Zagreb and Belgrade did not come at the most propitious time. Aside from distances, isolation, or lack of national interests, the fact remained that the failure to negotiate some equitable settlement between the Croatians and the Serbian political establishment would increase the likelihood that Yugoslavia might turn into another Czechoslovakia. American interests therefore would be best served if Yugoslav internal tension were somehow reduced to a minimum, without disturbances that in turn might affect the status quo of an otherwise potentially explosive area. Primarily because of Washington's desire to maintain the status quo and to watch the adverse interests of the Axis powers in Yugoslavia, American representatives in Belgrade turned their attention to Serbo-Croatian negotiations.

Apart from these considerations, the negotiations per se represented the most constructive attempt to sort out the internal life of the Yugoslav state. Few attempts were made earlier, but after the removal of Prime Minister Stojadinović from power, both sides came to believe that the time was right.[1] The American diplomats in Yugoslavia were therefore instructed to watch carefully the progress of negotiations. In keeping with the official policy, however, they were instructed not to demonstrate any visible interests and above all, not to intercede on anyone's (which in practice meant Croatian) behalf. They were still under strict orders to be "clerks on the other side of the wire" whose function was merely to be "listening posts"; i.e., American diplomats were to listen and to report to Washington, but under no circumstances were they to say or do anything that might involve the United States in the affairs of other countries.

At the time of the negotiations, only a handful of American diplomats were accredited in Belgrade and Zagreb, and they were not expected to understand the intricacies of Yugoslavia's internal politics. As Vladimir Petrov pointed out, there was no one in the U.S. State Department capable of evaluating them. Information Washington received from Belgrade was rarely read and instead was filed away.[2]

The instructions not to get involved in Yugoslavia's domestic affairs fit well with American global concerns to keep peace. Restricted by internal constraints emanating from the policy of isolationism, the overwhelming concern of the United States was to maintain the status quo. If any changes were to be made, they were to be negotiated; i.e., they were to be attained through peaceful agreements among the negotiating parties. Hence, there was much unwarranted praise for the Munich settlement. Undersecretary of State Sumner Wells enthusiastically endorsed the settlement, saying that it "represented the best opportunity . . . to establish a new world order based upon justice and upon law."[3] Secretary of State Cordell Hull, no less enthusiastically, instructed his "listening posts" to impress upon the European governments the importance of collective action in negotiating a peaceful settlement.[4]

Apparently, Washington agreed that the anschluss of Austria and the secession of the Sudeten region of Czechoslovakia constituted a solid basis for a new and just world order. In keeping with the pervasive isolationist mood, a distinguished Yale professor, Edwin M. Borchard, in the face of mounting European discontent, warned Roosevelt and the Congress as early as 1933 to stay away from Europe. Borchard's thesis was that the United States could accomplish nothing by another intervention in Europe; if Europe could not keep peace alone, he admonished: "Let us not be dragged down with them."[5] The same sentiments were expressed in press editorials. *The Chicago Daily News* commented a few years later that if Europeans were not willing to fight for their democratic principles, America should do even less.[6]

Behind American unwillingness to get "entangled" in foreign affairs lurked the fear of the "greedy" Europeans and the domestic "merchants of death," who served as convenient scapegoats for pushing America into war. This fear, compounded with economic depression, resulted in a number of protective legislative decisions that practically paralyzed American diplomatic initiatives.[7] Roosevelt, an old "internationalist" by conviction, was forced to concentrate his attention on the domestic scene, in particular on the New Deal designed to combat the Great Depression.[8] Restricted by a series of legislative constraints, Roosevelt managed to convey a casual attitude with respect to foreign affairs, but, as Robert Dallek pointed out, "behind the facade of indifference, he remained vitally concerned."[9]

The American isolationist mood notwithstanding, Washington could not afford to ignore the Serbo-Croatian negotiations altogether. As pointed out, negotiations surfaced at a time when the political landscape of Europe began, under the impact of the Axis powers, to change. The destruction of Czechoslovakia, the formation of a separate Slovak state, and the occupation of Albania bespoke of further changes that no "collective negotiations" could satisfy or avert. Without changing his facade, Roosevelt recognized early on the real threat to world peace. To preserve it, he extended diplomatic recognition to the Soviet Union in hope, as George F. Kennan indicated, of achieving an effective restraint against Nazi Germany in Europe and Japan in the far east.[10] As recognition of the Soviet Union fell short of his expectation, Roosevelt advocated a "moral embargo" against the "law-breakers," but maintained that all outstanding problems should be solved through negotiations.

Returning to Yugoslavia's elections, Stojadinović, in view of his success in foreign policy, especially with respect to Italy and Germany, never doubted that the outcome of the election would put the stamp of approval on his political achievements. The American minister in Belgrade, Arthur Bliss Lane, concurred with Stojadinović's views and reported to Washington that, given the Regency's support, the media, and the state apparatus, Stojadinović would indeed be the winner.[11] Under the impression that the election would not disturb the status quo, Lane left for his vacation in the United States shortly before the elections started. Although a career diplomat of considerable experience in Latin America and the Baltic, Lane was a novice in the art of Yugoslav politics. He had neither an adequate background nor was he sufficiently prepared for his job. In dealing with the regent Prince Paul and the government, Lane depended on his own "mental baggage." True, as his biographer Vladimir Petrov stressed, he recognized the existence of Slovenians and Croatians but never thought them very important and, in common with most of the foreign diplomats in Belgrade, Lane himself never understood the depth of Croatian bitterness.[12] Like most foreign diplomats, he too confused public opinion in Belgrade and Serbia as being Yugoslav. Consequently, his reports reflected a superficiality mixed with his own strong opinions. Similarly, those in the U.S. State Department were no better informed concerning Yugoslavia's domestic malaise.

Not surprisingly, it turned out that Lane's prognosis with respect to the elections was not accurate. Lane was still in the United States when his deputy and counselor, Robert T. Joyce, reported that judging by the election results, Stojadinović failed to get the mandate for his policy and that the Croatian question was "very much alive."[13] The next two dispatches confirmed his observations and added that the general mood of the country was strongly in favor of "fundamental negotiations with Maček." Maček had lost, but in light of the habitual malpractice of the regime in electoral procedures, it was generally assumed that he was the winner.[14]

Insofar as Prince Paul was concerned, Stojadinović's poor showing in the polls could not have come at a more propitious time. Taking advantage of the quarrel between Stojadinović and some of his ministers, Paul dismissed his prime minister, but the real reasons behind the dismissal were carefully hidden.[15] To meet the most pressing challenge, namely the Croatian question which simply would not go away, Prince Paul reshuffled the government and appointed Dragiša Cvetković as his new prime minister, a man of no particular political talent but one loyal to him and quite determined to bring negotiations between Zagreb and Belgrade to mutual satisfaction. Paul was accused of playing politics with such a pressing issue merely to avoid Yugoslavia's collapse and disintegration. This is partly true. Undoubtedly, he had dynastic interests in mind, but given his education and political outlook, qualities that would contribute to his fall from power, he was a world apart from Serbian political practices. One could even say that he understood Croatians and believed, unlike his Serbian compatriots, that their demands for self-rule and an equitable share of power in the central government had merit. By April 27, 1939, the first draft of the agreement was reached and presented to him for further discussion and approval. It was rejected without adequate explanation.[16]

In the meantime, Lane was back in Belgrade. He brought no new instructions from Washington. He was still to "listen and report" and to infer U.S. foreign policy from speeches and public utterances made by Roosevelt and Hull. The mere fact that Prince Paul formed a new government aroused Hull's interest, and he communicated to the legation in Belgrade while Lane was still in Washington to feel out Maček's feelings regarding the new government.[17] To comply with Hull's instructions, Joyce asked for help from the American consul in Zagreb, John Meily. Although he too was under strict orders not to have any connection with the Croatian opposition, Meily broke this rule and at his own risk contacted Maček before Hull's telegram arrived.[18] As Stojadinović at the time still clung to his post, Maček, rather disgruntled, told Meily that at this point he saw no solution to the Croatian question without "outside help." In case of war, Maček added, the Croatians would know how to take advantage of the situation for their own ends.[19] He, of course, never elaborated on what was meant by "outside help," but Meily knew only too well the extent of Italian propaganda as disseminated by the implacable foes of Yugoslavia who were led by Dr. Pavelić and encamped in Italy under Mussolini's protection. After Stojadinović's dismissal, Maček, in a more optimistic mood, reportedly said that it was now largely up to Prince Paul to find the solution (Doc. no. 860H.00/983).

Lane returned to his post in Belgrade at the beginning of March. The negotiations were still on the right track, but their unexpected derailment by Paul at the end of April 1939 coupled with Italian preparation to invade Albania, worried the American minister. The only instructions that helped him navigate safely through the treacherous waters of Balkan politics was Roosevelt's letter of the previous year (October 10, 1938) in which the president advised Lane to be on the lookout in Belgrade. Concerned with the decline of French and British presence in European affairs, Roosevelt cautioned Lane to pay closer attention to the Italo-German rivalry over the Balkans. There were reasons to believe that conflict might occur between the two powers should unilateral German influence continue to expand in the area. Therefore, as Roosevelt suggested, Belgrade was the key post and lookout for a rapidly changing European situation.[20] Now that the Italian invasion of Albania was imminent, Lane reported on both domestic and foreign aspects of Yugoslavia's position.

While the negotiations were still in progress, Lane assessed the situation in Yugoslavia as being conducive for talks with Maček, provided his demands for self-rule and other conditions were met.[21] He visited Prime Minister Dragiša Cvetković and Prince Paul on March 20 and 22, 1939, respectively. Cvetković assured Lane that on his forthcoming trip to Zagreb to visit Maček, he would find an acceptable formula to satisfy the Croatian demands (Doc. no. 860H.00/966). Prince Paul was not as optimistic. Anticipating a strong reaction from the Serbian opposition leaders and their deep disagreement among themselves with respect to the negotiations, Paul, to soften their anger, blamed Maček for being a hard negotiator with a propensity for stretching everyone's nerves beyond endurance. To illustrate the point, Lane complained in his report that Maček kept changing his set of demands (Doc. no. 740H.00/747). Nevertheless, he reported to Washington on April 4, 1939, that a tentative agreement relating to a revision of electoral laws, new general elections, and separate laws for Croatia was reached (Doc. no. 860H.00/999). The Italian invasion of Albania and Prince Paul's visit to Italy from March 11 to March 14, 1939, overshadowed the negotiations in Lane's report.

The Italian invasion of Albania confirmed Roosevelt's expectation of the Balkans turning into an area of potential Italo-German conflict. Cordell Hull held opposite views. For him, the invasion was a serious threat to peace. He therefore quickly instructed his "listening posts" in Balkan capitals to report immediately on the reactions, moods, and feelings of the people in the area. He fired an angry telegram to the American ambassador in Turkey, John V. A. MacMurray, for "failing in his duty." In view of the geographic position of Turkey, it was vital for the United States to know what action, if any, Turkey might undertake in this threatening situation.[22] Regarding a possible split between the Axis powers over the Balkans, the British were also hopeful. According to the American ambassador in Rome William Phillips, his British counterpart Lord Perth was saying that the Germans were not consulted in advance regarding the invasion. Lane immediately reported this piece of good news to Washington, adding that the Germans actually inspired the Italians to invade Albania in order to compromise them vis-à-vis London and Paris, and to keep them closer to Berlin.[23] Lane was partially right. True, German diplomacy made the most to embarrass the Italians, but for entirely different reasons.

Before the invasion, the Italians discreetly spread rumors in Paris and London that their aim in Albania was to stop the German penetration into the Balkans.[24] Aware of the consequences of the invasion regarding their own interests, the Germans sent Prince Philip of Hesse to Rome, to deliver Hitler's oral message to Mussolini. The latter was asked to postpone the invasion for another two years, when available Prussian divisions would amount to one hundred. Actually, Hitler was afraid that Italian action in Albania would spoil his designs on Danzig.[25] Another element that played an important role in shaping Mussolini's decision to invade Albania was the removal of Stojadinović. Disregarding Belgrade's explanation that Stojadinović was dismissed for domestic reasons (which was not quite true), Mussolini decided to act in Albania as quickly as possible.[26] He, therefore, with unexpected help from the Croatian leader Dr. Maček, again adopted a hostile policy toward Yugoslavia. To pressure Paul before the negotiations, Maček approached the Italians for help in case of a possible revolution in Croatia if the negotiations failed. Needless to say, the Italians were happy to oblige, but Maček turned them down when the talks with Cvetković started, claiming that he personally had no knowledge of such a request.[27]

By means of pressuring Belgrade, Maček sent his emissaries to other European capitals, including London and Paris, for the same reasons but were systematically turned down. When Mussolini heard that one of Maček's emissaries, August Košutić, was sent to recently occupied Prague, presumably to talk to the Germans, Mussolini believed that he was confronted with irrefutable proof of German duplicity. He therefore, yet again, reversed his policy toward Yugoslavia. In the context of Italo-German rivalry, Mussolini realized that a strong and unified Yugoslavia was actually to Italy's advantage. He even suggested a rapprochement between Yugoslavia and Hungary in the hope of creating a solid barrier against German penetration in the direction of the Adriatic.[28]

To assure Yugoslavia of his good will, Mussolini informed Belgrade of his imminent occupation of Albania and that he was prepared to honor the Ciano-Stojadinović agreement and reward Yugoslavia with territorial compensation in Albania.[29] Paul wisely declined Mussolini's offer lest he be regarded as

Mussolini's accomplice and, therefore, an aggressor. To dispel any suspicion in Mussolini's mind regarding German interest in Croatia, the Germans reassured him that, as in the past, they had no secret design on Croatia.[30] They even rejected the suggestion made by their ambassador in Belgrade, Viktor von Heeren, that in view of the forthcoming inclusion of Croatians in Yugoslav politics, Berlin should reconsider its present policy vis-à-vis Belgrade.[31] Danzig, however, was uppermost on the German mind. Not yet strong enough, Germany was still anxious to operate within diplomatic constraints to improve its strategic position vis-à-vis its neighbors. Therefore, Italian military aggression, the Germans feared, might, by reason of their own association with Italy, prejudice German claims on Danzig. Precisely because the Germans attempted to deter him from occupying Albania, it seems, Mussolini did so to defy them, and this act of defiance was to demonstrate Italy's independence and its mastery over the Balkans.[32]

British Prime Minister Neville Chamberlain, largely because of public pressure, required the Balkan states following the occupation of Czechoslovakia to declare openly their opposition to future German aggression. In view of the Italian hostility toward Yugoslavia after the dismissal of Stojadinović, Prince Paul considered Chamberlain's request "unwise" and "high-handed."[33] Dependent on trade with Germany and German credit for armament (which Belgrade could not secure from Britain, much less from France or the United States), the Yugoslav government, instead of making a public declaration, assured Germany that Yugoslavia would uphold unwaveringly its present friendly policy toward the German *Reich*.[34]

Since Chamberlain's request was induced by public pressure, Belgrade had nothing to worry about. For a while, the British government took a "dim view" of the occupation of Albania, but only because they feared that by invading Albania, the Italians might get greedy and violate the Status Quo Agreement in the Mediterranean signed by Britain and Italy in 1938. Having been assured that no changes would occur, the British made no attempt to deter Mussolini, and Chamberlain went fishing on the day of the invasion and was unavailable for comment.[35] The British foreign secretary, Lord Halifax, intimated to the American ambassador in London, Joseph Kennedy, that the Albanian situation, could not and should not, be taken as the cause of war. In view of Italo-German rivalry, Halifax explained, the invasion demonstrated Italy's resolve to keep its sphere of influence "while Hitler goes on his merry way" (387–88).

Indeed, the invasion of Albania was simply an Italian show aided by the tacit approval of both Britain and France. The Germans of course were apprehensive concerning the Italian military incursion into the Balkans, but Berlin kept a low profile. While in Belgrade, the German military attaché "volunteered," as Lane reported, to interpret the Albanian affair as the first step of the Italian drive to Salonika. The idea, obviously, was to scare the Balkan people and make them more dependent on Germany. Berlin, however, understood well the diplomatic game over the Albanian affair. Considering the danger involved, the Germans concluded that any upheaval in the Balkans could interrupt the smooth flow of raw materials from there, with dire consequences to their war effort. The showdown with Poland over the Danzig in mind, the Germans could not risk it; at the same time, they did not want to alienate Mussolini.

To smoothen relations with Rome, Hermann Göering was sent to Italy. Without saying exactly what was on his mind, he congratulated *Il Duce* on his military victory, and then tactfully warned his host that to repeat the Albanian action in the future might jeopardize the entire Axis strategy. Göering was aiming at Yugoslavia, which, after the invasion and erstwhile German reassurance that they had no secret designs on Croatia, again became the object of Mussolini's hatred. Therefore, continued Göering, to have Yugoslavia and the Balkans at peace and neutral, would be to their mutual advantage. *Il Duce* halfheartedly agreed, and a compromise was reached to the effect that a wait-and-see policy would be maintained toward Yugoslavia until its internal policy was more clear. In return, Yugoslavia was expected to demonstrate a more visible pro-Axis policy that Mussolini intended to use for gaining concessions from Paul on his forthcoming visit to Italy.[36]

Paul was aware of the diplomatic game surrounding the invasion of Albania. He also knew about Maček's contacts with the Italians, but was not sure about the extent of Maček's involvement, or was he certain if Maček acted in collusion with Pavelić. Paul had enough knowledge, however, of Mussolini's imperial dreams in the Balkans to be on guard during his visit. Contrary to Mussolini's original intent to pressure Paul, *Il Duce* behaved quite unobtrusively, but it made no difference. Paul remained calm and aloof and was quite noncommittal throughout the visit. Before Paul's return, Mussolini, with a profound sense of guardianship over the Balkans, advised him that in case of war, Yugoslavia should retain its neutral status, proposing a nonaggression pact between their two countries.[37]

Shortly after Paul's return from Italy, Lane came to see him on May 23, 1939. Anticipating some pointed questions about the status of the negotiations with Maček and his visit to Italy, Paul assailed Maček even before Lane asked him anything. He told Lane that Maček had lied in his statement regarding the failure of the negotiations. All Paul wanted was a "minor change" relative to the plebiscite in Bosnia and Herzegovina. Had he conceded to Maček on this point, the Croatian question would have been solved, but he would have had the Serbian one to deal with. He described Maček as a man with a "mean, ugly mind," who deliberately threatened to break off the negotiations on the eve of Paul's departure for Italy, and undermine his position vis-à-vis Mussolini. Although Maček claimed to be a democrat, Paul maintained that Maček wished to be a dictator and that his actions confirmed his refusal to accept the authority of the crown.[38]

Paul's assault on Maček was not entirely without foundation. To determine how deeply Maček was involved with Rome, especially with Pavelić, Count Josip Bombelles, a somewhat shady Croatian nobleman in Paul's pay, surfaced in Rome. In his diary, Ciano recorded that on March 9, 1939, Bombelles came with "grave" news from Croatia. The secession movement there was spreading quickly, and Bombelles requested to see Pavelić as soon as possible. Ciano authorized the meeting for April 1, 1939.[39] In the meantime, the German *Geheimedienst* (secret service), watchful of Italian machinations in the Balkans, discovered that Bombelles was a Serbian spy; this information, however, was not forwarded to Rome.[40] In the atmosphere of mutual suspicion, Maček, upon Paul's return from Rome, became even more mistrustful of Belgrade, fearing that some deal along the Ciano-Stojadinović line might have been struck between Paul and Mussolini at Croatian expense. To counteract the putative deal, Maček authorized Amadeo Carnelutti, a member of the Croatian Peasant Party with connections in Rome, to find out what commitments, if any, Prince Paul made that could affect Italo-Croatian relations. After Carnelutti was assured that there were none, he delivered Maček's proposal to Ciano which reads in part that Maček: (1) "no longer intend[ed] to come to any agreement with Belgrade; (2) he [would] continue his separatist movement; (3) he ask[ed] for a loan of 20,000,000 dinars; [and] (4) within six months, at our request, he [would] be ready to start an uprising."[41]

Since no official explanations were given as to the real reasons why the negotiations were interrupted, the government came up with the excuse that Catholic and Orthodox Easter holidays were the reason. Lane reported that the interruption had nothing to do with the holidays, but rather with the Serbian opposition. Although, he pointed out, the opposition originally supported Maček, they now sought to "scuttle his ship," because their primary aim was to use Maček to overthrow the government rather than to negotiate with the Croatians. "Like virtually all Serbs, they were primarily anti-Croat."[42] Furthermore, the military had their hands in it as well. According to Lane, they desired at all costs to maintain the "undisputed Serbian hegemony."[43]

Between Paul's return from Italy and his visit to Germany scheduled for the beginning of June, the situation in Croatia was tense and explosive. Aware of Yugoslavia's position between Rome and Berlin, the Croatian leadership believed that, by solving the Croatian question with the help of the democratic governments, Yugoslavia could become stronger and less dependent on Rome and Berlin. Croatian appeals to this effect sent to Washington, as well as to Paris and London, were turned down. What the Croatian leadership failed to understand (or pretended to) was that Yugoslavia, as an area of potential confrontation between Mussolini and Hitler, was more desirable than a Yugoslavia, which, by virtue of Serbo-Croatian rapprochement, might become less susceptible to manipulations by any outside powers.

Now that Prince Paul was soon to depart for his visit to Germany, the Croatian leadership voiced its apprehension regarding the negotiations. Lane reported from Belgrade that Germany might take advantage of the situation and "foment trouble in Croatia and Slovenia."[44] To size up the situation for himself, Joyce decided to visit Zagreb. Together with Meily, he talked to the vice president of the Croatian Peasant Party, August Košutić. Joyce reported to Washington that by breaking off the negotiations, the government made a serious mistake that would now require much more effort than originally anticipated. But regardless of the circumstances, Joyce, quoting Košutić, pointed out that the Croatians would find a "suitable settlement," even if it meant taking opposite sides in case of war against Yugoslavia.[45]

Košutić made a point by saying that Croatians were not looking for an outside "protector," but twenty years of stalled efforts to solve the Croatian question was no longer tolerable.[46] Košutić's threats and bold words notwithstanding, one could detect that the Croatian leadership was more concerned with the Serbians stalling than desirous of a solution outside of Yugoslavia. As in the case of the Italian visit, the Croatians were worried that Paul might strike some shady deal with Hitler that could be detrimental to Croatia. The British ambassador, Sir Ronald Campbell, also worried. He truly believed that Paul was a weak person and might cave in under Hitler's pressure. He stayed with Paul for two hours and tried his "best to stiffen him."[47]

There was no need for such worry. True, Hitler was unpredictable, but in view of the conflicting Italo-German interests in the Balkans, he managed remarkably well to control his temper and projected himself to Yugoslav leaders as a kind and understanding benefactor. That is precisely how Hitler acted with the Yugoslav foreign minister, Aleksandar Cincar Marković, during the Albanian invasion. He assured the foreign minister of Berlin's friendly policy toward Yugoslavia, suggesting improvement of relations with Hungary as a countermeasure to Mussolini's influence in the Danubean region.[48] The question of the Anti-Comintern Pact and withdrawal from the League of Nations was postponed until Prince Paul's visit to Berlin.

Both of these requests, if solved satisfactorily, insisted Hitler when Paul arrived in Berlin, would place Yugoslavia under Axis (i.e., German) protection, and at the same time would render Croatian "separatists" [*sic*] impotent (Doc. nos. 438, 474). Paul's argument was that to join the Anti-Comintern Pact would be rather pointless, since Yugoslavia was the only country having no diplomatic relations with the Soviet Union. As for withdrawal from the League of Nations, nothing could be done before the next session in September anyway. Actually, as Paul's foreign minister pointed out, Germany would benefit if Yugoslavia remained in the Council of the League of Nations. As a member of the Council, Yugoslavia was in a position to influence Rumania to stay within the confines of neutrality instead of drifting away.[49] There was nothing the Germans could do to change Paul's mind. It seemed that doing nothing was Yugoslavia's best defense and the most valuable contribution to German-Yugoslav relations.

Needless to say, Hitler was displeased with the outcome of Paul's visit. His displeasure was compounded by Paul's visit to Britain in mid-July, which he learned about from the press. Bearing in mind Paul's "duplicity," Hitler realized that his failure to bring Paul closer to the Axis might prove to be a blessing in disguise, and useful as bait for Mussolini.[50] To assure Italy's goodwill in the forthcoming campaign against Poland, Hitler proposed to *Il Duce* that during the campaign, Italy should protect Germany's back. In liquidating "uncertain neutrals," the Axis partners should protect each other. One such "uncertain neutral," Hitler pointed out, was Yugoslavia, which would not hesitate to go over to the other side if the opportunity presented itself.[51] The prospect of liquidating Yugoslavia overshadowed, but did not quite obliterate, Mussolini's objections over the war with Poland. Still, as Hitler predicted, Mussolini grudgingly acquiesced.

However attractive the prospect of liquidating Yugoslavia appeared to Mussolini, in practice, it had no value whatsoever. The preparation to attack Yugoslavia would extend, in view of Italian military weakness, beyond the Polish campaign. In fact, that was the most effective way to neutralize Mussolini without offending his delicate ego.

Paul's silence upon his return from Germany gave rise to all sorts of wild speculations, most of which were detrimental to him and the government. Paul's wife, Princess Olga, was believed to have fallen under Hitler's spell.[52] In Zagreb, the Croatian leadership suspected Paul of making a deal in Berlin to avoid further negotiations. None of this was true. In fact, Hitler's remark concerning the Croatian "separatists" weighted heavily on Paul's mind; he knew full well that by ignoring German wishes, Berlin would not hesitate to use them as leverage against Belgrade.

At any rate, the situation in Croatia worsened and Lane decided to visit

Zagreb. On June 8, 1939, Lane reported to Washington on the depth of Croatian bitterness toward Belgrade. While in Zagreb, he talked to Košutić but refused to see Maček as meeting the latter, Lane feared, might jeopardize his relations with Paul. Košutić was very blunt in his feelings toward Belgrade and repeated his old position as to future relations with Belgrade: "If Yugoslavia [sided] with France and Britain, the Croatians [would] go with the Axis." It was the same old story, namely that the Croatians would take the opposite side if it suited their national interests. If Paul made any deals in Berlin, Košutić emphatically stated, the Croatians would then turn to the democracies.[53]

Not quite sure what actually took place in Berlin, Lane paid a visit to the assistant minister of foreign affairs, Miloje Smiljanić. Smiljanić tried his best to assure the American minister that no secret deals were made in Berlin. To make it as plain as possible, Smiljanić told Lane that Yugoslavia's foreign policy was remarkably similar to that of the United States: to stay out of war, and under no circumstances, damage the cause of neutrality. Lane, however, was not convinced and reported to Washington that anti-German and anti-Paul feelings were strong in the country (Doc. no. 740.00/870). In his attempts to appraise the so-called Yugoslav public opinion, Lane never managed to attain much credibility. The reason, as his biographer pointed out, was that he habitually confused Belgrade's hearsay with overall Yugoslav opinion.[54] After talking to Paul, Lane changed his mind about the Berlin visit, and reported to Washington that the more he saw the prince, the more convinced he was that Paul's heart was with England and France.[55]

From a diplomatic point of view, Paul's visit to his "second homeland" was anything but a success. He poured his heart out to the members of the government. He entrusted the British with his assessment of Hitler and his immediate intentions over Danzig; i.e., that unless Hitler was stopped, he would unleash a conflagration of war in Europe. Paul therefore urged the British to consummate the pact with the Soviets before the Germans did so. He also divulged to them that Hitler told him of his intention to attack the Soviet Union.[56] In retrospect, that was a mistake. It merely reaffirmed Chamberlain's policy to use Hitler to attack the Soviet Union.[57] Ambassador Kennedy reported to Washington that Chamberlain did not feel any danger in consolidation of the Nazi-Soviet pact, and added that Hitler was "highly intelligent" in preparing to wage a world war.[58] Kennedy spoke with Prince Paul and in the next telegram advised Hull that the widely held views in Berlin were that the British Empire, due to its decadence, would not be able to fight, "even though [British] dispositions were courageous" (199–200).

The main British interest was that Yugoslavia should maintain the present course of its foreign policy. As far as the British were concerned, Stojadinović's dismissal by no means implied reversal of the Yugoslav foreign policy. The British ambassador in Belgrade, Sir Ronald Campbell, advised the Foreign Office that Yugoslavia's geographical position would constrain it to preserve neutrality for as long as possible, even if Germany and Italy were brought together in a future war.[59] The Foreign Office had no reason to disagree. The note, circulating within the Foreign Office, reflected identical views. Because the Croatians and the Serbians could not agree in the running of the centralized state, Stojadinović's policy would continue, albeit with less of a psychological bias in favor of the totalitarian states.[60]

According to his sympathetic biographers, Balfour and Mackay, Paul's trip to Britain was a splendid show, but devoid of any substance. The substance was replaced by lavish dinner parties and receptions. He was praised as "the trusted friend of England" and was expected to do exactly as he was told, but Paul was no fool. His attempt earlier in the year to improve trade with England to escape dependency on Germany had failed. The British offered "political credits," which would step up its propaganda in Yugoslavia and do nothing else.[61] The "political credits," coupled with the futility of the present visit, placed Paul on guard. Indeed, he would do nothing to compromise England, but his future policy to promote "understanding" between Germany and England would be inextricably linked to Yugoslavia's interests as well. As if he anticipated a fruitless trip to Britain, Paul, before his departure for London, told his Prime Minister Cvetković to resume negotiations with Maček.

Upon his return, Paul faced three immediate problems: (1) Serbo-Croatian negotiations; (2) trade negotiations with the United States; and (3) the combined Hitler-Mussolini anger over Paul's unannounced trip to London.[62]

The protracted negotiations were taking their toll. Mutual accusations of insincerity and bad faith flew back and forth. Germany, rather than Italy, was perceived as the cause of procrastination. Even Maček was suspected of having fallen under German influence.[63] August Košutić told the American vice-consul in Zagreb, Robert N. Memminger, that Germany was behind the disruption of the negotiations back in April 1939. It was in Germany's interest, he said, to keep Yugoslavia weak in the hope of turning Croatia into another Slovakia. Memminger met Košutić again on July 1, 1939. Košutić angrily informed Memminger that the Croatians had a "definite plan" in mind, should the negotiations continue to drag on.[64] In the second half of August 1939, however, Lane informed the U.S. State Department that the agreement was signed. On August 25 and 28, 1939, respectively, Lane reported on the new Cvetković-Maček government. Maček became the vice-premier and was joined by three more Croatian ministers, while Dr. Ivan Šubašić was appointed the Ban (viceroy) of Croatia.[65] In his initial reports, Lane was enthusiastic about the new ministers. In his subsequent confidential report, however, he reversed himself and reported that Maček, although he may be a clever politician, was essentially only a well-meaning farmer and the other three Croatian ministers were appointed, not because of their abilities, but because they were Croatians (Doc. no. 860H.00/1102). Nevertheless, Lane was the first of the foreign dignitaries to come and see Maček, and told the latter that because of the large number of Croatians in the United States, the American people were "particularly interested in matters dealing with Croatia" (Doc. no. 860H.00/1089).

Trade negotiations with the United States had no more success than those with Britain. Along with the trade, it was hoped that Yugoslavia also might import a quantity of arms from the United States. Neither was possible. Americans were not interested in barter for Yugoslav bauxite, while the shipments of arms were out of the question. In keeping with his economic appeasement policy during the Czechoslovak crisis, Roosevelt rejected the senate resolution that would have repealed the arms embargo and made it possible for American industrialists to sell arms on a cash-and-carry basis. The repeal eventually went into effect in November, but as far as Yugoslavia was concerned, it made no difference. An outstanding debt of $60 million from World War I hung over Yugoslavia. Because the debt was a very sensitive issue, the Johnson Act was enacted, designed to prohibit any financial transaction with those countries in default on their obligations to the United States.[66]

Informed that the Yugoslavs were interested in opening trade negotiations with Washington, Cordell Hull seized the opportunity, and in his telegram to Lane explained the advantages of reciprocal trade.[67] Although the Nazi-Soviet pact shattered any prospects for peace, Hull still believed that the network of a reciprocal trade agreement would create a solid basis for peace and the prosperous interdependency of all nations.[68] As a last ditch effort, the Yugoslavs applied for a credit loan with the Export-Import Bank, but on the advice of the U.S. State Department, were turned down.[69] Despite Paul's efforts, Yugoslavia again was left at Hitler's mercy, and in view of the Hitler-Mussolini agreement to deal with the "uncertain neutrals," Yugoslavia's future indeed was very uncertain.

Cognizant of Yugoslavia's precarious position, Lane reported that the agreement, signed on August 26, 1939, satisfied neither side. Croatians complained that the agreement fell short of their expectations, while Serbians felt that it went altogether too far.[70] Apart from these two basic complaints, the agreement was on rather unstable legal ground. Many points of the agreement were ambiguous and became the subject of various interpretations. The inclusion of the agreement into the constitution was another matter. It required parliamentary ratification when King Peter came of age in 1943. In the meantime, they were to wait and hope for the best, provided a peaceful internal consolidation was assured. Summing it up, Lane, as an afterthought, pointed out that no fair-minded person could have expected miracles. "[The] antagonism of centuries in race, religion, culture and political thought," could not be obliterated by the signing of a legal document (Doc. no. 860H.00/1102).

Chapter 3
Roosevelt's Peace Offensive and the Future of Yugoslavia

Roosevelt's facade may not have betrayed adequately his inner feelings, but the changes taking place in Europe worried him more than he openly dared to admit. Germany's pursuit of economic autarchy, coupled with restrictive European commercial practices, threatened the American economic future. The possibility existed that the United States could be excluded from European markets. The fear of European, especially German, economic hegemony pushed Roosevelt and the administration into the peace offensive. His peace strategy rested in part on an American policy of economic nationalism and a liberal economic system as practiced in the New World. Without such a system being universally applied, there would be neither peace nor prosperity. At least Roosevelt's administration thought so.

Further motivations for his policy were derived from the administration itself. There were those within the administration who carried an almost apocalyptic vision of war and its aftermath, one of destruction followed by revolution and chaos. The most reflective among them, Adolf Berle, depicted the future in the darkest of colors after the Nazi-Soviet pact was signed on August 23, 1939. In Berle's mind, the pact invoked the times of Genghis Khan. In the midst of such an enormous calamity, Berle lamented, there was nothing that the United States could do to avert a total disaster. Italy still might join the Allies, but the borders of the Western World would be pushed to the Rhine. The only recourse left was either to enter the war and defend France and England, no longer empires but small nations fighting for existence, or to fortify the western hemisphere and defend it against military, economic, and propagandistic attempts to establish domination over it. Not knowing the right answer, Berle concluded his lamentations by saying that "ultimately, of course, the new empire [would] break up as Genghis Khan's did, but so many things [would] break up with it that it [might] be said, without hyperbole, that an era of history [was] literally passing before us."[1]

Considering America's deep isolation, there were no other options for Roosevelt to pursue but the policy of peace. To discourage the war from spreading, Roosevelt was prepared to give full consideration to German and Italian territorial claims, while his economic package, if accepted, would scale down the differences among the belligerents. Believing that the cause of European upheaval was predominantly of an economic nature, Roosevelt's plan, as Robert Dallek observed, maintained a belief in the "interdependence of nations, that is, the dependence on each other for long term prosperity and peace."[2]

In April, messages were sent to Mussolini and Hitler following the invasion of Albania and the problems raised by Berlin over Danzig. To make sure that his messages would not be confused with "meddling" in European affairs, Roosevelt carefully elaborated his position in his press conference, stressing that the message was to open the avenues of international trade. Every nation should be free to buy and sell on equal terms on the world market, "as well as to possess assurance of obtaining materials and products of a peaceful economic life."[3] In turn, both Hitler and Mussolini were to give assurances that their armies would not attack the remaining independent nations of Europe or invade Turkey, Iraq, Syria, Saudi Arabia, Palestine, Egypt, and Iran (275–76). Always careful in dealing with the isolationists, Roosevelt once again stressed that he was not a "mediator" in the peace process, but an "intermediary," analogous to the "post office, the telegraph office—in other words, the methods of communication" (274–76).

The response to his message was less than negligible. Hitler responded to Roosevelt in his *Reichstag* speech. The speech was somewhat conciliatory, though not without sarcasm, which made the audience burst into laughter; it nevertheless left some slim hope for peace. Such a slim hope, however, was not due to Roosevelt's message, but to Hitler's fear of a possible military alliance between Britain and France on one hand and the Soviet Union on the other.[4] Göering, on his visit to Italy following the Albanian invasion, gave the impression to Ciano that Germany did not close the door completely to peace over Danzig.[5] In private, Mussolini characterized Roosevelt's message as a manifestation of the president's "infantile paralysis."[6] Chamberlain himself did not demonstrate any more enthusiasm over the message. In his view, the most desirable help from the United States would be an "appearance of American support"; otherwise, as he pointed out in a letter to Ida Chamberlain, "Britain should pay dearly if Americans had to be in on the peace terms."[7]

Other "independent nations" wisely kept their opinions to themselves. Accorded an appropriate coverage in the Yugoslav press, Yugoslav officials, although evasive, tried their best to explain Yugoslavia's precarious position between Germany and Italy.[8] Lane was not impressed by their answer and accused some of them, most notably Foreign Minister Aleksandar Cincar Marković, of being "enthralled" by Hitler. Whether or not the Yugoslav foreign minister was "enthralled" by Hitler was really beside the point. The point was that reorientation of the Yugoslav foreign policy toward Berlin (of which Lane knew nothing) originated with King Alexander and was continued by his successor, Prince Paul, as a precondition to sustain Yugoslavia and the Serbian preeminence.[9] Moreover, neither Washington nor Lane realized, although they should have learned something from previous policy vis-à-vis Latin America, to what degree "peaceful" economic penetration entailed German political control over Yugoslavia.[10]

Lane's reports notwithstanding, Washington could do nothing to change German political influence over Belgrade or in the Balkans at this point. As Arthur W. Schlesinger Jr. observed, Roosevelt, by applying his external and internal policies, was keenly aware of the distinction between "fundamental and profound," which he learned from Wilson, and "specific individual events" as practiced by Theodore Roosevelt, by which he always succeeded in stirring people into action.[11] The situation was not as yet favorable to specific individual events. Roosevelt therefore remained in the realm of the fundamental and profound. After the destruction of Poland by a joint Nazi-Soviet effort, the American fear of losing European markets increased. Exclusion from European markets was discussed in a meeting of the National Policy Committee in Washington during February 1940. The committee was in agreement that unless America took an active part in the war, no market for American products would be left in Europe. Debating this point, the committee decided that prudence required that some ground rules be laid down as preconditions for American entry into the war. Still, with the memory of the outcome of World War I fresh in their minds, Americans had no desire to repeat it. In his diary, Berle aptly described American concerns:

> To my mind we ought to go as far as we [can] towards keeping Finland, Sweden, Switzerland, Yugoslavia, Portugal, North America, and so on afloat. We ought do this on a common sense ground, if no other; it [would] cost the Germans time, money, men and organization to seize them. Most of all we ought to do it because our whole theory of life contemplates that these people [would] some day be free and I hope [would] cooperate.[12]

To assure cooperation after the war, the committee put forward: (1) that a peace settlement would have no secret treaties; and (2) that the postwar world would implement the principle of American liberal (open-door) economic policy.[13] Realizing that such a proposal then would not stir the American people into action, Roosevelt wisely opted for his original plan of economic appeasement. He sent his undersecretary of state, Sumner Welles, to Europe. Lest the trip be interpreted as warmongering, the President told the press on February 9, 1939, that the undersecretary was about to depart for Europe on a fact-finding tour for the purpose of advising the president and the secretary of state as to the present conditions in Europe.[14] The undersecretary's trip, however, entailed more than met the eye. Welles' main purpose was to persuade Mussolini to remain neutral. Considering Mussolini's mood after the Nazi-Soviet pact, and their joint dismemberment of Poland, the timing was favorable. *Il Duce,* as well as Ciano, viewed the pact between the Russians and the Germans as an act of "barbarism" directed against Rome and Catholicism, the defense of which, according to Ciano, was Italy's historical mission.[15] They jointly resurrected their old plan of constituting a bloc of Danubean Balkan countries together with Spain. Led by Italy, the bloc would act as the barrier against German and Russian penetration into the Italian sphere of influence (entry for September 15 and 19, 1939).

Already in a state of war with Germany over Poland, both London and Paris would have welcomed Italian neutrality with open arms. In practical terms, neutrality meant giving full consideration to Italian claims, especially in Croatia, which Mussolini would never allow to slide under German influence. Ciano in his diary, hinted on several occasions the willingness of the desperate English and French to extend tacit approval of Mussolini's ambitions in the Balkans (entries for September 20, October 19, and December 26, 1939). Before Welles came to Europe, Ciano, with Mussolini's consent, reestablished talks with Pavelić, who, since the Non-Aggression and Neutrality Pact between Italy and Yugoslavia on March 25, 1937, had been put on hold (entry for January 23, 1940). In the meantime, Ciano was informed by the French government that they were worried about Russian and German intentions in the Balkans. The French informed Ciano that if the Russians or Germans did make a move, General Weygand's army from Syria would intervene to repel any threats, although not without prior consultation with Rome (entry for December 24, 1939). General Maxime Weygand's army in Syria had been on Prince Paul's mind for some time. In late summer of 1939, the British and the French toyed with the idea of moving Weygand's troops from Syria to Salonika. Prince Paul was elated. In his mind, the French troops in the Balkans were the best deterrent against an Italian dash to Salonika, Yugoslavia's only link with the outside world. Before the war started, the British, thinking that Mussolini was about to take sides with Hitler, were in favor of turning Salonika into a fortress. Mussolini's neutral stance, and even hostile word toward the Nazi-Soviet pact, influenced the British to change their mind. To keep Italy neutral became an "all important factor" in British policy.[16]

When Welles came to Rome, Ciano vented his anti-German feelings. In addition to the distraction of Poland, the speech made by the *Statthalter* of Dresden only threw additional oil on the Italian fire. Slightly drunk (or so the Germans claimed), he said that Germany should be afraid more so of its friends than of its enemies.[17] In an atmosphere of mutual mistrust and suspicion of betrayal on both sides, it seemed that Welles' mission might attain a degree of success in Rome. These optimistic expectations were dispelled the moment Welles met Mussolini. Unimpressed by the British and French response to Germany during and after the Polish debacle, Mussolini had come to the conclusion that the democracies would surely go under. *Il Duce* demonstratively ignored the American undersecretary of state, and intimated to Ciano that Italy could not do business with the United States because Americans "judged problems on the surface while we [Italians] go deeply into them."[18]

In Berlin, Welles was even less successful. Before he arrived, Hitler had issued a secret order to German officials not to discuss or show any interest regarding the peace proposal. An official of the *Auswärtiges Amt* told the Yugoslav minister in Berlin, Ivo Andrić, that one should doubt Roosevelt's sincerity. If Roosevelt had followed his own inclinations, the United States would already have been at war with Germany. *Reich* Foreign Minister Joachim von Ribbentrop informed Welles from the start that Germany, like the United States, needed a Monroe Doctrine of its own in eastern and southeastern Europe. As for Hitler, he believed that peace could be attained only by a victorious German army.[19] He therefore told Welles that there could be no peace in sight until the resistance to national socialism was crushed on the battlefield.[20]

From Berlin, Welles returned to Rome again on March 16, 1940. Although the French and British leaders were certain by now that only military victory against Hitler could assure peace, they were still willing to negotiate with the Axis.[21] Regarding the Italians to be more rational than the Germans, Welles opened his talks with Ciano by saying that the mood in London and Paris was not as intransigent as press and official statements might suggest. If London and Paris had certain guarantees of their security, "they would be ready to give in more or less and recognize the fait accompli."[22] While Welles remained in Rome, Mussolini and Ciano were off to see Hitler in the Brenner Pass. War was discussed at the meeting, and Ciano recorded in his diary that *Il Duce* felt "more and more the fascination for the Fuehrer" and declared his unwavering solidarity with Germany, but the precise date to enter the war was left open (entry for March 18, 1940).

Upon his return, Ciano purposely downgraded the importance of the Brenner Pass meeting and told Welles that it was no more than an Axis "domestic incident," that left things as they were (entry for March 19, 1940). That was not quite so. The reaction in London and Paris was swift and serious, but Mussolini paid no attention to it. The French ambassador in Rome, André François-Poncet, expressed his disappointment to Ciano, saying that although *Il Duce* doubled his bet, he "put his money on the wrong horse" (entry for March 19, 1940). Chamberlain voiced his protest in Parliament while Ambassador Bullitt from Paris already predicted in January that Mussolini would be swayed by self-interests. Since Britain and France could not satisfy his ambition in North Africa and Syria, Mussolini believed Germany would.[23] This belief was further bolstered by the German occupation of Denmark and Norway in April 1940.

All hope, however, was not lost. Since entry into the war was still open, Welles concentrated his efforts on doing whatever he could to keep Mussolini out. He spoke of a possible meeting between Mussolini and Roosevelt in the Azores.[24] Mussolini, however, remained unmoved. Before leaving Rome, Welles spoke to his relative, Blasco d'Aieta. According to Welles, the war was already won by France and Britain because Germany would be exhausted even without undertaking any offensive, and the United States was there "with all the weight of [its] power to guarantee the victory."[25] In the meantime, under pressure from Washington, both France and Britain agreed to discontinue their restrictive trade practices in favor of an American plan based upon a liberal economic principle. The final draft of the American peace proposal incorporating these principles was about to be sent to the European neutrals, but Hitler's offensive in France impeded American intentions.[26]

Meanwhile, the American public had a vague notion as to the purpose of Welles' mission in Europe. Upon the undersecretary's return, Roosevelt held a press conference on March 29, 1940. He reiterated in part some of his previous statements made on February 9, 1940, adding that although there might be scant prospects for peace, the information gathered by the undersecretary would be of the greatest value when the time for peace arrived.[27] His explanations were, as usual, purposefully vague, leaving room for further secret negotiations with Rome. Privately, Roosevelt believed that Mussolini eventually would join Hitler, but only at the last moment, to amass as many spoils as possible for Italy with a minimum of effort on his part. To the desperate French and British, Mussolini's coldhearted realism looked like blackmail but, on the credit side, it did offer some possibility for further negotiations.

To that end, both the British and French representatives in the Vatican asked the personal representative to Pope Pius XII, Myron C. Taylor, to communicate the wishes of their governments to Roosevelt. In a further appeal to Mussolini, Roosevelt tried to convince him and other high Fascist officials that the nature of their regime would not be an issue in attaining cordial relations with Italy.[28] It was Cordell Hull, instead of Roosevelt, who answered Taylor, saying that the president saw no useful purpose for such an appeal at this point (689). Roosevelt, however, soon changed his mind. On April 29, 1940, he hinted in a message to *Il Duce* that in view of the present circumstances, one hardly could predict that the nations desiring to remain out of war "might yet eventually find it imperative in their own defense to enter the war" (692). The intent of the message was not merely to warn Mussolini, but to give Roosevelt leverage for further negotiations. Mussolini replied to Roosevelt's message on May 2, 1940, placing responsibility for war squarely on British and French shoulders. Mussolini singled out the British, who, as he pointed out, were the only European people in control of a large part of the world. In respect of the Monroe Doctrine, Mussolini therefore requested reciprocity with regard to European affairs (698).

With the war already progressing in France, and under considerable pressure from London and Paris, Roosevelt communicated yet another message to Rome on May 14, 1940. This time the president tried appealing to Mussolini's sense of decency. The world, Roosevelt stressed, was facing a "threat which appose[ed] every teaching of Christ, every philosophy of all the great teachers of mankind over thousands of years." Roosevelt impressed upon *Il Duce* the value of peace in the Mediterranean and asked him to stay away from war in the name of culture and civilization (705). Mussolini replied much as he had before, that he intended to remain allied with Germany and that Italy could not remain absent at the moment when the fate of Europe was at stake (706). As a last ditch effort, the French and British ambassadors in Washington jointly asked Roosevelt once again to intercede with Mussolini on behalf of their governments. On May 26, 1940, Roosevelt, with full agreement of the ambassadors, conveyed their wishes to *Il Duce,* to the effect that in exchange for Italy's neutrality and peace in the Mediterranean, the Allies were ready to consider all of Mussolini's outstanding claims (709–11).

On May 30, 1940, Hull authorized Phillips to communicate to Ciano that unless peace was preserved in the Mediterranean, the United States would accelerate its defense program and increase provisions of all supplies that the Allied powers might require (713–14). But Mussolini refused to be intimidated. He objected to American interests in the Mediterranean and told Phillips that Americans had as much interest there as Italy had in the Caribbean Sea (715). Instead of pursuing peace, Mussolini declared war against France and Great Britain on June 10, 1940.

In addition, there were still some aspects of Roosevelt's offensive for peace that had yet to be considered. In his message, Roosevelt talked forcefully of the importance of peace in the Mediterranean and how 200 million people around it would be tragically affected if Mussolini, by entering the war on Germany's side by military means, changed the status quo. Yet, without control over the Balkans, a point Roosevelt never mentioned, one could not imagine the safety of the Mediterranean area at all. The silence regarding Italian Balkan policy in talks with Mussolini was not therefore an honest omission but a well-calculated ploy. In addition to Italian claims in the Danubean-Balkan area, the Nazi-Soviet pact brought yet another player into the region. Many apologists for Soviet foreign policy saw in it a cunning diplomatic maneuver to further impede German penetration eastward. The cold-blooded dismemberment of Poland, the occupation of the Baltic states, and the war against Finland, however, in fact reinvigorated suspicion of the Soviet Union both in America and Europe. The Russian presence in the Balkans alarmed Mussolini and rekindled his desire to occupy Croatia.

Given Hitler's encouragement regarding "uncertain neutrals" and the acquiescent dispositions of London and Paris with respect to Mussolini's Balkan ambitions, no one would really stand in Mussolini's way if he really wished to acquire Croatia. Ciano informed the Rumanian president, Ion Antunescu, of Italian concerns and Mussolini's plan in the event of any Russian involvement in the Balkans. Antunescu was delighted and communicated to Ciano that, according to the French ambassador in Bucharest, Great Britain had recently sent a note to Paris couched in the following terms: "(1) Italy must again be won over to the British side; (2) Italy wants to go into the Balkans; [and] (3) if this is the condition for the realization of the first point, England is ready to let her go ahead."[29] Apart from his liberal economic policy, which was to be implemented sometime in the future, the immediate effect of Roosevelt's messages to Mussolini was to encourage the latter to undermine German influence in the Balkans. It could not be otherwise because the American president was a message deliverer for the Allies and wished to help them. Thus, during Roosevelt's message-sending engagement, the British ambassador in Rome, Percy Loraine, returned from London and informed Ciano that his instructions were "to do everything" to safeguard relations between London and Rome.[30] From Paris, Ambassador William C. Bullitt communicated to Washington on May 31, 1940, that the French government was prepared to examine Italy's claim with a view of satisfying them.[31]

From the Allied point of view, the timing of satisfying Mussolini's claims in Croatia was perfect. Germany would not be able to react to save Yugoslavia, because the bulk of German forces were already deployed along its western borders for an attack against British and French armies in France. When Welles was in Europe, Mussolini was in the process of preparing, although not very seriously, for his invasion of Croatia with the help of Pavelić and his followers.[32] Another element in this strategic equation was the nature of the Balkan Pact. Neither Greece nor Turkey, signatories to the pact, wished to embroil themselves in war against Italy, which they considered to be the major power in the Mediterranean and one that should be recognized as such. Drawing from the experience of World War I and the subsequent invasion of Turkey by the Greeks aided by the British, the Turks maintained that to keep their neutrality intact, their main concern was to foster friendly relations with the Soviet Union and Italy. As a partly Balkan and partly Mediterranean country, the Greeks felt that Greece, through negotiations, should protect its interests vis-à-vis Italy. As for Yugoslavia, one of the leading Croatian historians, Ljubo Boban, observed that by the end of 1939, the British out of necessity, focused their Yugoslav policy, despite a Serbo-Croatian agreement on the Serbian military and the Serbian oppositional forces who were against the agreement and its main architect, Prince Paul.[33]

Thus, when Welles was in Europe, the papal nuncio in Paris, Valerio Valeri, communicated to his secretary of state, Cardinal Luigi Maglione, that at the end of April 1940, the French government had decided not to intervene on Yugoslavia's behalf if Italy were to invade.[34] The papal nuncio assigned to the Italian government in Rome, Borgognini Duca, informed his chief, Cardinal Maglione, that according to government sources, war against Yugoslavia was inevitable, although it would be limited to the occupation of Croatia and that Croatia desired a separate status under Italian protection.[35] By the end of March 1940, Colonel Norman E. Fiske, chief of the Balkan and Near East military intelligence section, prepared a lengthy memorandum on Yugoslavia for the chief of military intelligence, General Miles. It seems to have been the first memorandum of its kind; therefore, one may assume that it was done for the purpose of briefing the president as well.[36]

The images from the Serbian caves overshadowed the memorandum. It was inaccurate and filled the "mental baggage" of those who read it. The most salient parts of the memorandum held that the Serbians, otherwise by their hearts and souls in sympathy with London and Paris, enjoyed a numerical superiority over the "minorities" who lacked the strength and cohesion to be of any value to the Allies. According to the memorandum, Yugoslavia was composed of a "fantastic mixture" of all the conflicting races and religions of the Balkans. With regard to the population, Fiske pointed out that there were 7,325,000 Serbians out of 14,275,000 Yugoslav citizens.[37] Analyzing the internal conditions, Fiske blamed the "minorities" for their lack of democracy and social cohesion, and asserted that however distractive their effect on Yugoslavia may have been, nothing came close to the hostility existing between Serbians and Croatians. To make his point more convincing, Fiske stressed that the Croatian culture was essentially German, whereas the Serbian was Turkish and definitely oriented toward the East.[38]

Although the Serbo-Croatian agreement tried to eliminate the enmity between them and furnish Croatia with a measure of autonomy (the map of which was attached to the memorandum), none of the domestic struggles could be eliminated. Fearful of losing their dominant position, various Serbian factions were opposed to the concessions made to the Croatians. Now that other "minorities" clamored for a similar autonomous life, the situation worsened and placed additional strain on the already fragile structure of the state. The concessions made notwithstanding, the revolutionary aspirations among Macedonians and Croatians were gaining strength. Fiske's unequivocal conclusion was that Yugoslavia, in the present state, was in no position to undertake any action, even if an outright dissolution of the state was no longer as previously imminent.[39] At any rate, the main value of the document was to demonstrate that Yugoslavia was not a viable state.

In short, Yugoslavia, compared to Italy and its strategic value in the eastern Mediterranean, had outlived its usefulness. Burdened by unresolved internal problems, Yugoslavia, in fact, was regarded as a liability for the Allied strategy whose aim at this point was to distance Mussolini from Hitler and turn *Il Duce* into another Franco, sympathizing with Germany but remaining neutral. To implement their plan, Mussolini's claims in the Balkans were viewed as the indispensable condition, the price of which was the western part of Croatia (especially the Adriatic coast).[40] In his effort to demolish the old "Versailles creature," Mussolini could count on the ardent support of Pavelić and his followers, while in Serbia, all factions were in opposition to the "concessions" made to Croatians. Considering the legal constraints on Roosevelt, his "profound" action disguised by his offensive for peace, arguably serves as a textbook example of machiavellian liberalism. Hence Mussolini would be rendered neutral, the Serbians would be awarded greater Serbia on the basis of the Ciano-Stojadinović agreement, and the Croatians would no longer remain an "embarrassment" to the Roosevelt administration. To put it in a broader perspective, Mussolini, aided by Serbians who were free of their "minorities" and other Balkan peoples, could forge a neutral barrier of sorts against German penetration toward the Mediterranean.

For a better understanding of Roosevelt's reasoning with respect to Yugoslavia, one has to know that in his view, Serbia was wronged by the creation of the new states in 1918. Subconsciously guided by his own particular mental baggage, he thought of Yugoslavia in terms of Serbia, which in his view, was the only entity capable of injecting life into the bloodstream of this ailing political creation; if not that, then separation was the solution. When Yugoslav Minister Fotić came to see Roosevelt after the Belgrade coup d'etat on March 27, 1941, Roosevelt addressed him as the Serbian minister and told the latter at the end of conversation: "Don't you think that it [would] be much better for you Serbs if you again became a homogeneous state by divorcing yourselves from your western provinces? You [would] again be strong and [wouldn't] waste your efforts in those endless domestic problems and discussion."[41]

On June 27 1941, the Yugoslav prime minister, General Simović, broadcasted the Yugoslav war aims on the BBC, saying that after the war, all territories inhabited by the southern Slavs and now under foreign jurisdiction, would be returned to Yugoslavia. Roosevelt reacted swiftly, warning Churchill against any trades or deals with the occupied nations, followed by the comment, "[a]s for example, the stupid story that you have promised to set up Yugoslavia again and the other story that you have promised Trieste to Yugoslavia."[42] Roosevelt expressed these same views in a conversation with the British foreign secretary, Anthony Eden, in March of 1943. Yugoslavia was discussed and Roosevelt voiced his opinion to the effect that he favored separating Serbia from Croatia.[43] The best testimony on this point came from Robert E. Sherwood. According to Sherwood, the president expressed his "oft repeated opinion that the Croats and Serbs had nothing in common and that it [was] ridiculous to try to force two such antagonistic peoples to live together under the same government."[44] According to the same source, Roosevelt's views were that Serbia itself be established as a separate state, while Croatia would be placed under a "trusteeship."[45] Roosevelt discussed numerous Yugoslav problems with Undersecretary Welles. According to Welles, Roosevelt talked to him for over an hour about the desirability of using plebiscites "to settle once and for all the friction between the Serbs, the Croats, and the Slovenes which had so clouded the history of Yugoslavia as an independent state."[46] Had Mussolini implemented his plan, his occupation of Croatia would have been very much in conformity with Roosevelt's idea of a trusteeship.

The greatest flaw of the entire plan was Mussolini himself. He decided that to attack Yugoslavia at this point "would be a humiliating experience, and besides," as he told Ciano after the victory was won, "we could obtain what we want anyway."[47] Irrespective of the failure of Roosevelt's peace offensive, the Allies, in their future policy toward Yugoslavia, remained faithful to their exclusive reliance on the opponents of the Serbo-Croatian agreement and its main architect, Prince Paul.

Chapter 4
Lane's Period in the
Diplomatic Wilderness

Roosevelt's offensive for peace had no chance of success. His economic solution was weak medicine for Europe's political ills. Political differences between the Axis powers and western democracies needed a radical solution that only war could bring. The Allied hope that Mussolini and his "seven million bayonets" and the sky "filled with planes" could be bribed into switching sides, was dashed by his joining belligerently against France. The Nazi-Soviet pact added a new dimension, thus complicating the European political agenda. It not only marked an active reentry of the Soviet Union into European politics but, from the Soviet point of view, the pact enabled Stalin to prevent further Anglo-French machinations against the "first land of Socialism," in collusion with Germany.[1] For security reasons, the pact reactivated interrupted Russian interest in the Balkans. The representative of the Soviet Press Agency (TASS) in Geneva, Rosenstein, and the Soviet undersecretary of the League of Nations, Sokolin, informed the Yugoslav press representative to the league that the Soviets would not tolerate a unilateral German initiative in Rumania, nor would they leave the guardianship over the Black Sea exclusively to the Turks. Suspecting that the British, in cooperation with Turkey, might repeat World War I as a military undertaking in the Straits and thereby involve the Soviet Union in a war with Italy and Germany, Moscow was in favor of keeping the Balkans neutral.[2]

Roosevelt's peace offensive caught Lane sitting on the sidelines. He was still a "listening post" without the authority to initiate anything other than listening and reporting. Other American diplomatic representatives in the area were in the same position. Whether they were in Belgrade, Budapest, Bucharest, Sofia, Athens, or Ankara, they all had the same task—report and do nothing that might involve the United States in European affairs. As diplomats, all except Lincoln MacVeagh, the minister in Greece, had one thing in common. Because of their educational background and diplomatic experience, they were uniquely unqualified for the job. They were shifted to distant places, unrelated to the Balkans, without any necessary training or guidance. Herbert C. Peal was transferred from Portugal to Hungary, George Earle, the former governor of Pennsylvania, from Vienna to Bulgaria, Franklin Gunther from Teheran to Bucharest, and Lane from the Baltic to Belgrade.[3]

Of them all, Lane was the most dynamic indeed, and wished to escape his daily routine by injecting some of his subtle feelings into his reports. Thus, when war started over Poland, he reported to Washington that Prince Paul was sad, and blamed the United States and its neutrality for the war. But for American neutrality, "the European war would have never started," Paul told Lane.[4] Lane tacitly shared his views, and to console the "melancholic" Paul, found the silver lining in the dark cloud of the Nazi-Soviet pact. In Lane's view, the Soviets signed the pact to prevent German advances rather than to help them. Paul agreed, but in contrast to Lane, shared the view prevalent in western capitals, that Soviet reentry in Europe marked the beginning of certain "far-reaching consequences," one of which was the bolshevization of Europe the moment opportunities were favorable. Lane, as a liberal democrat, could not see any sinister intent on the part of the Soviets, and he therefore disagreed and communicated to Washington that the Serbian people did not share Paul's feelings.[5]

For the most part, Lane concentrated his attention on Yugoslav domestic affairs. Forgetting about his erstwhile gloomy report pertaining to the agreement, he again assailed the Croatian leader Maček, along with the Croatian spiritual leader, Archbishop of Zagreb Aloisyus Stepinac. Apparently, Lane wished them to behave in an American fashion as when the president of the United States visited the capitals of Florida, New York, or some other American state, without controversy and strictly according to protocol. The occasion was the Serbian royal visit to Croatia in January of 1940. As a realist, Paul did not expect an outpouring of friendly emotions, but Lane was offended by the lack of it, and expressed his disapproval in lengthy reports to Washington. He actually accused Croatian leader Maček of behaving as a "lord and master" of an independent country, which in Lane's view, was an insult to the royal guests. Instead of demonstrating a show of unity, Maček deliberately turned the visit into a "Croatian show," leaving the unmistakable impression he was still "nothing more than a political opportunist and demagogue."[6] His displeasure reached a boiling point when he heard of Maček's interview with the official Italian paper, *Giornale d'Italia*. For tactical reasons, Maček gave the impression that Croatia, after the agreement with Belgrade, did not turn its back on Italy but together with Italy and Hungary, pursued a policy of neutrality in the Danubean region. Not knowing what motivated him to make such a statement, Lane branded him outright as "first and foremost" a Croatian nationalist and the champion of virtual independence from Belgrade (Doc. no. 860H.00/1097).

It took some skill and patience on the part of Stojan Gavrilović, Chief of the League of Nations Section in the Yugoslav Foreign Office, to calm Lane. Gavrilović confided to Lane's deputy Joyce that Maček's nationalistic show was more appearance than substance, that it was designed to pacify the opposition and maintain his position of preeminence in Croatia (Doc. no. 860H.00/1145). Lane was even less accurate in appraising the archbishop's speech, made before the entrance to the Zagreb Cathedral. According to Lane, the speech was "confusing and tactless." It was neither. For the benefit of Paul and his wife, Stepinac spoke of perennial human concerns regarding the power of the state versus human rights and freedom (Doc. no. 860H.00/1127). Lane, who understood not a single word of any of the southern Slavic languages, may have been somewhat misled by an exceptionally bad translation of the text.

Undoubtedly, his reports manifested his frustration and perplexity with regard to the Balkans and Europe in general. Nothing seemed to be moving in the right direction. The British expedition in Scandinavia ended in disaster. The Russo-Finnish War and British attempts to utilize the war against the Soviets never got off the ground.[7] The gradual concentration of German forces in the west, the period known in American historiography as the "Phony War," combined with the failure of Roosevelt's peace offensive, hung like a dark cloud over the European landscape. Furthermore, given that no appreciable improvement occurred within Yugoslavia only added to Lane's frustration. Yugoslavia still had to look to Germany for protection of its sovereignty. To that end, an additional secret protocol supplementary to the one of October 1939, was signed in Belgrade between Germany and Yugoslavia in mid-May of 1940.[8] Although this protocol placed Yugoslavia's exports largely under German control, Prince Paul was grateful, under the circumstances, to have Germany on his side.[9] As a result of Maček's "negative behavior," Lane attempted in his reports to reevaluate the Serbo-Croatian Agreement in terms of its "negative" influence on Yugoslav unity. Now that the Croatians had their autonomy, he reported, others sought the same status, spreading fear among Serbians that the agreement would turn Yugoslavia into a federated state.[10] Why this transformation would adversely affect Yugoslav unity, Lane did not elaborate. Instead, he illustrated the Serbian anger by quoting two Serbian politicians, Bogoljub Jevtić and General Petar Živković (both renowned as staunch supporters of King Alexander's dictatorship). These two gentlemen denounced the agreement as a Serbian "surrender" to Croatian demands, and consequently voiced their concerns over the "growing Croatian influence."[11] However in disarray the Serbians may have become compared to Croatians, they were moving closer together with respect to an autonomy of their own. The government (i.e., Prince Paul), however, stood in the way of Serbian aspirations, saying that it would widen the gap between Croatians and Serbians.[12]

With his limited knowledge of Yugoslav internal affairs, Lane had no idea how right Prince Paul was. Considering Serbian territorial aspirations, autonomy would have in effect given rightful recognition of greater Serbia within a Yugoslav state. It would not only have "widen[ed] the gap," but quite possibly would have invited an open rebellion against Belgrade, pushing Mussolini to intervene on Croatia's behalf. Even the Germans, who were in favor of keeping peace in the Balkans, were aware of the danger to their interests there. General Franz Halder, chief of the OKH, recorded in his April 1940, diaries that given Italy's neutral status, Mussolini was in a position to occupy Croatia, "without declaring war on anyone or taking the side of the one or the other party."[13] The American military attaché in Belgrade, Colonel Louis Fortier, reported to Washington that Yugoslavia was partially mobilized, but "exceedingly slow."[14] As previously pointed out, Hitler had Yugoslavia in mind as an "uncertain neutral," but Italy was unprepared and Mussolini was not about to plunge into war against its eastern neighbor while France, the bigger spoil, was next on Hitler's agenda. At any rate, Paul was cautious not to demonstrate any show of force that would provoke not only Italy but most likely Hungary and Bulgaria as well, both of which had territorial claims on Yugoslavia.

There is no evidence to confirm that Lane, or the U.S. State Department for that matter, knew what was really behind Roosevelt's peace offensive. They were still focusing their attention on maintaining the status quo in the Balkans. In this sense, the official Washington policy to keep peace in the Balkans was exactly what the Soviets and the Germans wanted. Roosevelt in his peace offensive never entertained the idea that Berlin would accept his economic solution for peace. Mussolini, however, was a different proposition altogether. His desire to occupy Croatia was a strong incentive to separate Italy from Germany. Even if the Italian invasion of Croatia did ignite war in the Balkans, so much the better. To protect their vital interests in the area, the Germans would have been compelled to rise to the challenge, as would the Soviets if they wished to secure the Black Sea. Although such expectations would seem unrealistic, one should bear in mind that the Balkans, for all powers concerned within the area, was a piece of real estate, which, with proper handling, could be used to some advantage.

For the Americans, Yugoslavia looked like a "crazy quilt of nationalities," uncontrolled and chaotic. For the British, and the Germans as well, the entire Balkan area was "trash," led by "chieftains, [who] could be made and unmade."[15] The idea of involving the Soviets against the Germans, however, existed for some time before the invasion of France, and was rooted in the belief that Germany could be defeated through isolation. Economic isolation of Germany, coupled with the "invincibility" of French arms behind the Maginot Line, would force Germany to surrender, just as in World War I. The unforeseen conflict in the north between Finland and the Soviet Union gave additional impetus to this illusion. If a similar war somewhere along the Soviet borders occurred, the effect might be disastrous for Soviet-Nazi relations. The Soviet engagement on two fronts, it was believed, would disrupt the German supply lines across the Soviet Union. Since the Soviet Union was Germany's principal commercial partner, the disruption would force Germany intervention to secure their supplies. This in turn would push the Soviet Union into war with its erstwhile partner. In short, to break the isolation, Germany would have no other choice but to wage war against the Soviets.

Most likely suggested by the British, a former colonel of the Russian imperial staff, Eugene Mossner, published an article of a similar nature in the Belgrade paper, *Vreme*. It dealt with the Finno-Soviet conflict and its ramifications on the Soviet system. Drawing on the Soviet imbroglio with Finland, Mossner came to the conclusion that General Maxime Weygand's forces in Syria were of considerable help to the Finns. His forces kept the Soviets in suspense and deterred them from concentrating on victory. The Allies, however, should go further and challenge the Soviets in a more serious conflict in Caucasus, near the rich oil fields. Such a conflict would not only endanger the Soviet system, but radically alter Soviet-German relations.[16]

Fortier translated the article into English, and added in his report that it deserved the "highest recommendation" for its "objective treatment and clear-cut strategic exposition of a much discussed subject."[17] In case the eastern front materialized under General Weygand's command, the Balkan nations would be included. But alas, the Balkan nations disagreed sharply on many important points. Rumanians were in favor of individual action, whereas Greeks pleaded for collective action in case of war. Yugoslav Foreign Minister Aleksandar Cincar Marković refused to become entangled in a military alliance that might prove detrimental to a neutral Yugoslavia. In the end, Fortier concluded that the Allies themselves bore the greatest responsibility for the failure of the eastern front.[18]

Although the eastern front faded away, the widening of the ongoing war in the north was very much on the British mind. With the highly unpopular Russo-Finnish war, both the French and the British were ready to spring into action.

Two British divisions with British bombers, fifty thousand French "volunteers," and a hundred bombers were ready to be sent to Finland. They would have been sent but for the fact that the Norwegians and the Swedes refused to co-operate.[19] Sir Winston Churchill (First Sea Lord at the time), himself one of the "rebels" against the "appeasers," was as enthusiastic as his boss Chamberlain about the Scandinavian expedition. In the war cabinet meeting, Churchill declared that if events forced Norway and Sweden into war with Russia, "we would then be able to gain a foothold in Scandinavia with the object of helping them, but without having to go to the extent of ourselves declaring war against Russia."[20] Recalling the events in retrospect, Churchill, in his memoirs shyly remembered those days, saying that such undertakings were beyond the dictates of "common prudence."[21] That may be so, but by no means less prudent than the entire notion that the "Huns" may be beaten through isolation and peripheral strategy.

When Churchill became the prime minister on May 10, 1940, he merely reversed Chamberlain's policy vis-à-vis the Soviet Union. Like Chamberlain, Churchill too was an ardent anti-bolshevik, tempered, however, by certain practical considerations. Unlike Chamberlain, he wanted the Soviet Union on his side. While the German armies were racing across the Ardennes, Churchill instructed his ambassador in Moscow, Sir Stafford Cripps, to undertake negotiations for a commercial agreement with the Soviets if the latter agreed not to resell the goods to the Germans. Cripps was further instructed to intimate to the Soviets that, in so far as Great Britain was concerned, the Soviet Union was "rightly" in a position to organize the Balkan states against German penetration into the area. To stimulate the Soviet appetite, the British were prepared to recognize Soviet interests in the Straits.[22] Although at first glance it might appear that Churchill and Roosevelt worked at cross-purposes, a closer look, however, showed their actions to be complementary, the possibility still existing that Mussolini might be persuaded to divide Yugoslavia with the Serbians. Churchill never mentioned the Italians. If, however, Mussolini refused to act (as he did), then the Soviets could serve the same purpose. The only difference was that the Germans would take military action against the Soviet presence in the Balkans.

British "generosity" could hardly fail to put Kremlin leaders on their guard. To make sure that they remained in Berlin's good graces, the Soviets divulged the British offer to the Germans. Communicating the British story to the Germans, Stalin very subtly interjected his own views on the matter. Although the Soviet Union, he said, was interested in Balkan affairs, no single power should be allowed to have an exclusive role in the region.[23] The Soviet attitude toward the Balkans was not a secret. They desired to keep it neutral for as long as they could because they were wary of both the Germans and the British. Cognizant of the Soviet position, Prince Paul decided to act upon it. He came to the conclusion that an agreement, even of a commercial nature, might serve as a deterrent against Mussolini. The agreement was signed on May 11, 1940, but fell far below the desired expectations. Realizing its impotence vis-à-vis Italy, Paul supplemented it with mutual recognition and the establishment of normal diplomatic relations between Belgrade and Moscow on June 24, 1940.[24]

Anxious to keep the Balkans as their very own, the Germans took rapprochement between Belgrade and Moscow much more seriously than it actually deserved. The legation from Bucharest communicated to Washington about the concentration of German troops in Slovakia. The troops were ready to spring into action to bar Soviet incursion into the Balkans.[25] Concerned that the peace might be shattered in the Balkans, Hull quickly instructed his people in Moscow to impress upon the Soviet government, the American views with respect to widening the war. At the same time, he requested clarification of Soviet intentions regarding the Balkans (Doc. no. 740.0011, European War 1939/3344). The Soviets denied any aggressive intention, and justified their troop movement toward the Black Sea on the grounds that it was a precautionary measure "to meet any eventualities" arising from the possible outbreak of hostility involving Italy, Great Britain, and Turkey in the Mediterranean (Doc. no. 740.0011, European War 1939/3447). As an incorrigible believer in reciprocal trade as a means of attaining lasting peace, Hull was fearful of any changes that might impair the prospects for peace. In a time of rapid changes brought about by military means, Hull was a remarkably unrealistic man, but still useful to Roosevelt's administration. His facade regarding legal adherence to the rules of international law in solving disputes among nations afforded, to the more practical Roosevelt and his undersecretary of state, Sumner Welles, the opportunity to make certain diplomatic moves, which under the surface were by no means in harmony with the postulates of American foreign policy still pursued by Hull.

Metaphorically speaking, Lane felt like a cricket under the waterfall. He felt voiceless and of no use while events were changing around him. Sitting on the sidelines in Belgrade, he was angry with everyone. He could not understand why such a slow response occurred on the part of the Allies to the Nazi challenge. There was, however, nothing he could do or change. The official policy to watch, listen, and report (with the emphasis on reporting) should any status quo changes take place, still held. Hungarians were about to square their account with Rumania over Transylvania, and appealed to Berlin for help. To consolidate their gains in the east, and to redeploy their troops successfully in the west, the Germans declined to intervene on Hungary's behalf. The Hungarians then turned to Sumner Welles for help. Since Washington officially still played the role of an "honest broker," Welles too declined, saying that the United States could not possibly inject itself into political problems of a purely European nature (Doc. no. 764.715/37). Why Welles really refused to take the role of mediator between Hungary and Rumania, one can only guess. I suspect that American intervention on Hungary's behalf would have helped Germany. By leaving the border dispute open to German arbitration, the chances of a German, Italian, and Soviet embroilment in the Balkans were enhanced.

In the absence of any meaningful instruction from Washington, Lane was compelled to adhere to his observations concerning the Yugoslav domestic scene. The lack of Yugoslav internal unity again cast a dark cloud over him. He doubted Yugoslavia's ability to resist the Axis pressure. This foreboding was confirmed by Meily, who in turn informed Lane that frequent bombings and street demonstrations in the Croatian capital were directed against Maček, Paul, and the agreement, and manifested great sympathy for Pavelić (Doc. nos. 860H.00/1130; 860H.00/1131). In another lengthy report from Zagreb, Meily implicated the Catholic Church in the fomenting of unrest in Croatia. In collusion with Rome, the Catholic Church in Croatia advocated from the pulpit, the separation of Croatia from Serbia. Transmitting Meily's report to Washington, Lane reiterated one of his previous observations. The differences between the two people could not have possibly been "blotted out by a political agreement arrived at under pressure of a dangerous international situation" (Doc. nos. 860H.00/1130; 860H.00/1131). Concerned about the situation in Croatia, Lane wished to confirm it firsthand. He spoke with one of the Croatian leaders, Košutić, who tried his best to convince Lane that the conditions there were not as bad as they seemed. In Lane's view, the Croatian Peasant Party's leaders were "in their heart satisfied" with the outcome of the agreement, but he doubted that others were (Doc. no. 860H.00/1136). In contrast to the Croatian Peasant Party leaders, there was a widespread opinion in Serbia against the agreement. The agreement, Lane pointed out, "threatened, if not totally destroyed" Serbian dreams of a greater Serbia. "All in all," he concluded, "the internal situation in Yugoslavia at the present moment appear[ed] highly uncertain, if not precarious (Doc. no. 860H.00/1136).

Fortier, who was much closer to the Serbian military than Lane, expanded in detail on the subject of greater Serbia in his report. His mentor on the subject was the "most informed" person and the "best political thinker" in Belgrade, Hungarian military attaché, Colonel Joseph Vasvary. According to Vasvary, the main source of present Serbian grievances was indeed the agreement. The agreement had shattered the unity of the Serbian political parties, and unless it underwent revision and Croatian "ambitions" were checked once and for all, the people of greater Serbia had absolutely no intention of cooperating with the government. Although unity among the Serbian politicians was desirable and necessary, there was unfortunately no one among them who could challenge Maček to attain this aim.[26] The military, also having been deprived of its traditional role of meddling in politics, felt disgruntled and disenfranchised. According to Vasvary, Fortier stressed, the situation was extremely delicate and requiring careful handling. At any rate, Fortier concluded in his report, the Croatians "must be reckoned with . . . , and [a]ny dream of a Great Serbia must vanish."[27]

In light of Allied diplomacy toward Italy and Welles' mission, Lane's reports were exceptionally useful because they corroborated the views of Roosevelt's inner circle that Yugoslavia was not a viable country, regardless of the agreements with the Croatians. Having misread the real intention behind Roosevelt's peace offensive, Lane did not see it that way. He also did not perceive Churchill's subtle diplomacy toward the Soviets. Discouraged, however, by the lack of a resolute response against the Axis, Lane decided to quit his post shortly after the fall of France. He was bored with his position, which offered nothing but passivity, routine, and disappointment. On July 13, 1940, he wrote a letter to Undersecretary Welles, asking to be transferred from Belgrade somewhere closer to the United States. His request was denied on the grounds of his "exceptionally helpful and useful" reporting.[28] Welles was not exaggerating. The undersecretary's letter injected confidence into Lane's depleted enthusiasm and quickly rejuvenated him.

The "Anglo-Saxon" (as Hitler often referred to the British and American) diplomatic strategy in the Balkans was not unknown to the Fuehrer. To keep Mussolini hopeful and on his side, Hitler revealed to the Italians, the existence of a number of documents captured in France, that incriminated certain Balkan states, including Yugoslavia, of duplicity. Indeed, some of them "appeared in a very interesting light," but at the same time, Hitler pointed out, "one had to be very careful" with regard to Yugoslavia.[29] Taking Hitler's revelations as a cue to settling his outstanding account with Yugoslavia, Mussolini ordered his generals to make all the necessary preparations to attack the "Versailles creature." In addition to military preparation, Italian propaganda intended to destabilize Yugoslavia from within, was to be intensified.[30] The renewed Italian propaganda could not escape Lane's notice. He immediately reported to Washington about new Italian support for the Croatian nationalists and Croatian communists. The communists, he reported, were exceptionally active against the Cvetković-Maček government.[31] While the communists may have had certain dealings with the Italians to destabilize the Yugoslav state, their concerns were primarily in line with the Comintern policy. They demanded a radical revision of Yugoslavia's foreign policy (i.e., complete independence from both "imperialistic camps") and urged a much stronger reliance on Moscow for protecting Yugoslavia's independence.[32] Lane reported frequent street riots and the killings of several people in Zagreb, for which he blamed the Germans and Italians. He also reported on Maček's dwindling authority and Pavelić's rising popularity. According to Lane, Pavelić was extolled as the coming savior of the "free," but in fact, "fascist" Croatia.[33] Fortier in turn dealt exclusively with the French debacle and its influence on Serbian morale. In June 1940, he reported that a mood of resignation and anger was much in evidence among the Serbians, but not among the others. The military could not believe that Yugoslavia was still out of the conflict. In meticulous detail, Fortier described Serbia's anti-German sentiments, claiming the Germans knew that the Serbian submissiveness at this point was dictated by necessity, but precisely because of it, would be compelled to liquidate the unreliable and discordant elements of the southeast earlier than anticipated.[34]

The fall of France was indeed a terrific blow to all who believed in the invincibility of French arms "behind the Maginot [L]ine." No one realized better than Churchill the grave situation in which England remained alone to fight the "Huns." Unlike his predecessor Chamberlain, Winston Churchill was sure that without America's active engagement on the Allied side, the war would be lost. He therefore reversed Chamberlain's American policy and tacitly recognized America's global aspirations. To a group of intimate friends, Churchill confided that "it was vital to our safety that the United States should be involved in totalitarian warfare."[35] As evident from their secret correspondence, Churchill was well aware of Roosevelt's inner feelings, but to manifest them openly would have been politically suicidal. Given American opposition to "getting into a European war," Churchill worded his requests to Roosevelt very carefully, giving the impression that Britain needed America's moral commitment, rather than its expeditionary forces. Ostensibly, Churchill desired only America's "moral engagement," knowing full well that a more drastic request would have serious consequences on Anglo-American relations.[36]

Concerned about British needs, Roosevelt desired to do more than the mere "moral engagement" required of him. Under the impression of the French debacle, which jolted America too, Roosevelt used scare tactics to maneuver the American public. The truth is that many Americans believed Britain would not be able to survive, and with Britain gone to defend the Atlantic approaches, America was next in line to face Hitler. Although one should take Churchill's laudable thinking during Dunkirk with a grain of salt regarding accommodations with Germany, the fact is that it did reflect (to an extent) his state of mind, which invariably made him more disposed to the possibility of accommodation. He contemplated peace only if he "could get out of this jam," providing peace with Germany was not sought by Britain and Hitler was convinced that Britain was unbeatable.[37] Certain evidence suggests that Churchill deceived the Germans into believing that peace between Germany and Britain was possible. Using the Duke of Windsor's Nazi connections, Churchill gave the impression that a negotiated settlement was being considered by the British. During the period of "negotiation," the British managed to withdraw their troops from Dunkirk. Once the withdrawal was achieved and the Duke of Windsor was whisked across the Atlantic, the British were no longer interested in "negotiation." The evidence also suggests that the Duke of Windsor was not the only one connected with the Nazis. British Intelligence used the contacts with Hess for the same purposes. "There can be no doubt that the intelligence services used the contacts with Hess to lead the Germans to attack Russia in the belief that Britain was about to seek peace."[38] The evidence further suggests that Hitler, having realized Britain's game plan, decided to invade the British Isles. With the element of surprise gone, Hitler no longer had his chance for an invasion. To make Americans conscious of the dangers facing them, Roosevelt, while France was on its last legs, pledged to "extend to opponents of force the material resources" of America. He depicted the war in Europe in terms of America's own security, conveying the impression that without the "Atlantic Wall," the invasion of North and South America would be imminent.[39] In reality, Roosevelt was not concerned with the invasion, but the prospect of a German-dominated Europe haunted him and his administration. A conquered Europe appeared in their minds as a gigantic German cartel, capable of pushing America out of the world market.[40] At a meeting with an impressive number of newspaper editors gathered at the White House, Roosevelt again spoke about the market. Unless America had a fairly free market, he told editors, we could end up behind bars. It is quite possible, he went on to say, to dominate the American continent, without sending troops over. By dominating the European Market, the Axis would be in position to hold America under the gun, and could do as they wished.[41]

Always the master of crowd psychology, Roosevelt translated Churchill's "moral engagement" into language easily understood by Americans still living under the shadow of the great economic depression. By using such language, Roosevelt hoped to avoid a politically costly confrontation with the still powerful isolationist groups. The caution he applied to his speeches and public utterances was a way of survival for him, but under the surface, as Berle pointed out, he was "emotionally engaged" in the Allied cause more than anyone around him.[42] His degree of emotional involvement is best illustrated by an unrealistic promise to King George, "[if] London was bombed [the] U.S. would come in."[43] In turn, when Churchill came to power, he reciprocated with his total trust in Roosevelt. He instructed his intelligence chiefs to act upon the assumption that Roosevelt was "part of the family, and to keep nothing from him" (72, 81). This trust was further deepened when Roosevelt allowed the British (without informing Congress) to establish their counterespionage center in New York, known as the British Security Coordination (BSC), under the leadership of the "quiet Canadian," William Stephenson. In addition to being a liaison between the British and Roosevelt, Stephenson performed other functions that were not, one might say, in harmony with American laws. One of those functions entailed the discovery and elimination of German espionage centers in the United States and the rest of the western hemisphere. The self-absorbed FBI chief, J. Edgar Hoover, had to swallow his pride, and by direct order from the president, dutifully cooperated with the British (84–85). The cooperation, under the surface, went so smoothly the president proudly boasted he was Stephenson's "biggest undercover agent" (136). Regarding the supplies of war matériel to the beleaguered British, Roosevelt was equally "emotional." He often circumvented the cash-and-carry laws, by which he was authorized to supply Britain, and frequently depleted the United States army reserve, which was prohibited by law.

Although on the surface, American neutrality officially was still present, under the surface, it was gradually eroding. In Belgrade, Lane tried hard to extrapolate, from public speeches and public utterances made by Washington officials, some tangible guidance. He came to the conclusion, and he was right, that from the viewpoint of the United States as well as Britain, the internal condition of Yugoslavia would continue to be the focus of their interest. The main feature of Belgrade foreign policy, devised by the Serbian establishment, entailed the preservation of Yugoslavia's territorial integrity. Such a policy required a powerful protector. For economic as well as for political reasons, Germany was the most logical choice. Nazi Germany was not interested in Yugoslavia's recalcitrant "minorities," as much as in trade, which Berlin skillfully used to keep Yugoslavia benevolently neutral toward Germany.[44] In light of the fact that the Serbo-Croatian agreement brought little practical improvement to relations between Croatians and Serbians, Maček himself, when he joined the government, recognized a practical need for such a policy. Any disruption of Yugoslavia, he feared, would not only end up in Yugoslav defeat, but worse still, in an open war between Croatians and Serbians. Not for any pro-fascist reason but for reasons of survival, Prince Paul and Maček considered it expedient to carry on the same policy vis-à-vis Germany. The British ambassador in Belgrade, Sir Ronald Campbell, recognized Yugoslavia's position relatively early on, and warned London that given economic and political conditions, plus a geographic proximity to the Axis powers, Belgrade might pursue a benevolent neutrality toward the Axis, for as long as it was possible.[45]

However useful for Yugoslavia's survival, neutrality, in the eyes of London and Washington began to acquire some sinister characteristics in the second part of 1940. Both Lane and his associates, with the exception of Meily, ascribed to the Croatian influences as if the Croatians were the architects of Yugoslavia's pro-German foreign policy. At the end of June 1940, Fortier again communicated to Washington his fear that Germany, having eliminated the possibility of two fronts by destroying France, was free now to settle the matter in southeastern Europe. Following this scenario, Fortier was in full agreement with the Serbian military that the Allies should apply stronger pressure on Paul to keep him in line.[46] The truth is that the Italians contemplated an attack on Yugoslavia, and the Germans were the ones who undermined Mussolini's plan.[47] From Germany, Fortier's mind wandered off to Bulgaria and the possibility of creating a "Slavic block" in the Balkans. His reasons for creating such a block were based on the fact that Bulgaria, sandwiched between German and Soviet interests, would greatly improve its position by improving relations with Yugoslavia. The improvement, however, hinged on Belgrade's willingness to cede some territory (presumably in Macedonia) to satisfy Bulgaria's claims, but the Yugoslavs refused on the grounds that it might encourage their neighbors with similar territorial claims to go against Yugoslavia.[48] The plan to create a "Slavic block" was later resurrected in conjunction with Mussolini's invasion of Greece; but at this point, Fortier conveyed the impression that the Balkan states were petty and jealous of one another, and too selfish and quarrelsome to see clearly the advantages of such an alliance.

Frequent communist riots and the Soviet influence associated with the July arrival of the Soviet ambassador in Belgrade, V. L. Plotnikov, prompted Lane to pay a visit to his Soviet colleague. Concerned about the riots, Lane asked Plotnikov who was behind the communist-inspired riots in Croatia. The Soviet ambassador was generally evasive and hinted that Italy was behind them. Lane sent his report to Washington without comments or doubts as to Plotnikov's hints. Reviewing the Yugoslav situation, however, both Lane and Fortier agreed that the Soviet presence in Belgrade improved morale within the country, especially for the army, which felt that "parallel action by Russians [could] give this country a fighting chance against Germany and Italy." Although better situated than Rumania, Yugoslavia too was in a precarious situation. Additional economic pressure from Germany onto Yugoslavia passed smoothly, but only because, Fortier believed, the Yugoslavs wished to forestall the conflict with Germany until the next year, when they expected the pendulum to swing back in Britain's favor.[49]

In mid-September of 1940, Fortier communicated an alarming report to Washington. It contained a "ten-point" text of Axis demands on Yugoslavia. If the demands were translated into practice, Fortier lamented, Yugoslavia would become an outright Axis colony. It purported to be the exact record of the conversation between Yugoslav Prime Minister Dragiša Cvetković and the German ambassador in Rome, Hans Georg von Mackensen. Because of its drastic demands, Fortier nevertheless cautioned with regard to the authenticity of the document. He found it, however, useful "for general information," and added that the train of events taking place corroborated, at least in tendency, the authenticity of the "ten-point" text.[50] Parenthetically speaking, one might add that so far no one has ever discovered where this alleged meeting took place, or was there ever any official record found. It is therefore quite logical to assume that the alleged document may have been a forgery. The question is whose forgery was it? It could have been Italian, intended to destabilize Yugoslavia given Mussolini's belief that an attack against the country could still be carried out; however, it is highly unlikely because the alleged plan surfaced shortly before the diplomatic impasse between Rome and Athens reached its apex. Before the document reached Washington, the old notion of Yugoslavia being a powerful deterrent against Italy circulated in Belgrade. Picking at the thread, Fortier reported that certain military circles in Belgrade believed that an attack on Italian forces in Albania would create havoc in Italy with dire consequences for Mussolini and his regime.[51]

Be that as it may, that was precisely the role Yugoslavia was assigned to play when Greece was invaded by the Italians, and the author of this strategy was Churchill, with the full backing of Washington. One may deduce, therefore, that the British themselves, in collusion with the Serbian military, were the forgers; some were already organized in conspiratorial groups with a view to removing by force, if necessary, Prince Paul and his benevolent neutrality toward Germany. Fortier personally attended the meetings of these groups at the invitation of an intelligence officer of the Yugoslav General Staff, Colonel Žarko Popović. Also present were the British military attaché, Lieutenant Colonel C. S. "Noby" Clark, and Colonel Draža Mihailović, future leaders of the Chetniks in wartime Yugoslavia as of the summer of 1940.[52] Therefore, irrespective of its authenticity, the document surfaced during a period when Yugoslavia's foreign policy could no longer be tolerated by the western powers. It was time for the Balkan "patriots" to do as they were told. Washington, too, would soon come with an arsenal of "friendly persuasions" to convince the Belgrade government that Yugoslav neutrality would have validity only if it was found to be satisfactorily in accordance with American standards.

Chapter 5
The Struggle for Yugoslavia's "Neutrality"

Mussolini's attack on Greece commenced on October 28, 1940. At that time, the attack was believed to have taken place with Germany's consent. Yet the truth of the matter is that Hitler was once again taken by surprise. The two historians of the Axis strategy in the Balkans, Martin Van Creveld and MacGregor Knox, are in agreement on this point. Mussolini indeed sprang Greece on Hitler at the most inopportune moment for Germany, which was in the process of redeploying its troops from the west to the east.[1] Italian sources agree with their views. Ill-tempered over Germany's move in Rumania to protect the oil fields from attempted British sabotage, Mussolini expressed his displeasure about the Germans to his son-in-law and foreign minister, Ciano. "Hitler always faces me with a fait accompli," declared Mussolini. It seems that this time he had enough and decided to pay Hitler back "in his own coin." As Ciano recorded, *Il Duce* rejoiced in the anticipation that Hitler would find out about the occupation of Greece from the newspapers.[2]

Actually, the Rumanian affair only served as a pretext. Mussolini never liked Hitler's strategy to dislodge Britain from the Mediterranean with the help of Spain and Vichy France. In case of victory, Italy would have had to share its mastery over the Mediterranean with France, Italy's former enemy. The negotiations for joint action in the Mediterranean were going nowhere, and Operation Sea Lion (the invasion of Britain) was postponed "indefinitely." Instead, Hitler decided to kill two birds with one stone by attacking the Soviet Union, which in turn would be a way of liquidating Britain as well. Interpreting the shift in German policy as a sign of weakness, Mussolini decided to act alone, to demonstrate that Italy could do a better job than Germany. Of course, the psychological underpinnings of his action meant reasserting Italy's independence and equality vis-à-vis Germany. By taking simultaneous action in North

Africa and Greece, Mussolini had no doubt that his endeavor, despite serious warning against such optimism by his military commander, would be triumphant. The action in North Africa was delayed; however, as MacGregor Knox pointed out, acting under the impression that it was going to be an easy undertaking, the invasion of Greece was almost on schedule.[3]

To make sure that Yugoslavia would not intervene on behalf of Greece, the Italians informed Belgrade of their impending invasion. Lane reported to Washington that the Italians assured the Yugoslavs as to the nature of their military buildup in Albania. The troops in Albania were earmarked for Greece, and Yugoslavia need not worry.[4] Foreknowledge of the attack was not much of a consolation. Given that the Italians already controlled the Adriatic, an Italian dash across northern Greece to Salonika (a free port) could deprive Yugoslavia easily of its last access to the Mediterranean. Not having time to waste, the Yugoslavs appealed to Germany for help. They stated unequivocally in their appeal that if Italy insisted on passage of its troops across Yugoslav territory in the direction of Salonika, the danger of widening the war in the Balkans would be very real. Transmitting their message to Berlin, von Heeren added that the Yugoslavs would indeed fight, although not for Greece but for their own vital interests.[5] The greatest irony associated with the invasion of Greece was that Mussolini not only became more dependent on Germany, but inadvertently gave new impetus to the as yet unclear Allied Balkan strategy. The Belgrade government immediately realized the seriousness of its new position. The gravity of the Yugoslav position was somewhat tempered by the fact that behind Mussolini's Greek adventure, there were no Germans. It was public knowledge, both in Belgrade and in Athens, that the Germans, in order to avoid all-out war, were in favor of a negotiated settlement between Italy and Greece. The British, however, would not hear of it. Consequently, they made sure that Greece would not come into any kind of agreement that might prove detrimental to British Mediterranean interests.[6] The invasion of Greece presented the British with two strategic decisions to make: (1) let the Greeks negotiate with the Axis, but occupy the island of Crete with British troops and turn it into a fortress for the defense of British commercial waterways in the eastern Mediterranean; and (2) organize the Balkan states into a unified front and challenge Hitler in the Balkans. It was, as pointed out, an old dream of embroiling Hitler and Stalin in the Balkans, an opportunity that Churchill would not forego, or let slip through his fingers—hence his decision to make a stand there as an "act of faith and humanity." By all accounts, the British decision to challenge Hitler in the Balkans was, from a military viewpoint, a colossal blunder.[7] Enough has been written of that blunder, but most historians still cling to the idea of an "act of faith and humanity." In reality, Mussolini's invasion of Greece was a stroke of good luck that fired Churchill's imagination beyond any reasonable expectation. As if by serendipity, things suddenly appeared to be falling into place. With a bit of luck and proper handling, the Balkan front might yet become a reality. The Italian reversal in Greece injected additional impetus into Churchill's Balkan strategy and the destiny of the Balkan peoples was sealed.

The changes in Rumania spilled over the Rumanian-Yugoslav border and had a considerable effect on Yugoslavia's domestic affairs. First there was a case of German refugee repatriation via the Danube from Rumania across Yugoslavia to Germany. To facilitate the repatriation, the Germans asked for permission to set up a rest camp for refugees near Belgrade. The camps caught Fortier's attention and he communicated to Washington that they were a camouflage for the German fifth column designed to control the area, and that they were there to stay.[8] Lane reported to Washington that Yugoslavia was faced with "immediate danger," one of which was German pressure on the Yugoslav government to allow them to transport their troops across Yugoslavia to Greece. Evaluating Yugoslavia's military readiness to resist German demands, Lane lamented over the lack of fighting spirit in general and among the Croatians in particular. "The Serbs, but no others would fight," reported Lane. He interpreted Maček's cautious view to resist the Italians and keep good relations with Germany as another clear "illustration of the lack of coordination in the government."[9]

On October 14, 1940, several days before the invasion of Greece, Lane (with some misgivings because of the bad state of the American diplomatic code), cabled another "immediate danger" message involving a "forthcoming military dictatorship" in Yugoslavia.[10] At about the same time, Sir Ronald Campbell communicated to his government of an impending coup against Paul and the government replacing him with a military dictatorship. The impetus for the coup was prompted by the replacement of King Carol of Rumania because of his "weakness" in dealing with the Soviets and Germans. The events in Rumania offered a very plausible cover for the putschists to act, but the British government was against it. Considering Italian reversals in Greece, the British thought it over and informed Sir Ronald that a neutral Yugoslavia would be more valuable now that the Germans needed passage for their troops. He subsequently was advised to put the project on hold for the time being.[11] Lane turned his attention to the situation in Croatia from that of the impending coup. Defeatism in Croatia was in full bloom. Maček was losing to Pavelić, and according to the chief of the general staff, General Petar Kosić, the Croatians could not be relied upon in case resistance was required.[12] The minister of war, General Milan Nedić, put it bluntly, the "Croatian terrorists," the "Italian government," and the "Catholic Church" acted in collusion and were collectively responsible for the deplorable conditions in Croatia.[13]

In mid-October, Fortier communicated another of his lengthy threnodies to Washington, inspired by the vanishing martial spirit even among the Serbians. The presence of German forces in Rumania greatly added to the Serbian lack of confidence in themselves. "What can we do?" asked General Kosić, and his question obviously implied surrender. If only Russia (very much on Fortier's mind) would go against Germany, Yugoslavia might find itself and fight. Fortier, a sincere admirer of the Serbian martial spirit, still believed it could reemerge, provided time was not running out. Unfortunately, the "fighting elements," the men who "value ideals and liberty more than life," were in a minority.[14] It is not too difficult to surmise who this "brave minority" may have been. So far, one could detect two major threads running through American reports from Belgrade—Yugoslav neutrality and the lack of fighting spirit among its citizens. Neutrality, however, became the focal point of Allied diplomacy, but for one reason only. Neither the British nor the Americans believed that Hitler would respect Yugoslavia's neutrality. Therefore, the "fighting elements," if ever brought to power would help to keep Yugoslavia within the bounds of a benevolent neutrality vis-à-vis Greece, and if necessary, fight for it. Bulgarians were expected to remain neutral, which in turn would encourage the Turks to join. Thus together they would close the ranks against Germans in an attempt to rescue the Italians in Greece.[15] However imaginative, the plan itself would not amount to anything unless the British offered the Balkan state some tangible help. Since the British themselves were in no position to help other than with verbal support, this encouragement, in their view, would meet the necessary requirement, even if only a handful of British troops landed in Greece. To compensate for the lack of adequate military support, the British of course had to pressure the Balkan states to find a common cause with the Greeks that would give them the leverage to keep the Germans away from Greece while the Italians, deprived of German help, could be pushed into the sea and knocked altogether out of the war. To be sure, the British military chiefs were highly skeptical of Churchill's plan, but none of them had the courage to oppose him.[16] The chiefs of course were right to be skeptical, but the propaganda aspect of the plan was invaluable with regard to Anglo-American relations. The Roosevelt administration needed at this point some proof of Britain's resolve to stay in the war and fight. The administration had to demonstrate that the policy helping to defend Britain was the best defense of the United States. To bolster American faith in Britain, Roosevelt sent Colonel William "Wild Bill" Donovan, an Irish American Catholic and future chief of the Office of Strategic Services (OSS), to London in July of 1940, to gauge the British commitment to war.[17] American neutrality required that the trip be publicized as a "private affair," but no one believed it; everyone knew that his mission to London was in an official capacity. The outcome of

Donovan's mission was highly favorable for the British and he reported to the president that the British resolve to stay in the fight was absolutely certain. In a series of successful lectures across America, Donovan depicted the British as the true bastion of hope and unconquerable spirit. The lectures inspired Walter Lippmann to say that Donovan "almost single-handedly overcame the unmitigated defeatism paralyzing the national capital."[18]

Offering additional proof of British resolve to stay in the fight, Churchill on December 16, 1940, wrote to Roosevelt about the Balkan plan. He carefully measured his words; the new situation in the Balkans made the possibility of an Italian collapse very real. With Italy out of the way, "our affairs will be more hopeful than four months ago," concluded Churchill.[19] As a response to the British resolve, Roosevelt not only initiated the lend-lease program (promulgated into law on March 11, 1941), but applied all his skill in implementing passage of the bill as well. Of exceptional importance is the fact that under the program, all the neutral countries willing to resist Hitler were eligible for American help. Thus, even before the Lend-Lease Act was promulgated into law, it became in effect, a powerful instrument of pressure against the Balkan neutrals to join the British. More of a hindrance than a help to the Balkan neutrals, the practical value of the Lend-Lease Act was that the British became the recipient of an effective leverage to push the Balkan nations into a war in which the British were in no position to participate. In the initial stages of the war against Greece, Yugoslavia's neutrality with all its ambiguity was beneficial to Greece. Thus, under cover of secrecy, Yugoslavia helped the Greeks with arms, food, and horses. At the risk of Yugoslavia's own security, the Greeks were given permission to establish secret supply depots on Yugoslav territory.[20] There is no evidence to suggest that the Germans knew of Yugoslavia's help toward Greece; however, there is plenty of evidence to suggest they were in favor of negotiated settlement rather than intervention, which might suggest that they did know and wished to use Yugoslavia's action as proof of their good intentions.[21]

Not knowing the broader implications of the Balkan strategy, the British plan made little sense to the Balkan neutrals. Indeed, even some American diplomats in the area were suspicious of the British intentions. The American ambassador in Budapest, Herbert C. Pell, privately informed Roosevelt that British "insouciance" demonstrated that they never had any desire to fight in the Balkans. According to Pell's assessment, the British were in a position to transfer one million men from the British Isles to North Africa and Greece. Such a transfer would change the situation in the Balkans and elsewhere in Europe dramatically, but the British were reluctant to do anything.[22] The ambassador's overestimation of the British strength verged on the ridiculous, but he was nonetheless right with respect to their "insouciance," compounded by the traditional British strategy of a hit-and-run mode of warfare somewhere on the periphery. With frequent repetitions of this sort of warfare, the British managed on many occasions in the past to exhaust their foes without submitting themselves to a major engagement, and they were prepared to repeat it here in the Balkans. British cajolery and the American lend-lease promises, however, were not enough. The Greek president, Ioannis Metaxas, said it very succinctly: "the British alone were too weak to exert any influence on anyone in the Balkans and everyone knew it."[23] The time came for more substantial American involvement.

Washington responded, but not with open pressure on Yugoslavia or any Balkan state. Considering American public opinion, that would have been too dangerous for Roosevelt and his administration. Under the guise of improving trade and other outstanding issues, American diplomacy turned its attention toward the Soviet Union. The ongoing talks between Germany and the Soviet Union to strengthen relations between the two countries, including the possible Soviet accession to the Tripartite Pact, ran out of steam because of excessive demands by the Soviets associated with their sphere of influence in Europe.[24] Aware of the military value of the Soviet Union, Washington kept relations with Moscow alive. Besides, any rupture in relations would have prevented the United States from gaining accurate firsthand information about the Soviet Union. Not to make relations any worse than they were, Washington initiated commercial talks with Moscow even before the Nazi-Soviet negotiations. Taking advantage of the now uncertain relations between Berlin and Moscow, Hull instructed his ambassador in the Soviet Union, Lawrence Steinhardt, in late October of 1940, to verbally communicate to the Soviet government that talks in Washington were going well between American officials and Soviet Ambassador Umansky. Steinhardt was further instructed to assure the Russians that any outstanding problems existing between the two countries could be eliminated by a free exchange of views. He was not to ask the Russians outright about the Tripartite Pact, but he was free to express American views on the subject as being a real threat to world peace.[25]

Replying to Hull, Steinhardt communicated that the Soviets were evasive in giving any answers. Molotov's deputy, Andrei Vishinsky, for example, pretended not to know much about what was going on in Washington but did listen carefully and offered a "glib exposition" of the Soviet foreign policy. Granted, the Soviet Union was well aware of the aggression taking place, but being primarily concerned with peace, it had no desire to limit its actions or to isolate itself from the rest of the world. As for the Tripartite Pact, Vishinsky thought he knew what Steinhardt meant and replied that the Soviet Union was strong enough to ward off any aggression against its sovereignty.[26] The point was that the Soviets mistrusted both the British and the Americans, and any advances by Washington to improve relations with Moscow were regarded ipso facto as a trap to push the Russian people into war.[27] The Russian mistrust was further aroused by the British. Steinhardt reported that the British ambassador, Sir Stafford Cripps, was using Soviet-American talks in Washington as a means of pressuring the Soviets. The British, he complained, spread rumors of an impending Anglo–American–Soviet alliance with obvious intentions of compromising the Soviets vis-à-vis Germany. Such intentions were "childish beyond belief," as long as the German armies were regarded by the Kremlin to be the main threat to the Soviet Union.[28] The Soviets, at this point, were not afraid of the German armies.[29] Their main concern was not to get involved in the Balkans and to resume negotiations with Berlin.

In October of 1940, the British made additional offers to the Soviets. This time they were ready to extend de facto recognition of Soviet acquisitions in the Baltic, Poland, Bessarabia, and Bukovina.[30] In contrast to the British, the Americans held slightly different views on the subject. They believed the recognition of Soviet acquisitions should be postponed to some later date and used as a bargaining chip when the time came to decide the future of Europe.[31] In the meantime, Soviet leaders instructed Umansky to clarify the Soviet policy to American officials. Their position was to pursue a policy of peace and stay out of any conflict, while at the same time the Soviet government would maintain normal political and economic relations with all powers, including those viewed as belligerent.[32] That did not stop the efforts made by the British and Americans. Both sides often "volunteered" (as a means of gaining Soviet confidence) to supply Russian officials with information concerning an "imminent" German attack on the Soviet Union.[33]

Mistrustful as ever, the Soviets, who had excellent sources of intelligence of their own in Germany, remained cool toward the unsolicited American and British information. Regarding the Balkans, official Soviet policy was to keep peace. In reality, however, they desired war there just as much as the British and Americans, albeit for different reasons. According to the Yugoslav ambassador in Moscow Milan Gavrilović, while the Soviets officially did not want war in the Balkans, privately it was altogether a different matter. From the viewpoint of Soviet ideology, war in the Balkans would incur a breakdown of the capitalist system—a disaster for others, but a boon for the Russians. In the chaos of war they could take over, weakening Germany at the same time.[34] In a much similar vein, Umansky privately explained the Soviet policy to the Yugoslav minister in Washington, Konstantin Fotić. The aim of the Soviet policy was to stay out of war until such time when peace negotiations were initiated. They would then appear as the strongest European power and could play a decisive role in shaping the new map of Europe.[35] Umansky was openly critical of American leaders for their failure to see the role the Soviets would play when peace was restored. True, the German drive into the Balkans was "very unpleasant," but by no means final. The final solution to the Balkan problem would be found after the war when the untouched strength of the Soviet Union would restore the balance of power.[36]

The upshot of negotiations with Moscow was that the Germans made their influence in the Balkans more forceful. Since Yugoslavia's neutrality depended on Germany's goodwill, the policymakers in Belgrade understood their precarious position well. Should that change, there was no other option but to face German military might. While there was still hope that the Balkan conflict could be localized, Belgrade preferred the German solution rather than confrontation with Germany. Concerned over the future of Salonika, several Serbian members of the government convened together with Prince Paul and deliberated as to what action to take if Salonika fell into the wrong hands. To prevent it, Prince Paul was in favor of the mobilization and deployment of troops along the Yugoslav-Greek border. Prime Minister Cvetković concurred with Paul's suggestion, but cautioned against unnecessary haste. The war minister, General Nedić, disagreed with both and proposed waiting until German intentions were clarified.[37]

Nedić's involvement in Salonika's affairs exceeded his authority and cost him his job. Behind Paul's back, Nedić, through his intermediary Colonel Vladimir Vauhnik, tried to feel out what the German reaction would be if Yugoslav troops occupied Salonika. Similar to Nedić, some members of the "Serbian Cultural Club"[38] in Belgrade pleaded with the Germans for their tacit support of Yugoslav claims on Salonika once young King Peter came to the throne in September of 1941. When the Italians heard of Belgrade's diplomatic maneuvers with the Germans, they "accidentally" bombed the town of Bitolj, located close to the Greek border. The bombing, however, passed without any official reaction from War Minister Nedić. Pretending displeasure over the lack of response, Paul confronted the general. To account for his lack of response, Nedić told Paul that Yugoslavia should revise its ambiguous policy and unequivocally state its position vis-à-vis the belligerents. His "unequivocal" position involved yielding (although he never was asked by the Germans) some of Yugoslavia's territory to Germany. Once it was settled, Yugoslavia would be left in peace, and more importantly, not need an army to defend itself. Paul, the real architect of Yugoslavia's foreign policy, saw Nedić's proposal as not only foolish, but utterly pro-German. He therefore asked the general to tender his resignation and General Petar Pešić was appointed his successor.[39]

That was the official explanation. The truth is that General Nedić, through his own initiative, developed rather strong relations with German intelligence and kept close contact with the German embassy in Belgrade. His actions were motivated by his anti-communist sentiments, believing that the Soviet Union was a real menace that was willing to overtake Yugoslavia and the rest of Europe. He also believed that in view of the formidable German power, one could not count on Anglo-American help. Nedić therefore advocated a pro-German foreign policy as the best solution for Yugoslavia's future. Nedić handed Prime Minister Cvetković an outline of the foreign policy drafted by Dimitrije Ljotić, a peripheral leader of the fascist movement "Zbor" in Serbia, to use as a guide. Most likely under Ljotić's influence, Nedić believed that Yugoslavia's salvation lay with Germany, which was to dominate Europe for years to come. Maintaining the sensitive balance in foreign policy, Paul was embarrassed by the sudden revelation of Nedić's connection with the renowned Fascist. His embarrassment was compounded by the printing of Ljotić's bulletin by Nedić's ministry press, whereupon he discharged the war minister. According to the same sources, Nedić, together with a group of like-minded officers in collusion with Ljotić's "Zbor," was suspected of hatching a plot to overthrow the government to implement a new policy drafted by Ljotić.[40] There is little doubt that the Nedić affair caused numerous difficulties for the Yugoslav government. Recalling the Stojadinović affair and his dismissal from power, the Germans naturally became suspicious, but wisely retained their sense of diplomatic propriety.[41] Fortier, who could never truly grasp the reality behind Belgrade's appearances, reacted swiftly. He reported his version of the events surrounding Nedić's dismissal to Washington. General Nedić, he maintained, had fallen victim to foul play instigated by the "appeasers" because he personified the Serbian "fighting spirit." He was "obstinate, direct and not afraid of Germans." In this atmosphere Fortier continued, created by an "appeaser triumvirate," namely Cvetković, Maček, and Korošec (the latter was the Slovenian leader), and the added problem of European FEAR (capitalized in the original), having a man like Nedić was indeed refreshing.[42] Although the Nedić affair caused negative reactions in London and Washington, nothing serious was undertaken to damage further Paul's position, which was still believed to be of use to the British Balkan strategy. As long as Paul kept within the bounds of a "strict" neutrality and refused passage to German troops across Yugoslavia's territory, he was regarded as a potential ally.[43]

The "strict" neutrality, however, would soon run out of steam. Now that the German-Russian negotiations were breaking down, largely because of Soviet interests in the Balkans, the British came to believe that the German drive southward might provoke the Soviets into action. This in turn would encourage the frightened Balkan states to resist the Germans.[44] The British gradually came to this conclusion. German strategy in the Balkans, from the time the German army moved into Rumania, was interpreted by the people in Whitehall as a deception concealing Germany's real intentions regarding Operation Sea Lion. They believed that these intentions were to draw British attention away from defense of the British Isles to the Balkans, and then to invade Britain. Their beliefs persisted even when the Italians declared war against Greece, except that the new situation presented new possibilities. If cooperation with the Balkan states was achieved, the British would be less anxious about the Germans turning against Britain prior to the invasion of the Soviet Union. Still, the subject of cooperation in the Balkan states was on Britain's mind for some time, but without much success. Thinking that the personal friendship between Paul and King George might be of some help, the Foreign Office drafted a letter for the king to send to Paul. In the letter, King George expressed his appreciation for Yugoslavia's friendly attitude toward Greece, and tactfully suggested that the time was propitious for talks with Greece and Turkey on the subject of closer cooperation.[45] A similar letter was addressed to King Boris of Bulgaria. With grievances against Serbia and Yugoslavia emanating from the Balkan Wars and World War I, Bulgaria gravitated toward the German solution. British concessions to the Soviets in the Balkans pushed the Bulgarians closer to Germany and moved Turkey into deeper neutrality. Bulgarian consent to let German troops pass across its territory (for territorial compensation in Greece), let Yugoslavia off the hook.[46] In his letter, King George referred to Bulgaria's territorial claims, stating that Britain would have nothing against border readjustments, provided they were brought about by means of free and peaceful negotiations.[47] Finally, the British resorted to empty threats to keep Bulgaria in line. The American minister in Sofia, George B. Earle, reported that the British had in mind to bomb Bulgarian airfields and railroad network, not to mention an invasion of the country with the help of Turkish troops.[48]

Although the passage of German troops across Yugoslavia was not an issue, the British nevertheless refused to accept it. London instructed Sir Ronald Campbell to impress upon Paul that if attacked, Yugoslavia should resist and refuse any territorial concessions. Most importantly, no German troops should ever be allowed to cross Yugoslavia. This, however, was not at variance with Yugoslavia's policy. What made it so dangerous was the provocative presence of the British in Greece. Both sides expected Yugoslavia to behave correctly, which in effect meant that any false move made by Belgrade might jeopardize its "strict" neutrality. To avoid such a predicament, Prince Paul warned Sir Ronald that while there was still room for a negotiated settlement in Greece, the British should refrain from their military buildup there. Otherwise, he said, the German armies will be provoked to overrun the entire Balkan peninsula.[49] Unfortunately for Paul, that was precisely what the British sought.

Not surprisingly, another document filled with ill predictions for Yugoslavia surfaced at this juncture. The Yugoslav military intelligence "discovered" a secret German plan to invade Yugoslavia and make it Germany's "tenth victim." The authenticity of the plan was in question, but the obliging British established that it was authentic beyond a shadow of a doubt.[50] The chief of the Yugoslav general staff, General Petar Kosić, was by no means convinced of it and was proved to be right. The circumstances under which the document was "discovered" brings to mind the "ten-point" plan to place Yugoslavia under Germany as a protectorate. All evidence shows that it was a British forgery to use the unsuspecting Yugoslav leaders without having to resort to a coup d'etat.[51] It seemed that Yugoslavia had no other choice but to join one or the other side. To avoid such a drastic decision, Paul made diplomatic overtures to Rome and Berlin. Together with his closest Serbian advisers, he sent two unofficial emissaries to Berlin and Rome. A Belgrade lawyer with excellent Italian connections, Vladimir Stakić, went to Rome, while the political director of the government paper *Vreme,* Danilo Gregorić, went to Berlin.[52]

Their instructions were basically the same. Yugoslavia was prepared to establish closer relations with the Axis in exchange for a joint Italo-German guarantee of Yugoslav territorial integrity. Here the similarities ended. In Italy, Stakić talked of an alliance between Yugoslavia and Italy with, as Ciano recorded in his diary, "far reaching guaranties."[53] To circumvent the humiliating German intervention in Greece, Mussolini again adopted the idea of strengthening relations with Belgrade. In Ciano's view, an understanding with Yugoslavia would create a solid basis in case Italy was compelled to adopt an anti-German and anti-Soviet policy.[54] In Berlin, Gregorić talked about Salonika and told the Germans that if it fell into Italian hands, it would amount to placing a "noose around Yugoslavia's neck." The implications were that to keep peace in the Balkans, the port should be given to Yugoslavia.[55] From Belgrade, von Heeren warmly recommended Serbian claims to Salonika, pointing out that the port under Yugoslavia's jurisdiction would have a calming effect on the Serbian people.[56]

In conversation with Ciano, Hitler was in favor of strengthening ties with Yugoslavia and was pleased that Mussolini was of the same opinion.[57] New Italian reversals in Greece urged Hitler to speed up the negotiations with Yugoslavia. He therefore invited Yugoslavia's foreign minister, Aleksandar Cincar Marković, to Berlin at the end of November 1940. Hitler told Cincar Marković that a nonaggression pact between Yugoslavia and Italy would eliminate all outstanding problems between them. Once it was achieved, he would affix his signature to the document, and irrespective of Italian wishes, Germany would guarantee that Italy followed its obligations to the letter.[58] After the meeting, von Ribbentrop instructed von Heeren to keep watch on the Belgrade scene and report back if any statements were made regarding Cincar Marković's visit. Because the Greeks were gradually pushing the Italians back to Albania, Yugoslav officials were not about to divulge the contents of their talks with the Germans. Yugoslav silence, coupled with their refusal to transport a thousand German trucks as a gesture of goodwill across Yugoslavia to Greece, chilled the atmosphere in Berlin. As a gentle reminder to Belgrade, von Ribbentrop instructed his subordinates that any future war matériel delivered to Yugoslavia would be subject to his approval (Doc. nos. 366, 465).

Ribbentrop's demarche swiftly caught the attention of Belgrade officials. As a result, Cincar Marković, to smooth things with Berlin, handed a four-page written statement to von Heeren to be forwarded to Berlin. In it he praised Germany very highly for having "correctly" understood that Yugoslavia was not a melange of peoples held together by force, but that their unity was a natural outgrowth of a long historical process. For this reason, as well as others, the royal Yugoslav government was ready to give full consideration to improving relations with the Axis. Belgrade was willing to discuss with Berlin and Rome the possibility of signing a nonaggression pact with Italy on the basis of the preexisting Italo-Yugoslav Pact concluded in March of 1937.[59] The preexisting pact between Yugoslavia and Italy, it will be recalled, was signed during the political honeymoon between Ciano and Stojadinović to keep Germany away from the Balkans and to liquidate the Ustaša organizations operating against Yugoslavia from Italy. What Belgrade wanted now was the inclusion of Germany into the pact to secure Yugoslavia, thus minimizing an obligatory need for compromise. There was, however, one serious flaw in this new proposal. It was not new, yet the situation in the Balkans had radically changed. It became clear to the Germans that the British would not leave the Balkans unless ejected by force. Berlin therefore informed Belgrade that the three-sided nonaggression pact, as proposed by the Yugoslav government, would no longer serve any useful purpose because such a pact would still leave open Yugoslavia's accession to the Tripartite Pact (Doc. nos. 549, 551). Reacting, as he put it, against the events set in motion by others, Hitler proposed to the Balkan nations to join en bloc the Tripartite Pact. Protected by the pact, the Balkan nations would no longer have to worry about the danger from without. They would be adequately protected by "240 unemployed German divisions" (Doc. no. 438). Apprehensive that Yugoslavia might slip through the Anglo-American net, Lane felt that the situation required a more decisive policy from Washington to guide his activities in Belgrade. His pleas notwithstanding, the U.S. State Department still believed that his position was to observe and report.[60] Officially, America still kept its neutral posture. After all, in his third-term preelection speech, Roosevelt still promised peace and not war. Pressure nevertheless came. In late November 1940, Lane's twenty-one-year-old daughter Margaret returned to the United States. Although she refused to give any comment to the press on her arrival, in early January there was a very damaging article written about the Yugoslav government in the *New York Times*. The headline read, "THE NAZI 'MODEL TOWN'; A BELGRADE PUZZLE," and was written allegedly by Miss Lane.[61] The content of the article had treasonous implications. The Yugoslav government, it seemed, had deliberately relinquished parts of its national territory to the Nazis for their subversive activities in the area. It was actually a makeshift camp for repatriated Germans coming from Rumania to Germany. Considering her tender age and lack of knowledge of Yugoslav affairs, one may safely say that it was not done without the approval of the administration. The Yugoslav press bureau chief in Washington, Bogdan Radica, informed Belgrade that the article left a "considerable impression" on American readers. In his reports, he kept warning Belgrade not to give much credence to American neutrality. One should remember, he warned, that the U.S. government was controlled by ardent Anglophiles determined to see Britain victorious, as demonstrated in Roosevelt's "Arsenal of Democracy" speech and his message to Congress at the beginning of January 1941.[62]

In the meantime, Washington asked Lane to survey the impact of the speech on Yugoslav public opinion. It was negligible at best.[63] The situation was bedeviled further by the fact that the Slovenian leader, Anton Korošec, died and was replaced by Fran Kulovec. Lane reported that unlike Korošec, Kulovec gravitated toward Zagreb, which in his view, would make Yugoslavia more vulnerable in the event of serious international complications.[64] The Yugoslav ambassador in Washington, Konstantin Fotić, was profoundly dissatisfied with the situation in Yugoslavia. Given his education and personal convictions, Fotić was not only a Serbian chauvinist but also a rabid Croatian-hater. Consequently, he hated the Serbo-Croatian agreement and the Croatians, who, in his view, were responsible for Yugoslavia not being actively engaged on the Allied side. Yugoslavia could not have any policy other than a Serbian one, or could the power be shared with anyone other than Serbians themselves.[65] Looking exclusively after Serbian interests, Fotić felt that Paul's policy, unless changed, would surely hurt Serbian interests in Washington. He therefore gradually merged his pan-Serbian aspirations with Roosevelt's global strategy. On this point, he had Roosevelt's and Welles' full cooperation.

In line with his Serbian project, Fotić engaged one of his ideological cronies. He brought in a broadcasting journalist, as Radica pointed out, of limited intelligence and limitless ambition, Svetoslav-Sveta Petrović, in a propaganda war against Paul and his government.[66] As Petrović proudly recorded in his book, in December 1940 he was given the opportunity to talk to his people through WRUL and WRUN, shortwave radio stations in Boston.[67] The propagandistic undertaking was financed (although denied at the time) by Fotić and the Yugoslav legation, clearly in violation of Yugoslav law.[68] Although Fotić never talked about Petrović's financial backing or broadcasting activities, he did mention in his book that because Yugoslavia was surrounded by members of the Tripartite Pact, the U.S. State Department and the president of the United States increased their interest in Yugoslavia's affairs.[69] There is no way of knowing to what extent the coup against Paul was influenced by Petrović and his broadcasts. They may have offered some moral encouragement to the putschists, but it is irrelevant at this point. What is relevant is that by the end of 1940, Yugoslavia was pressured from all sides, although it was not as yet strong enough to change official policy. As Greek President Metaxas correctly pointed out, the British alone were not strong enough to change the Balkan situation in their favor. The beginning of 1941 therefore marked the beginning of the United States' direct involvement in Yugoslav and Balkan affairs.

Chapter 6
Mutatis Mutandis

Donovan's Balkan Mission

To be sure, direct American involvement in Yugoslavia and the Balkans was still in its preparatory stages. Through William Stephenson, the British "master spy" in New York, London turned again to Roosevelt for help.[1] Roosevelt responded. The most logical means of helping the British was to send William Donovan back to Europe. By now his stature had grown in importance among the Washington interventionists. Donovan was known as a man of action and, although Irish and Catholic, was thoroughly devoted to the British cause. More importantly, he enjoyed Roosevelt's fullest confidence. Because of America's still-neutral status and strong domestic opposition to involvement in European affairs, Donovan's mission was shrouded in mystery to confuse the Axis and the isolationists. The press came up with all sorts of wild stories as to the purpose of his mission, but no one really believed that Donovan was on a "fact-finding" tour on behalf of the *Chicago Daily News*. They knew that President Roosevelt was, as during the first mission, behind Donovan, and that upon his return he would report his accomplishments only to the president.[2] While there was no need to press upon Churchill and his intelligence chief, Sir Stewart Menzies, the importance of the mission, Stevenson nevertheless pointed out to both that Donovan's mission could hardly be overestimated.[3] To make sure that the U.S. neutrality stand would not be exposed, Hull informed his "listening post" in Lisbon of Donovan's forthcoming mission at the end of November 1940. Hull insisted in his dispatch that the colonel would travel as a representative of the *Chicago Daily News,* and because all arrangements had been completed, there was no need to get involved unless some special requests were made.[4] Indeed, the British made all the necessary preparations.[5] Before leaving for London, Donovan secretly visited the Yugoslav legation in Washington on several occasions, although it was strongly denied at the time.[6] He had lunch with Churchill on his first day in London, followed by a long talk. Blowing smoke from his Cuban cigar, Churchill told Donovan how the United States, together with Great Britain, should defeat Germany. To defeat Germany together with the United States was fine, but to make any promises beyond "all the help short of war" was outside of Donovan's authority. That meant any outright war with Germany could not be promised by Roosevelt.

The talks turned to the Balkans. According to Donovan's account of the story, Churchill was sure that the Germans would soon attack the Soviet Union. He therefore explained to Donovan the importance of his mission in terms of the forthcoming Russo-German conflict. Donovan's mission was to encourage the Balkan nations to resist the Germans. The longer it took for the Germans to finish the Balkans off, the better the chances for the Soviets. Like Napoleon in 1812, German exposure to the Russian winter would come to the same inglorious end.[7] But this could not be taken very seriously. Which winter was Churchill talking about? By the time Donovan arrived in Belgrade in early January 1941, the winter had already set in, which meant that Churchill was referring to the next one. If so, how did he know that the next winter would be so severe as to paralyze German armor and men at the outskirts of Moscow? He had no way of knowing, and Donovan's account was a rationalization of the Balkan disaster after the fact. True, Hitler was anxious to settle the Balkan problem, but the timetable to attack the Soviet Union depended exclusively on the readiness of German army and, of course, the weather. The army was still in its preparatory stages. As for the weather, to make any predictions was as unrealistic as to read the future from a crystal ball.[8] With regard to British policy at this point, English historian Elisabeth Barker summed it up very accurately— the main object of the policy was "to exploit conditions which [were] likely to embroil Russia and Germany in the Balkans."[9]

Given British strategic needs, the first objective was to embroil the Russians in an explosion in the Balkans as a matter of British necessity. The British traditionally believed that the Balkans were a fertile ground for all sorts of impossible actions. It was a region teeming with plots, social and political upheavals, chronic disorders, and so forth, which, if skillfully handled, could be used to Allied advantage.[10] Donovan's mission was therefore to inflame the area against the Germans, which in turn would embroil the Soviets.[11] Before Donovan left London, the British instructed their diplomatic representatives in the Balkans to take the Americans into their full confidence.[12] Not by coincidence, Donovan's trip to the Balkans was preceded by Roosevelt's powerful message to Congress on January 6, 1941. The message was intended to bolster the morale of the Balkan neutrals; this in turn would make Donovan's job much easier. Ambassador MacVeagh reported from Athens that even the Bulgarians were interested in the message and asked if Roosevelt's fireside chats and messages could be taken seriously.[13]

Donovan flew to Athens from Egypt at the same time that Field Marshall Archibald P. Wavell also was ordered to fly there. Donovan attended the meeting at the British embassy between the Greek and British officials. On January 19, 1941, MacVeagh, circumventing the U.S. State Department, reported to Roosevelt about the situation in Greece. According to MacVeagh's report, all indicators pointed to a German takeover of the Balkan peninsula to cut Britain's commercial lifeline in the Mediterranean.[14] In light of the German strategy to dislodge the British from the Mediterranean, Salonika acquired additional importance for the Germans. The main topic of discussion at the meeting was the formation of the Salonikan front. The bad news was that the British promised more than they could deliver. To compensate for the lack of British aid, the Greeks appealed to the Americans for help. The timely arrival of Colonel Donovan, MacVeagh stressed, "did a grand job." He was scheduled to visit the Albanian front, but the anxious British rushed him to Bulgaria and Yugoslavia "to give the leaders in those capitals a very timely stir."[15]

While Donovan promised aid to the Greeks (which was never delivered), he tried a different tactic in Bulgaria. He brought along two documents revealing a British military plan in the Balkans and a promise of mass American assistance if Bulgaria decided to resist the Nazis. Needless to say, both documents were forgeries supplied by the British, and both, as intended, fell into German hands.[16] The intent of the forged documents was to deter the Germans from crossing Bulgaria and to choose Yugoslavia instead. German pressure, it was hoped, would bring Yugoslavia within the British fold. Talking to the Bulgarian leaders, Donovan drew their attention to the moral side of the conflict. The issues were clearly divided. Germany stood for "subjugation," and America was therefore compelled to take the side of those who fought against subjugation and freedom, and would not withdraw until Hitler was defeated.[17] The issues, as far as the Bulgarians were concerned, were not so simple. The editor-in-chief of the leading morning paper *Utro*, Stefan Tanev, told Donovan in no uncertain terms that although the Bulgarians wished to settle all outstanding problems with their neighbors peacefully, they were not prepared to give up their legitimate territorial claims in exchange for empty promises.[18]

Donovan nevertheless was pleased with his accomplishments. Earle shared Donovan's feelings and reported to Washington that the colonel's visit impressed the Bulgarians, especially the fact that the United States would stand by Great Britain.[19] Actually, they were not that impressed. No sooner had Donovan left for Belgrade than King Boris informed the Germans that the Bulgarians had no faith in England's "liberality and understanding." In a conversation with Fritz Twardowski, director of the cultural policy department of the *Auswärtiges Amt,* he spoke "derisively" about Donovan and his visit which, in his view, demonstrated how naive Americans really were.[20] There were no changes in Bulgaria's policy. If anything, the visit merely strengthened Bulgaria's resolve to stay with the Germans. The Greek ambassador in Sofia told Earle that the best way of winning the war would be to supply the Greek army on the Albanian front and to bring a speedy victory against the Italians. With their best troops in Albania, the Greeks feared that their unprotected borders along Bulgaria would offer an easy crossing for German troops into Greece in the direction of Salonika.[21]

Thinking quite highly of his powers of persuasion, Donovan left Sofia for Belgrade by train, but not before an "unpleasant incident" occurred. Donovan's passport, two letters of introduction, some American money, a letter of credit, and several photographs were "stolen." Responsible for the "theft" was no other than Earle's lover, a Belgian girl masquerading as a Hungarian dancer who worked for German espionage.[22] The whole "unpleasant incident" was staged so that the two forged documents would fall into German hands.[23] To avert public attention from Donovan's real mission, the Nazi press took advantage of the "incident" and condemned Donovan as a drunkard whose main purpose in Sofia was to visit the night spots, and a man of irresponsible disposition who could not be trusted.[24] He arrived in Belgrade on January 21, 1941. Lane was present at the Belgrade Railway Station and took Donovan to his home, where he remained until the end of his visit. By sheer intuition, Lane understood immediately the importance of Donovan's mission. Before Donovan's arrival, Lane pleaded with the U.S. State Department to use its authority to allay distrust and suspicions among the Balkan states and to make it easier for Donovan to bring about their joint defense policy. In keeping with his views, a somewhat irritated Hull replied that it was not the responsibility of the U.S. State Department to initiate such a policy, even though the chiefs in Washington from the southeastern European countries knew only too well the position of the United States.[25] To make sure that Ambassador John V. A. MacMurray in Ankara would not spring the same request on him, Hull made it quite plain that the colonel traveled as a representative of the Secretary of the Navy, Frank Knox, and not of the president. Hull therefore stressed that Donovan had no representative capacity but that indicated in the telegram (Doc. no. 740.0011, European War 1939/67). More in tune with the president than with his chief, Lane disregarded his instructions and made a conscious effort to make Donovan's visit an all-American show for everyone to see.[26] During their lengthy conversations in the evening, the two gentlemen discovered that they had much in common. Their views on the Balkan situation were identical, and both were experts on the "Slavs," Lane from his Baltic days in Riga, and Donovan as a former mayor of Rochester.[27]

Donovan's message to the Yugoslav leaders was in line with Churchill's strategy, which, as he emphasized, the United States backed. If embroiling the Soviet Union was not feasible, Churchill had another option in mind. He told Donovan that if Britain suffered the same losses as in World War I, it would flounder as a world power. He therefore built into his "grand strategy," the plan of so-called "circumference." He believed that Germany would be most vulnerable if attacked from the Baltic or the Mediterranean, rather than from the center across the English Channel as in World War I. Commenting upon this strategy, British historian Anthony Cave Brown pointed out that it was identical to the Duke of Marlborough's strategy used in the war of the Spanish succession. The difference was that now Churchill expected that it would be supported by a mass uprising in the occupied countries. In short, Churchill expected to beat the Germans (with a minimum of British involvement), or exhaust them at least to the point that the "armored legions" of Britain would have no difficulty in defeating them.[28]

Having said that, the United States stood behind Britain; Donovan's next step was to convince the Yugoslav leaders, however untrue, that America had already reached the level of wartime production. In line with American antipathy for Nazism, he stressed, the majority of Americans were determined to stop Germany from winning this war. The present course of the American policy was that "Hitler must be beaten at all costs, even though our peace can be endangered."[29] Having thus unequivocally stated the American position, Donovan wished to know how the government would react in case Berlin asked for passage of German troops across Yugoslavia. The answer was unanimous as in the past, that if attacked, Yugoslavia would resist; however, this was not a victory for him. Even the Germans knew that the Yugoslav government would view their demand for passage of their troops across Yugoslavia as a justification for war, and instead of pressing the point with Belgrade, they turned to Bulgaria for help. Bulgaria again became the focal point of Donovan's mission. He therefore asked if the Yugoslav leaders would challenge Germany should German troops move into Bulgaria.

Except for General Dušan Simović (the real leader of the conspiracy) and commander-in-chief of the air force, the rest were evasive.[30] Distrustful of Bulgaria, Prince Paul was originally in favor of military action, but soon retracted his views, claiming that his people were not in agreement on this point.

Maček was against military intervention from the start. They all agreed, however, on the commitment to defend Yugoslavia, and only Yugoslavia, should its sovereignty become endangered. That was not the answer Donovan wanted to hear, but by no means was he discouraged. Using Bulgaria as a symbol for the Yugoslav situation, he told the Yugoslav leaders that the Bulgarians were quite mistaken to assume that the United States would support them at the next peace conference, even though they might be occupied by Germany. The implications were clear. He warned Prince Paul that President Roosevelt expressed the will of the American people and that America was committed to aid Britain to the full extent of its capacity. No country, large or small, should complain later if they found themselves on the losing side.[31]

In his concluding remarks regarding Donovan's visit, Lane was hopeful. Apart from Cvetković, Maček, and Cincar Marković, who, Lane pointed out, expressed their views that the colonel's visit placed Yugoslavia in a compromising position vis-à-vis Germany, the general impressions were positive.[32] However distasteful his visit may have been to the "appeasement group," it certainly had a positive influence on the "military element" (Doc. no. 740.0011, European War 1939/7957). Lane's general impression was that even though the rest of Europe might do whatever the Germans asked, the Yugoslavs would resist, placing their honor before political expediency. If Yugoslavia organized a solid block with Bulgaria and Turkey, the Germans would think twice before launching an attack in the direction of Salonika (Doc. no. 740.0011, European War 1939/7889). In a separate report to the Military Intelligence Branch, Fortier came up with speculations of his own. He was sure that for economic reasons Germany would rather leave Yugoslavia alone; that, however, soon could change because of German troops in Rumania earmarked for Greece. The troop movement across Bulgaria would need, for logistic reasons, Yugoslavia's railways to the south. Yugoslavia must therefore take certain precautionary measures now, abandoning Croatia and Slovenia and setting up defenses south of the Sava-Danube line. With such a defense, Yugoslavia could launch an offensive in the direction of Sofia the moment German troops started crossing the Bulgarian border. While the offensive was in progress, the British Air Force from Greece would concentrate its attention on the river crossings, bridges, and other strategic points. There was no danger from Albania. Italians there could be kept in check with few Yugoslav divisions. Turkey would then be encouraged to act offensively while the wavering Bulgarians, caught in between, would be "assisted" by joining the Allies. Such a plan, according to Fortier was sound, but unless the unsuspected happened, or a strongman took over, Yugoslavia today was more apt to offer the performance of defeatism than to fight.[33]

It was actually an old plan, one frequently discussed among military and government circles. It was rejected, however, because of fear that application of the plan would drive the last nail into the Yugoslav coffin. Concurrently with the British decision to make a stand in the Balkans, the plan was revived and Donovan's task was to encourage its implementation.[34] In any case, Yugoslavia was doomed. To enforce his views, Donovan expanded his activities outside of the government circle. He talked to the conspirators, the Masons, the Military, as well as to Military Intelligence, and by some accounts even Tito, who supposedly was without guidance from Moscow.[35] His meeting with Tito is not certain, but he did talk with others. Critical of government policy, Donovan, in his conversations exalted the Serbian martial spirit. Visiting the General Staff School and Military Academy, Donovan left a distinct impression that only a restoration of the old Serbian fighting spirit could save Yugoslavia from shame and disaster.[36] Except for a short report on General Simović sent by Lane, there was no tangible evidence that Donovan made clandestine visits to the conspirators; but he did. On the basis of Donovan's report to the president (still unavailable to researchers), Dunlop irrefutably proved that Donovan had such meetings. Donovan talked openly with Simović about the coup and the war, in case the government made any concessions to Germany. They both agreed that given the rugged mountains of the country and the spirit of the people, Yugoslavia would have a great advantage over the invaders. Simović informed Donovan in no uncertain terms that the patriots would strike the moment Paul signed an agreement with Germany. They would then replace Paul with the seventeen-year-old Peter who supposedly had agreed with the conspirators that Paul had outlived his usefulness.[37]

In line with his mission, Donovan spoke convincingly about American material assistance. Speaking before a group of intelligence officers, Donovan not only promised American assistance but asked them in earnest to submit a requisition listing all the materials they needed. Observing the effect of Donovan's promises, the chief of intelligence of the Yugoslav general staff, Uglješa Popović, wrote that Donovan left an "extraordinary" impression on those "romantic dreamers." They all had the impression that Roosevelt spoke through Donovan. Yet Donovan knew that the deliveries, if any, would not be forthcoming.[38] Low-level American military production, in addition to distance and the submarine-infested Mediterranean, were hardly encouraging signs that help would arrive anytime soon. But his job was to disregard certain realities.

As to Donovan's guidance of Tito, one cannot be as sure. Various Tito biographers never mentioned a single word regarding his connection with Donovan or British intelligence. It is true, however, that most of the Serbian groups associated with the coup were infiltrated by the Communists or their fellow travelers who kept Tito and the central committee informed of the events behind the scene. The Serbian historian Vladimir Dedijer wrote that the Free-masons, renowned Anglophiles, were in touch with Tito at all times. Tito himself admitted that the Masons were the ones who supplied him with the exact date that the Germans would attack the Soviet Union.[39] While there is no dispute with respect to the Tito-Mason connection, Stevenson credited Donovan with Tito's opposition to Prince Paul's "pro-Nazi" policy and for the guerrilla warfare against the Axis. Stevenson could not make known how his contacts with Tito came about, supposedly because when he wrote in 1976, it was "still classified information."[40] Here one walks upon very shaky ground. If one takes Stevenson's assertions at face value, the conclusion is that Tito himself was a British agent. Stevenson's exaggeration in praising his hero prompted a Canadian historian, David Stafford, to observe that his book "on occasion only had a very tenuous connection with reality."[41] This also may be an exaggeration, but Stevenson in another book did admit that Tito's passport (which he used before the war) was not issued by Canadian authorities, as originally claimed by Stevenson, but was a forgery produced by the Yugoslav Communists. At the same time, Stevenson rewards us with still another "revelation," namely that Stephenson was "on speaking terms with Tito," partly because of his business interests in Yugoslavia.[42] Again, Stevenson does not offer any proof of these alleged meetings.[43]

The truth is perhaps less mysterious than Stevenson would like us to believe. It was no secret that the Communists manifested an intense hatred against Paul and his foreign policy. The British were also losing their patience with him. Acting upon the principle that the enemies of their enemies were their friends, both the British and the Communists could gain something useful from each other. Tito returned from the Soviet Union in March of 1940, almost at the same time that the Comintern master spy for the Balkans, Josip Kopinič, returned.[44] Shortly thereafter, the center for Soviet espionage was set up in Zagreb. To say then that Tito lacked "guidance" from Moscow was more than ludicrous. Rather, mutual interests required the elimination of Paul and his government. If Yugoslavia remained neutral, the usefulness of the Balkans as the potential spot for disruption and a conflagration of unforeseen dimensions could easily evaporate, unless Paul was removed from his position. Apart from that, the Soviets feared him because he was still on good terms with the British and the Germans, and they suspected him of trying to smooth things out between the two at the expense of the Soviet Union.[45]

Furthermore, the Soviets suspected Paul and the possibility that in case Yugoslavia did remain out of the conflict, it might be used as a bridgehead, not only against Germany, but as a deterrent against Soviet penetration in the direction of the Balkans and central Europe.[46] Viewed from a Soviet perspective, the outcome of Donovan's mission almost exclusively accommodated the Soviets. This accommodation, however, was not for the reasons Sir Winston Churchill came up with—to save the Soviet Union and give a free hand to Stalin with regard to penetration of the Red Army in the direction of central Europe and the Balkans when the time came. It seems rather odd, or perhaps not, that upon scrutinizing Donovan's mission, certain "rumors" started circulating in Belgrade shortly after the colonel's departure; this suggests that Donovan was going to disclose publicly his conversation with Prince Paul.[47] At the same time, "rumors" circulated in Moscow regarding the position Yugoslavia would take if the Germans occupied Bulgaria. Prime Minister Cvetković was upset and, suspecting the leak, asked Lane who was responsible for circulating such damaging information in Belgrade and Moscow. Lane naturally disavowed any knowledge of the leak. So did Steinhardt in Moscow (Doc. nos. 740.0011, European War 1939/8112; 740.0011, European War 1939/8158). Hull, who still maintained the posture of neutrality and regarded Donovan's mission as unofficial and outside his department's jurisdiction, concurred with both, adding that many stories of a speculative nature appeared regularly in the U.S. press (Doc. nos. 740.0011, European War 1939/8112; 740.00118, European War 1939/8112). That may have been so, but the "rumors" appeared at a most inopportune moment for the Yugoslav government. Talks with Italy and Germany were still in progress, and these "rumors" certainly did not help in negotiations. In fact, they were designed to increase mistrust among the negotiating parties in the hope that the talks would be abandoned. Donovan intimated to MacVeagh in Athens that the Germans would refrain from making any attack in the Balkans if they were convinced of a unified opposition on the part of Bulgaria, Yugoslavia, and Turkey. Although these nations were far from having any common aim, he was sure that with moral and material assistance from America, this unity might be actualized (Doc. no. 740.0011, European War 1939/8058). It will be remembered that Donovan, in his confidential message to Roosevelt from Ankara, communicated that only American armed involvement could save the Balkans from a German invasion. Without such armed intervention, there was no way of protecting the Balkans and Donovan knew it. What then was his real mission in Yugoslavia? The key to this question is Churchill. Before Donovan left London for his Mediterranean mission, Churchill told the colonel that there were reasons to fear Paul's anti-bolshevism, and that because of his attitude, the "patriots" might be deprived of any reason to form a resistance army.[48] Since British concessions to the Soviets in the Balkans and elsewhere failed to change Soviet foreign policy, the elimination of Paul, one might infer, was crucial for the British to accommodate the Russians without being obvious.

Reading the documents pertaining to the Yugoslav Communist Party's activities at the time, one cannot find any tangible evidence to link the British with the Communists—at least not on the surface. The Moscow party line was observed scrupulously and followed by the Yugoslav Communists. Their devotion to Stalin never faltered. With the ease of perfect chameleons, party members changed their protective colors every time a shift in Soviet foreign policy occurred. Switching, for example, from the policy of the Popular Front to the Nazi-Soviet pact, the Yugoslav Communists had no difficulty explaining it in terms of a necessary peace and as a victory for the small nations, which henceforth, by using peaceful means could avoid war and destruction. As the war gained momentum, the Communist Party propaganda machine was geared against both "imperialist camps," and the Yugoslav leaders were habitually branded as the "paid agents" of both camps. Criticizing Yugoslavia's foreign policy on the eve of Donovan's arrival in Belgrade, Tito accused the Yugoslav leaders of using both camps against the Soviet Union. He accused them of courting the Axis while desiring an Anglo-Saxon victory.[49]

Even after Donovan's departure from Belgrade, Tito wrote a blistering article against the "imperialist criminals" for trying to settle their differences at the expense of the innocent Balkan peoples, writing that we cannot allow those "criminals" to take advantage of us to reach their imperialist ends (356). Only the Soviet Union offered hope for peace and all-out security. In reality, neither Tito nor his Communists cared much about peace or security. Peace would be in the way of their ideological and political aims, which was quite evident from Tito's speech to the Fifth Party Congress held in October of 1940. "Comrades," he said, "we are faced with ... great decisions. Let us therefore march forward into the last battle!" The victorious end of this march would be liberation of the land, but the emphasis was placed on liberated land from the "foreigners and the capitalists."[50] For the same "anti-fascist" reasons, the Communists loathed Prince Paul and Maček. As long as those two remained in power, there was but a slim possibility that the Communists would realize their ideological aims.[51] Although on the surface they remained hostile to the "imperialistic criminals," below the surface, they desired war and the British knew it. On this point, British strategic aims in the Balkans were identical to those of the Communists.

Still mindful of the Soviet position, the Communists continued with their dual policy even after Donovan left Belgrade. Lane communicated to Washington how the Communists launched a propaganda campaign against the "pluto-democracies" and the war they caused. They preached allegiance to the Soviet Union for the benefit of the Yugoslav and Bulgarian masses, while in Greece, the party line was anti-German and anti-Italian.[52] Such caution hardly suggests that the Yugoslav Communists needed Donovan's "guidance." This is further ascertained by the fact that although knowledgeable about the coup, the Communists were nowhere in sight at the time of its execution. Communist visibility in the coup could have adversely affected the already strained Soviet-German relations.[53] Finally, that the Communists started an armed rebellion only after the attack on the Soviet Union, clearly testifies that they knew exactly, without Donovan's help, what they were doing.

Irrespective, however, of the claims and counterclaims made regarding the Tito-Donovan connection, the incontestable fact is that Churchill needed all the help he could get to bring about changes in Yugoslavia's foreign policy. Anticipating that the "factionalism" might paralyze Yugoslav resistance, Churchill was sure that the Communists would at least be at hand to "set Europe ablaze" once the Soviet Union was attacked. Thus, as so often in the past, the interests of various local groups ostensibly merged with the interests of the global powers, when in reality they all pursued their own separate agendas. In hindsight, one could say that to beat the "Huns," Churchill's Balkan strategy acted as a catalyst for a Communist takeover of half the European continent.[54] Although there is still no tangible evidence of the Tito-Donovan connection, the aims of both parties make this alleged connection rather credible.

Leaving Belgrade for Athens, Donovan was reasonably happy. He felt that the Yugoslav government would resist German aggression. Of course, there was never any doubt that it would, but it depended on Germany's intentions. While for the Yugoslav government, peace negotiations with the Axis were still possible, for Donovan, any negotiated settlement with Germany and Italy, however beneficial for Yugoslavia, constituted ipso facto an obsequious groveling to the Nazis.[55] He promised help and talked "tough," but as Higham observed after the fact, Donovan's toughness, in view of America's still-neutral position, amounted to a "mouthful of New York Irish blarney."[56] This was not a very charitable assessment, considering that Donovan put his heart and soul into the job, doing what he was told to do. More importantly, Donovan did "bolster" the conspirators who promised to undertake the coup should the government decide to "grovel" to the Axis.

By coincidence, General Metaxas died on the day Donovan returned to Athens, January 29, 1941. The new prime minister, Alexander Korizis, intended to continue Metaxas' policy of "watchful caution," but his lack of stamina and poor knowledge of military affairs made him more susceptible to Anglo-American influences. Wasting no time, Donovan visited the Albanian front to "bolster" the morale of the Greek soldiers, and as well, the civilians. Confronted with the poor condition of the Greek army, he made lavish promises of American assistance to the military and civilian leaders. A memorandum listing the most urgent needs of the civilian populations was submitted to the American authorities in Athens, while a separate requisition list for the military was immediately forwarded to Cairo.[57] There was no way that this aid could ever arrive in time, but no one considered that fact. Donovan informed MacVeagh that according to Field Marshall Wavell, the British were now interested, both offensively and defensively, in the Near East as a theater of operation.[58]

What Wavell meant by the "Near East" and how Donovan understood it is not clear. It is a well-known fact that Field Marshall was in favor of intensified warfare against the Italians in North Africa and less inclined to the transference of British troops from Africa to Greece. The controversy flared up in the American press after the fall of Greece. The press hinted that Wavell was skeptical regarding the wisdom of British military involvement in the Balkans, and blamed Churchill and the "interfering London politicians" for the Balkan debacle. Donovan was indignant. Speaking before the Union League of Philadelphia shortly after the fall of Greece, he was adamant that Wavell also favored military action in the Balkans, but that its success would depend upon certain logistics to transfer troops across the Mediterranean. That was true, except that Wavell knew only too well that there were neither available troops nor the available ships to transfer them across the Mediterranean. Even if the troops were available from elsewhere, it was very often impossible, sometimes for a whole month at a stretch, to transport them through the Suez; access to the Mediterranean was infested with Axis mines.[59] Perhaps Wavell was not too candid with Donovan regarding the logistics, but by defending the field marshall ex post facto, Donovan was really defending the British Balkan strategy, which he himself strenuously labored to implement.

Precisely for this reason, Donovan paid no attention to the misgivings of the Turkish ambassador in Athens. Before Donovan left for Ankara, the ambassador told MacVeagh that the Turks were satisfied with the talks already under way in Ankara between the British and the Turks; in Ankara's view, however, the British should defeat the Italians in Libya first, to face any developments in the Balkans that required more strength.[60] The sad point was one that the ambassador may have been vaguely aware; namely, the "interfering London politicians" acted upon the assumption that British success in the Balkans would ipso facto eliminate the African front. It will be recalled that one aspect of the Balkan strategy was to defeat the Italians in Albania and push them altogether out of the war. With talks already in progress in Ankara, Donovan was not about to discourage the British, but to pressure the Turks, as with others in the region, into joining the Balkan front against the Axis.

In line with his mission, Donovan told the Turks that to win the war, Hitler must first and foremost invade and hold the British Isles. The Axis action in the Balkans was therefore designed to strangle British commerce and force

Britain to surrender.[61] As previously pointed out, Higham ridiculed such views and ascribed them to "British egocentricity." The British were inclined to believe that everywhere, even in the Balkans, they were the object of German action. In reality, they posed a mere potential threat to the German southern flank once war with the Soviet Union was under way.[62] While Higham was right to ridicule British "egocentricity," the truth (which seems to have escaped him) was that the strategy of the "interfering London politicians" went beyond the real and immediate danger for the security of the British Isles, and was undertaken as a calculated risk to make others absorb the main brunt of German military power. This was the reason why Churchill "lost sight" of the gradual German incursion into North Africa. From the British viewpoint, it was a risk worth taking.

With the strangulation of Britain, Donovan switched to the Balkan front, making promises that he knew he could not deliver. The formation of the unified Balkan front appeared as a highly idyllic proposition to the Turks. Not only were the Bulgarian grievances an obstacle that refused to go away and which stood in the way of achieving any Balkan unity, the Turks were quite aware, as intimated by their ambassador in Athens, that the Allies would not be ready for any offensive warfare for at least another year. They therefore told Donovan that if preparations for offensive warfare in the Balkans could be achieved, the initial Allied successes could draw even Soviet support. The pugnacious Donovan, however, believed that it could be done much sooner. MacMurray communicated a watered down version of Donovan's secret message to the president, insisting that the Balkan front was feasible, provided "some outside impulse from a nation that [had] no interest in the Balkans" came to the rescue.[63] Neither the secret message nor its watered down version to the U.S. State Department could have had any practical effect on the president. Dunlop, Donovan's biographer, pointed out: "Even with Europe on fire, politics in Washington went on as usual."[64]

The American press, however, was elated. The Yugoslav Press Bureau Chief in Washington, Bogdan Radica, sent several dispatches to Belgrade. The salient points of his dispatches, as they appeared in the American press, were that Donovan made it clear to the Balkan countries that America stood 100 percent behind Britain and was determined to prevent a German victory every means at its disposal. Donovan was the messenger of hope, not only to the Balkan nations, but to all of Europe. No American before Donovan brought such an unequivocal message to the doubting Europeans, one clearly demonstrating where America stood in the current conflict.[65] Reflecting upon the American scene, Radica stressed how Donovan's mission lifted the American spirit as well. Americans finally realized that the Balkans were the last bastion of European resistance. The Greek resistance against Mussolini's forces gave rise to the hope that the Axis could be beaten if the Balkan nations were assisted by Britain and the United States.[66] Of special interest, as Radica observed, was that the American press took it for granted that the Balkans belonged in the Soviet sphere of influence, believing that the German invasion of the region would compel the Soviets to take counteraction. The impression that Radica conveyed to Belgrade was that improvements in relations with the Soviet Union was undertaken by Washington to help the Balkan peoples. "The prevalent beliefs in the country [were], that the Balkan peoples could resist the aggression only if the Soviets stood behind them."[67] It seems then that the "guidance" of the Communists could have been attributed to the joint Anglo-American effort. At any rate, Donovan's mission, Radica stressed, convinced Americans that the Balkan peoples were decidedly against any capitulation to the Axis, and that they would defend their independence.[68]

In conclusion, one might say that Donovan's mission in the Balkans in general, and in Yugoslavia in particular, was not his crowning success as later lauded by Churchill. True, he used Roosevelt's authority, no doubt a powerful incentive to back the British plan. Even so, no one took it very seriously except those who had already consented to undertake a coup if Yugoslavia acceded the Tripartite Pact. The coup itself failed to mobilize Yugoslavia into action against the invading Germans. It did, however, offer legitimacy to the pan-Serbian elements (involved in the coup) to reclaim their dominant position lost due to the Serbo-Croatian Agreement.

Chapter 7
Yugoslavia between Scylla and Charybdis

According to Serbian sources, Donovan's mission in Yugoslavia left behind lasting consequences for the future of the country. Before Donovan's arrival, the precise date of the coup was still being debated among the putschists. Initially, General Simović was not in favor of war against the Axis. He merely wanted the inclusion of the Serbian oppositional parties into the new government. Such a government, in his view, would have the backing of the military, and therefore provide Yugoslavia with a stronger position in negotiations with the Axis. Another group involving the Knežević brothers was in favor of letting the existing government manage the negotiations and compromise itself in the process; i.e., allow the government to dig its own grave.[1] Simović reversed his decision when he met Donovan. Colonel Donovan informed the general that his impressions of Paul and Cvetković were that both of them would give in to Hitler's demands without a fight. Emboldened by Donovan's assurances of America's moral and material help, Simović changed his original views and declared that the military would act to prevent the government from compromising Yugoslavia vis-à-vis the United States and its Allies (14). Hearing such a resolute answer, Donovan was satisfied. Before leaving for Greece, he appointed George Radin, an American lawyer of Serbian descent and Simović's friend, as a liaison between him and the general (15).

Whispers about the forthcoming coup thereafter circulated in Belgrade. Simović himself told Paul that the military would, under no circumstances, accept any compromise with the Axis (17). While in a semi-drunken state, General Bora Mirković, Simović's right-hand man in the conspiracy, boasted in Zemun how he would, together with his officers, take care of Paul who had the unfortunate habit of making arbitrary decisions (17). The Germans too heard about the whispers and were naturally concerned about the government's ability to keep itself in power if Yugoslavia acceded to the Tripartite Pact. In the past, the Germans had been quite tolerant toward such whispers. Opponents of the government knew how to camouflage them as a purely domestic affair. The Germans, on the other hand, were not concerned with the power holders in the government, being more interested in Yugoslavia retaining its neutral status and trading with Germany. But this time was different. Donovan's mission, coupled with the crossing of the German troops over Bulgaria, made the Germans less inclined to regard the coup as a purely Serbian domestic squabble with no influence on Yugoslavia's foreign policy.[2]

With the pressure on Belgrade mounting from all sides, the question was which course Yugoslavia should take that would prove least detrimental to its interests. One option was to reopen simultaneous but separate negotiations with Rome and Berlin. After some deliberation, the decision was made to send Stakić and Gregorić back to Rome and Berlin, respectively. While Donovan was still in the Balkans, both emissaries resurfaced in the Axis capitals. As instructed by Court Minister Milan Antić (Paul's confidant), Stakić was to query Mussolini as to the possibility of improving Italo-Yugoslav relations based on the treaty between the two countries signed in 1937.[3] In Berlin, Gregorić was to clarify some points concerning a "misunderstanding" between Ribbentrop and Aleksandar Cincar Marković. Cincar Marković's "misunderstanding" was that Yugoslavia could better its position vis-à-vis the Axis if a nonaggression pact was signed between Belgrade and Rome, with an option to accede to the Tripartite Pact. If that was still possible, Yugoslavia would be ready for further negotiations. The "misunderstanding" was immediately cleared up, with the understanding that Germany could no longer be satisfied unless Yugoslavia acceded to the Tripartite Pact. Now that matters were clarified, Gregorić had no choice but to ask permission for Cvetković and Cincar Marković to visit Germany.[4]

In the meantime, the Italians notified Berlin of the new Yugoslav proposal. True, the Italians felt the proposal was somewhat stale, but the military operations in Greece were on the verge of a collapse, making them less critical of the Yugoslav approach. Given the improved relations with Yugoslavia, Il Duce in his message to Berlin, pointed out that it would cause the "moral and military collapse of Greece," terminate British intrigues in Belgrade and Sofia, and, of course, isolate the Turks. With such optimistic expectations, Mussolini was sure that German intervention in Greece would indeed be "superfluous."[5] The Germans, however, were not of the same opinion. Suspecting that the Yugoslav-Italian negotiations might again have an anti-German edge, Berlin objected on the grounds that talks with the Yugoslavs were already in progress in Berlin.[6] To placate Mussolini, State Secretary of the Foreign Office Ernst von Weizsäcker informed Italian Charge D'affaires Guiseppe Cosmelli that talks with the Yugoslavs were of common interest to both Berlin and Rome because they dealt with Yugoslavia's accession to the Tripartite Pact (Doc. no. 45). Both Mussolini and Prince Paul realized that further negotiations would be of no use. Mussolini instructed his ambassador in Belgrade to break off any further talks with the Yugoslav officials, while Paul realized that any agreement with Italy would be no more than a "curtain-raiser" for Yugoslavia's succession to the Tripartite Pact.[7] Cvetković and Cincar Marković were scheduled to visit Germany on February 14, 1941.

On February 2, 1941, Lane informed the U.S. State Department that Prime Minister Cvetković and Foreign Minister Aleksandar Cincar Marković were going to visit Germany.[8] To confirm the story, Lane visited Cincar Marković. Concerned about the outcome of the visit, Lane took the occasion to remind the foreign minister that countries that did not resist aggression were not worthy of independence. He therefore repeated Donovan's warnings that such countries in no way should count on American support when political and geographic readjustments were made after the war.[9] To make sure that the Yugoslav government got the point, Lane suggested that the state department deliver a similar message to Fotić in Washington as a corollary to the president's message of January 6, 1941, in which he unequivocally expressed American support to those nations willing to resist aggression (943). In line with the president's instructions, Hull prepared the message for Fotić, who in turn transmitted it to the Yugoslav government. In the message, Hull emphasized the need to resist the Axis, stressing that any victory, diplomatic or otherwise on part of the "predatory" powers, would only pave the way for new demands and in the process undermine human freedom and independence (954).

To make it more effective, an identical message was communicated to Lane, whereupon he immediately requested to see Prince Paul and Prime Minister Cvetković. Cvetković refused to see him, and Court Minister Antić told Lane that Paul was "too busy." Feeling uncomfortable about Lane's patriotic lectures, one official asked him point-blank why Washington was so anxious to push such small nations to fight, while the United States had no intention of entering the war. Lane became indignant and snapped back that it would if attacked.[10] Considering the strength of the United States it was hardly an inspiring answer, but he managed to secure an interview with Paul on February 18, 1941, after Cvetković and Cincar Marković returned from a meeting with Ribbentrop. In a strictly confidential message to Hull and Welles, Lane reported that Paul was in a very pessimistic frame of mind; twice, he repeated that he wished he were dead. Paul admitted that the Germans asked Yugoslavia to join the Tripartite Pact, but he had refused. Paul's pessimism was compounded by the Bulgarian-Turkish Nonaggression Declaration, hatched in Berlin due to the incompetence of the British minister in Sofia, George W. Rendell. To make things worse, the Germans remained "frightfully amiable" which, in Paul's view, was designed to suit their "fiendishly cunning" plan. Before Lane could advise Paul on what to do, Paul himself concluded that even American help would be of no use. Yugoslavia would be destroyed before it could arrive. Prince Paul, however, like other Yugoslav leaders, believed in an ultimate British victory.[11]

When Paul said that he had refused to join the pact, he was not quite candid. The meeting between the German and Yugoslav officials in Salzburg eliminated any possibilities for further "misunderstandings." Yugoslavia's accession to the Tripartite Pact was on the agenda. Given that Yugoslav officials were not authorized to discuss accession to the pact, the joint decision was made to wait for Prince Paul's visit to Germany scheduled for March 4, 1941.[12] Lane did not quite believe what he heard from Paul, learning from "two diplomatic colleagues" that the final decision to join the pact was to be made in Belgrade, presumably by Paul alone.[13] In the next dispatch to Washington, Lane described the rapid preparation for the crossing of German troops into Bulgaria. The urgency notwithstanding, there was no sign of mobilization; yet Lane cautioned Washington.[14] Hearing such disquieting news, Hull sent another message to Paul. "I am confident," Hull reminded Paul, "that our type of civilization and war in whose outcome we are vitally interested will definitely be helped by resistance on the part of the nations which suffer from aggression."[15] Lane reported back the effect the message had on Prince Paul. The message was received rather positively according to Lane, and he asked the American minister to assure Washington that Yugoslavia would never sign any agreement with Germany that proved detrimental to Yugoslavia's sovereignty.[16]

Considering the military situation, the question of troop withdrawal from Croatia and Slovenia (of which Fortier had spoken in past dispatches) again resurfaced. The problem of pulling troops from Croatia and Slovenia was not merely a military move but a political one as well. In reality, it meant the disintegration of Yugoslavia, and Paul said so to Lane. To vent his feelings, Paul blamed British "stupidity" and Bulgarian "perfidy" for the situation Yugoslavia faced. To ameliorate it, he tried to initiate talks with Bulgaria, but it was useless. He understood Bulgarian perfidy from the start better than anyone else. Not even the Turks understood it, which was why they signed the "stupid pact" with Sofia.[17] Secretly, Lane was pleased with Paul's remarks regarding British diplomacy. Although not indifferent to his British colleague Campbell in Belgrade, he nevertheless regarded him as a "poor little man."[18] Knowing that Roosevelt stood behind the British, however, Lane never hesitated to support British interests in Belgrade.

Paul's difficulties were compounded by the fact that the British no longer considered the disintegration of Yugoslavia as a valid excuse to stay neutral. In his memoirs, Churchill complained about Paul's wishing so stubbornly to "maintain a fictitious internal cohesion" of Yugoslavia by upholding a neutral policy vis-à-vis the Axis.[19] Commenting on the British frame of mind from the middle of 1940 to the time of the coup, Phyllis Auty, best known for her work on Tito's biography, stressed that the British leaders were so desperate that they considered a radical change in British policy irrespective of the consequences for Yugoslavia.[20] As Paul's biographers, Balfour and Mackay correctly pointed out that Churchill was actually convinced that Britain, as a great power, had every right to sacrifice small neutral nations for the sake of an ultimate victory.[21]

Concerned about Paul's forthcoming trip to Germany, Lane warned Washington that the meeting with Hitler would determine Yugoslavia's status during German intervention in Greece. Given that the Germans assured Belgrade of Yugoslavia's sovereignty in advance, the Germans, to have a free hand in Greece, hoped to undermine Yugoslav resistance.[22] Lane reported that the "better informed sources" in Belgrade believed that it was of mutual interest to keep Yugoslavia out of the conflict and to maintain the status quo. In Lane's view, the neutral status made Yugoslavia all the more vulnerable, and now that troop withdrawal was out of the question, the role of the Croatians and Slovenians would be more visible in Belgrade (Doc. no. 740.0011, European War 1939/8652). Regarding Turkish-Yugoslav relations, the Turkish ambassador in Belgrade told Lane that the Yugoslavs had no intention of improving relations with Ankara; in discussing the subject with Campbell, the latter believed the lack of seriousness to be mutual (Doc. no. 740.0011, European War 1939/8652).

From the British point of view they were, of course, mutually responsible for the absence of serious negotiations. Speaking objectively, however, why should they be blamed for looking after their own respective interests? True, negotiations never went beyond an ambassadorial level, but the main issue was to determine which act committed by Germany would be regarded as a justification for war. Both countries agreed that a direct violation of their national territory would lead to war, but such an understanding was not good enough for the British. To assuage the British prime minister, Cvetković asked the Turks in March of 1941 if a simultaneous German attack on Yugoslavia and Greece would be considered in Ankara as cause for war. The answer was no! The Turks would defend themselves but would never send their troops outside of their territory.[23] Turkish views were well-known to the British who finally agreed to let them be, but only because they held, geographically speaking, a key position in the Balkans. MacMurray reported from Ankara that the British agreed to keep Turkey out of the conflict even if Greece was attacked, but that Britain would nevertheless continue to prepare Turkey for its eventual participation in war.[24]

As agreed, Paul visited Berghof at the beginning of March 1941. On March 4, while Paul was still in Germany, Lane visited Court Minister Antić. Guessing the nature of Lane's visit, Antić avoided any discussion of German-Yugoslav relations at this crucial point and changed the subject by attacking Bulgarian "perfidy." Antić informed Lane that since the past November, he had known that the Bulgarians would let the Germans in without a fight. Antić deliberately talked about Bulgaria in the hope that it might soften the impact of Paul's visit with Hitler when the story broke in the press. He was right. The coverage of Paul's visit was tempered in the American press by Yugoslavia's exceptionally difficult position; as a result, the Turks and the Russians got most of the blame.[25] The German troops started pouring into Bulgaria on March 2, 1941. The Yugoslav authorities were duly notified yet demonstrated no visible reaction, which worried the German commanders. Without formal Yugoslav assurances, the commanders were not at all sure that their right flank would be immune from Yugoslav attack.[26] With German troops in Bulgaria, Paul had to face a showdown with Hitler unless Yugoslavia was to enter the war.

Anticipating a confrontation between Paul and Hitler, Prime Minister Cvetković, together with Justice Minister Mihajlo Konstantinović (otherwise a British agent), drafted a proposal that they forwarded to Paul to be used for guidance in his talks with the Germans. Although the authors of the draft were not quite sure regarding the exact demands the Germans would make, they tried to anticipate them and furnish appropriate answers. The Tripartite Pact was not even considered, but if forced upon Paul, Germany should then guarantee Yugoslavia its sovereignty and independence. As a possible counterproposal to German demands, Paul was to offer Yugoslavia's intermediary role in the Greco-Italian conflict and, with German arbitration, help to establish peace. If peace was established, then the Balkan states would guarantee jointly that no military operations by any foreign power would ever take place there.[27] In essence, the draft did not differ much from the proposal made by Cvetković on his visit to Salzburg. It was so far-fetched that few people believed Hitler would even consider it.

In his meeting with Paul, Hitler addressed the same subject as he had previously with Cvetković and Cincar Marković. This time, however, the subject concerning Yugoslavia's accession to the Tripartite Pact was unavoidable. By joining the pact, Hitler stated forcefully that Yugoslavia would be exempt from military involvement while its territorial integrity and independence would be fully guaranteed by the Axis powers. Hitler's proposal was by far better than anyone had expected. Still playing for time to avoid making any final commitments, Paul remained noncommittal by saying that such an important decision could not be his alone; if it were, he would, in view of Yugoslavia's domestic situation, not be sitting there six months later. True, Hitler replied, but if this opportunity slipped by six months from now, he might not be there either.[28] Still acting the part of a benevolent protector, Hitler agreed to wait until the members of the Crown Council were consulted. No sooner had Paul left than von Ribbentrop communicated to von Heeren from Fuschl and Berlin that the Prince was "wavering" in making his decision, and if it were necessary, he would like to see the Paul again in Bled (Slovenia) to expedite matters. In the meantime, von Heeren was instructed to do everything in his power to hasten Yugoslavia's accession to the Tripartite Pact.[29]

Returning home, Paul realized that the time had finally arrived to decide on Yugoslavia's future one way or the other. The meeting of the Crown Council was set for March 6, 1941. In attendance were Prince Paul with two other regents, Radenko Stanković and Ivo Perović, as well as Prime Minister Cvetković, Foreign Minister Aleksandar Cincar Marković, Croatian leader Vladimir Maček, Slovenian representative Fran Kulovec, War Minister General Petar Pešić, and Minister of the Royal Court Milan Antić. Paul recapitulated his talks and impressions of the meeting. Hitler, he declared, requested Yugoslavia's accession to the pact. No one was surprised. Aleksandar Cincar Marković repeated the German request. If the pact was accepted, Yugoslavia would retain its territorial integrity. Moreover, the pact would exempt Yugoslavia from any military obligation, including the passage of military transports and wounded German soldiers. After the war in Greece was brought to a successful end, Salonika would be ceded to Yugoslavia.[30]

After the reports were heard, an intense discussion followed. Cincar Marković contended that unless Yugoslavia was prepared to accept its own destruction, there was no other way out but to accede to the pact. Fearing for the future of his native Slovenia, so close to Germany, Kulovec concurred with Cincar Marković and declared himself in favor of the pact. Cvetković's concerns were directed toward Salonika. His argument was that if they acceded to the Tripartite Pact, it meant that in reality, Yugoslavia would become part of the German political system and consequently would have no grounds on which to claim the city. Unless Salonika was secured for Yugoslavia, he was prepared to go to war against Germany.[31] The second regent, Stanković, was also against the pact on the grounds that it would break Yugoslavia's relations with the Western Allies. To avoid such a predicament, he proposed to wage a symbolic war against the Axis. His symbolic war involved the king, the government, and a hundred thousand soldiers, who would join the British in Greece, and then, as in World War I, return as victors. Cvetković assailed Stanković's symbolic war, calling it a selfish act that would expose defenseless people to the mercy of the German invaders needlessly.[32]

Then it was Maček's turn. A pacifist by conviction, but not at any price, he needed some convincing answers to clear his own conscience. His first questions were directed to Cincar Marković. If Yugoslavia refused to sign the pact, would it really mean war with Germany? The answer was yes! Then he questioned General Pešić about Yugoslavia's defense capability. General Pešić put it very succinctly. In case of war in northern Yugoslavia, the three major cities of Ljubljana, Zagreb, and Belgrade, would come under German occupation in a matter of days. The remaining forces defending the mountainous region of Bosnia, without adequate supplies, would be finished within six weeks. The reality was indeed bleak and could get even worse. Claiming impartiality, Paul remained noncommittal while the council voted in favor of accession to the pact, although with several provisions.[33] The decision of the council was submitted to the government for deliberation. With three members against, the rest of the members accepted the council's decision.[34]

The government deliberately procrastinated in signing the pact for the following two or three weeks. Cognizant of Germany's desire to liquidate the British in Greece and their preparation to attack the Soviet Union, the Yugoslav government, by delaying its final decision, and in a rather skillful manner, used the German predicament to its advantage. Giving various plausible excuses, Belgrade insisted on the publication of the clauses relative to Yugoslavia's military exemptions, together with other important points covering territorial integrity and national sovereignty. Belgrade also insisted that a separate clause recognizing Yugoslavia's interests in Salonika be drawn and kept secret for the time being.[35] Motivated to preserve Yugoslavia (most likely to avoid sharing it with Mussolini), or as Hitler told Paul, "*aus eigenen egoistischen Gründen*" (for selfish reasons), the Germans agreed to accept all provisions put forward by Belgrade.[36] The Yugoslavs achieved more than they had ever expected. An experienced German diplomat, Urlich von Hassell, could not have said it better: "*Im Grunde haben sie [the Yugoslavs] wenig versprochen und allerhand Sicherungen bekommen*" (promised little and received all sorts of guarantees).[37]

To take a closer look at the Balkan situation, Foreign Secretary Eden came to Athens two days before Paul was scheduled to meet Hitler on March 4, 1941. The situation was not very promising. Without Britain's knowledge, the Greeks themselves still kept in touch with the Germans through their connections in Belgrade.[38] Although time was running out, the Greeks were still hopeful that Berlin would be interested in arranging peace between Athens and Rome. The Greco-German connections in Belgrade encouraged Prime Minister Cvetković and Prince Paul to plead with Hitler for a united Balkan region, free of any foreign power. As previously pointed out, however, Hitler was sure that the British would never leave the Balkans peacefully. Upon Eden's arrival, British forces, although few in number, accelerated their landing in Greece. Mindful of Yugoslavia's key position in the enfolding Balkan drama, Eden asked Campbell to visit him in Athens. Reviewing the Yugoslav domestic scene, Campbell informed the foreign secretary that the Serbians were generally pro-British, whereas the Croatians were in sympathy with the Germans. Campbell was not quite accurate. The problem was not so much that the Croatians sympathized with the Germans but, rather, they could not reconcile themselves with the notion of dying for a Yugoslavia which they still considered their prison, regardless of Maček and his agreement with Belgrade. They both, however, glibly agreed that the Yugoslavs feared the Germans, but that it all might change provided Belgrade was properly informed with respect to the British plan to aid the Greeks.[39]

What was supposed to be Eden's "secret" visit to Greece came to Sulzberger's attention, whereupon he decided to go to Athens and interview the "elegant and courageous" foreign secretary. Cyrus Sulzberger was one rare American correspondent who came to the Balkans from Prague in 1938 and remained there. He established excellent connections with anybody who was important, especially with the Serbian underground (e.g., the Serbian putschists). With intimate knowledge of a Serbian conspiracy, he told the "surprised" and "pleased" Eden that the Serbians were ready to fight, no matter what the government might decide. Chatting informally, Eden, knowing the value of the press, informed Sulzberger about the Balkan front. There were difficulties, of course, while the "old dictator" Metaxas was alive, but now that he was gone, the situation was more favorable for the British. As a precondition to the Balkan front, Metaxas had insisted that the British forces amount to two hundred thousand well-equipped men; otherwise, there was no point in their coming to Greece. Now that the "price stipulation" was no longer an issue, the British would send Greece whatever they could.[40] The actual number of available British troops was skillfully avoided by Eden.

To prevent any accurate assessment of the their strength, the British tried to camouflage it in any way they could. Several weeks before the coup took place, the British sent their emissary on a "diplomatic mission" to Belgrade. In Belgrade, a young Greek "journalist" known as Papas talked about there being three hundred thousand British soldiers in Greece with "plenty" of tanks, planes, and ammunition.[41] Although the British officially denied his stories, unofficially, they smiled politely, giving the impression that they were true, but that they were in no position to confirm anything.[42] Such stories were intended to deceive anyone concerned with the Balkans, especially the press. American correspondents, who by now swarmed to Belgrade from all over, were especially eager to fill their papers with stories of the mighty British armies landing in Greece. The British stories had a considerable influence on the Serbian putschists as well.[43] In quest of their aims in the Balkans, the British even succeeded in fooling their own people. As Sulzberger pointed out, General Sir Henry "Jumbo" Maitland Wilson, the commander-in-chief of the British expeditionary forces in Greece, was promised fourteen divisions and ended up with less than three.[44]

The American ambassador in Athens, MacVeagh, was not spared from British deceptions. Summing up his conversation with Eden, MacVeagh sent a glowing report to Washington about British aid to Greece. They would help Greece with everything they had. When asked about the numbers of British troops, Eden, with masterful equivocation, replied that on this particular point he was saying nothing, not even to the United States or the British ambassador in Athens.[45] Instead, he talked of how "delighted" he was with his reception in Ankara, and added that in case of a German attack on Greece, the Turks might declare war on Germany and allow the British to use their airfields and other facilities to wage war against Germany. Although Yugoslavia was still indecisive, he was nonetheless sure that Belgrade would eventually come in, and together with Greece and Turkey, would fight the Germans.[46] MacVeagh undoubtedly was impressed. In a separate dispatch to Roosevelt, he reported how British help toward Greece would encourage the entire Balkans to forge a unified front stretching from the Bosporus to the Adriatic. If, however, Yugoslavia joined the pact, the Germans would make use of the Monastir Gap in Macedonia, and the well-laid plans for the Balkan front would "go agley."[47]

This "well-laid plan" reported by MacVeagh added additional pressure on Yugoslavia. Eden dispatched Campbell back to Belgrade with a personal letter for Prince Paul. In it he outlined the most salient problems facing the British in their defense of Greece. Of all the problems, the most pressing was Salonika. Well aware of Serbian interests associated with Salonika, Eden pointed out how impossible it would be for the Greeks to defend the city along the Aliakom Line (running south of the Yugoslav border to the Aegean Sea), because the Germans could always swing to the left through the Monastir Gap and outflank the Greek forces in the region. The city would then fall into German hands. The German strategy, Eden stressed, was to subdue Greece, immobilize Turkey, occupy Salonika, and, by gaining control over the Straits, to place Yugoslavia at Berlin's mercy. All this, however, could be prevented if Yugoslavia took the necessary steps, along with Britain and Greece.[48]

Eden purposely left out what the precise British role would be, and instructed Campbell to outline verbally Britain's aims for Prince Paul. According to

Campbell's oral outline, the British forces eventually would take the position west of Salonika temporarily covered by the Greeks, but a successful defense of the city would depend largely on Yugoslavia. True, Campbell was careful not to press Paul for any concrete answers, but he pointed out that the British would be glad to discuss their plan, provided a Yugoslav staff officer came to Athens. To win over the Croatians and Slovenians, Campbell was also instructed to say that a "case could be made" at the peace conference for revisions to the present Italo-Yugoslav frontier if Yugoslavia became a British ally.[49] Paul declined Eden's personal invitation to Belgrade but agreed to send a staff officer, Major Milisav Perišić, to Athens for further talks with the British. Suspicious of Britain's motives for pushing Yugoslavia into war, Perišić, in talks with the British, did not disclose Yugoslavia's military plans but rather asked what the Allies would do if Yugoslavia became belligerent. Since they had no precise knowledge of Yugoslavia's intentions, Perišić was told the Allies could not give him any answer either. A protocol was signed regarding Yugoslavia's self-reliance, which entailed the old idea of attacking the Italians in Albania. If the Yugoslavs wished to know more about the Allied plan, then Major Perišić should return to Greece with something more concrete. General Kosić, thinking it over, decided that the whole project should be postponed for the time being.[50]

Pressed for time and quite anxious not to complicate the Balkan situation more than it already was, von Ribbentrop instructed von Heeren to inform the Yugoslav authorities that their provisions to the pact were acceptable, with an exception relative to Article 3 covering military assistance which was required from all the signatories of the pact. Article 3 was singled out in an effort to extract some concessions from Yugoslavia, but von Ribbentrop cautioned von Heeren to drop it if Belgrade objected. From the government point of view, the German offer could not have come at a more opportune time. Acting on the assumption that a bird in the hand was worth two in the bush, Belgrade, without slamming the door on the Allies, decided in favor of a final negotiation with Berlin.[51]

Well acquainted with the decisions made by the Yugoslav government, Campbell again sprang into action. This time he was instructed by London to go to Zagreb and talk with the Croatian leader, Maček. The meeting was held at the home of Croatian artist Ivan Meštrović, who had important connections in Britain. In addition to Maček, Campbell, and Meštrović, two of Maček's closest associates, Dr. Juraj Krnjević and August Košutić, were present, as well as the British consul in Zagreb, Thomas G. Rapp. Campbell came straight to the point and asked how Yugoslavia would act in the forthcoming conflict in the Balkans. While asking this and similar questions, Campbell kept referring to the Yugoslavs as a "fine military race," and quite naturally wanted to see them on the British side as soon as possible.[52] As usual, Maček was on guard and carefully measured every word he said. Croatian sympathies for the Allied cause notwithstanding, Maček replied to Campbell that the Croatians were not in the least bit responsible for the situation Yugoslavia now faced, or were they ever, which was true, in a position to influence Belgrade's actions with respect to foreign policy. True, Maček agreed, the Yugoslavs were a "fine military race," but the point was that an unarmed people could not fight tanks, or ordinary rifles silence heavy guns. Only a German invasion of Russia would offer Yugoslavia a chance to prepare for war. Then at some future date while the German armies were busy in the Russian plains, Yugoslavia could enter the war on the Allied side. Campbell disagreed of course and insisted that the only way Yugoslavia could extricate itself from the present situation was to attack the Italians in Albania and reequip the Yugoslav Army with arms captured from the Italians. The meeting was quite fruitless, with both sides merely recapitulating their old positions.[53]

Meanwhile, Lane communicated to Washington that he increased his efforts along with the British to strengthen Paul against accession to the Tripartite Pact. His task was difficult, Lane complained, because so many "Anglo-American opponents" were exerting influence over Paul. To complicate matters still further, the government itself was divided into three different groups: (1) the appeasers; (2) those who wanted to take Salonika before the city was occupied; and (3) the compromisers who mediated between the first and the second group.[54] At the same time, Steinhardt transmitted Gavrilović's message to the U.S. government from Moscow. The Yugoslav ambassador was certain that with proper handling of the situation, Washington still might play a decisive role in averting Yugoslavia's accession to the Tripartite Pact.[55] Lane, by coincidence, shared an identical view with Gavrilović. In an unprecedented move, Lane held interviews with the leaders of the Serbian oppositional parties. Such a move was interpreted by the Yugoslav government as meddling in the internal affairs of Yugoslavia. Minister of the Royal Court Milan Antić expressed strong disapproval, but Lane insisted that in the absence of official information he was forced to contact the opposition.[56]

On March 10, 1941, Churchill sent a letter to Roosevelt informing him that the British forces were being redeployed from Africa to Greece. It was perhaps regrettable that redeployment of the British could not finish the Italians off in Africa. Being duty bound to stand by the Greeks was the only honorable move to make. The letter was a mixture of British self-sacrifice and a disguised cry for help. The joint actions of the American representatives in Moscow, Ankara, and Belgrade, Churchill pleaded, would be no less valuable than Donovan's "magnificent work" in the Balkans, for which Churchill profusely thanked

Roosevelt.[57] Roosevelt understood Churchill's pleas, but to be on the safe side, asked Foreign Secretary Hull for advice on what the United States could do next to help the British. Hull replied that it was up to the British to give the Balkan nations the help they needed. If the British desired success in the Balkans, Hull told the president, they should give military aid to Turkey and Yugoslavia in the event they needed to resist German aggression.[58] Roosevelt did not argue with his foreign secretary for tactical reasons, but when he left for his extended vacation in the Caribbean, he left Sumner Welles, his alter ego, in charge of foreign policy.

On March 19, 1941, Lane sent an urgent message asking for the president's help for his next meeting with Paul; a personal letter from the president would be of great help, Lane pleaded (959–71). Authorized by Roosevelt, Welles replied that in the president's absence he was in charge of foreign affairs. Therefore, in the president's name, Welles instructed Lane to impress upon the regent that the president followed every development in Yugoslavia more keenly than ever before (954). Welles talked to Fotić as well. To make sure that the message was properly understood in Belgrade, Welles informed the Yugoslav minister that any step taken by Belgrade viewed as detrimental to Yugoslavia or the Allies would place Yugoslavia beyond the pale of U.S. government sympathies (954–55). In subsequent dispatches, Welles authorized Lane to use his instructions as "emphatically as he considered desirable." He was to tell Paul or anyone else in the government that in case of war, the Italian forces in Albania would not be any threat to them. The rugged terrain and the landing of British forces ahead of schedule offered full advantage to withstand any German thrust against the position held by the Yugoslavs. His views, Welles pointed out, should be taken seriously by Yugoslav authorities, not only for the sake of present relations, but for future ones as well.[59]

That his words were not seen as empty threats was demonstrated sooner than expected. To assure some independent action abroad, the Yugoslav government requested to convert $22 million worth of gold deposited in the United States into dollars, half of which was to be transferred to the Bank of Brazil. Secretary Hull swiftly communicated his disapproval both to Lane and Fotić, demanding an outright clarification. Unless satisfactory clarification was received, Hull pointed out, the freezing order of Yugoslav assets might be considered.[60] Neither Paul nor Prime Minister Cvetković had any knowledge of the request, and Finance Minister Juraj Šutej was absent from Belgrade. Lane therefore recommended that the treasury defer its decision until further notice (954–55). Welles, however, was quite explicit on this point and informed Fotić that should Yugoslavia make any false move, the United States would freeze all Yugoslav funds immediately. In addition, the United States would refuse to consider Yugoslavia's request for assistance under the terms of the Lend-Lease Act (960). Welles spoke incessantly about Yugoslavia's "independence," and it seemed that any course Belgrade might take to keep Yugoslavia out of war could be construed as violation of Welles' undefined canons on "independence." In keeping with Welles' instructions, Lane impressed upon Paul that American aid to Yugoslavia would be considered only if Yugoslavia retained its independence. As to what constituted independence, Lane told Paul, would be for Americans to decide and not for Cvetković and Hitler.[61] Accordingly, Yugoslavia had no choice but to follow what Washington deemed the right course to take, irrespective of the consequences.

His overbearing attitude notwithstanding, Lane saw himself as an innocent bystander concerned only with Yugoslavia's political virtues such as honor, national dignity, independence, and integrity. Exasperated by Lane's insensitivity to Yugoslavia's position, Maček's chief of cabinet, Ilija Jukić, told the American minister that Yugoslavia would have taken a stronger stand vis-à-vis the Axis if the United States were already in the war. Several hundred American bombers in Turkey would have made it easier to face the Axis. Why was there now such a determination to push Yugoslavia down the "Nazi monster's gorge?" Jukić very calmly pointed out to Lane that the Yugoslav government was aware of its awesome responsibility, and it made no sense to push the entire nation into jeopardy simply because the Americans insisted that it was the right course to take. Counterarguments, however sound, were of no help. The formation of the Balkan front by Turkey, Greece, and Yugoslavia was firmly fixed in Churchill's mind, and Roosevelt's diplomacy stood firmly with the British. The Balkan front, as Jukić observed, was but the initial step in turning Stalin against Hitler.[62]

The fixation with the Balkan front made the British change their tactics vis-à-vis the Soviets. By the end of January 1941, Eden wrote the British ambassador in Moscow, Sir Stafford Cripps, that Britain needed some tangible success in the field, to compel the Soviets to change their attitude toward them.[63] Cripps agreed but since there was nothing that the British could do to impress the Soviets, he instead proposed joint Anglo-American economic pressure on the Soviet Union. Even then, Cripps cautioned, one could hardly expect miracles, because the "nature of things," meaning the war, was not strong enough at the moment to make any difference. Reopening the question of Anglo-Soviet relations in association with Russia's economic needs, however, might yield results.[64] Judging by the results, it was hardly worth the effort. Instead, the pressure on Yugoslavia as a means of attracting the Soviets became stronger.

Hoping that things would somehow fall into place, Eden, along with Sir John Dill, chief of the Imperial Staff, and Field Marshall Archibald Wavell, commander-in-chief of British forces in the Middle East, agreed at the meeting in Athens that the worst possible scenario at that point would be the British withdrawal from the Balkans. Now that they were in Greece, withdrawal would be even worse than a possible defeat. On the other hand, Wavell pointed out, a measure of success "would be incalculable and might alter the whole aspect of war."[65] Eden agreed and added that British failure to make a stand in the Balkans would result in losing Yugoslavia and by a chain reaction, Turkey as well. Consequently, Eden communicated to London that "in spite of the heavy commitments and dangers involved, especially in view of . . . limited naval and air resources the right decision had been taken in Athens."[66] The decision made in Athens, coupled with Cvetković's proposal to Ankara to regard the German crossing in Bulgaria as a justification for war, prompted Eden to fly back to Cyprus for a meeting with Turkish Foreign Minister Şükrü Saracoğlu. Despite Eden's arguments, however, the Turkish position remained unchanged. By citing the opinion of his general staff, Saracoğlu tried to convince Eden that Germany would not risk attacking Greece if the Yugoslavs stood firm and fortified the Monastir Gap in Macedonia. Pretending that fortification of the gap might redirect a German assault across Turkish territory, Saracoğlu said that Turkey was ready to take such a risk.[67] In reality, there was no risk involved for Turkey at all. The Turks already had German assurances.[68] In short, they were ready to go to war, but only if directly attacked, which in view of German aims in the Balkans and the forthcoming invasion of the Soviet Union (of which Ankara knew), was highly unlikely. Eden, however, was not prepared to leave Cyprus empty-handed and pressed for a message that would indicate Yugoslav-Turkish resolve in regarding an attack on Salonika as cause for war. Saracoğlu flatly refused to draft such a message and opted for an "emasculated" version, suggesting an exchange of views with Belgrade in regard to the threat to Salonika. "Pretexting," as Eden recorded in his memoirs, "political uncertainties in Belgrade, the Turks never delivered even the emasculated version to the Yugoslav authorities."[69]

Objectively speaking, the Yugoslav government chose the Tripartite Pact. The choice was not for any ideological reasons; for Yugoslavia to survive, they had no choice but to accept the German offer, which indeed was better than anyone expected. The only other option was to reject the pact and incite a war that could not be fought. It was a simple decision; Yugoslavia was militarily weak and unprepared. Apart from a military consideration, the internal political situation was even less conducive for military action. The political considerations may not have been the same for all members of the government, but their decision to accede to the Tripartite Pact was motivated by their common fear of destruction from without and explosion from within.

Chapter 8
Yugoslavia Chooses the Tripartite Pact

In the second half of March 1941, Lane realized that the Yugoslav government was faced with the final and irreversible decision to accede to the Tripartite Pact. Concerning the accession, he felt that neither diplomacy nor his powers of persuasion was enough to influence the course of events unfolding around him. Under different circumstances he might have reconciled this as his own limitation, but the stakes this time were too high to sit and watch Yugoslavia pass into the "Axis orbit." The idea that the war in the Balkans could act as a catalyst to bring in the Soviets was the challenge that Lane could not avoid despite his limitation. He therefore doubled his efforts and, as his biographer observed, turned his Belgrade post into a veritable "battle station."[1]

To compensate for his diplomatic and personal failure, Lane turned to the American news reporters stationed in Belgrade. Knowing full well how influential the press could be in making and reporting the news, he gathered reporters around him and fed them confidential information carefully selected to create an atmosphere of mistrust and suspicion against the Yugoslav government in Washington and the Axis capitals. Anxious to retain a semblance of neutrality vis-à-vis the Allies, the Yugoslav government was reluctant to interfere with news gathering or to censor outgoing reports.[2] As intended, the tailored news exacerbated Yugoslav-Axis relations. The Italian news media, careful not to provoke Belgrade, carried reports selected from German, Hungarian, and other pro-Axis sources accusing Americans of their provocative behavior in Belgrade. William Phillips reported from Rome that the newspaper *Il Messaggero* carried the summaries of stories published in Hungary of American machinations in Belgrade and the nocturnal visits of Yugoslav Minister Fotić to the private residence of Sumner Welles. Hiding its own feelings, *Il Messaggero* warned that Berlin was cognizant of American goings-on and gave them "particular attention."[3] Indeed, the reports from Belgrade were designed to shape American public opinion, especially those of various national groups from Yugoslavia residing in the United States and Canada. Yugoslav Press Bureau Chief Bogdan Radica reported how the mood of the Yugoslav immigrants changed under the impact of the press reports. Irrespective of their internal divisions and intergroup hostilities, the immigrants identified themselves with the Allied cause and were strongly in favor of preserving Yugoslavia's independence by force of arms if necessary.[4] The tension between Belgrade and Washington made immigrants from Yugoslavia nervous. Burdened by the complexities of being foreigners, they felt guilty that their "old country" adhered to the policy of not keeping with the interests of their adopted homeland. President Roosevelt was for them the champion of freedom and world democracy. They strongly advised Prince Paul, Maček, and Cvetković in their telegrams to follow in his steps, for one should never submit to tyrants without a battle. In a telegram to Croatian leader Maček, Louis Adamic, a well-known writer of Slovenian descent, expressed his readiness to sacrifice four brothers still in Yugoslavia. He would grieve over the shedding of Yugoslav blood, but the heroic action of Greece was by far more preferable to him than the ignoble and melancholic fate of Rumania and Bulgaria.[5] The fighting spirit of the immigrants was enhanced further by passage of the Lend-Lease Act on March 11, 1941, and by several powerful speeches delivered by Roosevelt in which he depicted masses of plain people taking up the torch of freedom who would rather die as free men than live ingloriously as ordinary slaves. America, Roosevelt stressed, was faced with a task so worthwhile that he envisioned future generations of Americans calling them blessed.[6]

While the Balkan crisis was reaching its peak, Yugoslavia's importance was highlighted on a daily basis. The Serbians enjoyed a reputation for being uniformly anti-Axis; parallels therefore were drawn between the Serbian role in World War I and the present.[7] The reality, of course, was considerably different. The patriarch of the Serbian Orthodox Church and the "guardian of Slavic souls," Gavrilo, was among those who originally had urged Paul to accede to the pact and free Stojadinović, whom the Germans wanted in power instead of Dragiša Cvetković. When Paul handed Stojadinović to the British, the patriarch changed his mind and became an ardent supporter of the putschists.[8] The press expected the Serbians to repeat their past glory with or without the Slovenians and Croatians, and carry the torch of freedom for the peoples of Europe and the world. On March 21, 1941, Lane rehashed Fortier's view favoring the withdrawal of the Yugoslav troops from Slovenia and Croatia and concentrating them in Serbia. With eight divisions, the report suggested, the Yugoslavs could attack the German right flank in Bulgaria and as a corollary action, could launch a four division offensive against the Italians in Albania.[9] Enthusiastically, Welles discussed the same plan with Fotić. Fotić naturally was in favor of it, but to be on the safe side, he criticized Paul for having dismissed the best Serbian generals from their posts.[10] In several of his reports, Radica aptly depicted the press-war against the Belgrade government, whose policy according to the American press, was designed to satisfy Croatian and Slovenian demands. To offset such a policy, the *Christian Science Monitor* pleaded for a more meaningful U.S. engagement in defense of the Balkans, and stressed that Roosevelt's promises to help Yugoslavia already had galvanized the Serbian peasants into resisting Axis demands.[11] The resignation of the three Serbian ministers in protest against Yugoslavia's accession to the pact was interpreted in terms of a collective Serbian resistance. In honor of these three ministers, the *New York Times* carried the story of "traditional Serbian valor" and questioned the "dubious behavior" of Vladimir Maček and the Croatian ministers in the Yugoslav government.[12] As a Croatian, Radica felt the anti-Croatian slant of the American press and suggested to Dr. Juraj Krnjević, secretary of the Croatian Peasant Party, that Croatian interests demanded at this time for one of the Croatian ministers to resign, to demonstrate solidarity with the Serbians. Radica asserted that "only then might you secure the sympathy of the United States and Britain."[13]

The press attack was not restricted merely to that of foreign policy but also encouraged the hope of an open rebellion against the Yugoslav leaders. The press announced the possibility of Fotić's resignation; Oleg Cassini, in his gossip column "These Charming People," speculated that Fotić might resign to secure his social position in the United States.[14] While the majority of U.S. reporters stationed in Belgrade were uniformly pro-Serbian in their outlook, some, in their praise of the Serbian martial spirit, became irrational. Ray Brock of the *New York Times,* much like the romantics of the last century, rediscovered the collective soul of the Serbian folk. While one may sympathize with Brock's anti-Nazi feelings, it may not be as easy, as his colleague Robert St. John pointed out, to understand how Brock, within just a few days, became a greater Serbian than anyone he had ever met.[15] Ignorant of the so-called Yugoslav past and present, Brock truly believed that only the Serbian folk and their Chetniks were capable of making things right. Frustrated by daily events, he went about Belgrade as if in a dream, singing and whistling Chetnik songs as if they had some cathartic effect on him.[16] He depicted them as being a unique people. Those "bald and gray-haired men were fighters, bomb-throwers with blood on their hands, and all of them were ready to kill again," etc.[17] Contrary to popular belief, however, in the United States, the Chetniks throughout the war were more concerned with the creation of greater Serbia than fighting the war. All their actions were subordinate to that end. In theory, they were on the Allied side; in reality, they made all sorts of "accommodations" with Nedić's quisling government, the Germans, and the Italians, to say nothing of the Ustašas.[18] The outcome of their policy brought them into a collision with the British who rejected them in favor of Tito and his partisans. The Chetniks felt betrayed by their former friend and ally. Their leader, Draža Mihailović, according to some accounts, gradually turned against the English. He often referred to them as an "ordinary merchant of human flesh," and linked them to the Germans in terms of their inhumanity. The ideological leader of the Chetnik movement, Dragiša Vasić, labeled the English the "grave diggers of the Serbian people," and frequently expressed the need to establish a special department at the University of Belgrade after the war promoting hatred of the English.[19] The truth was that in contrast to the German war machine, these people looked like antiquated relics of the past; that thought, however, never crossed Brock's mind. Assembling news reporters at his residence, usually after conferences with government officials, Lane deliberately fed their illusions. His stories were misleading and designed to inspire passion against the Axis and the "appeasers." As always, the main appeasers were Maček and the Croatians, and although not as frequently, the Slovenians. Consequently, the pages of the major American papers and radio reports were teeming with the Serbian martial spirit, while the Croatians were depicted as a "passive" people favoring accession to the Tripartite Pact. Annoyed with Croatian "passivity," the *New York Times* in its popular column, "The Topics of the Day," printed an extremely demeaning account of the Croatians as a superfluous people "eternally discounted," standing in the way of Serbia's courageous resistance to the Axis.[20] Such a flippant view fit well with the propaganda generated by Fotić and his staff in the Yugoslav legation. Throwing his arms in the air, Fotić never failed to say, "You see, we Serbians are willing, but the Croatians are not and so we can do nothing either" (105). Fotić was only preaching what Washington wanted to hear. It was therefore not hard for him to convince his listeners that the Serbians would never be swayed from their historical mission to fight. "Serbians were not in the habit of taking their liberty to auction. The least now, to satisfy . . . Croatians and Maček." In the end he would usually exclaim: "Remember, we Serbians are not about to sell our freedom for the sake of Croatians" (109). Although officials in Washington knew that the Croatians were not the only "appeasers," Fotić, however, refused even to consider it.[21] In Fotić's mind, Prince Paul, because of his foreign education, was not a Serbian, while Cvetković and Cincar Marković were his and Maček's docile tools.[22] The real Serbians were the common Serbian folk, the Serbian intelligentsia, the Serbian Orthodox Church, and so forth. In fact, it included every Serbian outside the

Yugoslav government. It is not an exaggeration to say that the Serbians had acquired an image in America akin to that of a modern Prometheus chained to the Croatian rock.

A few Americans did see a different picture. One of these was the Senator from Wisconsin, Robert M. LaFollette. As an ardent proponent of domestic social reforms, he was not in favor of Roosevelt's foreign policy. In a conversation with Radica, LaFollette vehemently assailed Roosevelt's foreign policy, calling it a device with which to push small nations into war and disaster. Roosevelt's policy was not only at variance with the American tradition, but was in fact, dishonest and immoral. In LaFollette's view, Maček was absolutely right in guarding his country's neutrality, but instead of being appreciated in Washington, he was tarnished as a German sympathizer. Neither Lane nor Donovan demonstrated any more sense. They both should have listened to Maček (117). You Croatians were ignored and persecuted and why on earth should you fight now for Serbian interests? Fotić looked exclusively after Serbian interests in Washington and worked on the president through Sumner Welles in an effort to push Yugoslavia into war. The U.S. State Department was filled with warmongers. As a matter of fact, American foreign policy was not American; it was British, having been designed by Winston Churchill. Having strong isolationist feelings, LaFollette naturally felt ill-disposed toward Roosevelt's involvement in the "European War," but he was absolutely accurate in assessing Fotić's activities. In the end Radica and LaFollette agreed that they were powerless to change the course of events that led another small nation straight to destruction (117).

The black-and-white approach toward Yugoslav affairs remained unabated, although some signs appeared that should have warranted reconsideration. Vladimir Ribnikar, editor-in-chief of the influential Serbian daily, *Politika,* informed Ray Brock that there were no British troops in Greece. He emphasized that the whole story was questionable. There were only a few British, Australians, and New Zealanders, a token force of sorts to reassure the Greeks. "All you Americans in Belgrade were dreamers."[23] Although Ribnikar was an unimpeachable source, his views, however, sounded like a sacrilege to Brock and his colleagues. None of them could or wanted to see the connection between Yugoslavia's "pro-Axis" policy and the extant reality. As far as they were concerned, Yugoslavia's foreign policy was strictly the handiwork of the "appeasers." As proof of their faith, they supplied stories of misguided Belgrade high school children revolting against the government chanting, "war rather than the pact" and "grave rather than the slaves." The unanimous conclusion was that the children revolted not only against the sins of the government, but the cowardice of their parents as well. Such stories in turn emboldened the policymakers to apply stronger pressure on the Yugoslav government; for purposes of domestic consumption, however, the administration managed to retain an appearance of neutrality. Such appearances could not deceive experienced columnist Drew Pearson, who wrote that but for the White House, the U.S. State Department, and Minister Fotić, Yugoslavia would have already "surrendered" to the Axis.[24]

As the day for Yugoslavia's accession to the Tripartite Pact was approaching, Eden made another attempt to pressure Paul by sending a letter from Cairo. The carrier of the letter was the British minister in Cairo and Paul's personal friend, Terence Shone. Lane talked to Shone and reported that Eden had asked Paul not to accede to the pact, now that the British were doing so well against the Italians in Africa.[25] There was nothing new in the letter. The Yugoslavs were still expected to attack the Italians in Albania and use the captured materials in defense against the Germans.[26] Exasperated, Paul again promised that Yugoslavia would never allow passage of German troop across "Southern Serbia" (Macedonia) in order to cut off the Greeks in northeastern Greece.[27] Meanwhile, Churchill and King George directed their attention toward Cvetković and Prince Paul, respectively. Churchill lectured Cvetković on world demography and the productive capacity of the British Empire. There were only 65 million Huns, while the combined population of the United States and the British Empire amounted to 200 million. The productive capacity of the two exceeded the rest of the world.[28] He therefore advised Cvetković to see the truth and "rise to the height of world events," which Cvetković apparently was too ignorant to grasp.[29] King George was not as direct, but was nonetheless concerned about Yugoslavia's future. He told Paul, as one would tell one's "best friend," not to trust the Germans, especially now. The king was sure that Paul would make the right decision in conforming to the interests of his country and his trusteeship, and would leave no doubt as to where his interests lay. As King George's biographer reproachfully observed, however, instead of taking "friendly counsel," Paul and his government decided to take "their fatal course."[30] Churchill's much-quoted description of Paul resembling an "unfortunate man in the cage with a tiger" was accurate, but none of his "friendly" advisers ever saw themselves in the role of such tigers.

Concurrently with pressuring Paul, contacts were intensified with the putschists and the oppositional parties associated with the putsch. The Serbian Agrarian Party was especially active. The leaders of the party were for some time in the pay of the British. One of the Agrarian Party leaders, Miloš Tupanjanin, boasted after the coup how he received over twenty million Yugoslav dinars from the British before the coup.[31] Along with the bribe money, British intelligence smuggled arms and explosives into Serbia from the beginning of 1941. Much of this smuggled material was then distributed among Tupanjanin's friends in Belgrade and elsewhere.[32] Although the Americans were not engaged in arms-smuggling and bribing Serbian politicians, their influence in the coup was nonetheless effective, perhaps even more so than one could have imagined. Analyzing the Serbian scene before the coup, Damaree Bess, an astute American journalist who retained her sense of reality when all her colleagues took flight into the realm of dreams, wrote how "every carpenter and clerk in Belgrade knew about American pledges given to Yugoslavia." Americans were guilty because they took advantage of Serbian credulity. The common Serbian folk "mystically" believed in the power of the United States. On the other hand, the American people "credulously" accepted the so-called "expert opinion" that insurrection would explode within Germany and that the Soviets would stab Germany in the back. According to Bess, the most guilty among the Americans were Roosevelt, Welles, the American representatives in Belgrade, and of course, Donovan, who was singled out for his self-righteous arrogance.[33]

By "expert opinions," Bess most likely had the British in mind, but such "expert opinion" could be traced to Fortier as well. His authoritative reports did betray an unusual faith in the concentration of Yugoslav troops in Serbia and Serbian willingness to fight the Germans. Moreover, Fortier was overly impressed by the Chetniks. He made inspections of their "secret" hideouts and caches of arms in the mountains.[34] Based on his findings, Fortier concluded that Yugoslavia could significantly contribute to the Allied war effort.[35] Although Paul and the government knew about the clandestine activities in Yugoslavia, he pretended not to notice them. In fact, he issued a strict order that "neither the British Legation . . . nor any of its officials were at any time to be monitored or in any way interfered with."[36] Such naivete elicits a suspicion that Paul may have played a duplicitous game. To keep Yugoslavia intact, he was compelled to accede to the Tripartite Pact, while at the same time, he allowed clandestine activities to go unchecked. In effect it meant undermining his own position, but whatever the outcome, he could not be blamed personally, either for the accession to the pact or the coup.

With fresh instructions from Welles to keep a sharp lookout for events unfolding in Belgrade, Lane reported on March 20, 1941, that the Yugoslavs were in an "embarrassing" position because the Germans accepted all their terms. No one was more embarrassed than the British, who were sure that the Germans would reject the terms put forth by Belgrade. Discussing German acceptance of these "seemingly absurd terms," the British consoled themselves by viewing this situation as positive proof of Germany's weakness; therefore, Yugoslavia should be encouraged not to sign the act of accession.[37] To offer such encouragement, the Lanes invited Paul and Princess Olga to dinner on March 24, 1941. If Lane thought he could help change Paul's mind, he was sadly mistaken. The atmosphere during the dinner was "depressing" and the princess was in tears all evening. To make it more relaxing, Paul again enumerated the reasons for accession to the pact. Croatians and Slovenians, although in agreement with respect to resisting Germany's forceful entry into Yugoslavia, were not considering Salonika. They believed that any dash toward the city would embroil Yugoslavia in war. If, however, Germany did violate the guarantees with Yugoslavia, the entire country would be united in fighting them. Politically, therefore, an attack on Germany would be impossible, not to mention a defensive war that would be fatal as well (962–63). Paul accurately conveyed the existing state of affairs, but Lane would not be mollified. The Yugoslavs, as Lane's counterargument went, were not looking toward the future but only at the present. Using Hitler's arguments, which he heard from Paul, Lane turned them against the pact. In view of the Italo-German rivalry, he argued, Germany would not destroy Yugoslavia so as to share it with the Italians; therefore, there was no need to sign the Tripartite Pact. On the other hand, if Germany were to attack Yugoslavia (and they agreed on this point) at some future date, why bother signing the pact now? It would destroy Yugoslavia's neutrality, to say nothing of its reputation abroad. Lane talked about the Lend-Lease Act and America's love of small nations, but Paul remained distant and said wearily, "You big nations are hard. You talk about our honor but you are far away" (962–63). Lane's verdict was that the prince was a man "lacking in strength," and a diplomat rather than a statesman, who was using the Croatians and Slovenians as an excuse to cover his own position (962–63).

The impression one gets of the conversation between the two men was that it fulfilled a need to explain themselves, rather than influence each other. The arguments Lane used were stale and superficial, and promised nothing but war and destruction. He never understood or cared much about the rift among various Yugoslav nationalities, especially that between the Serbians and Croatians. While Paul was still at Lane's residence, the government was in a meeting, deliberating about accession to the Tripartite Pact. Out of seventeen ministers, three, as previously pointed out, were against it and resigned on the spot. Justice Minister Mihajlo Konstantinović withdrew his resignation, and at Paul's request remained in the government.[38] In the next several reports, Lane communicated a somewhat confused and contradictory account of the pact. First, he reported on March 21, 1941, that the pact guaranteed Yugoslavia's territorial integrity and noninvolvement in military affairs, as requested by Article 3. Furthermore, full consideration would be given to Yugoslavia's interest in Salonika. In the same dispatch, he reported on some nonexisting "Annex to the Pact" that guaranteed the German transport of wounded soldiers from Greece across Yugoslavia.[39] On March 23, Lane corrected himself with respect to the transport, but reported on the "rumors" circulating in Belgrade about Paul's betrayal of Greece.[40]

Lane immediately confronted Cvetković and Prince Paul. He accused Cvetković of "backing down" on his word. The pact, he told Cvetković, was directed against the United States. Cvetković disagreed and retorted that the pact was strictly of a political nature and was not directed against either the United States or Great Britain. A heated debate ensued and Lane lost his diplomatic composure, ranting about the Yugoslav parliament. If the parliament existed, Cvetković would soon find out what the Yugoslavs thought of his pact.[41] He attempted to frighten Paul via Yugoslav public opinion, insisting that not only were the Serbians against the pact, so were Croatians.[42] The public opinion argument was not very effective; there was no such public opinion and the argument ceased to be effective. Lane's relentless pressure, however, left Paul visibly exhausted and on the verge of losing his self-control. "I am out of my head. I wish I was dead," Paul told Lane, and spoke bitterly about Bulgarian perfidy, British stupidity, and the opposition of the Croatians. Despite Lane's pressure, Paul refused to reconsider signing the pact and "capitulation" to Germany (967).

While the events in Belgrade were moving in the direction of the pact, President Roosevelt was still on his fishing trip in the Caribbean. He was, however, kept informed about the events taking place in Belgrade and the Balkans, almost on a daily basis.[43] The summaries of Lane's dispatches were immediately forwarded to him. Lane's last-ditch effort to influence Paul and Cvetković against the pact brought the issue of Yugoslavia's assets to the surface. Without waiting for further clarification, as originally suggested by Lane, the U.S. State Department advised Roosevelt to instruct the Treasury to place all of Yugoslavia's assets in the United States on hold until a written presidential order arrived. The order eventually arrived on March 24, 1941.[44]

The day after, March 25, Dragiša Cvetković and Aleksandar Cincar Marković were in Vienna in the old Belvedere to affix their signatures on Yugoslavia's accession to the Tripartite Pact. The cold atmosphere of the old building fit the occasion. To put the Yugoslav representatives at ease, Hitler told them that he very well understood their sentiments and hostilities, because he himself was not free of them. What actually mattered was that the reasons of state triumphed over personal feelings.[45] According to American reports, the German press welcomed Yugoslavia's accession to the pact and informed readers that the Axis powers would not demand passage of their troops or transports of war matériel across Yugoslav territory during the present war.[46] German reports from Belgrade expressed moderate optimism. Not being sufficiently informed, the general public was bewildered, but more informed segments of the Serbian people soon realized the advantages of the pact for Yugoslavia's future.[47] One day after the accession to the pact, Campbell handed a note to the Yugoslav government. According to Lane's report, the British, although sympathetic to Yugoslavia's geographic position, were nonetheless "surprised" by Yugoslavia's defection to the enemy camp. As Campbell told Lane, the British would not condone it.[48] On the same day, Lane sent a summary of an article published in the Serbian daily *Politika,* which he labeled an "apology" for Yugoslavia's accession to the pact. It was actually a plea for calm and understanding rather than an outright apology. The ongoing war, the article read, was of global proportions and could be brought to a desirable conclusion only by the participation of the major world powers. If, however, Yugoslavia's accession to the Tripartite Pact entailed Yugoslav "subjugation" and "enslavement" in any way, the government would never have taken such steps, and all Yugoslavs would have preferred a "heroic death" in conformity with their tradition. The pact guaranteed Yugoslavia's independence, integrity, and above all, peace.[49] But an understanding of its decision was in short supply. Before Campbell handed the note to the Yugoslav government, he advised London on March 21, 1941, to threaten them with a rupture in relations to pressure Paul and encourage the coup should Yugoslavia sign the pact. There was a glimmer of hope that Paul might change his mind and that the Germans would reject Yugoslavia's terms, but neither Churchill nor Eden favored Campbell's advice. Churchill instructed Campbell "not to let any gap grow between [him] and Prince Paul or [his] ministers," but if the Yugoslav government had "gone beyond recall," then the "alternatives" would take precedence. By "alternatives," Churchill meant a coup. In the meantime, Campbell was to "pester, nag, and bite" and not take NO (emphasized by Churchill) for an answer.[50] Eden too wished to know more detailed information with respect to the coup before he made the final decision. If Yugoslavia was determined to accede to the pact, Campbell was authorized to use the coup as a preventive measure. He was further authorized to impress upon the conspirators that the new government would enjoy "full support" of His Majesty's government. Campbell proceeded to discharge his instructions very carefully. Before he took the first step, Campbell requested new information regarding British military assistance from Eden. Since there was no new information on the subject, Eden instructed Campbell to inform the "prospective leaders" that the Yugoslavs would be fighting side by side with British forces armed with modern equipment. Delivery of such modern equipment would be impossible because the training to use it would take too much time.[51] There were no British armies. There was no equipment and no supplies of any kind, but the "prospective leaders" failed to notice that British help amounted to zero.

Neither "pestering" nor "biting" were of any help. Therefore the British decided to use other "alternatives" on March 26, 1941. The British air force attaché, Group Captain A. H. H. McDonald, requested an urgent interview with General Dušan Simović. The text of the conversation was immediately forwarded by the British to Washington, and received by the president the same day. McDonald's impressions were that Simović was as good as his word. The general felt strongly against the pact and was ready to repudiate it, as was the government; he had complete confidence in his associates. In turn, Simović requested that the Allies extend the same confidence toward him. He promised to attack the Italians in Albania immediately after the coup and wanted to know the number of British troops in Greece, hoping that the number would increase and that the Turks would come in. McDonald avoided any straight answers and told Simović that the defense of Salonika would depend a "great deal on the Serbs." As for the Turks, "it was very positive" that they would come in, but McDonald was not sure as to when and how.[52] In short, McDonald repeated the same old insubstantive stories.

Whether or not the lack of substance in McDonald's promises aroused Simović's suspicions, the general ventured to ask more about British help. McDonald refused to be more specific and kept repeating Eden's promises of "fighting side by side" and sharing a "common pool of materials" with the British. Simović appeared disappointed to McDonald, but in the end agreed that the Yugoslavs would do well with the loot taken from the Italians in Albania. At any rate, McDonald concluded in his report that the "general was now committed to a course of action from which nothing could deter him."[53] Reading McDonald's report, one is struck by Simović's insufficient grasp of the Balkan situation from an Allied point of view. Perhaps for that reason, he died denying any contacts with British intelligence or any other agency prior to the coup. The general maintained that the coup was a patriotic endeavor in conformity with the heroic tradition of the Serbian people.[54]

On March 27, 1941, Churchill informed Roosevelt that the coup d'etat in Belgrade was an accomplished fact. The British could not foresee any problems in extending recognition to the new government or any difficulty in assisting it in any way, provided the Yugoslavs were ready to join the Greek resistance. Churchill then asked Roosevelt to adopt the same policy backed by powerful support.[55] Washington quickly responded, although not necessarily because of the British. Independent of British desires, Lane was instructed under triple priority to congratulate General Simović for an act worthy of "self-congratulation for every liberty-loving man and woman," along with the promise of immediate assistance in accordance with Lend-Lease provisions.[56] Roosevelt wired Hull from the Caribbean to keep him informed of every event unfolding after the coup. The president also instructed Welles to send, on behalf of the White House, a congratulatory message to King Peter and to inform Simović that a revocation of the freezing order would be considered as soon as the situation in Belgrade became clearer.[57]

Regarding recognition of the new regime, the administration took the position that the coup was a patriotic act designed to preserve Yugoslavia's "integrity" and "independence." Welles instructed Lane that his recognition of the regime should be accorded outright on the grounds that Simović's government was set up by King Peter and because the U.S. government never withdrew its recognition of the Yugoslav monarchy.[58] The administration also strove publicly to give the impression of Yugoslav unity, interpreting the coup in such terms. Privately, however, Welles talked about Serbia and its war against Germany.[59] The insistence on giving an all-Yugoslav character to the coup was a clever device to push Maček into joining the new regime. The alternative would have been to stay away and incur the wrath of the Allies against himself and the Croatian people.[60] Before joining Simović's government, Maček nonetheless managed to put forth certain demands as a precondition for his cooperation. He demanded recognition of the Serbo-Croatian Agreement, control of the police in Croatia, the promise not to harm his former colleagues, especially Cvetković, and assurances that Simović's government would adhere to the policy of peace and neutrality.[61]

Thus, after brief negotiations, Maček's demands were accepted and he joined Simović's cabinet and assumed his old position as vice-premier. Hull was delighted and praised Maček's "wise statesmanship." Hull sent a message of congratulations which, rather ominously, was never delivered.[62] Yet Maček was not blind to the terrible situation caused by Simović and the coup.

Chapter 9
The American Press and the Coup

The articles appearing in the American press with respect to the coup may be best described as an advertisement for war. The frustrated reporters who were hopping from one occupied European country to the next, chased by the victorious German army, wished themselves into believing that Yugoslavia (actually Serbia) was the place to stand up to the Germans and fight. In addition to their frustration, the realization that Roosevelt stood behind the British added fuel to the fire. Here was Roosevelt's "specific event" that would inflame the masses and spring them into action. The Americans and the British had two aims: to exalt Serbian courage, and by doing so, shaming American isolationists and galvanizing America into some action "short of war." Largely because of the misperception, to say nothing of the reasons for political expediency, the coup was applauded in the leading papers as the victory of naked valor over the mechanized and goose-stepping Huns. Serbs were made larger than life. In honor of the coup, Serbian plum brandy was turned into a patriotic American drink. Toasts were drunk to celebrate this daring deed, viewed as the turning point of the war against the Axis powers.

Reuben Markham, an astute appraiser of the sociopolitical conditions in the Balkans, wrote about the Serbs just three days prior to the coup as if he were writing about the brotherhood of chosen people, held together by an exceptional sense of duty and honor. In his somewhat flowery style, Markham described the Serbs quite skillfully through questions and answers, as though they were mythological heroes of ancient Greece. Although they were only semiliterate, Markham wrote that the Serbs knew more about freedom than professors of other lands. He obviously was referring to his own compatriots who, in the face of danger, still wished to retain their neutrality. In answer to his own question, Markham replied that the Serbs understood Hitler and his demonic plans much better than diplomats and learned senators. All the professors, senators, and diplomats were fools compared to the Serbs, who, because of their exceptional virtues, were not only exemplary warriors but philosophers as well. Readers could not help but notice the didactic implications of the message. It was as if Talvi spoke through Markham's pen. The Serbs did not acquire such virtues, Markham pointed out, by reading "wise" books, but rather from their tradition and their experience, preserved in their folk tales and folk poetry. Markham also attributed the shaping of the Serbian national character to the Serbian landscape. Every mountain and every hill, every valley and every ravine spoke to them of tyrants and the evil they caused throughout their history.[1]

Around the same time, Ray Brock sent his "scoop" from Belgrade. As an admirer of the Serbian martial spirit, he heralded a spontaneous revolution of the masses that could not be deterred by any amount of suppression from the government. Serbian orthodox priests and peasants were the front-runners of the imminent revolution; they preached their message and no one could stop them.[2] Brock was about to be deported because of such inaccurate and provocative reporting, but the coup prevented that possibility. Reports by others were also in the same vein. The *New York Times* broke the story regarding the Yugoslav ambassador in Moscow, Milan Gavrilović, who supposedly was determined to depose Prince Paul if Yugoslavia acceded to the Tripartite Pact. The reports no doubt were tailored according to British policy and Donovan's mission; they were also fueled by the personal frustration of the news reporters. Instead of being driven by the German army from place to place, they wanted Yugoslavia to take a stand in conformity with Serbian martial valor and tradition. Wishful thinking rather than reality turned Yugoslavia into a deus ex machina whose "formidable" military power could destroy easily the Italian forces in Albania before the Germans could rescue them. Such a victory would have caused a chain reaction in the Balkans, forcing the Balkan nations to take a stand against Germany.

As the diplomatic games in the Balkans were becoming more complicated, the faith in Serbian valor grew accordingly, ranging from the fantastic to the ridiculous. Edgar E. Mowver emphasized in the *Chicago Daily News* the seriousness of the situation facing the Belgrade government, but he was sure that the tested patriots would find a way to replace the present government with that of "free men."[3] Convinced of Serbia's military resolve, the *Washington Post* editorialized that Hitler should know that Yugoslavia was a volcano whose eruptions he would not be able to contain.[4] Other "expert" opinions were of this view and went much further, predicting that because of Serbian resistance, a politically explosive incident within Germany itself might ensue. Perceiving the Yugoslav scene as they wished, especially the Serbian resolve to stand and fight, the news was filled with admiration for Yugoslav Ambassador Konstantin Fotić. He was, according to some, an uncompromising enemy of fascism, and for that reason, had been "exiled" to the United States in 1936, to a post that was only of minor importance to Yugoslavia at the time. Drew Pearson, in his column "Merry-Go-Round," lauded Fotić as a "genuine political giant" who was destined, in spite of his humble origins, to make his mark on history beside Roosevelt for his unflinching anti-fascist stand.[5] It will be mentioned that two of Fotić's relatives, General Milan Nedić and Dimitrije Ljotić, were willing collaborators of the Nazis, but Fotić kept silent regarding them. He was in fact responsible to a great extent in portraying Nedić as a Serbian Petain who sacrificed himself to save the Serbian people—someone who deserved pity and admiration, but never condemnation as an outright collaborator.

After accession to the pact, the *New York Herald-Tribune* openly threatened the Yugoslav government, saying that only blood can wash the sins of such "criminal irresponsibility."[6] According to Ray Brock, Serbian peasants were already organized for war.[7] Markham attributed such swift readiness to the regenerative spirit of the Serbs' indomitable national character. "Freedom they saw in the hills, freedom they breathed in the air, freedom they heard in the songs of the birds" and so on.[8] Fotić again was praised lavishly. Bertram D. Hullen considered him one of the main initiators of the coup because he was in constant touch with the conspirators in Belgrade.[9] Needless to say, it was true. Fotić had very cordial relations with President Roosevelt and Sumner Welles, and had his own way of transmitting their sentiments to the right people in Belgrade. He, however, publicly declined such honors for fear that the coup would be interpreted by the public at large as a purely Serbian endeavor. Caroll Binder, himself a great admirer of the Serbian martial spirit, considered it quite normal that the Serbs took exclusive control of the government after the coup. He viciously assailed Prince Paul for his "softness" and his lack of courage in using force against the opposition (presumably Croatians) to secure Yugoslavia's position on the Allied side.[10]

Clearly, the press was not merely recording the events, but in most cases, manufacturing them by advocating the need for rebellion against the Belgrade government. Gerard André Pertinax, a French journalist residing in the United States, considered Prince Paul an outright traitor. He accused Paul of destroying the Little Entente, allowing the Italian occupation of Albania, and most of all, his "duplicity" toward the British. In Pertinax's view, the coup should have taken place the moment the Italians marched into Albania. Had that happened, the martial spirit and patriotism of the common people and soldiers would have surfaced sooner.[11] The majority of opinion makers, however, were in agreement that the coup occurred at a very propitious time. It ushered in new hope for opening the second front, which it was believed Hitler wanted to avoid at any cost. True, nationalist passions were still shaking the fragile foundation of Yugoslavia, but it was assumed that these particular passions would forge "all the Yugoslavs" into a unified nation in the struggle against the invaders. According to some enthusiastic dispatches, Yugoslavia was already being transformed into a mighty battlefield where the future of the Balkans and even the war in Europe would be decided.[12] Such unwarranted optimism grew in strength the moment the story broke out about Maček deciding to join the new government.

In any case, the euphoric state created by the coup often went beyond the boundaries of reasonable expectations, owing in most part to the remarkably muddled picture of Yugoslav affairs in the minds of the writers. For example, during a reception in honor of the coup, the master of ceremonies for the Society of the American Friends of Yugoslavia, introduced Ambassador Fotič to a sizable crowd with a short exposition of Yugoslavia's history. According to his exposition, Yugoslavia was an "ancient kingdom" with a long and honorable history. Yugoslavia had thrown off the Turkish yoke in 1878. In 1914, an Austrian crown prince was assassinated in Sarajevo and Austria blamed the Serbian nationalists. Because of the assassination, an impossible ultimatum was delivered to Serbia. The country was overrun, yet owing to the superb military efforts of the Serbians, it was restored in 1918.[13] It was not uncommon for Yugoslavia to be confused with Serbia and vice versa. The euphoria of the coup was manifested in Sonja Tomara, a woman of Russian descent. In a lengthy article, Miss Tomara recounted her trip to Yugoslavia several months before the coup occurred. She wrote of seeing with her own eyes that every Serb was a born prince; everyone was a stubborn individualist, a free man having no idea of what it was to sell one's soul for material gain. As far as the Serbs were concerned, the Kingdom of Heaven was uppermost on their minds and could not be replaced by earthly pleasures. She picked an old man by the name of Sava Pešić to demonstrate her point. Sava was a Chetnik in the Balkan Wars and in World War I. He fought alone and went into enemy territory, killing many enemies behind the lines. Now that the coup took place in Belgrade, Miss Tomara remembered the old man, not only because he was a brave soldier, but because he had considerable foresight as well. He told her that the Russians were Serbian brothers and, as in the past, would come to their rescue. Miss Tomara did admit that all Yugoslavs were different from one another but it hardly mattered because the heroic spirit of the old Serbia hovered above their heads.[14]

No matter how naive the stories may have sounded or whether the reports were real or imaginary, all the ingredients were ripe for propaganda. They extolled Serbian physical and moral virtues, giving readers the unmistakable impression that the Serbs were predetermined to be leaders and assume the destiny of Yugoslavia and the Balkans in their able hands. Lest someone take a dim view of the legality of the coup, views were expressed (quite untrue except in Serbia) that changing government by force was in fact an acceptable sociopolitical mechanism in the history of the Serbs, Croats, and Slovenes.[15]

In line with the spirit of the old Serbia, Brock filed another lengthy report from Belgrade. He too was an eyewitness to the "Serbian national regeneration." According to his testimony, out of sheer pride, every Serb grew an inch or two taller during the process of regeneration.[16] Walter Lippmann came to the conclusion that because of the coup, the situation in Europe had radically changed. It became clear, he asserted, that Hitler was beatable without the need for several million American soldiers in Europe.[17] Similar views were expressed by Devitt Mackenzie who warned Hitler not to rush headlong into the Balkans to gratify his "bruised ego." Were he to do so, he would be stopped by the Yugoslav and Allied armies entrenched along the Bulgarian borders.[18] An expert on military affairs, Colonel Frederick Palmer, was certain that given the new circumstances, Hitler would negotiate with Belgrade rather than fight. Time for negotiations would be time enough for the Yugoslavs and the Greeks to liquidate the Italians in Albania.[19] To what extent such flippant opinions permeated the American journalistic scene is further illustrated by Cyrus Sulzberger. He wrote that the time for Slavic power in the Balkans stretching from the Black Sea to the Adriatic, had finally arrived.[20]

With such grandiose plans in the making, no internal quarrels among the Yugoslavs would be tolerated. The Croats in particular were under the watchful eyes of the press. In this historical moment, unity was by far more important than "ethnic" interests. "Unity: now or never!"[21] Maček's return to Belgrade to join the government was therefore highly praised. Sulzberger, who otherwise never cared for the Croats and their leader, declared that it was Maček's most intelligent move in his entire political career.[22] Dorothy Thompson could not agree more and concluded that the unity of Yugoslavia was an accomplished fact. According to Miss Thompson, it seems that unity was attained by Hungarian greed in the past. Hungarians, Miss Thompson pointed out, wanted to dominate Croatians like they did the Croatian soldiers in the Austro-Hungarian army. Because of that greed, King Peter now had a unified state solidly behind Belgrade's policy. Her best prediction was that if the Russians came to Yugoslavia, there would be no need to panic. Yugoslav peasants were the sole owners of their land and therefore immune to Communism.[23] The flippancy of these and similar views are hardly deserving of any clarifying comments. Most likely because Markham was a sincere admirer of the peasant movements, he paid special attention to Maček's return to Belgrade. Maček, for him, was a man of simple yet penetrating views. His decision to join the putschist government was equated with the wisdom and courage of Leonidas at Thermopylae and William of Orange before the Spanish Inquisition. Like them, Maček also secured the future of Croatia in the belief that democracy would triumph.[24] Along with the spirit of Serbia, the glorification of the Chetniks was very much in the press. According to certain estimates there were approximately thirty-eight thousand Chetniks already armed. Other sources estimated that in addition to this figure, there were "several hundred thousand" secret members. The Chetnik saga was told in several versions, all of which were in agreement—the Chetniks were a people of exceptional strength and valor.

To enlighten its readers, an Associated Press correspondent described in very dramatic terms the rituals of accession to the Chetnik organization. The person being described was Ruth Mitchell, sister of the well-known American air force general, "Billy" Mitchell. The oath of accession was administered by none other than the "legendary" Chetnik, Kosta Pećanac. It is worth mentioning that Pećanac became a Nazi collaborator. Pećanac handed Mitchell a vial of poison in case she fell into enemy hands. He then crossed her name from the list, saying that when someone becomes a Chetnik, that person was no longer among the living. "We Chetniks do not think much of our lives," Pećanac warned her, and we may all be dead very soon. I myself, Pećanac went on, expected to die this time. "What about you Miss Mitchell?" asked Pećanac. Of course, Miss Mitchell was ready to die as well.[25]

Apparently, however, Mitchell had second thoughts about dying. Although no one knows exactly how, she fell into Nazi hands shortly after the German attack. Although a sworn Chetnik, the Germans, after keeping her for several months in detention, let her go. Upon her return to the United States, Mitchell wrote a book called *The Serbs Choose War*[26], which the reviewer Bennett Cerf aptly described as being a "cheapjack device for snagging a little free publicity."[27]

To paraphrase Napoleon, there is indeed but one step from the sublime to ridiculous. The press was very liberal in taking that step. It was not that they were deliberately deceitful. It was rather that they were too eager to change the bleak reality and fell victim to their own wishful thinking. As the saying goes, truth is the first victim of every war.

In pursuit of his vision, Robert K. Shellaby wrote in his column, "The Week in Focus," that Yugoslav unity was evident and that it would be, regardless of German intentions, well used in defense of Yugoslavia's freedom and independence.[28] Numerous articles came out in praise of Yugoslav military strength. The rugged mountains were seen as a natural barrier against the German armor. Every mountain and mountain passage was turned into an impenetrable fortress. Actually, the whole of Serbia was seen as a mountainous fortress that the Germans could neither pierce through nor conquer.[29] Andrè Visson, another French journalist in the United States, wrote of 2.5 million Yugoslav soldiers who, in his mind, were the best proof that Yugoslavia was not an artificial country but an organic growth of history.[30] Swept up by unwarranted optimism, many editorials were written in the spirit of an immediate Yugoslav victory. In connection to this, Yugoslavia's resistance was seen as the salvation of Great Britain. A grateful Englishman, Harold J. Laski, publicly expressed his gratitude to Yugoslavia for its resolve in resisting the aggression, and added that for such an unselfish act, every Yugoslav could easily measure up to every Englishman.[31]

German advances in the south toward Skoplje and the Greek borders were viewed as a tactical withdrawal, not altogether unlike that of the Duke of Wellington's during the Napoleonic Wars.[32] When the bubble of "Serbian valor" and the "spirit of old Serbia" finally burst, the responsibility was placed squarely on the shoulders of Prince Paul for neglecting the armed forces, and on the Russians, Turks, Croatians, and, to a lesser degree, the Macedonians and Slovenians. In the midst of the confusion, a *Christian Science Monitor* editorial attempted to be more tactful. If we built castles in the air of Serbian military valor, the editorial reasoned, we would still not be discouraged. After all, the Yugoslavs alone decided to resist the aggressors, knowing full well whom they were facing. Instead, one should praise them as the victims of their democratic convictions. At any rate, one should give them credit for saving Britain from a German invasion.[33]

Rumors persisted, however, that the whole Balkan front and the Yugoslav involvement in the war was more than met the eye. Robert L. Hullen exposed some of these "rumors." He broke the story of existing tensions within the U.S. State Department after Yugoslavia's collapse. According to Hullen, the State Department disavowed any connection with Donovan's mission at the time. Moreover, the people responsible for pushing Yugoslavia into war were Donovan, Roosevelt, Sumner Welles, and Konstantin Fotić.[34] Responding to these "rumors," Fotić wrote a letter to the *New York Times,* which was published the same day as Hullen's article. Fotić bitterly complained that anyone would think that Yugoslavia was pushed into war. Rather, Fotić insisted, Yugoslavia never hesitated to pay a "gruesome price" for the salvation of Britain, Greece, and most of all, for its own honorable place in history.[35] Markham agreed with Fotić. Markham was somewhat perplexed by such a rapid collapse of the "mountain fortress," but he still believed that Yugoslavia remained a "symbol of courage." Centuries of foreign rule, Markham lamented, left undesirable footprints upon the landscape of Yugoslav history, which, in the final analysis were responsible for Yugoslavia's rapid collapse. The agony of collapse notwithstanding, future generations would remember the Serbs in terms of the Spartans; in fact, they would be regarded more highly than the Spartans. For in addition to military valor, they demonstrated moral courage, and like Socrates, who sought answers to his moral dilemmas, the Serbs too had to find their answers. Indeed, like Socrates they chose the path of honor; they chose the poison.[36]

The rapid collapse, however, could not be pushed under the carpet with a few journalistic eulogies, not without some plausible explanation. The real reasons, namely the Yugoslav army and the nature of the coup, were themes still taboo to the journalists in the midst of total ruin. Under the circumstances, the most plausible reason for collapse was the Croats. Their "treachery," demonstrated by proclamation of the Croatian state, offered "tangible" proof of their malevolent and pro-Nazi behavior. Sulzberger blamed Macedonians as well for the collapse of the Yugoslav army in the south, suggesting that because of their treachery, the Germans practically were able to walk into Greece.[37] The Croats were the main villains. No words were spared to demonstrate their base and treacherous nature. They were portrayed as eternal malcontents, an immature people, and the victims of their own obsession generated by their own ideological and political lunatics.[38]

The return of American Ambassador Arthur Bliss Lane shed little light on Yugoslavia's rapid collapse. In his lengthy article "Conquest in Yugoslavia," he made Prince Paul the sole culprit responsible for Yugoslavia's collapse. According to Lane, Prince Paul knew that the Germans were going to attack the Soviet Union, yet refused to do anything. Instead, he acceded to the pact in the hope that the Germans would take revenge against the killers of his royal relatives in Russia. Lane found yet another flaw in Paul's character that contributed to Yugoslavia's disaster—Paul's aversion to war and the shedding of human blood. In short, Prince Paul was a coward.[39]

Still, irresponsible reporting can be seen in the reports by Ray Brock and Robert St. John. Before the war was over, they both reported on the killing of Croatian "Ustašas" and "spies." Forty-nine of them were killed in Sarajevo and thirty-two in Mostar.[40] Whether or not the reports were true is beside the point. Reading the reports, one derives the unmistakable impression that these killings of civilians were seen as a moral act of retribution against the "treacherous" Croats.[41]

Chapter 10
Coup d'Etat
Myth and Reality

Without a doubt, the coup stirred powerful human emotions on both sides of the Atlantic. Sir Winston Churchill announced to the world that Yugoslavia had found its soul. Much was written about the Yugoslav soul and expectations were great. The reality, however, barely merited such expectations. In fact, when the dust of the coup settled, one could see clearly that the putschists were in no hurry to do anything spectacular, least of all fight. So what was the purpose of the coup? Compounded by such a rapid destruction of Yugoslavia, the coup became an object of intense speculation. Many observers guessed that it was not purely a Serbian patriotic endeavor as official propaganda maintained, but that it was not entirely without outside help. As the evidence gradually emerged, it became clear that both the British and the Americans were instrumental in pushing the Serbian putschists into action. The moment the coup was over, Hugh Dalton, head of the Special Operation Executive (SOE), recorded in his diary how "well our chaps [had] done their part" in bringing about the coup.[1] The truth was that Dalton's "chaps" were not the only ones. There were other branches of British intelligence associated with the putschists. The Secret Intelligence Service (SIS) had operated in Yugoslavia ever since its creation. With Germany's gradual economic penetration into the area, the SIS intensified its activities. In the late 1930s, section D (for Destruction) was separated from the SIS and designed for acts of sabotage against German economic interests in the region, specifically with regard to river transportation on the Danube. In July 1940, section D was attached to the newly established SOE. The function of the SOE, as Churchill hoped, was to set all of Europe "ablaze." Because of its limited success and unorthodox methods, traditionalists in the SIS questioned the wisdom of its existence. To prove its usefulness, the SOE made Yugoslavia, with tacit agreement from Belgrade, the testing ground for its unorthodox activities.[2]

The other branches of intelligence, not nearly as flamboyant as the SOE, were actually more productive. Lieutenant Colonel C. S. Clarke of military intelligence and A. H. H. McDonald, the air attaché, had long-standing relations with various Serbian groups deemed of interest to the British. Others, such as T. G. Mappleback and Julius Hanau, although businessmen and civilians, were both British agents, and kept in touch with numerous Serbian organizations and political leaders. Mappleback, for instance, was a close friend of General Bora Mirković, second in command of the coup.[3] These intelligence groups and the individuals working for them were in close contact at all times with the various centers of the Serbian military, including its political and cultural ones, which were known to be in opposition of Prince Paul. Some of these centers were supplied with British money, arms, and information, or rather misinformation, concerning Britain's strategy in the Balkans. The Serbian Agrarian Party was a typical case in point. One also should not forget the BBC. The BBC broadcasts against the "appeasers," together with British newsmen assigned to Belgrade, became a "guiding light" of the conspiracy. Last but not least, there was Campbell himself who evaluated every intelligence report before it was communicated to London. As a traditionalist, Campbell often relied on his own judgment.[4]

In the previously mentioned article, David A. T. Stafford argued that the initiative came from the "Yugoslavs," and only by a stretch of the imagination could the British be said to have planned or directed the coup.[5] A Serbian author, Dragiša N. Ristić, held similar views, except that he confined himself to the execution of the coup.[6] Still another Serbian author, Nikola Milovanović, came to yet another conclusion—that the coup was first linked to the French and then to the British and Americans.[7] To substantiate his point, Milovanović cited two instances when the British delayed the coup on the grounds that its execution would be more detrimental than helpful (402). The fact that the coup was carried out via the orders of McDonald and Mappleback is itself proof of Serbian dependency on British intelligence. The Allied influence was so pervasive that the Serbians were told after the war that they had no right to claim the coup as their own endeavor because it was bought by the Allies.[8]

Perhaps the biggest omission was to ignore the American contribution. Donovan's visit, Welles' and Lane's pressures, Roosevelt's promises, and Fotić's maneuverings with Welles, to say nothing of the American media, were too obvious to be ignored. Above all, Professor Stafford ignored the "mystical" faith the putschists and Serbian peasants had in America. This faith was demonstrated on the pages of leading American newspapers. The Serbian Chetniks and the spirit of the common Serbian men and women were set as an example to those who lacked faith and valor. The best journalistic minds in America were on the job in Belgrade. Among others, the names one frequently encountered were Hanson W. Baldwin, Daniel T. Brigham, Turner Catledge, Walter Duranty, Guido Enderis, G. R. R. Gedey, George F. Horne, Bertram D. Hulen, Edwin L. James, Arthur Krock, Girard A. Pertinax, and Cyrus L. Sulzberger. They were all sincere and patriotic Americans who believed in freedom and hated tyranny and oppression, but they all had more enthusiasm than sense about the subject they were covering. George Radin's role was of considerable importance as well. He had a reputation for his excellent connections with influential Americans, including President Roosevelt.[9] Radin befriended General Simović and became one of his most trusted friends. Rumors circulated in Belgrade (and they were never denied) that Radin exercised a tremendous influence on Simović, promising American help if Yugoslavia switched to the Allied side.[10]

Professor Stafford made still another omission. In building their state, Serbians masterfully managed to enmesh their internal revolts with their foreign policy, providing them with the necessary protection from without. In the twentieth century alone, Serbia lived through several protectors—Russia, Austria, Britain, and France. After World War I, Belgrade was closely associated with France and the Entente, but with the decline of the French influence in European politics, King Alexander, as protection against a hostile Italy, inaugurated closer relations with Germany. By fostering these close relations, Belgrade's diplomacy succeeded in keeping Yugoslavia intact under Serbian domination, while at the same time it kept Croatians cut off from the opponents of the Versailles order. The mere illusion, however, that the Serbo-Croatian Agreement spelled out the end of Serbian domination, led the ultranationalistic Serbian groups to fuse their nationalistic aspirations with the Allied cause. Thus, for Professor Hugh Seton-Watson, the men who carried out the coup were a handful of daring officers, "true heirs to the tradition of great conspirators 'Apis' Dimitrijević. But they were only carrying out the will of the nation." The will of the nation, it seems, "preferred destruction to treachery."[11] Their action nevertheless proves that the Allies provided the conspirators with the stamp of legitimacy and made them appear as the true champions of human freedom. Under these deceptive appearances, the coup was in fact an attempt to regain Serbian dominance as a reward for taking Yugoslavia away from the Tripartite Pact—if not immediately, then certainly after the war.[12]

Irrespective of the nature of the coup, the future course Yugoslavia was to take hinged on the capability of Yugoslav military strength. The army that the Serbians were so proud of was in fact in such a poor state that any war, offensive or defensive, was out of the question. It is said that the generals at the beginning of every war are actually ready to fight the one that ended. The Yugoslav generals were not ready to fight even World War I. It is generally recognized in Yugoslav historiography that the Yugoslav army was far below standard. Even some foreign observers realized the shabby state of Yugoslavia's military. When, for instance, French General Franchet D'Esperey visited Yugoslavia in 1933, he confided to Ivan Meštrović that in case of war, the French General Staff would not be able to communicate with its Yugoslav counterpart, because the latter was totally ignorant of the needs of modern warfare.[13] The condition of the army provided the putschists with yet another excuse not to fight. Vice-Premier Slobodan Jovanović told Ilija Jukić that had the putschists known about the real terms of the Tripartite Pact, they never would have carried out the coup.[14] Cognizant of Yugoslavia's deplorable condition, the first thing Foreign Minister Ninčić did was to instruct the Yugoslav diplomatic representatives that Yugoslavia's policy would be a policy of peace vis-à-vis the Axis—to uphold Yugoslavia's international obligations, including that within the Tripartite Pact.[15] The resumption of the old policy was explained to the Allied governments in terms of time needed for the preparation of war, while to the Axis, the coup was explained as a purely domestic affair directed against Prince Paul.[16] Whatever happened, the hidden aims of the putschists would be secured.

Acting on the assumption of Serbia's patriotic defiance against Hitler, not only Welles, but the entire administration, especially Stimson and Knox, urged President Roosevelt to help Yugoslavia as soon as possible. Secretaries Henry Stimson and Frank Knox suggested loading twenty-five Yugoslav ships in American ports with essential supplies destined for Yugoslavia, Greece, and the British in North Africa. Details concerning the shipments were not as important as the effects they would have on the Balkan states.[17] Roosevelt personally instructed Welles to make every effort to speed up the loading of the Yugoslav ships.[18] All these noble gestures were done strictly to help Yugoslavia. Yet there was no way to send these ships to their destinations. The Suez Canal was closed (at times for the whole month) because of German mines dropped from the air. The U-boat-infested Mediterranean became even more so with the gradual arrival of fresh German forces in North Africa.[19] Wavell himself complained to London about the transports America promised but never delivered.[20] To make things worse, the request of the Yugoslav military attaché in Washington, although modest, could not be filled without depleting U.S. military reserves. The request was partially filled with materials taken from the military reserves; by then, however, it made no difference. The Germans were already the masters of the Balkans.[21]

The lack of help clearly suggests that the Allies, their promises notwithstanding, counted more on their original blueprint for the Balkan front than the help they promised to send. They were quite mistaken in believing that the Putschist government would rush headlong into war because it was expected of them. Actually, having discovered the "abysmal truth" with regard to the token British forces in Greece, Simović refused to do anything that would have further infuriated the Germans. He refused to attack the Italians in Albania and declined any military accord with the British on the grounds that it might alienate the Croatians and Slovenians. Yugoslavia would go to war only if the Germans attempted to penetrate Greece through the Monastir Gap.[22] Under pressure from the Axis press accusing Washington of its complicity in the coup, Lane suggested to Welles that Welles send a message to Simović assuring him that the policy of the United States was not to push Yugoslavia into war but to prevent the Yugoslav government from relinquishing its independence.[23]

To placate the new government, Lane visited Foreign Minister Momćilo Ninčić. His impressions of Ninčić were anything but accurate. Ninčić appeared to Lane as a man with a "superior mentality and cultural background."[24] Undoubtedly, the foreign minister once was such a man, but he was now old and nearly deaf. Ninčić was assigned to this important post primarily because of his Italian sympathies, which the Simović government wanted to use in pressuring Germany. Although the present government, Ninčić told Lane, was more in tune with Yugoslavia's interests, the Tripartite Pact was nevertheless an accomplished fact and needed no ratification. Any deviation from the peaceful policy toward Germany would alienate the Croatians, the Slovenians, and the Bosnian Moslems.[25] Lane realized that Ninčić was using the same arguments as the ousted foreign minister, but remained silent. No matter what Ninčić thought and said, the war with Germany was no longer wishful thinking, but rather a matter of time. Lane knew it, and as a precautionary measure, ordered all codes and ciphers destroyed except the Gray Code.[26] Both Lane and Fortier knew of the German and Italian concentrations along the Yugoslav borders. Lane communicated Fortier's views to Washington that Germany would first attack Yugoslavia and then Greece.[27]

Lane's suggestion to Welles had no effect on Washington. To compensate for British military weakness in the Balkans, the press extolled Serbia's military virtues and their readiness to fight; this led to the administration exerting pressure by praising Simović and promising help. Such praise, along with empty promises, were designed to exacerbate the already tense Yugoslav-German relations. An exasperated Ninčić tried his best to use Rome to assuage Berlin, complaining to Lane that American pressure tactics and expectations placed Yugoslavia in a difficult position vis-à-vis Germany.[28] Ninčić's complaints were naive to say the least. After all, Simović promised war, and above all, an Italian defeat in Albania. Acting on Simović's promise, Churchill, after the coup, immediately sent a message to the Turks asking them to make Greece and Yugoslavia a "common front which Germany [would] hardly dare to assail."[29] He dispatched a similar message to Eden who, at the time of the coup, was in Malta and on his way back to England.[30] Churchill's message authorized Eden to resume negotiations with the Turks, and to send Sir John Dill to Belgrade to help the Yugoslavs put the final touches on their military plans. Inflamed by the coup, Churchill was already operating with "seventy Balkan divisions" versus "thirty German divisions." He was sure the Yugoslavs would destroy the Italians in Albania. Numerically weaker and faced with a rugged terrain and poor communications, the Germans might be deterred from entering the Balkans. Since the Russians refused to get involved in the war, Churchill speculated, there was a chance the Germans might turn against the Soviet Union instead.[31] Churchill could not overlook the Russians. This time, however, he hoped the Germans would attack the Russians and would leave the Balkans alone.[32]

The military talks with Belgrade were useless as in the past. Both sides demanded more than the other could possibly deliver. The Turks too were less inclined to risk German guarantees and stood by their old decision to fight only if they were attacked by German forces.[33] Meanwhile, the Yugoslav government informed Campbell that in order for it to gain time, it would renew contacts with Berlin and Rome. When he heard of it, Eden's comment was (and he was right this time) that such maneuvering would achieve nothing.[34] As a first step in renewing negotiations with Berlin and Rome, Simović asked the Italian minister in Belgrade, Francesco Mameli, to come and see him. In the meantime, Simović held lengthy talks with Campbell and Soviet Charge d'Affaires Lebedev. While Simović was in conference with Campbell, Ninčić was busy in his office with von Heeren, trying hard to convince the Germans that the coup was a domestic affair directed only against Prince Paul and his unpopular government. Ninčić went on to say that as a friend of Italy and Germany, he guaranteed that no changes in foreign policy vis-à-vis the Axis would be taken, and especially with Germany.[35]

Concurrently with Ninčić's efforts, Campbell too was after Simović. Of course, Campbell approvingly told Simović that there was nothing wrong with attempting to gain time, especially now that Eden experienced such a brilliant success with Turks. They were ready to declare war on Germany as soon as they received a sign from Belgrade. Wavell in Alexandria was waiting for ships to transport his division to Greece. Another piece of good news was that the Russians' attitude was "completely clear" and Viktor Z. Lebedev himself would come to tell Simović that.[36] No sooner had Campbell left than Lebedev arrived. Lebedev told Simović that he came to see him by direct order of Vishinsky. The Soviet Union was ready to offer an agreement of a military and political nature. He promised arms and suggested that Simović send someone to Moscow to sign and finalize the agreement.[37] The diplomatically inept Simović, all puffed up with "good news" and encouragement, waited for poor Mameli to come in. Still thinking that the Italians might be useful in pressuring the Germans, Simović told Mameli that in case of a German attack, Yugoslav forces would not hesitate to make a dash across Albania to Valona in order to save themselves from German captivity. To make sure that he heard correctly, Mameli asked if this meant a declaration of war. To give the impression that Yugoslavia really meant business, Simović merely shrugged his shoulders and said nothing. Although the conversation was not for the Germans to hear, Mameli, as intended, told them the whole story.[38] On April 2, 1941, Steinhardt in Moscow reported that according to British sources, the Italians had made several diplomatic efforts in Berlin during the past three days, pleading not to attack Yugoslavia because attack at this point might jeopardize their position in Albania and Trieste.[39]

In contrast to the Germans, the Italians, most likely due to their military weakness in the Balkans and their growing dependency on Germany, were not nearly as upset about the coup as the Germans were. Although critical of it, the Italian press for the most part restricted itself to paraphrasing German, Hungarian, Bulgarian, and Rumanian views while lavishly praising the new foreign minister, Ninčić, as a valuable friend of Italy.[40] Italian ambivalence gave additional impetus for Belgrade to use them as an intermediary between Belgrade and Berlin. So as not give the impression of insincerity, Ninčić informed Gerhard Feine, counselor of the German legation in Belgrade, that he was scheduled to travel to Rome but that he would much rather negotiate directly with Berlin.[41] Obviously, Ninčić desired an invitation to visit Germany but in view of Germany's resolve to deal with Yugoslavia militarily, no response from Berlin was forthcoming. In the meantime, Mameli informed them (but not before he talked to Feine) that the Italo-Yugoslav negotiations would make sense only if an "adequate basis for negotiations were assured beforehand" (Doc. no. 253). Since no one came up with an "adequate basis," Ninčić turned to the Germans yet again.

Ninčić sent his brother to deliver a message to Feine in the German legation, which by now was almost empty. The message was that the foreign minister still favored negotiating with Berlin, which was why he delayed his talks with Mameli (Doc. no. 271). Less than two hours later, Ninčić sent his brother back with an eight-point proposal to be communicated to Berlin. Had they been accepted, Yugoslavia would have been in a much worse position than before the coup. He apologized via his brother regarding the Yugoslav-Soviet talks. They were, he said, undertaken without his knowledge. With respect to rapprochement with Germany, the government was on his brother's side and was willing to visit Germany. Yugoslavia received many proposals from abroad but the foreign minister would accept only those coming from Berlin (Doc. no. 272). However desperate Ninčić was to place relations with Germany back on the right track, his efforts proved completely useless. The Yugoslav-Soviet talks put additional oil on the German fire. In a letter to Mussolini, Hitler expressed his concern about Soviet meddling in the Balkans and, having taken into consideration the entire situation, had decided to attack Yugoslavia with "fanatic determination" (Doc. no. 281).

Hitler was determined. When Hitler heard of the coup, he had burst into a rage. He told his assembled military and political leaders that he had decided to destroy Yugoslavia without waiting for any possible declaration of loyalty from the new Yugoslav government. In view of the forthcoming invasion of Russia, to destroy Yugoslavia now was more favorable than later. The operation would be carried out in cooperation with the neighboring states, which would be compensated with territories at Yugoslavia's expense. Hungary would be awarded Banat, Italy the Adriatic coast, and Bulgaria would receive Macedonia, while later, Croatia would be given autonomy.[42] In separate talks with the Hungarians, Hitler was more specific. He reaffirmed his promise to cede Banat to Hungary and added that for tactical reasons, Croatia had to be independent but in alignment with the Hungarian state. In view of Italy's interests in Croatia, Hitler cautioned the Hungarians with respect to their desire to acquire an outlet on the Adriatic; he, however, expressed his willingness to back their claims.[43] On the same day of the conference with the German military and political leaders, Hitler issued his Directive No. 25. Here, he outlined his plan of operation to destroy Yugoslavia as a military and political entity (Doc. no. 223).

Henceforth, the preparation to attack Yugoslavia moved with lightning speed. On March 27, 1941, the Fuehrer communicated his decision to Mussolini. Explaining the reasons for his decision, Hitler insisted that the policy shift in Belgrade left him no choice but to act quickly and decisively to avoid any further mistakes. He then advised Mussolini to interrupt his offensive in Greece and concentrate his forces along the Albanian-Yugoslav border (Doc. no. 224). Although concerned about Italian troops in Albania, Mussolini accepted Hitler's decision, as long as Croatian "separatist" (which meant Italian) aspirations were met. Hence, Mussolini informed Hitler that a meeting with Pavelić was arranged for the next day.[44] On March 30, 1941, von Heeren was recalled to Berlin. He attended a meeting of experts to plan the bombing of Belgrade. Vehemently against war with Yugoslavia, von Heeren pleaded for peace and the need for negotiations. When he realized that he could do nothing, he left the conference room and burst into tears.[45] Privately, von Heeren was sure that the coup was no more than a Serbian affair, precipitated by young officers, mostly fliers, for purely adventurous reasons. Even the so-called outrages supposedly perpetrated against Germany and against him personally, von Heeren told his friends, were highly exaggerated by Berlin.[46]

Obviously, von Heeren was not clever enough to penetrate deep into the labyrinth of the Serbian mind-set, but his heart was in the right place. There was nothing he could do, and in the words of Ernst von Weiszäcker, Hitler, from the moment he heard about the coup, was bent on revenge and the total destruction of Yugoslavia. To make things worse, Hitler had decided to place Croatia under Hungarian domination, and the entire Adriatic coast of Croatia was to be taken over by Italy.[47] Without von Heeren in Belgrade, Charge d'Affaires Feine was instructed to remain completely aloof, no matter what the Yugoslavs wanted. On April 2, 1941, the legation staff was reduced drastically. Only the charge d'affaires, the military attaché, the radio operator, the code clerk, and the chauffeur remained in Belgrade. Once they received the code word "Tripartite Pact," they too were to leave the legation. They were to advise their German allies to do the same, but under no circumstances were they to mention the code word to anyone.[48]

With the doors closed from all sides, the last trump card Belgrade still could use was the Soviet Union. Although Ninčić claimed the talks were initiated behind his back, he in fact was the one who informed Yugoslav Minister Milan Gavrilović about the two colonels (Božin Simić and Dragan Savić) coming to Moscow for talks with the Soviets. When the colonels arrived in Moscow, Vishinsky flatly denied any knowledge of Lebedev's promises. In fact, such a treaty, Vishinsky told Gavrilović, would be detrimental to Soviet-German relations. He proposed instead (which was Moscow's intention from the start), a treaty of friendship and nonaggression. Even this emasculated version of the original promise did not go so smoothly. Article II of the treaty became contentious. Gavrilović insisted that in case of an attack on one of the contracting parties, the others should refrain from aiding the aggressor. The Soviets, however, found it unacceptable. They rephrased it into "the other contracting party [would] preserve its policy of neutrality and friendship." In Gavrilović's view, the treaty was worthless and he rightly refused to sign it. Only on Simović's insistence did he sign it and then only after the Soviets agreed to reword the clause into "the friendly relations [would] continue to exist."[49] The treaty was signed on April 6, 1941.

The Soviets had played their part well. Under the guise of friendship for their "little Slavic brother," they in fact reinforced Hitler's determination to decimate Yugoslavia and kept Soviet-German relations intact. The signing of the treaty was a joke. After numerous toasts, Stalin took the stage. According to some sources, he made the sign of the cross (aping the patriarch of Moscow) on Gavrilović. When Anastas I. Mikoyan saw Stalin blessing Gavrilović, he could barely control himself and hid his face in his handkerchief. "A fit of coughing seemed to be choking him."[50] When Yugoslavia collapsed, the Soviets forgot about the toasts, the "little Slavic brother," and the continuation of friendly relations. Mindful as always of their relations with Germany, the Soviets informed Gavrilović that the Soviet Union no longer regarded Yugoslavia as a political entity.[51]

The drastic situation created by the coup urgently required reconciliation with Maček. His presence in Belgrade would legitimize the Putschist government and give the appearance of domestic unity desired by the Allies. Moreover, now that the putschists switched their policy back to peaceful relations with the Axis, Maček's pacifism would be useful to assuage Hitler's anger. Maček was in Zagreb when he heard of the coup, and his initial impulse was to challenge it with forces loyal to Paul, who also happened to be there. In view of the meager forces on the putschist side, the coup could have been crushed, but Paul rejected Maček's proposal on the grounds that his family in Belgrade would suffer.[52] Instead, Paul appealed through the British consul in Zagreb, Terence Rapp, to have Campbell intervene on his behalf and let him and his family out of Yugoslavia. He would leave the country for Greece and would eventually settle in England.[53] Paul was allowed to return to Belgrade and resign in favor of King Peter. Together with his family, he was flown to Greece. England was out of the question. He was immediately taken to Rhodesia and branded as a "traitor." Paul languished there in virtual isolation for the rest of the war.[54]

To prevent Maček's return to Belgrade, Berlin advised him not to join Simović and to stay in Zagreb.[55] Bent on their destruction of Yugoslavia, Maček would have made an ideal candidate as head of an emasculated Croatian state for two reasons. The Germans needed his authority to expose Pavelić as an Italian pawn, and his democratic orientation would have considerable propagandistic value. Maček was in a difficult position, and irrespective of the steps he would take, was bound to make someone angry. He tried hard to make the Germans understand that to separate Croatia from Serbia at this point meant bloodshed and war. Such a solution was against his principles because he was a Christian and mindful of the words of Christ: "Blessed are they who build, for they shall be called sons of God."[56] His real motive, however, was his belief that Croatian national interests were inseparable from the interests of the western Allies. After some political horse-trading with Belgrade, Maček decided to join Simović.[57]

Whether because of his Christian principles or his naivete, Maček remained a firm believer in peace and he also wanted further negotiations with Berlin. Before he left Zagreb for Belgrade on March 4, 1941, he told the Berlin emissaries in Zagreb that peace was possible because the majority of Serbian leaders desired peace with Germany. In quest of his aims, Maček even bypassed the official German channels and contacted the Nazi youth leader Baldur von Schirach in Vienna, to intercede in Berlin on behalf of peace between Germany and Yugoslavia. In sympathy with Maček's peace mission, von Schirach agreed to send a Croatian residing in Vienna to Berlin with the proper recommendations and a plea for peace; but it was much too late.[58] Regardless of Maček's intentions, Meily warned from Zagreb, the Croatian people were apprehensive of the coup and remained detached from the events in Belgrade.[59] Reports from Meily somewhat tempered Lane's initial enthusiasm about the coup being an all-Yugoslav endeavor. Lane stated that in spite of the government's efforts to give the impression of national unity, many uncertainties with regard to Croatia remained unsolved. Reporting on some of these uncertainties, he pointed out that the Croatians were not involved in the coup, which in the Croatian mind, destroyed the basis of equality. Lane further maintained that the government, composed of Serbian nationalist elements, was symbolic of a recrudescence in the spirit of greater Serbia (Doc. nos. 740.0011, European War 1939/1242, 1250, and 1264). At some later point, Lane became quite skeptical that the relations between Zagreb and Belgrade would work, and hinted about the possibility of an alignment between Croatia and Germany (Doc. no. 740.0011, European War 1939/1264).

In line with his newly projected image as a diplomat concerned only about Yugoslavia's "neutrality" and "independence," Lane was not quite pleased with the "high spirit" of the Serbian Orthodox Church or the military. Such a spirit might compel the government to accept separation from Croatia, rather than cooperation with Germany as a unified country. One of the Serbian bishops was quite explicit on this point. The policy of the church was "the cross and independence." If the Croatians could not accept this principle, Serbia would let them go (Doc. no. 740.0011, European War 1939/1264). When Maček dropped one of his demands, namely "control of the National Bank," Lane was delighted. Maček's moderation, in Lane's view, expedited the process of reconciliation and merited praise for not taking advantage of the critical situation by pressuring the government for further concessions (Doc. no. 740.0011, European War 1939/1271). Secretary Hull also was generous in praising Maček for his cooperation to bring unity to the country in such trying times (Doc. no. 740.0011, European War 1939/1276A).

Rapidly unfolding events soon pushed aside this show of dubious unity. Maček went to see General Simović the moment he arrived in Belgrade. Anxious to retain peace, Maček asked Simović if there was still a possibility of averting war. Simović assured Maček that such a possibility did exist. Although pressure from Berlin precluded any meaningful negotiations between Rome and Belgrade, the Italians nevertheless kept communications open with Simović prior to when the Germans became ready to attack Yugoslavia. Mameli therefore informed Foreign Minister Ninčić that, as mediators between Belgrade and Berlin, the Italians were assured that Berlin would respect its obligations under the Tripartite Pact. This, however, was contingent upon Yugoslav troops being deployed in the south along the Yugoslav-Greek borders, to guard the German and Italian flanks in Bulgaria and Albania against Allied penetration through Yugoslav territory.[60] The meeting of the government to consider the Italian proposal was scheduled for the next day, April 5, 1941. Since any further negotiations with the Italians depended on Germany's preparedness to attack, Maček asked Simović how long it would take for the Germans to launch an offensive against Yugoslavia. Simović replied that if the Germans wished to prepare themselves well, it would take two weeks; if they wished to risk it, they could start right away.[61]

Ninčić gave his report on the Italian proposal at the meeting. The fact that the Yugoslav troops had to be deployed in the south against Allied penetration rendered the Tripartite Pact somewhat unclear. Upon reflection, they agreed that deployment of troops would not violate Yugoslavia's neutrality because their aim was to guard Yugoslavia against the entry of foreign troops. Simović had no objection against the occupation of the Greek frontier and proposed to occupy Salonika at the same time. Ninčić, who was neither for nor against the Italian proposal, observed that a dash for Salonika meant war. The other ministers were in favor of accepting the Italian proposal as a basis for further negotiations, and were willing to drop claims on Salonika. When Simović realized that no one was on his side, he literally became uncontrollable. He stood up and unleashed his emotions. He ranted about the Serbian past, the bones of Serbia's heroic military ancestors, the battle of Kosovo, the legendary princes of Serbia, the Serbian epic struggle against the Turks, and on and on.[62]

Maček was upset and exasperated with such an outburst. To calm Maček, however, Simović declared that no definite steps would be taken until the next day. In the meantime, Ninčić was authorized to ask Mameli to wait until noon of the following day for an official reply concerning troop redeployment.[63] Had

Maček known about Simović's obligation to enter war, he certainly would have understood the emotional outburst of his prime minister. Maček, however, soon realized that Simović was bent on war, on the "token war" raised by Regent Stanković before the coup. At any rate, Maček understood that Mameli's proposal provided Simović with an excuse to repeat Serbia's World War I military experience without being too obvious—take a small portion of the army out of the country and then, with the help of the Allies, return as victors. Actually, to give any consideration to the Italian agenda was an exercise in futility. No one really believed that peace with Germany could be possible.[64] Mameli never received the official reply. On April 6, 1941, at 4:00 in the morning, von Ribbentrop fired the code word "Tripartite Pact" to the German legation.[65] By 5:15, squadron after squadron of German planes roared over Belgrade. Yugoslavia was at war.

Chapter 11
War and the Aftermath

In contrast to the news accounts, the reality was devastating. The swift German air attack on Belgrade on the morning of April 6, 1941, jolted most of the people of Belgrade out of their beds. Wave after wave of German planes roared in the early morning air, showering death and destruction. In concert with the air assault, German forces entered Yugoslavia from Austria, Rumania, and Bulgaria. The combined land and air attack sent the entire structure of the Yugoslav state crumbling. Hungarians joined the hostility on April 10, the day the Croatians proclaimed their independence. This offered the Hungarian government a convenient excuse to regard the Yugoslav-Hungarian Treaty of "eternal friendship" null and void. On the same day, Italian troops crossed the northwestern Yugoslav border. Although the attack, compared to the spectacular German advances, lacked the necessary aggression and initiative, the Italians managed to move slowly ahead virtually unopposed.[1]

While the bombs were falling, Lane lost his nerve. The result of his diplomatic efforts could not have been more frightening. He took refuge in his room, "not wishing to see anyone and dulling his senses with whiskey."[2] His dark moods soon changed. After all, he was merely doing his job as any conscientious diplomat would have done in his place. He decided to make the best of it. Together with an American businessman in Belgrade, George H. Schellens, Lane arrived at what he saw as a practical idea. He sought to help the people of Belgrade by opening several soup kitchens and placing them in the care of the Red Cross. Through the American legation in Budapest, he asked for financial aid from the U.S. State Department in the amount of $100,000.[3] Considering the damage, it was by no means a large amount, but the response from Washington was nonetheless negligible.[4] Of the initial request, Hull authorized $25,000; upon Lane's further insistence, he added an additional $25,000. Petrov was not far from the truth when he observed that the U.S. government "was in fact less concerned about the fate of Yugoslavia than it publicly claimed to be."[5] Having lived through a humiliating experience in the fall of Belgrade (taken by a single SS infantry platoon on April 12, 1941), Lane returned via Budapest, Berlin, Geneva, and Barcelona to the United States on June 8.

The spectacular German victories, however, made no impression on the reporters in the field. They remained faithful to their original prognostication of victory over the "Huns." The rapid German advances were interpreted as a "tactical withdrawal" that would force the Germans to fight for every mountain and every narrow defile, thus ultimately demonstrating the fallacy of Hitler's military genius.[6] Others believed that the "tactical withdrawal" meant, in practice, turning Serbia into a formidable "fortress," and with 2.5 million well-trained Yugoslav soldiers, the Germans were expected surely to suffer defeat.[7] The entire press shared this basic view and relentlessly lulled its readers into believing in some nonexistent and indomitable fortress that would never permit a quick German victory.[8] Some editorials credited the "fortress" with saving England from an invasion, and therefore made a strong appeal to the U.S. government to honor its promise to Yugoslavia; otherwise, Americans might find themselves defending those very lines.[9] Thus, in addition to forcing the Italians out of the war, this "fortress" acquired two additional functions—keeping Britain safe from invasion and America out of war.

While hype about this fortress ran unchecked, chilling reports emanated from Berlin. These reports offered a different picture of the Balkan front, indicating that the German drive from Bulgaria across southern Serbia toward Skoplje in Macedonia cut off the Yugoslav forces from the Greeks and the British.[10] Although the Berlin reports were true, the press dismissed them as German propaganda. The Yugoslav military attaché was an intelligent Slovenian, Colonel Mirko Buria, who was of a different opinion. Unlike his Serbian boss Fotić, Buria was an experienced soldier with no faith in or admiration for Yugoslavia's military capability. Buria quite rightly regarded the Yugoslav army as an antiquated institution led by military fossils from World War I and the Balkan Wars. Minister Fotić was aware of Buria's views, but living under the illusion that the world was about to witness another *Gesta dei*, and this time *per Serbos*, he dismissed Buria's views as those of an "Austrian" who never learned that "we Serbians never capitulated, nor were we about to do it now."[11] When news of the German drive toward Skoplje reached Washington, Buria, together with other Legation members, was in the Washington Press Club listening to Fotić's oratory on Serbia's invincible valor. Having heard the news, Buria turned to Radica and whispered that Yugoslavia was as good as dead.[12]

The truth, however, could not be suppressed for long. Other reports reluctantly mentioned Yugoslavia's military "reversals." These reversals were attributed to Prince Paul and the former government who undermined the army by so frequently shifting commanding officers.[13] Some went beyond the notion of "shifting" and linked Germany's victories with the technological backwardness and general unpreparedness of the Yugoslav army. They again blamed Prince Paul and Cvetković, who refused to talk to British military authorities before the coup.[14] The truth of the matter was that the British never offered any help, and they themselves secretly made plans in Cairo to withdraw their meager troops from the Balkans before they were even sent there.[15] Still, the myopic vision of the "mighty armies" and the "spirit of the old Serbia" could no longer be maintained. Some bolder journalists dared to ask if it was wise to expect a victory in the Balkans and the defeat of Germany without American military engagement. Some reports reflected embarrassment permeating the U.S. State Department. Secretary of State Hull, as well as other officials of the department, were quick to disavow any knowledge of Donovan's mission. The War Department had not been consulted and there were indications that "privately [they might] have been dubious" of the whole endeavor. The conclusion drawn from the reports was that Roosevelt, Welles, Donovan, and Fotić were instrumental in precipitating war in the Balkans.[16]

Similar charges against Roosevelt and the administration came from Rome. Ambassador Phillips reported that the Italian news agency *Stefani* revealed the story of captured documents purporting Roosevelt's culpability for war against Yugoslavia. American maneuvering in Belgrade followed Donovan's instructions, and the result was that Yugoslavia ended up fighting "the Colonel's war." Now, commented Virginio Gayda in *Giornale D'Italia,* Roosevelt, Churchill, and Eden should sit back and admire the sight.[17] The sight was catastrophic indeed from the very start. Robert St. John ex post facto wrote of "ox-cart outfits" and "[o]xen, oxen, oxen" everywhere.[18] His description of the war was perfect. It was a war of oxen versus panzers. The so-called "invincible" Fifth Army (predominately Serbian) was pierced by the Germans on April 7, 1941, and the road to Greece was wide open.[19] In the midst of total collapse, Maček tendered his resignation. His place, as prearranged, was taken over by the secretary of the Croatian Peasant Party, Dr. Juraj Krnjević. Rather than escaping abroad, Maček decided on returning to Zagreb, to "share the fate of his own people."[20] Cut off from the field commanders, and having no communication with one another, other ministers ran from place to place in an effort to reach Montenegro and thence to fly away from the country with the young king.

A group of ministers headed by Vice-Premier Slobodan Jovanović reached Montenegro on April 15, 1941. Waging war was the last thought on their minds. As an outstanding Serbian legal historian, Jovanović, ex cathedra, lectured them instead on two types of surrender that would enable them to surrender and still be at war. If the army surrendered without the government's involvement, from a legal point of view, Yugoslavia would still remain a belligerent on the Allied side. With the "token war" on his mind (which was originally rejected), Jovanović believed Yugoslavia could repeat the Serbian experience of World War I, and with the help of the Allies, return as a victor. Under the circumstances, his view sounded quite plausible, because rumors were circulating that two Yugoslav divisions already had crossed the Greek borders and joined the Allies.[21] The rumors, however, were not without foundation. In the Greek campaign, the Germans captured ninety thousand Yugoslav soldiers.[22] It turned out that Simović himself initiated these rumors. A protagonist of the "token war," Simović in the meantime, without consulting anyone, ordered one of the commanders, General Kalafatović, to sound the Germans out about a surrender of the armed forces.[23] Verbally assaulted for his arbitrary decision, Simović repeated Jovanović's argument in his own defense, clearly indicating that the putschists had the "token war" in mind all along and had never intended to fight.[24]

The act of surrender was as shoddy as Serbia's military valor. Having sounded the Germans out, General Kalafatović authorized General Mihajlo Bodi to negotiate the terms of surrender. Lacking the proper authority, the Germans refused to negotiate with Bodi until proper representatives were found. Since these representatives were already in Greece, the question was who would fill their place. Desperate to find someone, General Bodi remembered the erstwhile foreign minister, Aleksandar Cincar Marković. After his initial reaction against it, Cincar Marković changed his mind and together with yet another general, the head of the Operational Division of the General Staff, General Radivoje Janković, signed the document of unconditional surrender.[25] As of April 17, 1941, Yugoslavia de facto ceased to exist. The reasons for such a sudden collapse, however, were not as clear as the collapse itself. While the war was still on, there was a tendency to blame Prince Paul, Cvetković, and the old regime—the Russians and the Turks. If the Russians and the Turks intervened, proclaimed the *Chicago Daily News,* the whole Balkan situation could have been altered; but they would rather wait, "like birds hypnotized by a snake, fluttering and helpless, to be devoured one at a time."[26] Now that the Germans were winning, the Turks might even be amenable to joining the Nazis and attacking the British position in the Suez area, while the Russians would be less inclined than ever before to challenge Hitler.[27] Thus, the "Independent State of Croatia" was proclaimed on April 10, 1941, which offered new, though not more insightful, justifications for Yugoslavia's collapse.

Numerous articles covering the "Free Croat State," ranging from the confusing to the ridiculous (and venomously anti-Croatian), appeared in the press the moment Croatia was proclaimed. Considering the timing, one could not really expect any understanding of the Croatian national cause, and the contemptuousness reduced these interpretations to pure bigotry. The reasons for these vitriolic attacks were more than just "Croatian treason." It was a face-saving attempt to cover their own journalistic flights into the realm of pure fantasy, to say nothing of attempting to rationalize the failure of American and British policy in the Balkans. True, a majority of the Croatians welcomed the establishment of a Croatian state; yet the idea of an independent statehood was associated with the Ustašas and their leader Dr. Ante Pavelić, "criminals" and "arch-terrorists" who plotted indiscriminately on the orders of their Axis masters.[28] The truth is that they would have welcomed anybody, including Dr. Maček, if he agreed to assume the leadership of the Croatian state. The guiding idea was to rid themselves of the Serbs and to attain independence from Belgrade and the Balkans. In so doing, however, they lost sight of the fact that they were actually jumping from the frying pan into the fire. Yet the truth about Pavelić was that he left Yugoslavia several months after the assassination of the Croatian leadership in the Belgrade Parliament in 1928, and not as a terrorist but as a parliamentarian. In conformity to his mission abroad, Pavelić signed the Sofia Declaration, in which he, together with some Macedonian leaders, declared to undertake every "legal action . . . in order to secure human and national rights, political liberties, and complete independence for Croatia and Macedonia." Pavelić also submitted an appeal on behalf of "suffering Croatia" to the League of Nations. His appeal, however, like many before and after, were totally ignored. In it, Pavelić outlined the Croatian resolve to struggle for freedom and independence, and, he stressed, although Croatians would prefer to fight for their freedom and independence by legal means, they would not hesitate to resort to "more drastic measures" if Croatian grievances were not taken into consideration. With the death sentence on his head in connection to the Sofia Declaration, and to avoid assassination by Serbian agents, Pavelić fled to Italy—right into Mussolini's arms. That crimes were perpetrated by Pavelić and his followers is not questionable. The numbers and their accuracy are questionable. The exaggerated numbers of crimes are repeated even today, frequently without any tangible proof.[29] The fact is, although it is not an excuse, were it not for Yugoslavia having been held hostage to the idea of a warped Serbian political vision, neither Pavelić nor the Ustašas would have ever appeared on the stage of history. Covert and overt Serbian propaganda fed such views. As far as the Serbians were concerned, the Croatians were an antiquated people, fossilized in their medieval Catholicism, and who, much like Rip van Winkle, woke up to the modern world of which they had no understanding whatever.[30] The "sinister figures" came to the helm of Croatia, lamented an editorial. The new leaders were all members of the "murderous" Ustaša organization that operated a "Murder School" abroad and trained bands of professional assassins.[31]

The psychological underpinning of the Ustaša movement was traced to the Croatian national ideology of the last century. This ideology was originated by the Croatian "madman," Ante Starčević, whose ideas reflected symptoms of dangerous megalomania.[32] Since it was assumed that all those who favored an independent Croatia were followers of Starčević, the dangerous lunatic who created a generation of "embittered and degenerated Croat intelligentsia," they were all mad. From this polluted source, Pavelić and his henchmen sprang into the political life of Croatia. Croatian-Americans were told that although the majority of them were loyal citizens, approximately seventy-five thousand of them were in sympathy with Pavelić and his regime.[33] Minister Fotić also held similar views. The proclamation of the Croatian state appeared to be exactly what Fotić needed, saving him from the humiliation of a speedy collapse. For Fotić, the appearance of Croatia was visible proof that Croatians had stabbed the Serbians in the back. He therefore wasted no time explaining the Yugoslav military debacle in terms of Croatian treachery. In line with his "stab in the back theory," he informed the U.S. State Department officially that the quick disappearance of Yugoslavia was possible only because of Croatian treason. Instead of fighting Croatian officers and soldiers, simply let the Germans walk in unopposed.[34]

Fotić's theory referring to those "treasonable" Croatians gained in currency, especially among Serbian-Americans. The outcome was that the principal Serbian newspaper, the *Srbobran,* became Fotić's mouthpiece, fomenting hatred against Croatian people.[35] Other members of the legation followed Fotić's lead. His wife, Tatjana Fotić, sought to castigate every Croatian in the United States. One evening at the home of Sumner Welles, Mrs. Fotić lectured the guests about Croatian "disloyalty." The Croatians, according to her, were as disloyal to America as they were to Serbia. They therefore should all be placed under surveillance. "Yes, it was necessary to bring it out. Let everyone know how disloyal the Croatians were" (115). Concerned about American unity, the U.S. government was finally compelled to intervene on behalf of Croatian-Americans. Although the *Srbobran* had diminished its hate-propaganda, other papers continued to write along the "stab in the back" line. Indeed, Yugoslavia's collapse, the readers were told, could be fully attributed to "traitors." Treason in the south enabled the Germans to make an easy breakthrough in Macedonia.[36] An interview with the commander of the Fourth Army in Croatia, General Nedeljković, was published in full. According to Nedeljković's story, the Croatians refused to serve, reducing his army from two hundred thousand to twenty-five thousand soldiers. Because these soldiers were mostly Croatian, they turned their arms, not against Germans, but against the Serbians, causing "wholesale slaughter" on both sides, Serbian and Croatian.[37]

Nedeljković's story, like most of the stories in the press, had little basis in reality. True, there was reluctance on the part of the Croatians and some did refuse to join the army, but it was not only for national reasons. The main reason was the general state of confusion that gripped the entire country. Thinking that the Germans would avoid risking a premature attack, General Simović dismissed information regarding an imminent German attack as "unreliable," and refused to consult the government or take the necessary steps toward mobilization.[38] By the time any move was made, it was too late. No reasonable person would have responded to such a mobilization and be caught unarmed by the advancing German units. The Serbians themselves, although in absolute command of the army, deserted their posts, even before seeing the enemy. For example, a Serbian general in command of the coastal city of Sibenik left the Croatians to fight "for their own country," and along with his Serbian officers and men, defected to Serbia.[39] There were many cases like this in which Serbian officers defected, leaving the Croatians to defend "their" country. As for General Nedeljković, the truth was slightly different. Although numerically inferior, Croatian soldiers of the Fourth Army twice repelled the Germans, and were the only ones to demonstrate a degree of courage in the face of total collapse and disorder (166). The navy also suffered the same misfortune, but not because Croatians were in the majority. Rather, it was because of a government order to wait for refugees. In the meantime, the government fled, the refugees never arrived, and with the sudden capitulation of the military forces, the navy had no other choice but to surrender (166).

The total military confusion is further illustrated by the fact that even in Serbia, as well as elsewhere, high ranking officers left their posts. The commander of the army in Skoplje, General Ilija Brašić, left his designated command and took refuge in a nearby vineyard. The commander of the First Army, General Milan Radaković, together with his chief of staff, General Todor Milićević, relinquished (without authorization) command and disappeared into the woods of the Fruška Gora. In addition, the commander of the Second Army in Sarajevo, General Dragomir Stojanović, along with his entire staff, surrendered to the Germans before the capitulation was signed. The commander of the Fifth Army, General Vladimir Čukavac, lost contact with his troops and had to be replaced. Lastly, the commander of the Kosovo Division sent his messenger on April 9, 1941, to the town of Peć to negotiate with the Germans regarding the surrender of his unit.[40] This was the bulk of the Yugoslav army, commanded exclusively by the Serbians. So what reporters witnessed and reported were not merely "Croatian defectors," but soldiers of an army in total disintegration. The most striking example of Serbian "military valor" was General Nedić himself. Two days after the coup, Nedić was reactivated by Simović. On March 31, 1941, he was sent to Skoplje to command the strongest military force—the Army Group South, consisting of eight divisions. The war minister, Army General Bogoljub Ilić, ordered him to organize the command and undertake preparations for the units under him to fight the Germans at the start of the war. He hesitated in leaving Belgrade, giving all kinds of implausible excuses. Finally, when he did leave, it took him five days to get to Priština in Kosovo, away from Skoplje. By then, the entire Army Group he was supposed to lead had been penetrated, and was subsequently dispersed.[41]

The question one might legitimately ask here is, why was Nedić reactivated and given the most important post in the army? Given his views and his dismissal, one may safely assume that Simović was either inept or else used Nedić as a ploy to placate the Germans. I am inclined to believe that Simović used him, for how is one to understand that after the capitulation of the Yugoslav army, Nedić was not, like others, taken prisoner and transported to Germany? He was exempted from his prisoner status (the only general in the Yugoslav army) and was given a limousine to return back home to Belgrade. Furthermore, to camouflage Nedić's role, the Germans kept him confined to his home until he was called upon to form the Serbian government, which, according to some of his associates, the Germans prearranged in collusion with Nedić before the war even started.[42]

Thus, these soldiers were without leadership, without communication, and often without arms and supplies. In short, the soldiers left behind were in the mercy of the enemy.

Several weeks after capitulation, the Yugoslav government (the Serbian part) in exile advanced the thesis that Croatian culpability was instrumental in the collapse of Yugoslavia. This thesis was preceded by the king's proclamation in which he asserted that, because of fraudulent information and fictitious promises, a number of Croatians were swayed by the Germans.[43] The deep-seated suspicions about the Croatians, plus the concern about Serbia's future, led the theme of culpability to become the official line of Yugoslav foreign policy, which continued to be dominated by the Serbians.[44] The official line of the Yugoslav government reinforced the culpability of Croatians in the American press. Stories were filed, well after the war was over, detailing Croatian treason, defection, and pathological behavior. One of these stories could be viewed as apocryphal, depicting the killing of thirty-two "Ustašas" by a single Serbian officer before he took to the mountains to struggle against the invader.[45] Another described how one of the Serbian policemen in Sarajevo singlehandedly captured and killed forty-nine "traitors" and "spies," and looked around for the fiftieth. Apparently, it was not hard to find them because "spies" were everywhere, even among the newspaper vendors.[46] Irrespective, however, of its substance, the most fascinating aspect was their moral content. It seemed that the Serbians were morally obliged to take retribution against "traitors" and "spies" because they were betrayed by Croatians, Moslems, and "some" Slovenians.

The apex of Croatian "treason" was portrayed in a story published three months after the collapse. It was the synthesis of treason and the pathology of human behavior. The story took place in Donji Vakuf in Bosnia, where the author, together with Military Attachè Colonel Louis Fortier, were in German "captivity" for several days. The reason for the speed of the German advances, the author found, lay in the still unsoiled guns of German panzers. The Croatian "traitors" let them through. These "traitors" were everywhere, literally under "every rock." Lest some might excuse the lack of enthusiasm to defend Yugoslavia, the Croatians were depicted as an abnormal people. Croatian independence was lodged in the heads of children and adults of an inferior intelligence. There were four or five boys, no more them sixteen-years-old, with swastikas on their shirts. Puffed up with a certain authority, these boys were led by a man of forty-five, a "big, brutish type, the small town bully who had never grown up."[47]

Lane's return to the United States clarified none of the events surrounding the collapse of Yugoslavia. If Lane had any qualms about the war, he, as his sympathetic biographer Petrov pointed out, soon lost it in the atmosphere of the warm welcome he received from the administration. As a good and conscientious public servant, and above all, loyal to Roosevelt, he could not implicate anyone from the administration in the Yugoslav fiasco. His public statements were therefore designed to fit the existing Washington pattern. The "Yugoslavs" were responsible for the course of action they took on March 27, 1941. In return, Welles praised Lane for his "ability, energy, and tact" in handling Yugoslav affairs while on the job in Belgrade.[48] The president also appreciated Lane's efforts in Belgrade and promised him a new job in Mexico.[49] In the meantime, Lane was sought after for speaking engagements across the country. The theme of his speeches, of course, was Serbian heroism and the determination of all "Yugoslavs" to carry on the struggle. When briefed by administration officials in measuring his words, Lane dutifully praised all "Yugoslavs." In private, however, his personal feelings were considerably different.

At the invitation of *Life* magazine, Lane wrote his own version of the German conquest of Yugoslavia. Rumors of American involvement in the coup were false, and if he made some protestations now and then, it was because the Tripartite Pact was directed against the interests of the United States. Rather,

Prince Paul, Lane argued, was to blame. His aversion to bloodshed and his determination to avenge the death of his relatives in the Russian slaughter by the bolsheviks were the main reasons why he decided to accede to the Tripartite Pact.[50] One of his speaking engagements brought Lane to Libertyville, the Serbian stronghold near Chicago. The invitation came from Fotić and Serbian Orthodox Bishop Dyonisius. The occasion was a double celebration, the Fourth of July and the "heroic Serbian resistance" to the Nazis. The whole celebration soon turned into an anti-Croatian demonstration, with the gathered Serbian-Americans demanding punishment of the "treacherous" Croatians.[51] Mindful of official policy, Lane ostensibly remained impartial. In conversations with private individuals, however, he gave the unmistakable impression that Serbians, for quite understandable reasons, no longer desired to live with Croatians. The Croatians were indeed their greatest enemy.[52] Speaking about the coup, Lane explained it to his listeners in terms of American elections. The Serbians merely wished to elect the government of their choice, with Croatians and Slovenians represented in it. "It is the right which is in harmony with the principle of our own Declaration of Independence and our practice of holding an election for the Presidency once in every four years."[53] No less extraordinary, to say the least, was Lane's reasoning concerning Simović's peace efforts, entailing all the obligations with respect to the Tripartite Pact. That Berlin rejected Belgrade's overtures toward reconciliation, for Lane, was positive proof that the Germans never wanted peace with Yugoslavia.

It seemed then that the Germans disliked the Serbian "election" and therefore decided to attack Yugoslavia, which otherwise had no intentions of joining the belligerents.

Two views stood in sharp contrast to the prevailing opinions. John Meily, the American consul in Zagreb, and William H. Smyth, a long-standing representative of the American automobile industry, markedly disagreed regarding Croatian culpability. Both, however, were prohibited from expressing their views in public. When Smyth visited the Yugoslav legation, Fotić asked him not to confide his views to anyone, least of all to Bogdan Radica. Nonetheless, Smyth made an effort to contact Radica outside the legation and told him that the war in Yugoslavia was a catastrophe for which Roosevelt and Donovan were responsible. He believed that Maček and Prince Paul were right to stay out of the conflict. Smyth was sure that Yugoslavia would slide into an internecine war, that in the long run, would pave the way for the communists' rise to power.[54] Meily was equally explicit. In his report from Zagreb on June 13, 1941, he detailed the events surrounding the Ustaša takeover; it was smooth with no resistance from anyone. The reason for such a smooth takeover was the Serbo-Croatian Agreement itself. As far as the majority of the Croatian people were concerned, the agreement was made as a concession to the monarchy. The uncompromising stand by the Ustašas against Yugoslavia acted in their favor and made them champions of Croatian independence.[55] The final rift between Maček and his people, according to Meily, came when Maček decided to join Simović. No longer paying any attention to Maček's policy, Colonel Slavko Kvaternik proclaimed the rebirth of Croatia on April 10, 1941, shortly before the German units entered the Croatian capital. The colonel also read a proclamation drafted by Maček, appealing to his followers to cooperate with the new regime. The "bloodless revolution" (only one policeman was killed) was carried out; when the first German units entered Zagreb, thousands of enthusiastic citizens "widely acclaimed" their appearance.[56]

Why Meily remained in Zagreb after other American diplomats left is an open question. When Croatian authorities, under pressure from Berlin, asked Meily to leave Croatia, he considered the expulsion "regrettable" and allegedly told the foreign minister, Dr. Mladen Lorković, that the U.S. State Department "acknowledged the declaration of independence of Croatia," and that de jure recognition would follow as soon as the international situation became more clear.[57] Although his testimony remained uncorroborated, it should not be summarily dismissed. Meily's alleged statement was not at variance with Roosevelt's views concerning the future of Yugoslavia. It was along the lines of Roosevelt's idea of making Serbia stronger without "its" western provinces, which may very well account for the fact that the Americans, unlike the British, expressed a lukewarm "indignation" when Croatia was proclaimed.[58] The undisputed fact is that Roosevelt discussed in earnest, the separation of Croatia from Serbia, with Welles, Fotić, Eden, and according to the Italian historian Gaetano Salvemini, with King Peter.[59] Under pressure from some of his close advisers, including Welles and especially Eden, who all held that the future of the small states was in their "groupings" rather than in their separation, Roosevelt became noncommittal.[60] Facing opposition, Roosevelt adopted his usual approach to controversy. He just pushed it aside, hoping that a solution would somehow manifest itself in the future.

In a last-ditch effort to justify the American Balkan policy, the opinion was expressed that Roosevelt's Balkan policy, coupled with the Lend-Lease Act, saved the British in the Mediterranean and the Soviets from collapse. It seemed that passage of the Lend-Lease Act was instrumental in "knocking the German timetable haywire." The British resistance in North Africa in late September was somehow connected with Belgrade's coup. "Thanks to American diplomacy and Yugoslav heroism, the Middle East is still secured."[61] Similar views regarding the breakdown of the German offensive at the outskirts of Moscow were expressed and associated with the American Balkan policy. It all started with Donovan's visit to the Balkans. His assurances were sufficient for the "Yugoslav patriots and the Greek heroes" to resist Hitler. The Balkan events used up two-and-a-half months of Hitler's valuable time, and the result was that he invaded the Soviet Union in June instead of April. The delay and the dreaded Russian winter saved the Soviet Union. In light of the Soviet victory outside Moscow, Donovan's mission was lauded as having "contributed" to a considerable extent to the success of the Russian arms.[62]

These journalistic rationalizations of the Balkan fiasco were uncritically displayed in the pages of World War II historiography, and the credit should go to Sir Winston Churchill. Given his authority and reputation, few historians ever questioned his delay theory in regard to the invasion of Russia. Hitler himself gave some credence to Churchill's views on the subject. Once Barbarossa (code name for the invasion of Russia) failed, Hitler, in excusing his own failure, blamed the four-week delay as having been caused by the Belgrade coup d'etat. It will be recalled that the Israeli military historian Martin van Creveld, on the basis of German military sources, established that the date for the invasion of Russia was pushed forward because the German Army was not militarily ready to launch its offensive vis-à-vis Hitler's May prediction.[63] Among the first to challenge Churchill's delay theory, however, was the British historian B. H. Liddell Hart. Studying the weather conditions at the time of the invasion, he concluded that Barbarossa could not have started before June because the ground was too wet for mechanized warfare.[64] Another British historian, Trumball Higgins, argued quite rightly that the delay theory was politically motivated from the start. Barbarossa's failure allowed both Churchill and Hitler to claim that the Balkan campaign saved Moscow and the Soviet Union. Rather than face the embarrassing truth, Churchill turned Barbarossa into his victory, while Hitler discovered that were it not for Mussolini's "idiotic" campaign in Greece, he could have destroyed the Red Army during the brief summer and autumn of 1941.[65] Contrary to Hitler's rationale, Belgrade's coup shortened the Balkan campaign. By swinging to the right from Bulgaria into the Vardar Valley in Macedonia, the Germans found the Greek borders completely unprotected and wide open for their easy crossing into Greece.[66] Nevertheless, Americans were instrumental in saving the Soviet Union. This, however, had no connection to America's Balkan policy. America's intransigence toward Japan led the Japanese leaders to believe that their "co-prosperity sphere" could be attained only by advancing southward in the Pacific, instead of attacking, as they contemplated, the Soviet Union in the summer of 1941. "The asset freeze, soon a complete embargo, decided the leaders of the [Japanese] Imperial Army that war against the Soviet Union was not feasible in 1941 and that the navy's version of the Southward advance—which included an attack on the United

States—had to be endorsed."[67] Whether by accident or by design, the U.S. policy denied Japan a co-prosperity sphere, rendering the two-front war against the Soviet Union a virtual impossibility. Apart from the Russian winter, Washington's far eastern policy, rather than the Balkan policy, was the most important factor in saving the Soviet Union. America, having been attacked, was propelled into war.

The consequences of Yugoslavia's defeat, however, were actually worse than the defeat itself. The people of Yugoslavia certainly got more than they bargained for, irrespective of their national and political orientations. Slovenia was divided between Italy and Germany. Mussolini having taken "his" share of Croatian territory along the Adriatic, Croatia was then proclaimed "independent" (unarmed), meaning that it very much depended on Italian goodwill and military protection. In negotiations between Italy and Germany, it was agreed (on Italy's insistence) that Croatia had no need for military forces other than police units to maintain the peace.[68] The Serbian and communist insurrections forced the Italians and Germans to allow a gradual buildup of the Croatian armed forces, although they were never strong enough to meet the challenge. To make things worse, from the beginning, Croatia was divided into two military zones of approximately equal size. The western part was under Italian control and the eastern was under the Germans. The Germans were interested in guarding and protecting the railway lines running southward toward Greece. Italian interests on the other hand were somewhat different. They became involved in the internal affairs of Croatia. Suspicious of the Germans and afraid that a strong Croatia might diminish Italy's influence in the area, the Italians, in their military zone, behaved like a conqueror of enemy territory.[69] Due to the blood relations with the Italian Royal House (the Queen of Italy, Elena, was the daughter of the last Montenegro's King Nikola), Montenegro became an Italian protectorate. Macedonia was given to Bulgaria, Kosovo to Albania, and parts of Vojvodina were annexed by Hungary. Serbia, the mighty "mountain fortress," was reduced to a pre-Balkan War territory. After a few months of occupation, a quisling government, as previously pointed out, headed by General Milan Nedić, was established in Serbia. The government of "National Salvation," as it was euphemistically called by Serbian apologists of the war regime, was supported by an ardent Fascist, Dimitrije Ljotić, and his "Volunteer Corps."[70] The policy of Nedić's government was ostensibly to keep Serbia quiet and to save Serbian blood from being spilled. In reality, its function was to carry out every German demand faithfully, in order to secure Serbia's place in the new European order under the Nazis.

Apart from these openly nationalistic programs, two supranational movements appeared on the scene. The Chetnik movement, under the auspices of the Yugoslav government in exile, was led by Draža Mihajlović; the Partizan Movement organized by the Communist Party of Yugoslavia (KPJ) was led by Josip Broz Tito. There were some attempts at the beginning to integrate these two movements, but due to their irreconcilable ideologies, no progress was ever made. In fact, open hostility between them broke out as early as 1941. The reason for the failure was because the Chetniks, ostensibly supranationals, operated on two levels. One entailed the recreation of the prewar model of Yugoslavia with the Serbs again in the domineering position, while the other carried an exclusively Serbian program of creating a greater Serbia. Such a policy required a delicate balancing act that involved secret accommodations with the enemy, including Nedić. It also involved fighting the Partizans while simultaneously, through intercession of the Yugoslav government abroad, maintaining the Chetnik's reputation as genuine freedom fighters.[71]

In truth, the occupation, as Maček and Prince Paul feared, enabled the Yugoslav peoples to settle their scores with one another. It was the bloodiest act of nationalistic and ideological passions. Since the Croats were "independent," they got most of the blame from all sides—especially from the Serbian and Communist propaganda machines, both of which desperately needed to project themselves as the martyrs of the right causes. In reference to the wartime Yugoslav scene, Professor Hugh Seton-Watson, except on one point, was quite right when he said that the casualties from famine and starvation were fewer in Yugoslavia than elsewhere in Europe, but that it "[was] more than compensated for by the frightful scale of the massacres carried out by Germans, Italians, Hungarians, Bulgarians, Croatians and Serbian Fascists."[72] I do not know whether or not he included the Chetniks among the "Serbian Fascists," but without them, the picture would not be complete. Moreover, he "forgot" to mention the Communists. True, they were "anti-Fascists," but in their struggle for "freedom" (to realize their ideological agenda), they left trails of blood and nameless graves, which by their magnitude, could easily be measured up to that of the crimes perpetrated by their opponents in wartime Yugoslavia.

Chapter 12
Conclusion

Every student of diplomatic history is aware that diplomacy is a highly elusive proposition. Appearances are often confused with realities and vice versa. Hence, my main concern was to illuminate that opaque world of motives behind diplomatic actions hidden in the shadow of diplomatic verbiage and charged with resounding words of justice, dignity, freedom, etc.

American diplomacy toward Yugoslavia in its initial stages, in many instances, was a continuation of Washington's relations with the kingdom of Serbia. There was no pressing need to change it, simply because the new state of Yugoslavia amounted to very little on the scale of American national interests. For a brief period while President Wilson was still in power, however, Yugoslavia was of considerable importance to him, in relation to the secret London agreement in which Italy was entitled to get parts of Croatian and Slovenian territories as a reward for entering the war on the Allied side. Being an outspoken opponent of all secret agreements, Wilson's agenda was set up to impose his vision of the future onto the quarreling Europeans. His vision was based upon, among other things, international cooperation through the League of Nations, guided by the principle of self-determination for all peoples under foreign domination. This was to be viewed as the most effective impediment against future wars. His unorthodox vision collided with old European practices, and indeed, with many of his powerful compatriots who believed that Wilson's ardent internationalism might prove detrimental to the sovereignty of the United States. At any rate, Wilson's vision in foreign affairs came to an end with his untimely death. His Republican successors in the White House supplanted it with calculated isolation, and the American withdrawal from the League of Nations was seen as a necessary precaution against all European alliances and political entanglements.

Consequently, American diplomacy became more static. Diplomatic representatives were instructed, no matter where they were, to simply listen and report back to Washington, but to never get involved in the internal affairs of other countries. When Franklin D. Roosevelt came to power in 1933, he replaced the Republican administration, but it seemed as though nothing had really changed in Washington. The mental state of most Americans was still clouded by President Calvin Coolidge's vision of world order. He firmly believed in the continuation of world order by keeping still.[1]

Although an internationalist, Roosevelt, by necessity felt compelled to blend in with the political landscape. The sentiment from his famous speech to "fear nothing but fear itself," was not applied to foreign affairs, for he knew only too well that any deviation from "keeping still" would cost him his reelection. Yet the beginning of the war in Europe recorded an imperceptible change in Roosevelt's attitude vis-à-vis the fascist powers. By the end of 1940, Yugoslavia had become the object of American attention in relation to Italy's intention prior to the war against France, and later in relation to Mussolini's invasion of Greece.

The rise of the fascist powers in Europe and the danger of imminent war compelled Roosevelt (still restricted by the imposed isolation) to shift somewhat the American policy, from "keeping still" to a policy of containment of the "law breakers"—again without direct American involvement. The "shift" in his policy involved recognition of the Soviet Union in the hope that it would effectively restrain Nazi Germany in Europe and Japan as well, and promote open and free access to economic resources to all. Apart from his cautious moves, most Americans still believed that keeping peace in Europe was exclusively a European problem. Although recognition of the Soviet Union fell short of his original expectations, Roosevelt sought a kind of "moral embargo" as a means of restraining the "law breakers," and he strongly advocated a peaceful solution through negotiations of otherwise highly complicated social and political issues. The outcome of his moral exhortations was that no one took them very seriously. Relations toward Yugoslavia changed with Donovan's mission to Belgrade, but due to American neutrality on the surface, remained the same.

Elsewhere in Europe, the lack of common policy between Britain and France, as reflected in their relations vis-à-vis the Axis powers and the Soviet Union, benefitted both Hitler and Mussolini from the start. For years, Britain looked upon Mussolini's policy toward the Danubean region with benevolent neutrality. When Germany became a serious threat to the Versailles order, Britain continued to pressure France to be evenhanded toward their former foe, and publicly defended the policy that Germany's recovery would be beneficial for all of Europe. In fact, British capital investments in Germany made Hitler's rearmament policy a success, given that both the French and British business world regarded the Nazis as a useful tool and a bulwark against the Soviet Union.

Caught in the net of European power politics and riddled by a host of internal problems, Yugoslavia depended heavily upon the protectors of the Versailles order for its very existence. With the gradual decline of the French defense system directed against German and Austrian "revanchism," Yugoslavia almost imperceptibly found a new guardian. Mussolini's hostility toward Belgrade, not to mention the Croatian national question and the economic crises, were compelling factors in seeking closer relations with Nazi Germany. As an agricultural region, Yugoslavia became a significant exporter of food and raw materials for the German rearmament industry. In return, Yugoslavia imported industrial goods from Germany, including military equipment that Yugoslavia could not procure from either France or Britain. Most importantly, Germany's commercial predominance in Yugoslavia, which Mussolini regarded as his sphere of influence, provoked a rivalry between Rome and Berlin. This in turn offered the Serbian establishment some breathing space, and even a false sense of security.

Germany, in view of its strategic needs, unlike Italy, was satisfied to trade with Yugoslavia and keep peace in the region, regardless of who was in charge in Belgrade. Believing that the Germans wanted to undermine Yugoslavia by satisfying the national aspirations of the Croatians, is sheer nonsense and has no basis in reality. Gradual dependency on German trade and military hardware, however, created Yugoslavia's political dependency as well. The pro-fascist prime minister Milan Stojadinović realized the danger of Germany's growing influence on Yugoslavia and tried to balance it by improving relations with Italy. The main purpose of his smoothing relations with Italy entailed, as a precondition, the liquidation of the Ustašas camps in Italy. Afraid of undue German influence in his *spazio vitale,* Mussolini responded positively to Stojadinović's diplomatic overtures. For more elevated reasons concerning the future of Italy, he pushed the Ustašas aside in exchange for a more "far reaching" agreement with Belgrade—one involving the curbing of Albania and possibly Croatia, should the opportunity present itself between Rome and Belgrade. An agreement with Italy, good relations with Germany, and the impression that Yugoslavia was still a good friend of the Versailles powers, made Stojadinović believe that he finally had solved the Croatian question without making any concessions to them. If any were to be made in the future, it would be on his terms. A few ministerial posts would be the maximum he was prepared to offer them. In spite of Stojadinović's wishes and calculations, however, the Croatian question would not go away, as the forthcoming election clearly would demonstrate. Contrary to Stojadinović's expectations, the election result turned out disappointing for him, which in turn offered a good excuse for Prince Paul to dismiss his overly ambitious prime minister. The real reasons for dismissal were hidden from the public. In his secret maneuvering with Rome and Berlin, Paul, the real architect of Yugoslavia's foreign policy, was convinced that Stojadinović not only exceeded his authority, but threatened to undermine his position as well. It was no secret that Stojadinović harbored a strong desire of becoming a Yugoslav Mussolini (whom he consciously aped in his speeches and political gatherings). The Stojadinović incident, coupled with the dismemberment of Czechoslovakia and the forthcoming showdown with Poland, forced Paul to initiate more serious negotiations with the Croatians.

Prior to these events, the Croatian-Americans, responding to the pleas of their compatriots in the "old country," busied themselves with sending memoranda to the newly elected Democratic president. In their minds, Roosevelt was a resurrected Wilson who would finish the work of his distinguished predecessor. In reality, the Croatian appeals to Washington proved to be "embarrassing" to the administration, as they were directed against the "friendly country." True, America was still uninvolved and as yet had no desire to get entangled in European affairs. If, however, the Americans wanted the Europeans to take care of peace and defend their own freedom, one would expect demonstration of a requisite amount of sympathy for those who struggled for freedom and justice before the advent of war. In keeping with American policy, Arthur Bliss Lane in Belgrade turned down the pleas of Maček's representatives for help in negotiating with the government. The Croatians received the same treatment in London and Paris. On certain occasions in the past the Americans had counseled Belgrade to settle the Croatian question, but their counsels were never taken very seriously.

The Serbian establishment could not imagine Yugoslavia as being anything other than what it was—an extension of greater Serbia. As far as they were concerned, the inclusion of some Croats in the government was the maximum they were prepared to concede. By negotiating with the Croatians, a less intransigent Prince Paul proved to be far more clever than commonly perceived. His main concerns were dynastic interests, to say nothing of the fact that he needed Maček's pacifism for the success of his future foreign policy. Although undertaken too late, the negotiations, if successful, would in Paul's view, reduce Croatia's susceptibility to dangerous manipulation by outside forces such as Italy and Germany. Maček, although for different reasons, shared Paul's fears and responded positively to negotiations in the hope that war might be averted and Yugoslavia kept neutral. To succeed, they both needed peace.

History, however, was not kind to either of them. A fragile autonomy, plus the partial sharing of power gained by the Croatians, failed to consolidate the country, which seems to account for why the Allies, through Roosevelt's good offices, were prepared to split Croatia between Rome and Belgrade in exchange for Mussolini's neutrality in war against France. The crumbling of France and Mussolini's costly adventure in Greece drastically changed Yugoslavia's role in the game of global politics. Churchill's ascendance to the position of prime minister in the midst of the French disaster, coupled with Mussolini's subsequent invasion of Greece without Hitler's approval, set a new British strategy in motion.

Under the guise of "strict neutrality" of the Balkan states, Britain's new strategy, formulated by Sir Winston, was to prevent German forces from coming to Italy's rescue in Greece. Anticipating (quite correctly) that Hitler would have no intention of letting Mussolini play out his destiny, Churchill's plan, in reality, envisioned an all-out war in the mountainous region of the Balkans. The war would have three distinct, yet interconnected, aims: (1) the engagement of German forces in the mountainous region of the Balkans, which would (2) precipitate not only an Italian collapse in Greece but would change the face of the Fascist regime in Italy; and, more importantly, (3) draw the Soviets into the conflict against Germany.

To translate the plan into action, the British realized that they were in no position to do it alone. The only logical choice was to turn to the United States for help. Donovan's arrival in the Balkans at the beginning of 1941, supposedly on behalf of the *Chicago Daily News,* under the surface, marked a decisive shift in United States foreign policy. To be sure, Washington officially counseled neutrality for the Balkan states, but Donovan's mission injected new meaning to it. By giving full support to the British policy, Donovan not only endorsed it, but encouraged the coup as well, in case the Yugoslav government deviated from the expected line of "strict neutrality."

In his talks with the Yugoslav leaders, Donovan was quite explicit on this point. The only neutrality acceptable by the United States was a benevolent one toward its Allies. From this formula that Donovan spelled out for them, it was not hard to detect that the Yugoslav government would be held accountable if they chose not to comply. Given the situation in the Balkans, it meant Yugoslavia's engagement in war against Germany. The ensuing diplomatic pressure on Belgrade, compounded by British troop redeployment from North Africa to Greece, only heightened Hitler's resolve to move more quickly to the rescue, but avoiding the British trap. Unfortunately for the British, Hitler retained his original plan, which was to rush to Greece across Bulgaria rather than Yugoslavia, which from a logistic point of view, would be much easier. Yugoslavia's accession to the Tripartite Pact, in effect more political than military, required Yugoslavia's neutrality with no military engagement on the Axis side. By instigating the coup, the British intended to reverse the situation in their favor. They expected the coup to provoke German retaliation, but counting on resistance from the new putschist government, they thought their plan would fall into place. The new situation appeared to be favorable for the Germans as well. Instead of crossing the Bulgarian-Greek borders, highly unfriendly to mechanized warfare, the Germans swung to the right from Bulgaria into Yugoslavia with lightning speed. Within a day or two, they managed to cut the Yugoslav forces from the Greeks and the British; the result was an open and unopposed German move into Greece.

Contrary to popular belief persisting in the historical literature, Belgrade's coup d'etat, rather than helping Greece, precipitated its fall, and had no influence on Germany's timetable with respect to invading the Soviet Union. One might conclude from the evidence that the idea of the Balkan front was an exercise in four-sided deception (the ends justifying the means). The British, the Soviets, the Americans (Donovan), and the Serbian putschists were deceiving one another for their own secret aims. The only sincere people in the Balkan conflict were the Greeks, and that was because they were real victims of unprovoked aggression. They were determined to stand and fight, provided the help promised to them arrived. Assuming that there was any truth to the delay theory of attacking the Soviet Union, the most logical assumption would be to give the Greeks their due, given that the hostility in Greece had lasted to June 1, when Crete was finally taken by German forces. Perhaps the entire credit belongs to Mussolini's ambition, without which the Balkan campaign would never have taken place.

To retrace the course of Yugoslavia's downfall, the Yugoslav army, a strictly Serbian institution, comes to mind. The condition of the army merely reflected the general state of the Yugoslav body politic. The state was run by the pan-Serbian establishment and regarded as an extension of greater Serbia. The "concessions" Paul made to the Croats (Serbo-Croatian Agreement) were given to save the monarchy on the eve of the rapidly approaching war. The agreement came too late to do any good. Neither the Croats nor the Serbs were satisfied. The Serbs outside of Paul's circle regarded it as an outright capitulation to the Croats.

Furthermore, most of the people involved in the coup were pan-Serbian in outlook, which justified Croatian suspicions that the coup was directed more against the agreement than against the Tripartite Pact and the Germans. The war records of the putschist government fully support the Croatian suspicions. The first move Foreign Minister Ninčić made was to run to the German Embassy and transmit full acceptance of the Tripartite Pact by General Simović and his government to Berlin, claiming that the coup was the internal affair of Yugoslavia and had nothing to do with Germany. When the invasion did occur, the resistance was supplanted by a "token war"—withdraw some units to join the British, and when victory was secured by the Allies, return as victors to restore the prewar model of Yugoslavia. In retracing the course of Yugoslavia's collapse, the evidence clearly demonstrates that the main cause was the nature of the Yugoslav state. As Hans Kohn has pointed out, the Serbians imagined themselves in the role of the Prussians, without the numerical and administrative superiority of the Prussian state.[2] To compensate for the lack of Prussian abilities, the Serbian establishment resorted to brutality and aggression to maintain their dominant position. "This aggressive overflow of misguided energy expressed itself . . . in Serbian policy towards . . . Croatians and Macedonians."[3] In short, Yugoslavia fell under the weight of its own weaknesses and the German forces merely pushed it into the grave.

To retain their heroic image, however, the Serbians with the help of the Allied press, shifted the blame of the Yugoslav collapse upon their former victims. The Allied and American news reports were filled with reports of Croatian treason, in which the Serbians were excused for killing "traitors" and "spies" before the war even ended. The rapid collapse of Yugoslavia was to protect Serbian pride, ostensibly explained in terms of Croatian treachery, or else trivial nonsense, such as Arthur Bliss Lane's account of Prince Paul's accession to the Tripartite Pact, purportedly to avenge his relatives in Russia who were killed by the bolsheviks.

The continuous bashing of Croats, accused not only of treason but of killing hundreds of thousands of innocent Serbs in NDH (Independent State of Croatia) even before the end of 1941, was propelled not only by the peculiar Serbian need for martyrdom, but more importantly, to cover their own misdeeds and crimes.[4] To keep their war record untarnished, they had to cover their collaborations with their enemies. Nedić, Ljotić, Kosta Pećanac, even Mihailović, all collaborated with the Germans and the Italians. While Nedić and Ljotić counted on a German victory, the others collaborated in order to liquidate the Partizan Movement and to undermine the Croatian state. Nedić's regime "distinguished" itself through the use of exceptional cruelty. Thanks to Nedić and his anti-semitic internal policy, only several months after the occupation, Belgrade was proclaimed as the first *Judenfrei* (free of Jews) city in Europe.

This peculiar Serbian inclination toward lies and deception proved hard to understand. Perhaps it is best explained by the Serbians themselves. Dobrica Ćosić, a leading Serbian writer, in his World War II novel *Deobe,* gives us a remarkable rendition of this unique Serbian phenomenon. Through his alter ego in the novel, Ćosić takes the reader through the frightful circles of an authentic Serbian soul:

> Slavery, it's what it is: deadly is the truth. For that reason, lies are told aloud and in whisper. To all and everyone. The occupiers tell lies, and the fighters for freedom tell them. We tell lies to deceive ourselves, to comfort others; we tell lies out of compassion, we tell lies to avert fear, to conceal our own misery and the misery of the others. We tell lies out of love and humanity, for the sake of honesty. We tell lies for the sake of freedom. Lie is the vision of our patriotism and the proof of our inborn intelligence. We tell lies creatively, imaginatively and inventively. Under the occupation a lie of an ordinary idiot has more imagination than of many romance novelists put together. Lie is a necessity, biological, psychological, national, political. Belgrade in these days—is an apocalypse of lies.[5]

Several chapters after the above passage, Ćosić provides another rendition of the truth, this time using an English captain who was with the Chetniks during the war. As an expert on Serbian history, he describes the Serbian national character as being exceptional and unique. "They (the Serbs) are the most veritable liars. The system of lies they use is complex and very comlicated, and for our American and British mind is quite incomprehensible."[6] Ćosić, with his reputation of being the "conscience of his time," wrote with the intention of celebrating the physical and psychological virtues of his people. For most civilized people brought up to believe that truth is a moral category and the only one that leads humanity to its deliverance, it is hard to understand, to say nothing of accepting and practicing this perversion of truth. It is also true that a novel of history such as *Deobe,* cannot replace history or historical fact, or is it intended to do so in this case. Ćosić's artistic vision of Serbia, however, does offer remarkable insight into the Serbian mind-set.[7]

In retrospect, the entire Balkan campaign was an unmitigated disaster. There were few heroes and many villains. The greatest "heroes" (the Serbians) were not any better than the villains. They had neither the strength nor the desire to fight. Their main concerns were to repudiate the "concessions" made to the Croatians, to wage a "token war" on the Allied side only to reestablish the prewar model of the Yugoslav state under their domination. Indeed, the war was not inspired by good and evil, or by right or wrong as subsequently claimed. Rather, it was ignited by a whirlpool of conflicting interests and hidden expectations that may be properly understood within the broader scope of international diplomacy. Although the Germans were made the sole scapegoats of the war, the evidence countervails such views and shows that the powers involved in the Yugoslav drama all practiced the art of deception, carefully concealed under an ideological garb that pushed Yugoslavia into war. Neither liberty nor independence, even less neutrality, can be construed as the cause of war. Rather, the power politics shaped by individual national interests proved to be the prime mover in the Balkan drama. The United States, otherwise naively perceived by most of Yugoslavia's people as the sinless giant, in practicing its brand of power politics, excelled no less than the others.

Robin Higham has given us a day-to-day account of the British policy vis-à-vis Greece. His conclusion was that Britain would have been better served if the British had fortified themselves in the Greek islands and concentrated on defending the eastern Mediterranean—thereby leaving the Balkans alone. I fully agree with Higham's assessment, except for the fact that he lost sight of Britain's motivation behind its seemingly confused strategy. In contrast to Higham, Phyllis Auty's thesis was that despair shaped Britain's policy toward Yugoslavia, and that they jumped headlong into an action that they could not control properly. By far, the best conclusion and the one closest to my own was reached by Elisabeth Barker. She concluded that Churchill's Balkan strategy reposed on the belief in Russian intervention in the Balkans. Indeed, it is demonstrated throughout the book how the strategic needs of Britain and the United States were enmeshed in an effort to create a Balkan front, in order to wage a war by proxy against Hitler's Germany. It was undoubtedly a clever gamble involving high stakes, but one based on an illusion.

In short, the policies of the major powers toward Yugoslavia were subordinated to their strategic needs, which were suitable for achieving their desired aims. When it became obvious that the communists would emerge on top, Churchill was quite explicit on the point. He told Britain's representative with the Partizans, Fitzroy Maclean, not to worry about it. After all, he was not going to live there.[8] Consequently, the interpretation of such policies was (and still is) explained in terms of their expediency in serving the needs of those victorious powers whose relation to the truth was nothing short of tenuous.

Appendix A

MEMORANDUM
Presented to
His Excellency, Franklin Delano Roosevelt
President of the United States of America
by the Croatian National Representation for the
INDEPENDENCE OF CROATIA

Pittsburgh, Pennsylvania
MAY 25, 1939

Memorandum

While the whole world trembles with the fear of war which may break out in Europe at any time, and the consequences of which cannot be foreseen, we, the CROATIAN NATIONAL REPRESENTATION, in the name of the Croatian immigrants of North and South America, representing one-fifth of the Croatian population, bring to the statesmen and the public of the world the conditions under which our people live in Yugoslavia.

We also wish to present the plea of the Croatian people, as it has been expressed in five general elections in Croatia in 1920, 1925, 1927, 1935 and 1939, for an end of the unbearable conditions in Yugoslavia. If these pleas continue to be ignored, and are not taken into consideration seriously, the terror and oppression practiced by the Belgrade government, will ultimately lead to an explosion and provoke a new world conflagration.

The Croatian People, Through Machination,
Became a Part of the Kingdom of Serbs, Croats, and Slovenes.

After the world war, by machination and against the will of the people, Croatia was annexed to Serbia, thus forming the Kingdom of Serbs, Croats, and Slovenes. The Croatian Party of Rights, and the Croatian Peasant Party, representing a majority of Croatian people, protested this illegal annexation to Prince Regent Alexander. The same protest was lodged in 1919 with the Peace Conference in a memorandum bearing 500,000 signatures. The sixty-three Croatian representatives, with Stephen Radich as their leader, who in spite of the pre-election terror received the majority of the votes of the five provinces, sent to the Geneva Conference Feb. 1922, another memorandum with which they repeatedly protested the illegal annexation of Croatia to Serbia, and refused to recognize the right of the Serbian parliament to adopt a constitution which would give all power to the Serbian government and impose the rule of the Serbian Prince Regent over Croatia.

From the very beginning the Belgrade government deprived Croatia of its local self-government and terminated its thirteen hundred years of existence as a state. Its official policy was to exploit Croatia economically, to hamper her cultural development and educational facilities, while the same government was very generous in its expenditures of State funds for the cultural and economic development of Serbia. The ultimate goal of all these policies was to weld the Croatian and Serbian people as one, while in blood, culture, and history they are not only foreign to each other, but also widely separated by their social and religious beliefs.

How Belgrade Ruled over Croatia

The Croatian Diet was closed and dissolved, and the Croatian army (Home Defenders) was disbanded through the support of the allied troops. The Croatian government with the Ban (Governor) at Zagreb was dissolved and 95% of the Croatian money was, by the order of the Belgrade government, taken out of Croatia. When the Croatian people legally protested, Belgrade answered with brute force, which was the only Serbian method of settling internal questions. The Croatians shared the fate of Macedonians, Albanians, and Montenegrins, and other national minorities. On December 5, 1918, Croatian soldiers who refused to recognize the Serbian king and the union with Serbia were shot in Zagreb at Jelachich Square. This act initiated a wave of terrorism which has kept Croatia in turmoil ever since. The Croatian Republican Peasant Party in a memorandum to Prince Regent Alexander, under the date of February 11, 1921, protested the atrocities perpetrated upon individuals during this wave of terrorism. Along with the military and the police persecutions, the Belgrade government controlled chauvinistic organizations **"Orjuna"**, **"Narodna Obrana"**, **"Srnao"**, **"Komitadjis"**, and others terrorized the whole of Croatia and committed an innumerable number of murderous attacks on prominent Croatian patriots.

Croatian Representatives Quit Parliament

Beside all the written and verbal protests against these methods throughout Croatia, as a final and most effective protest, the Croatian representatives abstained from the Belgrade Parliament from 1918 to 1925, thus refusing to participate in the governing body of Yugoslavia, and share any responsibility of governmental acts in the country.

In 1925 Stephen Radich, persuaded by English political circles, entered to the Belgrade parliament with all Croatian representatives, although the majority of the Croatian people were against such a move. Belgrade's answer to this act of reconciliation was a premeditated murderous attack on the Croatian representatives in Parliament. This attack was organized by the Belgrade Government through the Court Minister Yankovich and carried out by one of the Government representatives, Punisha Rachich, on June 20, 1928. While Parliament was in session, Rachich shot and fatally wounded Stephen Radich, his nephew Pavle Radich, and Gjuro Basarichek, while two other representatives, Dr. Pernar and Grandja barely survived their critical wounds.

This premeditated murder stunned public opinion. The Croatians and the whole cultural world expected that the Belgrade oppressors would cease to hinder the Croatian people in the realization of their national liberty. However, on January 6, 1929, King Alexander proclaimed a military dictatorship, making himself a supreme ruler, and appointed as head of the Government General Pera Zhivkovich, the commander of Royal Guard.

The military dictatorship started with the most brutal methods and with the slogan **"Destroy and wipe out Croatia from the face of the earth"**. To realize this aim the Government issued decrees which were called "laws", in order to legalize some of the worst misdeeds performed by the King.

The Reaction Against the Dictatorship

After all the terror to which the Croatian people were exposed, Dr. Vladko Matchek, the successor of Stephen Radich, while on trial in 1930 for "treason" before the Court for the Protection of the State and from the defendant's chair declared: "I am accused of creating propaganda to sever Croatia from the State and to create an independent state. I did not have to create any such propaganda, your Honor, because it would be folly to propagate something that is already here! It is not necessary to evolve any propaganda for that which starts to blaze in the hearts of our children when for the first time they sing 'Our Croatia Has Not Yet Perished'. . . It is not necessary to promulgate any propaganda for an idea with which our old men and women go to their graves...."

No, Judges of the Court, it is not necessary to propagandize something that the whole nation carries in its heart. That should not be considered as a fixed idea, but as a political conviction of a whole nation. The Croatian nation wants its INDEPENDENT STATE".

The elections of 1935 and 1938 show that the Croatian people are determined to remain true to their ideal of Independence. The twenty year "Union" of the Croatian people with Serbia has recorded thousands of murders, complete loss of all political, cultural and human rights. It has been estimated authoritatively that over 150 billions of dinars has been taken out of Croatia and carried over to Serbia. ("The Economic Foundation of the Croatian Question", by Rudolph Bićanić.) The only benefit which this "Union" produced is an unyielding determination of the Croats to fight and a stronger faith in their ideal for independence.

Terrorism

In recent years, the Belgrade Government in its struggle against the Croats has resorted to the Byzantine methods of fighting—lies and intrigue, insinuations and calumny. Croatian patriots and the whole Croatian nation were proclaimed "terrorists".

Even the League of Nations branded the Croatians as terrorists, and by doing so it supplied some states of Europe with the excuse to incarcerate and intern hundreds of Croatian patriots.

Although the enlightened public knows the real state of affairs in Yugoslavia, we wish within the limits of possibility to restrospect in detail about this slander.

Serbia—The Incubator of Terrorism

Serbia has been and is a country of terror. This fact has been corroborated by all who know the Balkan conditions, as Lady Durham, Lord Buxton and Noel Buxton; the English members of Parliament, Davis and Riley; Dr. George Desbons, French barrister; Henri Pozzi, French writer; Professors v. Loesch, Einstein, Kuziela, v. Leers, Behm and v. Bajza; Virginio Gayda, Italian Editor; Berkes and Lahman, German journalists; Miss Stimsonova, Gedye, Stephens, and Fodor, English journalists; the Carnegie International Commission to investigate the conduct of the Balkan Wars, etc.

"**Murders are the means of political strife in Serbia**", wrote Gayda. "**Belgrade believes in war as a regular means of its politics. Belgrade will again set fire to Europe**", wrote George Young, in the "New Leader" on May 29, 1928. That these assertions of an Englishman and an Italian, who are today friendly inclined toward Serbia, are truthful, we cite facts which speak clearly for themselves.

1. The Serbian diplomat and historian, Milosh Boghichevich, writes about the dynasty of Kara-George among other things, as follows:

"Kara George, the founder of the Dynasty of Karageorgevich, was a man who got mad very easily and could not control himself. In his madness he put a hive of bees on the head of his mother... He killed his father and shortly after—this time, unsuccessfully—tried to kill his brother.

"During the reign of Milosh Obrenovich, Karageorgeovich returns to Serbia but Milosh has him killed at the behest of Constantinople and sends his head to the Sultan as a gift. The Duke Milosh had to leave in 1839 on account of internal political fights in Serbia. He was succeeded by his son Mihailo, who after a short time had also to flee from Serbia. When, after the fall of Alexander Karageorgevich Mihailo Obrenovich again became Duke, he was murdered in 1868, leaving a free field for the personal ambitions of Alexander Karageorgevich, who, as is shown by official reports of the Serbian Parliament, was the master mind of this murder.

"He was succeeded by his nephew Milan, who to save his head, had to resign his succession in the year of 1903. Alexander Obrenovich Mihailo's son, and his wife, Draga, were murdered in their bedroom and the nude and mutilated bodies of the royal couple were thrown out of the window to the street. Prince Peter Karageorgevich, later King Peter, knew of the plot in its smallest detail. As proof, the meeting of the plotters at Linz, their stay at the Hotel Bigler, near Vienna, their meeting with Nanadovich, Prince Peter's cousin, who as a reward became later Minister to Constantinople." (M. Boghichevich: Colonel Apis Dimitrievich.)

2. After the Balkan wars, 1912–1913, in those parts of Macedonia and Albania which were occupied by Serbia, over 10,000 persons were killed by the Serbian officials.

The International Commission sent by the Carnegie Endowment for International Peace to investigate the conduct of the Balkan Wars in its report of 1914 writes as follows:

"From the first day of the Serbian victory at Kumanovo, there were army officers who agitated openly for the annihilation of the Albanians. The army took to this idea, and it became its slogan. Between Skopie and Kumanovo (October 1912) 3,000 Albanians were killed, women and children included;

at Terizovik (October 1912) — 5,000 Albanians beside women and children; at Senitza (October 1912) — 750 prominent Albanians; at Istok (district of Pech) in December 1912 — 90 Albanians were tortured, their hands and feet bound and then thrown under wheels of a village mill. All were dismembered alive: at Pech, (1912–1913) — 1,300 persons were killed".

3. The Montenegrin Dynasty of Petrovich-Negush was to have been annihilated before the Great War. This plot was hatched in 1908 by the Serbian Premier Pashich, but it was discovered at Podgoritza. It is interesting to note that one of the leaders of this conspiracy was Punisha Rachich who in June, 1928, massacred the Croatian Leaders in the Belgrade Parliament. (Boghichevich—"Auswertige Politik Serbiens", Report of the Foreign Minister of Montenegro P. Plamenatz, and Report of the Serbian Minister to Cetinie.)

4. A second plot for the assassination of the Montenegrin King Nikola in Paris after the World War failed only through the vigilance of the French police and the protest of the French Government. After a successful war, King Nikola, his government and his army which had saved the Serbian army, government and court from complete annihilation in their retreat through the wilderness of Albania, were not allowed to return to their country. Montenegro was occupied by Serbia through fraud and deceit.

5. When, during the World War the Croatian prisoners refused to heed the inducement of Serbian officers to leave their Russian prison camp to fight for Serbia, they were submitted to most horrible outrages and tortures and then thrown into the Black Sea. This fact, based on reports of Lieutenant Marion, was revealed by Alexander Horvat in his speeches before the Zagreb Assembly in 1917. If, at the end of 1917, the Russians themselves had not intervened in this matter, it is doubtful whether any of the Croatian war prisoners would have been saved.

6. The murder of Archduke Franz Ferdinand, in 1914 at Sarajevo, which brought about the World War, was plotted and carried out by the Serbian terroristic organization "Black Hand", a member of which was the successor to the throne, the late King Alexander. It is confirmed by the writings of the confidential counselor Goohs, Milosh Boghichevich, and especially by Ljuba Yovanovich, Serbian minister of Internal Affairs in his pamphlet, "Krv Slavenstva" (Slavic Blood), that Colonel Dimitrievich-Apis, chief of the General Staff was the leader of the organization, and Major Tankosich of the Serbian army trained the terrorists; that the participants in this murder were personally introduced to and greeted by then Prince Regent Alexander; and that the Pashich Government was fully informed about the plot. The exultation of the murderer, Gavrilo Princip, and the erection of a monument in his honor by

the Serbian Government is clear proof that his act was not the work of an individual but of the Government itself.

7. In 1917 Prince Regent Alexander and Prime Minister Pashich, at Solun (Macedonia), ordered Colonel Dimitrievich-Apis to be court-martialed. Since he knew too much about the Sarajevo crime, only death could silence him. Three of allied great powers intervened in his behalf but the Prince Regent decided to delay the delivery of their telegrams to the Government until the next morning and the great powers were told that the sentence was carried out "to their regret, at night".

8. On June 20, 1928, the Croatian leader Stephen Radich and his associates were killed in the Belgrade Parliament by Punisha Rachich, a Government member of Parliament. He was the physical murderer, but the judgment over the unfortunate Croatian representatives was pronounced by the Royal Court. This is the reason why Stephen Radich while still alive and the Croatian National Representatives brought suit against the Minister of the King's Court, Yankovich, the President of Parliament, Dr. Perich, Dr. Milan Stoyadinovich and the representatives Popovich, Boyovich, Dr. Lazitza Markovich and others as the intellectual plotters. It might be mentioned that Punisha Rachich, owing to this murder, was praised as a Serbian hero, honored by the Serbian Society, and, while in prison, openly visited by representatives of all the Serbian parties.

9. The massacre in the Belgrade Parliament of June 20, 1928, gave the signal for new terror, new persecution and new murders. Thus on January 6, 1929, the King suspended the constitution, dissolved Parliament, proclaimed military Dictatorship, and initiated the "new order". Croatia became a veritable hell. She shared the fate of Macedonia and Montenegro.

On November 6, 1930, the Croats residing in Germany presented a memorandum to the League of Nation which described the conditions in Croatia as follows:

"The process against Dr. Matchek ending in July, 1930, before the Court for the Protection of the State, brought to light and confirmed that the political prisoners had their hands and their feet chained behind their backs, were beaten on their heads till blood flowed from their mouth and nose: the guards trampled with boots over their toes, kicked the manacled prisoners, not sparing the most sensitive parts of their bodies."

"After such beatings the prisoners were thrown on the floor, with their hands and feet fastened over their backs, and then their bare feet beaten with leather straps till blood flowed. Some were tortured by hanging them on hooks on the walls or on a rifle suspended between the backs of two chairs till they fainted. To quiet the shrieks of the tortured victims, gramophones were playing at full blast while wet towels and blankets were thrown over their heads to deafen the shrieks and moans. All these tortures which the chief of police at Zagreb, Dr. Bedekovich applied on political prisoners, were confirmed by police and court physicians, but no one was held responsible for them. On the contrary, the performers of such deeds, including Dr. Bedekovich, were promoted to higher positions and rewarded. It is confirmed that in the Zagreb prison alone from the proclamation of the Dictatorship, until July 1, 1930—that is in 18 months—seventy-six persons were killed; at the 69 political trials three persons were condemned to death by hanging, one given life imprisonment, while 319 persons were sentenced to a total of 1,201 years and nine months at hard labor".

Another memorandum sent by the Croatian National Representatives, on May 12, 1931, to the League of Nations among other things, we read:

"The last twelve months, thousands of political prisoners underwent the most horrible tortures. The Zagreb City representative Dr. J. Tot, who was arrested two months earlier, was so outrageously tortured at the Zagreb police station that they had to carry him to court. The pharmacist Carlo Denes and the lawyer Dr. Ivan Lebovich also incarcerated a few months earlier had their hands and feet tied to their heads and were left in this position until they fainted. With terrible pain caused by their torture, they were not able to take any food for days. The peasant Juro Ilianich succumbed on February 17, 1931, in the Zagreb Hospital of his wounds inflicted by the police. The Technician Poropat committed "suicide" by jumping from the third floor of the prison, but it was proven that before his "suicide" he had broken ribs and other wounds. Similar treatment was given the women. Janja Oreski was beaten at the Zagreb police station although she was pregnant. Anna Mihota critically ill of tuberculosis was tortured to unconsciousness. The same happened to Mileva Birtl, Mika Yankesh, Magda Nalich, and others.

A band organized by the government, consisting mainly of police members calling themselves "Young Yugoslavia", performed atrocities in broad daylight. In such manner on February 18, 1931, the well-known Professor Milan Suflay was murdered in Zagreb. Similar was the attack on the well known Croatian writer and lawyer Dr. Mile Budak. The murder of Dr. Suflay was organized at the residence of General Belimarkovich the Military Commander at Zagreb. The Government papers, NASA SLOGA and ZASTAVA reported this murder as intended to frighten the Croatians under the caption "Prskati će čelenke". ("Skulls will burst").

10. Former Prime Minister of Yugoslavia, Dr. Milan Stoyadinovich, admitted in his pre-election speeches, December 1938, that prior to his government and since the proclamation of the Dictatorship there were 18,000 political trials, while during his tenure in office 2,000 new trials took place involving altogether over 80,000 men and women! This admission shows best what conditions prevail in contemporary Yugoslavia.

11. This state of affairs still continues. In May, 1937 at the occasion of a festival at Senj, Captain Koprivitza and the County Clerk Anton Stalio ordered their gendarmes to fire without provocation and without any warning at the 33 visitors from Gospić when the latter were returning home in a bus. The bus was riddled with bullets. Six persons were killed instantly, while, of the six wounded seriously, four later died. The investigation established that the gendarmes used "dum-dum" bullets. On some of the bodies were found as many as twenty-six wounds.

Such unbelievable atrocities took place at Virovititsa in 1936, at Posavski Brod in 1935 and at Maria Bistritsa near Zagreb in 1938, but still worse in the region of Lika in 1932–33. Here an attempt was made by the Yugoslav police to kill Dr. Andria Artukovich, who had just been released by the State Court as being innocent. The bullets aimed at Artukovich missed him, but they killed Karlo Brklachich, a Croatian member of Parliament.

Serbian Terror Outside of Yugoslavia

The terror of King Alexander's dictatorial government was not only confined to Yugoslavia, but it reached across the state borders, so that the prominent families of Kvaternik, Hranilovich, Jelich, Pavelich, Herenchich, and many others were persecuted. It is hard to describe all that was done to them.

12. Miss Eva Klapka, an American citizen from Chicago, Ill., who had gone for a visit to Yugoslavia was beaten to death. **"Died on November 22, 1921, from the abuses of the border authorities of the kingdom of Serbs, Croats and Slovenes on her return home"** — is the inscription on her tombstone in a Vienna cemetery. This is a most eloquent indictment against the Yugoslav police on the treatment of a U.S. citizen.

13. In 1929, the Italian police arrested in Livorno a Belgrade agent who was sent to kill the Croatian leader, Dr. Ante Pavelich. Pavelich and Perchec were condemned to death by Belgrade just because they visited the capital of Bulgaria and declared themselves for Croato-Macedonian friendship and cooperation.

14. In 1929, the police of Graz, Austria, Forbade Dr. Jelich to appear on the street because of the information that three Serbian commitadjis had arrived

in Graz to kill him. For his protection the police placed a guard before his residence.

15. In 1930 the Viennese police arrested three Serbian police agents who had arrived in Vienna with the intention of assassinating the Croatian patriot, Gustav Perchec.

16. In 1931 the Viennese and Graz police arrested two different bands of Belgrade hirelings, one of which was to kill the well known Croatian staff officer, Colonel Stevo Duich, and the other—Gustav Perchec. These bands were tried and sentenced in Austria.

17. In 1932 the agent provocateur Peter Gruber, with three associates arrived in Munich with the intention of killing Dr. Pavelich. Only Dr. Pavelich's self-possession and heroism saved his life and that of Colonel Perchevich, whom a Serbian reserve officer was supposed to kill in his apartment on the same day. Vjekoslav Servatzy, another Croatian patriot, was marked to be killed on the same day by a Serbian prisoner sentenced to 16 years in the penitentiary but released by the police to carry out this order. This prisoner was promised his liberty, money and other favors.

18. After these unsuccessful attempts, a certain consul-general of Yugoslavia, approached a physician (the name is withheld because his life is still in danger) to either poison Dr. Pavelich and Dr. Jelich, or to give them **scopolamin** and render them unconscious, and then transport them across the border to Yugoslavia. Besides the reward of 2,000,000 dinars, this physician was promised many privileges and favors.

19. In 1931, the Viennese police established the fact that the Serbian attaché, G. Ujchich, half an hour before the attentat on Albanian King Zog, drove with the would-be assassin through the Ring, in a taxi.

20. In November, 1934, Colonel Duich was killed at Karlsbad by the Serbian police attaché Milichevich, now with the Yugoslav Legation in Rome. He confessed before three witnesses that he organized this assassination at the order of the Belgrade government. (From the testimony of Pospishil, Raich and Kralj at the trial at Aix-Les-Bains, France).

21. In 1934 the "suicide" of the Montenegrin nationalist Petrovich in London, and the "suicide" of the prominent Serbian diplomat Milosh Boghichevich in Berlin in 1938, who uncovered the conspiratory work of the secret Belgrade forces, speak for themselves. Milosh Boghichevich, the day before his alleged suicide, wrote a letter to one of his friends about his future plans. His "suicide" took place in the house of a man whose acquaintance he made only a short time before. It is interesting that not being a lefthanded man, Boghichevich "shot himself" into his left temple and that only half an hour after the "suicide" the police attaché Ujichich, of the Yugoslav Legation in

Berlin, searched the apartment of Boghichevich, gathered his papers and sent them to Belgrade by a special courier.

Are Croats Terrorists?

While terrorism, as we have shown is the way of conducting politics in Serbia, Croats in their political life from the time of their settlement in Croatia up until 1918 did not have any idea of it. Under their kings, Tomislav and Kreshimir, in the tenth and eleventh centuries, Croatia as an independent state had signed a pact of non-aggression with the Popes, and this pact was religiously respected. History has recorded great Croatian victories, but Croatia has never attacked anyone. (Sakach: "Croatia Sacra"). In the later middle ages when the Croatian National Dynasty became extinct, Croatians formed a personal union with Hungary and from 1301 elected diverse kings. In 1526 Croats elected, on account of their fight with the Turks, that branch of the house of Habsburgs for the Croatian lands which was in power in the southern German provinces. During the time of the Turkish wars in Europe nobody gave the Turks so much resistance as the Croats. The great Byzantologue Gfrörer says that the Croats saved European civilization and Christianity. As a reward they got from the Pope the title **"Antemurale Christianitatis" (The Wall of Christendom).** When after the French Revolution and the fall of Joseph's absolutism, the Magyars wanted to place Croatia into a state of submission, the Croats did not resort to terrorism but stood up in their defense and proclaimed in 1848 war on Hungary and fought an open fight.

In the pre-war history of Croatia, when the Croatians were embittered with the politics of the Habsburg dynasty and the Magyar hegemony, they led a bitter fight, but always by legal means. The heroism and military capabilities of the Croatian people have been lauded by the foremost army leaders and statesmen of the world. **"Croatians are the best soldiers in the world. If I had 100,000 Croats, I would have conquered Europe"** — said Napoleon. Frederick the Great, Empress Maria Theresa, Commander-in-Chief Eugene Savoyski, General Montecuculi, Ahmed Cuprili Pasha, Hindenburg and Ludendorf were unanimous in their praise of Croatian heroism. Croats are peace loving people, but they could not stand with folded arms when persecuted, maltreated, dishonored, or murdered without provocation. That in self-defense they made use of the means which the existing conditions forced upon them is only natural.

Considering these facts on one hand, and on the other that King Alexander in proclaiming his dictatorship formally accepted all the responsibilities, it should be clear that his end in Marseilles was only the logical consequence of his misrule.

The task of the League of Nations was to create a friendly association of nations. Its failure is due to the partiality towards some of the victorious nations, while it completely disregarded the complaints of the vanquished states and oppressed minorities. After the Marseilles event Yugoslavia made an attempt in the League of Nations to place the blame on Hungary, although neither state, nor any other had anything to do Alexander's assassination. The Council of the League of Nations refused to hear the facts of the unbearable conditions and the reign of terror in Yugoslavia. Such revelations could cast the shadow of guilt and responsibility not only on Yugoslavia, but on the League of Nations as well. The Hungarian representative Dr. Eckhardt was prevented from exposing the material and psychological reasons that brought forth the King's death.

The League of Nations ignored all the memoranda and complaints of Croatians, Macedonians, Montenegrins, Albanians, Magyars and Germans, dealing with the violation of the peace treaties which the Yugoslav government had signed and pledged to respect. Their numerous appeals for protection and justice brought no results. To their legal efforts for a peaceful solution of all the differences, the Serbs answered with unheard of terror. The only open way left to them for the protection of their properties and rights, honor and lives, was **armed resistance. They had no alternative but to meet force with force.**

Croatia Demands Freedom

Today when the world looks for a way to prevent a new war, we wish to call your attention to the appaling state of affairs in Yugoslavia and to present to you our demands:

That the historic 1300-year-old Croatian state rights and inalienable rights of self-determination of the Croatian people to proclaim their independence be recognized. These rights could be best ascertained and expressed through the principle of self-determination to which the Croatian people in the five Croatian provinces of Bosnia, Herzegovina, Slavonia with Srem, Dalmatia and Banovina, have always been ready and willing to ascribe. To secure the fullest freedom of expression of the people's will, the recall of the Serbian army from the above mentioned five provinces should be imperative.

That the Serbian troops should be recalled from Macedonia, Montenegro and Voivodina and that in these countries plebiscites should be also held under an objective neutral control so that the respective people's can decide for themselves about their future destiny:

That the representatives of Croatia and Serbia and of all other peoples of Yugoslavia should meet under the control of the great powers regarding agree-

ments and compensations which Serbia, by its plundering and the confiscating of the property of these nations, is due to repay to them.

All these governments, institutions and individuals, which either actively or passively support the present Yugoslav government and oppose our demands, do not have the moral right to speak of liberty, democracy and righteousness, while their eventual support of some oppressed nation is nothing but a new subterfuge for their hidden imperialistic aims.

The Croatian people, in collaboration with other nations and the national minorities of Yugoslavia numbering over ten millions, will not any longer endure the oppression and destruction of a slight minority of four million Serbs. But, in their struggle for self-preservation, Croats will be forced to avail themselves of any means which will secure their freedom and independence.

Respectfully submitted,
Croatian National Representation for
THE INDEPENDENCE OF CROATIA

Dr. J. F. Skafec, President
Rev. Oscar Suster, Detroit, Mich.
Nikola Sulentich, Waterloo, Ia.
Rev. Dobr. Sorich, Pittsburgh, Pa.

Karlo Krmpotich, Wlkinsburg, Pa.
Rev. Ivan Juricek, Omaha, Neb.

Frank Budak, Campbell, Ohio.
Rev. Karlo Stimac, Kansas City, Kan.
Pavle Starcevich, Keewatin, Minn.
Rev. Hugo Feis, St. Louis, Mo.
Ing. Slavko Duich, Chicago, Ill.
Rudolf Erich, Akron, Ohio.
Rev. F. Pehar, St. Louis, Mo.
Stjepan Salopek, San Francisco, Cal.
Ivan Artukovich, Los Angeles, Cal.
Rev. Bono Andacich, St. Louis, Mo.

Mirko Jalsich, Secretary
Jack Jakovac, Youngstown, Ohio
Ivo Metkovich, Los Angeles, Cal.
Rev. A. Sliskovich, Farrell-
    Sharon, Pa.
Josip Sulentich, Eveleth, Minn.
I. Horvatinovich, New York,
    N.Y.
Ana Tuskan, Chicago, Ill.
Pavao Kufrin, Chicago, Ill.
Louis Matanovich, Omaha, Neb.
Mile Persich, So. Chicago, Ill.
Stjepan Jukovcich, Detroit, Mich.
Josip Bogdanich, E. Chicago, Ill.
Steve Kukuruzovich, Gary, Ind.
Daniel Duich, Chicago, Ill.
Ivan Budak, N. Chicago, Ill.
Luka Grbich, Pittsburgh, Pa.

Appendix B

British Embassy,
Washington, D.C.
March 27th, 1941.

I enclose herein two copies of the further telegram from Belgrade which the Prime Minister wishes communicated [*sic*]to the President. Would you therefore please be kind enough to attach these copies to the two letters, one for the President and one for Mr. Welles, which I left with you earlier this afternoon.

Mr. R. Atherton,
  United States Department of State,
  Washington, D.C.

*Telegram Sent by British Minister in Belgrade
to Foreign Office on March 26th, 1941.*

At my request I was afforded an interview with General Simovitch (chief of Yugoslav Air Force) this morning. As this officer is head of an organisation intending to carry out a coup d'etat meeting was arranged with great secrecy. The General seemed to be in very good health and had an appearance of alertness, energy and ability which I have rarely observed among senior officers in Serbian Army. He was confident in his speech but cautious in his utterances and gave the impression of sincerity, truthfulness and a belief in what he said. For the sake of simplicity in recording a conversation which ranged over various subjects it is summarized as follows:

(a) He stated that there was no doubt that the country felt very strongly about signing of pact with Germany and wished to repudiate both the pact and present Government. They understood that this almost certainly meant war and they preferred this alternative to continuing on present lines.

(b) There existed an organisation which was working for the overthrow of the present Government. General had confidence in its success and he asked us to have confidence in it and him. We should not have to sit more than a few days before coup d'etat.

(c) He was anxious to know how many troops we had in Greece and hoped that we would send a great many there and that we intended to defend Salonica. I replied that we must consider our left flank and this depended a great deal on the Serbs.

(d) He foresaw that Yugoslavia would go to war in Albania immediately after the coup d'etat. He asked if Turks would then join in to which I replied that it was very possible but that I had no positive assurance regarding exact circumstances he described.

(e) He then asked what could the British do to help Yugoslavia if she went to war against the Italians, Bulgarians, and Germans. I replied in the sense of Secretary of State's telegram from Cairo of March 25th. He seemed impressed by conception of a common pool for materials and asked if it included supply of food to which I replied that although I spoke on this matter without precise authority, I felt sure that it did.

(f) He appeared to be disappointed that we could not promise precise numbers and quantities of war material but agreed that they should do well out of Italian loot in Albania. He feared however that types of weapons were not the same and that Italian ammunition could not therefore reinforce Yugoslav units. Reserves of 76.5 and 75 mm. ammunition for field artillery would be required.

(g) In answer to a question he replied that the Prince Regent and even the President of the Council appeared to be very depressed over the signing of the pact. This may indicate that the Prince Regent intends to try and remain in power in the event of the Government being overthrown. From an officer on General Simovitch's staff I hear that it is intended to hand the Prince Regent over to the British.

The impression I gained from journalists as a whole was that the General was now committed to a course of action from which nothing would deter him. Please inform General Wavell for his own secret information, but otherwise regard as highly secret as any leakage would compromise chance of success for the *coup d'etat*.

Notes

Introduction

1. Harding's secretary came to see the author and asked for the copy. Franjo Dujmović, *Hrvatska Na Putu k Oslobodjenju* (Rome-Chicago: Ziral, 1976), 70. The book was translated into Croatian in 1943. After the war, the communists shot the translator, indicating how damaging the book was for Yugoslavia.
2. Henri Pozzi, *Black Hand over Europe* (London: Mott, 1935), 75.
3. Ibid., 245.
4. In his political reminiscence, *Političke Upomene i Rad Dra Branimira Jelića* (Cleveland: Mirko Šamija, 1984), 82–85, Dr. Branimir Jelić, one of the closest associates of the head of the Ustaša Movement, Dr. Ante Pavelić, made some interesting observations about Pribićević, whom he met in Paris in 1933. According to Jelić, Pribićević underwent such a personal and political change that he was personally prepared to accept confederation and even an independent Croatia, although he would much rather have found a solution to the Croatian question within the frame of the Yugoslav state. In his letter to August Košutić, vice president of the Croatian Peasant Party, Pribićević confirmed his meeting with Jelić but clearly emphasized his belief in the solution within Yugoslavia to avoid more serious complications. See Ljubo Boban, *Svetozar Pribićević u Opoziciji*, 222–25. Most historians agree that Pribićević was sincere in changing his mind and that he was steadfast in his belief in Yugoslavia, providing Serbian hegemony was removed. They also agree that he had a negligible influence on his followers in the Independent Democratic Party (mostly Serbs from Croatia) who were in favor of maintaining a closer association with Belgrade. See also Hrvoje Matković, *Svetozar Pribićević*.
5. *Manchester Guardian*, December 24, 1932. The signatories were James Berry, Edward Boyle, Roland Bryce, Victor Cazalet Cushendun, Sir Arthur Evans, H. A. L. Fisher, G. P. Gooch, Ellinor F. C. Grogan, Harry Lamb, Gilbert Murray, H. W. Nevinson, Noel Buxton, Ben Riley, R. W. Seton-Watson, Wickham Steed, and Gertrude F. Wilde.
6. *R. W. Seton-Watson and the Yugoslavs: Correspondence 1906–1941* (London-Zagreb: British Academy and University of Zagreb — Institute of Croatian History, 1976), 2: 193–200.
7. Ibid., 202.
8. Ivan Meštrović, *Uspomene na Političke Ljude*, 249–50.
9. Ibid., 173–75.
10. Ante Smith-Pavelić, "Jugoslavija i Trojni Pakt," *Hrvatska Revija* (Buenos Aires, 1956), 1: 65–88.
11. Ibid.

Chapter 1. The American Perception of Yugoslavia on the Eve of World War II: Origins of an Illusion

1. Frieda Fordham, *An Introduction to Jung's Psychology* (Baltimore: Penguin Books, 1954), 69–82.
2. Herbert Butterfield, *The Whig Interpretation of History* (London: G. Bell, 1959), 110.
3. Raymond W. Stedman, *Shadows of the Indian Stereotypes in American Culture* (Norman: University of Oklahoma Press, 1982), ix.
4. Talvi, *Historical View of the Languages and Literatures of the Slavic Nations with a Sketch of Their Popular Poetry* (New York: Putman, 1850).
5. *North American Review*, 70, nos. 146–47 (January, 1850): 78–136, 369–91, and 473–520.
6. Reginald Horsman, *Race and Manifest Destiny: The Origins of American Racial Anglo-Saxonism* (Cambridge: Harvard University Press, 1981), 67.
7. Following the romantic aesthetic canons, Talvi elevated Serbian epic poetry to unimaginable heights, saying that such poetry had no comparison in the history of literature since Homer's time.
8. Herbert Adams Gibbons, *The Foundation of the Ottoman Empire: A History of the Osmanlis up to the Death of Bayazid I, 1300–1403* (Oxford: Clarendon, 1916), 86.
9. Stephen L. E. Lazarovich-Hrebelianovich et al., *The Servian People: Their Past Glory and Their Destiny*, 2 vols. (New York: Scribner, 1910). The author claimed that his family name could be traced to the last medieval Serbian ruler, Prince Lazar. He was married to a great grandniece of the well-known senator from South Carolina, John Calhoun. Inspired by Serbian patriotism, they wrote these two volumes together. With the same patriotic zeal, Lazarovich-Hrebelianovich wrote another book based on his lectures at Stanford University in 1912, under the title *The Orient Question To-day and To-morrow* (New York: Duffield, 1913). His princely origin was ridiculed among the Serb community in the United States, but because of his connections to American high society, he was used in propaganda against the Croatians, especially by the Yugoslav ambassador to Washington, Konstantin Fotić, during World War II.
10. An impressive work dealing with the relations between the Yugoslav Committee and the Serbian government was written by a Czech historian: Milada Paulova, *Jugoslavenski odbor. Povijest jugoslavenske emigracije za svjetskog rata od 1914–1918* (Zagreb: Prosvjetna Nakladna Zadruga, 1925); see also Ivan Meštrović's account of the events. Meštrović, *Uspomene na Političke Ljude*, 41–132. See also Vaso Bogdanov et al., *Jugoslavenski obor u Londonu* (Zagreb: JAZU, 1966).
11. Woislav M. Petrovitch [Petrović], *Serbia: Her People, History, and Aspirations* (London: Harrap, 1915), 7–14. Petrović also wrote other books covering the Serbian language and literature, all of which followed Karadžić's philological formulas. He therefore promoted Karadžić's views of Serbia's territorial claims. Accordingly, Serbia consisted of "Old Serbia, Macedonia, Bosnia and Herzegovina, Montenegro, Dalmatia, Batchka, Banat, Croatia, Sirmia, and Istria." In short, the whole territory of Yugoslavia, minus Slovenia. His other contribution to the Serbian cause was that by his insistence, the name of Servia was changed to Serbia for the first time. After World War I, Petrović left Yugoslavia, claiming that the Serbian police were after him for having discovered a Serbian plot to

assassinate Franz Ferdinand. Under somewhat mysterious circumstances, Petrović died in London a broken man (November, 1934).

12. Leon Dominian, *Frontiers of Language and Nationality in Europe* (New York: Holt, 1917), 174–91.

13. Ibid., 185. Basing his views on purely fictitious findings of Serbian scholars, Dominian also concluded that Serbian was spoken in the "provinces of Croatia, Slavonia, Bosnia and Herzegovina, and Dalmatia." Ibid., 182.

14. C. Townley-Fullam, "Panslavism in America," *Forum* 52 (August, 1914): 185. The author disliked the South Slav Movement in America and advised Croatians to stay within the Habsburg monarchy. "Concentrate on the logic of the situation and the temper of the age. Work for federation, in which not only you but the components of the monarchy itself must ultimately seek salvation. That is true service to the Crown. Pause before throwing in your future with a civilization admittedly upon the lower plane: salvation never yet lay in descend. Above all, come before the world with clean hands; blood is hopelessly out of fashion, at best a vulgar argument."

15. In 1916, Father Martin Krmpotić published his well-documented pamphlet, "Croatia, Bosnia and Herzegovina, and the Servian claims" in Kansas City, Kansas. He exposed Serbian claims on Bosnia and Herzegovina as unfounded. He also wrote the first article on Croatia in an American encyclopedia, *The Catholic Encyclopedia* (New York: The Encyclopedia Press, 1907), s.v. "Croatia." It was, without doubt, the most serious article about Croatia that had ever appeared in the United States. The Croatian immigrants were disunited and disoriented on the topic of a future common state with the Serbs. See James J. Sadkovich, "The Mobilization of Croatian Immigrant Opinion," 94–120.

16. Paul R. Radosavljevich, *Who Are The Slavs?*, 2 vols. (Boston: Bagder, 1919).

17. The literature on Stjepan Radić is extensive. Apart from theses and dissertations, however, no books have been published on his life and work in English. Some useful books in Croatian are: Vladimir Radić, *Zločin 20. Lipnja i Medjunarodna Štampa* (Zagreb: 1931); Zvonimir Kulundžić, *Atentat na Stjepana Radića;* Stjepan Radić, *Politički Spisi, Govori i Dokumenti: Izbor* (Zagreb: Dom i Svijet, 1994); Ivan Mužić, *Stjepan Radić;* Franjo Tudjman, *Stjepan Radić.*

18. George J. Prpić, *The Croatian Immigrants in America,* 247. See also Mužić, *Stjepan Radić,* 70–71.

19. Pozzi, *Black Hand over Europe,* 77.

20. For a better understanding of the Italo-Yugoslav conflict, see Ivo J. Lederer, *Yugoslavia at the Paris Peace Conference;* Rene Albrecht-Carrie, *Italy at the Paris Peace Conference;* James H. Burgwyn, *The Legend of the Mutilated Victory.*

21. The best account of Italo-Croatian relations can be found in James J. Sadkovich, "Italian Support for Croatian Separatism."

22. Ivan Meštrović, *Uspomene na Političke Ljude,* 259.

23. Pozzi, *Black Hand over Europe,* xi–xxii; Ljubo Boban, *Sporazum Cvetković -Maček,* 31.

24. As an agricultural land, Yugoslavia was among the first to be included within German *Wirtschaftraum.* The initial stages were facilitated by Franco-English rivalry. While the French, for military reasons, feared the German economic recovery, the British took the position that the recovery would be beneficial for all. Disliking French control of Europe, the British, acting in conformity with their

economic policy, tacitly approved German economic penetration into the area. See Paul Kennedy, *The Realities behind Diplomacy*. Other literature on the subject: Dietrich Orlow, *The Nazis in the Balkans;* Johann Wüescht, *Jugoslawien und das Dritte Reich;* Dušan Lukač, *Treći Rajh i Zemlje Istočne Evrope*. The rearmament industry that the Nazis initiated after they came to power served two purposes—to arm Germany and to export arms as a means of gaining political influence. For a detailed account of German export of arms to Yugoslavia, see Leposava Cvijetić, "Prodaja Naoružanja," 172–253.

25. Rev. John Stipanivić to Senator Robert J. Buckley, September 23, 1933; O.F. 364A, Box 1, F.T. Yugoslav crisis, 1939–40, Franklin Delano Roosevelt Library, Hyde Park, New York. Hereafter, FDR Library. In their frequent appeals to Roosevelt, the Croatians exhibited not only tenacity but naivete as well. They never seemed to have understood that in American foreign policy, Wilson was the exception rather then the rule. Whatever Wilson's merit, the truth of the matter was that when the Inquiry Commission was set up in New York in 1917, no one mentioned Croatians or their rights to self-determination. According to the plan devised by the commission, the Austro-Hungarian Empire was to remain intact, and only Serbians and Czechs were assured of internal autonomy within the empire. Other nationalities, including Croatians, were encouraged to push their claims, but Vienna was "given assurance that no dismemberment of the Empire [was] intended." Ronald Steel, *Walter Lippmann and the American Century*, 134–36. See also Arthur S. Link, ed., *The Papers of Woodrow Wilson*, 51: 383. Under pressure from the emigre groups (Croatian and Slovenian) operating in the United States and other Allied countries, and aided by an impressive number of British intellectuals—Sir Arthur Evans, Wickham Steed, R. W. Seton-Watson, etc.,—Wilson changed his mind and took upon himself to champion the cause of the southern Slav nationalities. His ardent support brought him in conflict, not only with Italians over the secret London Treaty, but with his own people as well. Almost all nonacademic members of the U.S. Peace Delegation were solidly against Wilson. They worked hard behind Wilson's back to support Italian claims on the eastern shore of the Adriatic. Their argument was that the Italians were racially superior and therefore should be awarded the promised territories. Robert J. Kerner, "Yugoslavia and the Peace Conference," 96. Walter Lippmann, a prominent member of the Inquiry Commission, looked with apprehension upon the new course of American policy vis-à-vis Vienna, and many years later said that it "destroyed the political balance of Central Europe and opened the way to Hitler." Steel, *Walter Lippmann and the American Century*, 135.

26. Hamilton Fish Armstrong, "After the Assassination of King Alexander." As a young man, Armstrong was sent to Belgrade where he befriended King Alexander. He considered the Serbs to be the main force in Yugoslavia and used *Foreign Affairs* as the forum for his views and ideas. While refusing to write anything negative about Yugoslavia, he considered Croatians weak, and therefore, of no importance. Bogdan Radica, *Živjeti-Nedoživjeti*, 2: 151.

27. Henry C. Wolfe, "Yugoslavia's Design for Democracy."

28. Harold L. Ickes, *The Secret Diary*, 2: 54.

29. Stephen E. Ambrose, *Rise to Globalism*, 1.

30. Armstrong, "The Royal Dictatorship in Yugoslavia," 601–603.

31. Marie S. Good, "International Politics," 77.

32. Vladimir Petrov, *A Study in Diplomacy,* 104–105.
33. Reuben Markham, "Croats Revolt Against the Serbs."
34. Charles A. Beard, "Autobiography of Stephen Raditch," 84.
35. Pozzi, *Black Hand over Europe,* 96.
36. Ivan Meštrović, *Uspomene na Političke Ljude,* 188.
37. Ibid., 189–91. In a desperate attempt to improve his cause, Radić sought support throughout Europe. The support, however, was denied; hence the reason for his trip to Moscow. Ideologically they were worlds apart; Radić told the Soviet commissars that his Peasant Party's ideology was superior to theirs. For tactical reasons, Radić included the Croatian Peasant Party into the Peasant International. Belgrade took advantage of this and accused him and the party of being communists.
38. Prpić, *Croatian Immigrants,* 247.
39. Robert J. Bulkley to Louis M. Howe, September 29, 1933, O.F. 364A, Box 1, F.T. Yugoslav crisis, 1933–40, FDR Library; Louis M. Howe to Robert J. Buckley, October 4, 1933, O.F. 364A, Box 1, F.T. Yugoslav crisis, 1933–40, FDR Library.
40. U.S. State Department to Louis M. Howe, December 7, 1933. O.F. 364A, Box 1, F.T. Yugoslav crisis, 1933–40, FDR Library.
41. James C. Dunn to Colonel McIntyre, December 12, 1934, O.F. 364A, Box 1, F.T. Yugoslav crisis, 1939–40. FDR Library.
42. Ibid.
43. A. J. Sabath to Brig. Gen. Edwin M. Watson, May 25, 1939, O.F. 364A, Box 1, F.T. Yugoslav crisis, 1939–40. FDR Library.
44. Edwin M. Watson to George T. Summerlin, June 1, 1939, O.F. 364A, Box 1, F.T. Yugoslav crisis, 1939–40. FDR Library.
45. Ibid.
46. Croatian National Representation Memorandum Presented to Franklin D. Roosevelt, May 25, 1939, O.F. 364A, Box 1, F.T. Yugoslav crisis, 1939–40. FDR Library. For the full text of the Memorandum, see Appendix A.
47. Moffat to Roosevelt, U.S. Department of State, Doc. no. 860H.00/1021. National Archives, Washington, D.C.
48. U.S. Department of State, Doc. no. 860H.00/1024. National Archives, Washington, D.C.
49. Moffat to Roosevelt, U.S. Department of State, Doc. no. 860H.00/1021. National Archives, Washington, D.C.
50. Barbara W. Tuchman, *Practicing History: Selected Essays* (New York: Alfred A. Knopf, 1981), 289.
51. Radica, *Živjeti-Nedoživjeti,* 2: 426.

Chapter 2. Croato-Serbian Rapprochement in Light of American Diplomacy

1. Maček was released from prison at the end of 1934, after the assassination of King Alexander. Prince-Regent Paul sounded out the Croatian leader regarding the Yugoslav crises. The conditions that Maček put forth entailed starting anew from the way things were in 1918. Given the political situation and the fact that Paul was a novice in the art of Yugoslav politics, Maček's conditions could hardly be considered. Maček's demands notwithstanding, Paul let him express his views freely. Informing R. W. Seton-Watson about the talks with Paul, Vice President

of the Croatian Peasant Party August Košutić pointed out that Paul was a man of culture and, unlike Alexander, no enemy of the Croats. Although nothing of substance was achieved, contacts were kept open through various channels between Maček and the Prince, with the intent of finding an equitable solution when the situation permitted. See Boban, *Maček i Politika,* 172–79.

2. Petrov, *Study in Diplomacy,* 103–10. It is regrettable that no one read the reports sent to Washington by Ambassadors John D. Prince (1926–33) and Charles S. Wilson (1934–37). Their reports, although often permeated by a pro-government bias, nevertheless demonstrated a keen observation of Yugoslavia's internal affairs. Most of the reports are invaluable for study, not so much for American-Yugoslav relations, but more so for their concern of the sociopolitical conditions in Yugoslavia. Both ambassadors often referred to the Belgrade regime as being brutal, resting on crude military power. John D. Prince was particularly eloquent in condemning Belgrade for the assassination of the Croatian leadership in 1928. See also N.A., Records of the U.S. Department of State Relating to the Internal Affairs of Yugoslavia, 1910–29 and 1930–34. Microfilm.

3. Ambrose, *Rise to Globalism,* 1.

4. Petrov, *Study in Diplomacy,* 110.

5. Edwin M. Borchard to Senator Key Pittman, May 22, 1933, Committee Papers, U.S. Senate Committee on Foreign Relations, SEN 734-10 (112B), N.A., Washington, D.C. Taken from Edward M. Bennett, *Franklin D. Roosevelt and the Search,* 4.

6. *Chicago Daily News,* September 21, 1938.

7. For a detailed analysis of the period, see Wayne S. Cole, *Roosevelt and the Isolationists.*

8. William L. Langer and S. Everett Gleason, *The Challenge to Isolation,* 11–15.

9. Robert Dallek, *Franklin D. Roosevelt and American Foreign Policy,* 20.

10. George F. Kennan, *Memoirs: 1925–1950,* 57.

11. Lane to U.S. Department of State, Doc. no. 860H.00/974. National Archives, Washington, D.C.; Joyce to U.S. Department of State, Doc. no. 860H.00/985.

12. Petrov, *Study in Diplomacy,* 106.

13. Joyce to U.S. Department of State, Doc. nos. 860H.00/985 and 860H.00/978.

14. Stojadinović won by 279,259 votes.

15. From "reliable sources," Paul found out that his overly ambitious prime minister had committed outright treason. In case of war, Stojadinović and Ciano had agreed to dissect Croatia. The western part would go to Italy, while the rest would be incorporated into greater Serbia. Furthermore, Stojadinović had struck another deal with Ciano (again without Paul's knowledge) to trade Yugoslav neutrality in the forthcoming Italian invasion of Albania for some of Albania's northern territories. Unfortunately for Stojadinović, that was not all. Paul discovered from his German sources that Hitler also had far-reaching plans for the Yugoslav prime minister, having ordered a diadem for Stojadinović's wife, who incidentally, was a German. See Dragoslav Georgevich [Dordević], *Na Raskrsnici,* 132. The British supported Paul in dismissing Stojadinović, but not so much for his treasonable activities as for his psychological propensity for fascism. Stojadinović, on the other hand, defended (in his boastful manner) his policy on the grounds that it would have enabled Yugoslavia to stay away from the Tripartite Pact, while enjoying all the benefits accorded to the member states. In keeping with this view and given Yugoslavia's catastrophic end, Stojadinović blamed

Paul for his dismissal from power. See Milan Stojadinović, *Ni Rat ni Pakt*. Prince Paul informed Ivan Meštrović that according to Ciano-Stojadinović agreement, Italy was prepared to give full support to Serbian aspiration to create Great Serbia. The new Serbian state would include the territories in Greece (Salonika) and the northern half of Albania. In return, Belgrade would relinquish the western parts of Yugoslavia to Italy. When Meštrović remarked that such an act was a tantamount to treason and required punishment outright, Paul agreed, but added that because of Stojadinović's Italian and German protectors he was not in position to do anything. All he could do was to hand him over to the British. Ivan Meštrović, *Uspomene na Političke Ljude*, 290–91.

16. The draft of the April 27 agreement was short and contained only three provisions, relative to territory, jurisdiction of the central government in Belgrade, and the formation of a joint government. "The definite borders of Croatia were to be determined by a plebiscite on the rest of the territory of Bosnia and Herzegovina and Srijem." For the full text of the proposed agreement, see Branko Pešelj, "Serbo-Croatian Agreement," 15–16.

17. Hull to Joyce. Doc. no. 860H.00/982.

18. Prior to Hull's telegram, American diplomatic representatives assigned to Yugoslavia were under strict orders not to have any contact with the Croatian opposition. See Pavle Ostović, *The Truth about Yugoslavia*, 128. See also Vladimir Maček, *In the Struggle for Freedom*, 265.

19. Joyce to Hull, Doc. no. 860H.00/980.

20. Petrov, *Study in Diplomacy*, 110–11.

21. Lane to U.S. Department of State, Doc. no. 860H.00/991.

22. Hull to MacMurray, Doc. no. 860H.00/966.

23. Lane to U.S. Department of State, Doc. nos. 860H.00/1001, 860H.00/1005, and 860H.00/1007.

24. Martin Van Creveld, *Hitler's Strategy*, 188, 23 n.

25. Prince Philip of Hesse delivered Hitler's spoken message to Mussolini—postpone the invasion for another two years, at which time the Prussian divisions would number one hundred. DGFP, Series D, Vol. 5, Doc. no. 5. Mussolini told Ciano that if he relayed the message to the Italian people, they would laugh at him. Galeazzo Ciano, entry for March 15, 1939.

26. On February 7, 1939, Ciano told *Il Duce* that without Stojadinović, the "Yugoslav card" decreased by 90 percent of its value for Italy. Furthermore, since the invasion would not be undertaken in conjunction with Yugoslavia (but without it, or perhaps against it), the speed of action was essential, so as not to give time for Yugoslavia to strengthen its political, diplomatic, and military position. Ciano, entry for February 7, 1939.

27. Boban, *Sporazum Cvetković-Maček*, 111–19. Maček never admitted that he initiated contacts with Ciano. For his side of the story, see Maček, *In the Struggle for Freedom*, 157. Contrary to Maček's denial, it has been established in the historiography relating to Italo-Croatian and Italo-Yugoslav relations that Maček used the Italians to pressure Belgrade (to settle the Croatian question). For the same reason, Maček kept secret contacts with Pavelić and his Ustaša groups abroad for as long as it was useful to his political program in dealing with Belgrade. No less opportunistic were the Italians who used the Croats to settle their differences with Belgrade. It was a marriage of convenience on both sides. Maček, however, unlike Pavelić, never seriously considered breaking away from Belgrade

by bringing the Italians to Croatia, especially after Prince Paul became the regent. The best reading on the subject can be found in Sadkovich's previously cited dissertation and in his numerous articles: James J. Sadkovich, "Oportunismo Esitante: Appogiare Il Separatismo Croato: 1927–1929," *Storia Contemporanea* 16(3) Bologna (1985): 401–26; "Terrorism in Croatia"; "The Use of Political Trials." For Italian authors dealing with the same subject see Antonio Tasso, *Italia e Croazia;* Alfredo Breccia, *Jugoslavia, 1939–1941.* Croatian author Ljubo Boban dealt extensively with the subject of Maček's connections to the Italians in his book, *Maček i Politika.* Ante Smith-Pavelić too shares the views that Maček's connection with Rome were designed to pressure Belgrade and to show Prince Paul that Zagreb too can negotiate with Mussolini. Smith-Pavelić, "Jugoslavia i Trojni pakt," 72. See also Milan Martinović, "Moje uspomene na veliko doba" in *Kalendar Hrvatskog glasa,* Winnipeg, 1958.

28. Prince Paul told Lane that Germany would not take Croatia, but the cynical Italians were now endeavoring to bring the Serbs and Croats together. Some "responsible" Italian official confided to Lane that the Germans had intentions of taking Croatia in order to gain access to the Adriatic. FRUS, 1939, 1: 82. In conversation with Ciano, Mussolini pointed out that German "power mania and arrogance" might lead Berlin to strike at Italian interests as well. He therefore suggested setting the objectives that would guide Italo-German relations. Ciano, entry for March 22, 1939.

29. Ibid., entry for February 5, 1939. Fearing the Germans, Mussolini even contemplated an Albanian invasion because it might disturb the unity of Yugoslavia and favor an independent Croatia under German rule. Ibid., entry for March 16, 1939.

30. Ibid., entry for March 17 and March 20, 1939. The Germans informed the Italians that they had no interests whatsoever in Croatia, or had they any desires for independent actions that might be detrimental to Italian interests. The Germans were adamant that no Croatian emissaries make contacts with any official German agencies in Prague. See also DGFP, Series D, Vol. 6, Doc. no. 15.

31. DGFP, Series D, Vol. 5, Doc. no. 310.

32. Van Creveld, *Hitler's Strategy,* 7.

33. Balfour and Mackay, *Paul of Yugoslavia: Britain's Maligned Friend,* 172.

34. DGFP, Series D, Vol. 6, Doc. nos. 262, 271, and 279.

35. FRUS, 1939, Vol. 2, 370–71. At the request of the British foreign secretary Lord Halifax, Mussolini extended formal assurances to Greece, which was instrumental in guarding British commercial lanes in the eastern Mediterranean. *Il Duce* communicated to the effect that Italy would respect Greece's independence and its territorial integrity, both continental and insular. Ibid., 392–93. Similar information was given to Cordell Hull by the British ambassador in Washington on April 11, 1939. Ibid., 397–98.

36. DGFP, Series D, Vol. 6, Doc. no. 205.

37. Balfour and Mackay, *Paul of Yugoslavia,* 173–74; Breccia, *Jugoslavia, 1939–1941,* 103–105.

38. Lane to U.S. Department of State, Doc. no. 740H.00/1714. After the agreement, Paul reversed his opinion about Maček and considered him to be reliable and the most honest of all Yugoslav politicians, 605–11.

39. Ciano, entries for March 30 and April 1, 1939. When Bombelles visited Ciano on March 9, 1939, the latter was careful not to reveal his suspicions that Bombelles

was Paul's agent. If Ciano really suspected Bombelles, then why did Ciano arrange for him to meet with Pavelić? Almost a year later, Ciano found out from Pavelić that Bombelles was Paul's spy. Introducing himself as Maček's agent, Bombelles needed to find out the full extent of Maček's involvement with the Italians and Pavelić before Paul visited Italy. Breccia, *Jugoslavia, 1939–1941*, 46–49. Another curious matter was that Bombelles introduced himself as Maček's agent, but in the English translation of Ciano's *Diario*, his role was translated as being Pavelić's agent. In his book, Antonio Tasso came to the correct conclusion that Bombelles was a triple agent, working for Paul, Maček, and Pavelić. *"Come ben si vede, il conte Bombelles faceva un doppio, anzi un triplo giuoco."* Tasso, *Italia e Croazia*, 1: 151.

40. Walter Hagen, *Die Geheime Front*, 119–20.

41. Ciano, entry for May 26, 1939; Breccia, *Jugoslavia, 1939–1941*, 110–14. Carnelutti, together with Bombelles, translated Ciano's response to Maček's request into Croatian. Bombelles requested a meeting with Pavelić, supposedly to sound him out regarding Maček's proposal. Breccia, *Jugoslavia, 1939–1941*, 113. Given Bombelles's role, there is no doubt that Paul was well-informed on the state of Croato-Italian relations. cf. Tasso, *Italia e Croazia*, 1: 150–52.

42. Lane to U.S. Department of State, Doc. no. 860H.00/1028.48; Ibid., Doc. no. 860H.00/1040.49; Ibid., Doc. no. 860H.00/1037.

43. FRUS 1940, 2: 714.

44. For the text of the agreement between Ciano and Pavelić, see DDI, Nova Series, 1939–43, vol. 3. It is worth noting that Pavelić spoke of the Italo-Croatian union as a powerful deterrent (*un colpo di arresto*) against German penetration in the region. The British ambassador in Belgrade, Sir Ronald Campbell, communicated to London that Maček looked upon Paul's visits to Rome and Berlin with displeasure. Consequently, Maček was prepared to do precisely the opposite of what Belgrade was doing. Campbell's remark was that Maček's idea of himself exceeded his importance, and he advised London to refrain from giving any support that he might interpret as encouragement for his obstinacy. Boban, *Maček i Politika*, 109.

45. Joyce to U.S. Department of State, Doc. no. 860H.00/1046.

46. Ibid.

47. Sir Ronald Campbell to the Foreign Office. Taken from Balfour and Mackay, *Paul of Yugoslavia*, 174.

48. DGFP, Series D, Vol. 6, Doc. nos. 262, 271, and 274.

49. Ibid., Doc. nos. 474 and 539. Recalling his visit to Germany, Paul told Dragoslav Georgevich that by listening to Hitler, he came to the conclusion that the Fuehrer was a homosexual maniac. "I see thousands of young, beautiful dead Englishmen, and thousands of dead, beautiful, young Germans, but I am a war machine, and I must go forward." Hitler also divulged to Paul that he was going to "settle the account with the Soviets." Georgevich, *Na Raskrsnici*, 88–89.

50. Balfour and Mackay, *Paul of Yugoslavia*, 178. Hitler's displeasure was even greater when he heard of Paul's visit to England. He called Paul a "slippery eel," hiding behind the sanctuary of his parliament, while his wife, Princess Olga, was an "ice-cold" English woman, interested only in high society life. The Italians of course watched the outcome of Paul's visit to Berlin rather carefully, and concluded that Prince Paul refused to be intimidated by the Germans. *"Il principe Paolo non si lascio intimorire."* Breccia, *Jugoslavia, 1939–1941*, 129.

51. Ciano, entries for August 6, 11, and 12, 1939; DGFP, Series D, Vol. 7, Doc. nos. 43, 47, and 71.

52. David Irving, *The War Path,* 209–10.

53. Lane to U.S. Department of State, Doc. no. 860H.00/1053.

54. Petrov, *Study in Diplomacy,* 210.

55. Lane to U.S. Department of State, Doc. nos. 860H.00/1116 and 860H.00/116.

56. Balfour and Mackay, *Paul of Yugoslavia,* 179–81.

57. In an interview many years after the war, Chamberlain's former private secretary, Sir Alex Douglas-Home, revealed some characteristic peculiarities of his former superior. "I think that the main thing to grasp is that Chamberlain, like many others, saw Communism as the major long-term danger. He hated Hitler and German Fascism, but he felt that Europe in general and Britain (in particular) were even in greater danger from Communism." See Margaret George, *The Warped Vision,* 20; DGFP, Series D, Vol. 7, Doc. no. 405.

58. FRUS, 1939, 1: 287–88.

59. DBFP, 1919–39, Third Series, Vol. 3, 102–103.

60. Balfour and Mackay, *Paul of Yugoslavia,* 171–72.

61. Ibid.

62. Hitler told Ciano that Prince Paul "sought guarantees from the Western powers" on his visit to England. DGFP, Series D, Vol. 7, Doc. no. 43.

63. Biddle to U.S. Department of State, Doc. no. 740.00/1870. Biddle corrected such opinions and pointed out that Maček was merely in a "huff" over Belgrade's procrastination regarding the negotiations. One cannot dismiss the fact that the Serbo-Croatian Agreement was concluded shortly after Paul's return from England, suggesting that pressure may have been applied on Paul while in England. Boban, *Sporazum,* 190–92. Other facts, however, may have influenced Paul to conclude the agreement with the Croats upon his return. On the way to England, he met Yugoslav War Minister Petar Pešić who was with the government mission in France to sound the French about a preventive war against Italy. Pešić advised the prince to put aside any illusions he had involving the British to conduct a preventive war against Italy. Well-informed about Maček's activities with the Italians, Paul, under French influence, thought that a preventive war with French and British help would avert any possible danger coming from Italy. In talks with the British officials, Paul nevertheless tried to convince them that Italian Fascism (but not Italian people) presented a danger to Yugoslavia. The British had no intention of disturbing Mussolini at that time and rejected the French initiative, telling Paul that Yugoslavia's difficulties were of a domestic nature stemming from unsolved relations between Zagreb and Belgrade. Breccia, *Jugoslavia, 1939–1941,* 160; Tasso, *Italia e Croazia,* 2: 59–70.

64. Memminger to U.S. Department of State, Doc. no. 860H.00/1059.

65. Lane to U.S. Department of State, Doc. nos. 860H.00/1073 and 860H.00/1079.

66. U.S. Department of State, Doc. nos. 660H.1115/10, 740.00/1923, and 611.60H31/173.

67. Hull to Lane, Doc. no. 660H.1115/19.

68. George Peck, a well-known proponent of economic nationalism, argued at the time that in view of the world situation, Hull's reciprocal trade would have about as much effect on preserving peace as it would in curing leprosy. See Patrick J. Hearden, *Roosevelt Confronts Hitler,* 51.

69. Berle Memorandum, Doc. nos. 6716.60H31/182 and 660H.1115/32.

70. Lane to U.S. Department of State, Doc. no. 860H.00/1103.

Chapter 3. Roosevelt's Peace Offensive and the Future of Yugoslavia

1. Adolf A. Berle, "Navigating the Rapids, 1918–1971," from *Papers of Adolf A. Berle,* eds. Beatrice Bishop Berle and Travis B. Jacobs (New York: Harcourt Brace Jovanovich, 1973), 254.

2. Dallek, *Franklin D. Roosevelt and American Foreign Policy,* 482.

3. Franklin D. Roosevelt, *Complete Presidential Press Conferences of Franklin D. Roosevelt,* 3: 275–78.

4. Hans-Heinrich Herwart von Bittenfeld, *Against Two Evils,* 144. According to Jonathan Haslam, one of the most compelling reasons for Stalin's acceptance of the pact with Hitler was that "London was still reluctant to accept the need to deter German expansion into Eastern Europe at the price of risking Soviet hegemony in that region." Jonathan Haslam, *The Soviet Union and the Struggle,* 221. William C. Bullitt reported from Paris that the Soviet proposal to go to war in case Germany attacked any country was unacceptable to Britain, and because France depended on British support, Paris rejected it too. French Foreign Minister Georges Bonner and his subordinate, Alexis Leger, informed Bullitt that it would be quite impossible to get French soldiers to march in case of a German attack on Estonia, unless an attack first involved Poland. Bullitt to U.S. Department of State, Doc. no. 740.00/1068. For Kennedy's reports from London, see FRUS, 1939, I: 199–200, 287–88. Other valuable works dealing with Chamberlain and his relations with the Soviets are: Keith G. Feiling, *The Life of Neville Chamberlain;* George, *The Warped Vision;* T. R. Fehrenbach, *F.D.R.'s Undeclared War.* On page 179, Fehrenbach aptly pointed out that in the 1900s, the dominant men in Britain were men of narrow vision. Sir Samuel Hoare, Sir Arthur Balfour, Sir John Simon, and Chamberlain himself were in fact provincial British businessmen rather than aristocrats. "Their instinct was that the historical fears, hatreds, emotions, and ultra-rational drives of nations and people could be managed the same way capable and sensible men managed business." Some authors have brought out that through Soviet espionage, which Britain knew only too well, the British by virtue of their weakness, were in no position to offer any effective resistance to Hitler. This was one of the reasons why Stalin opted for the Nazi-Soviet pact. See Andrew Sinclair, *The Red and the Blue;* Keith Middlemas, *The Strategy of Appeasement.*

5. Ciano, entry for April 16, 1939.

6. Ibid., entry for April 15, 1939.

7. Cameron Watt, *Succeeding John Bull,* 87.

8. Lane to U.S. Department of State, Doc. no. 740.00/870.

9. King Alexander was one of the first European rulers to realize the importance of Nazi Germany in European politics. Two compelling factors operated in Alexander's decision-making process—Mussolini's hostility toward Yugoslavia and the Austrian desire to restore the Habsburg empire. Thus the disappearance of Austria as a political entity was considered beneficial to both Yugoslav and German interests. Alexander expressed his sympathy for some features of the

National Socialist regime. He wished to improve trade with Germany and establish closer relations with Berlin. Germany responded in kind. To assure trade and good relations with Belgrade, Hitler outlawed activities of the Croatian political emigre in Germany. For the initial development of Nazi-Yugoslav relations, see DGFP, Series C, Vol. 1, Doc. nos. 99, 279, and 345; Vol. 2, Doc. nos. 43, 72, 91, 92, 309, 318, and 381. In the unsuccessful 1934 putsch against the Austrian government, the Yugoslav authorities collaborated with the Austrian Nazis. After the putsch, the Austrian Nazis crossed the Yugoslav border and found safe haven in Yugoslavia. Pozzi, *Black Hand over Europe,* xvi. Prince Paul continued the same policy after Alexander's assassination, and according to Aleksandar Cincar Marković, secretly visited Germany in 1936. Boban, *Sporazum,* 31. Apart from these practical considerations, Serbian sympathy for the Nazi leader was expressed in part by one of the leading theologians of the Serbian Orthodox Church, Bishop Nikolaj Velimirović. These reflected more than practical considerations. "One has to give respect to the nowadays German leader, who as a simple artisan and man of the people, clearly saw that nationalism without religion is an anomaly, a cold and uncertain mechanism. And here in the Twentieth Century he came upon the same idea, practiced by Saint Sava, and as a layman took upon himself the mission, worthy of a saint, a genius, and a hero. This mission was accomplished by Saint Sava, a long time ago . . . It's therefore safe to say that Serbian nationalism, as a reality, is the oldest in Europe." Nikolaj Velimirović, *Nacionalizam Sv. Save* (Belgrade: Udruženje srpskog pravoslavnog sveštenstva Arhiepiskopije beogradsko-karlovačke, 1935), 27–28.

10. As an agricultural country par excellence, Yugoslavia came within the main economic orbit from the very beginning. The initial stages of German economic penetration were aided by the Franco-British rivalry. Regarding the German post–World War I economic recovery from a military standpoint, the British took an economic position and, unlike the French, regarded German recovery as beneficial to all. Looking at the French political hold on the Balkans as potentially dangerous to peace and prosperity, the British, in line with their policy, tacitly allowed German economic penetration into the region. See Kennedy, *The Realities behind Diplomacy.* Furthermore, the penetration was sped up by imposing sanctions against Italy because of the Italian conquest of Abyssinia. The Yugoslav trade with Italy was absorbed by Germany. The annexation of Austria and dismemberment of Czechoslovakia, Yugoslavia's former trade partners, added considerable weight to further German penetrations. For further readings on the subject, see also Lukač, *Treći Rajh;* Orlow, *The Nazis in the Balkans;* Wüescht, *Jugoslawien und das Dritte Reich;* Hans-Jurgen Schroder, "Süedosteuropa als 'Informal Empire' Deutschland," 233–66.

11. Arthur M. Schlesinger, Jr., *The Age of Roosevelt: The Crisis of the Old Order, 1919–1933,* 1: 482.

12. Adolf Berle, "Navigating the Rapids, 1918–1971," 363.

13. Hearden, *Roosevelt Confronts Hitler,* 142–43.

14. Roosevelt, *Complete Presidential,* 15: 139.

15. Ciano, entry for September 26, 1939.

16. Balfour and Mackay, *Paul of Yugoslavia,* 190–91.

17. Ciano, entry for November 26, 1939.

18. Ibid., entry for February 26, 1940.

19. DGFP, Series D, Vol. 8, Doc. no. 637. For Welles's account of his mission, see

Welles, *The Time for Decision* (New York: Harper, 1944), 71–147.

20. Langer and Gleason, *The Challenge to Isolation,* 356–70.
21. Ibid.
22. Ciano, entry for March 16, 1940.
23. Bullitt to Hull, January 25, 1940, Franklin D. Roosevelt Papers, P.S.F., Box 26.
24. Ciano, entry for March 19, 1940.
25. Ibid., entry for March 20, 1940.
26. Hearden, *Roosevelt Confronts Hitler,* 147.
27. Roosevelt, *Complete Presidential,* 15: 210; FRUS, 1940, Vol. 1, 27–117.
28. FRUS. 1940, Vol. II, 687.
29. Ciano, entry for December 26, 1939.
30. Ibid., entry for May 8, 1940.
31. FRUS, 1940, Vol. 2, 714.
32. For the text of the agreement between Ciano and Pavelić, see DDI, Nova Series, 1939–43, Vol. 3, Doc. no. 194. It is worth noting that Pavelić spoke of an Italo-Croatian union as a powerful deterrent (*un colpo di arresto*) against German penetration in the region.
33. Boban, "Britanija, Hrvatska."
34. Pierre Blet et. al., eds., Vol. 1, Doc. no. 296.
35. Ibid., Doc. no. 291.
36. Norman E. Fiske, Memorandum for Chief, Intelligence Branch, Military Intelligence, March 28, 1940. National Archives, Washington, D.C.
37. According to the present Yugoslav sources, the total number of Serbians was 5,848,000 out of 14,457,000 Yugoslavs. See Milovan V. Radovanović, *Enciklopedija Jugoslavije.* Even this number may be questionable because the population census in the kingdom of Yugoslavia was always taken by religious affiliation. Among the orthodox population, in addition to Serbians, there were Macedonians, Rumanians, Montenegrins, and Bulgarians in Yugoslavia. To prove their numerical superiority, the Serbian census takers manipulated the census figures as they wished.
38. Fiske, Memorandum for Chief, 3.
39. Ibid.
40. The exiled Italian politician Count Carlo Sforza and the historian Gaetano Salvemini strongly believed that Mussolini was after the best part of Yugoslavia, the Croatian Adriatic, and that neither Paris nor London would deter him to take Croatia only to keep him away from Hitler Radica, *Živjeti-Nedoživjeti,* 1: 443.
41. Konstantin (Fotić) Fotitch, *The War We Lost: Yugoslavia Tragedy and the Failure of the West.* Roosevelt extended very similar advice to King Peter when the latter visited Washington and finally asked him, "Peter, would you prefer to be the beloved king of Serbia rather then the hated king of Yugoslavia?" Radica, *Živjeti-Nedoživjeti,* 2: 174. Peter, because of his young age and not being very bright, was unable to give a sensible answer. Although Roosevelt sympathized and admired the Serbs, he was nevertheless very disappointed with Peter's mental acumen. The president sarcastically remarked to some of his associates that the boy (Peter) would never make it as the king. Roosevelt continued by saying that since Peter was going to visit Detroit, he might as well learn some suitable trade to have a job later when he needed it (this later became public). Ibid., 2: 189. Fotić, who ran the Serbian show in Washington, was against the division of Yugosla-

via. Fotić had two policies that complemented each other with regard to Yugoslavia. In private, he was for the creation of greater Serbia. In public, he spoke of Yugoslavia, but without a Serbo-Croatian Agreement. The Croats were to be kept in perpetual quarantine under Serbian control. Fotić's "Yugoslavism" may have been motivated further to some extent by Dr. Otto von Habsburg's political activities in the United States. Otto's agenda involved the restoration of the former Habsburg monarchy in which Croatia and Bosnia and Herzegovina would be included. His agenda was regarded by some influential Americans as the best postwar solution, since they believed that grouping the land of the former Austro-Hungarian monarchy could offer a political cure in the area and after the war could become a bastion against bolshevism in Europe. Because Archbishop of New York Francis Cardinal Spellman (the "American pope") supported it, and some believed that the pope himself was behind it, there was some reason to worry. Moreover, it was not a secret that Otto had access to the White House as well. Radica, *Živjeti-Nedoživjeti*, 2: 170–78 passim. At any rate, Fotić's Yugoslavism was identical to his pan-Serbianism.

42. FRUS, 1941, Vol. I, 343; Loewenheim et al., eds., 149.
43. Anthony Eden, *The Reckoning: The Memoirs of Anthony Eden*, 432.
44. Robert E. Sherwood, *Roosevelt and Hopkins, an Intimate History*, 711.
45. Ibid.
46. Welles, *Seven Decisions That Shaped History*, 136. Welles's main argument against Roosevelt's views was that it failed to take into account the "fractionalization" effect upon the economy, which Welles saw as the chief cause of Europe's woes.
47. Ciano, entries for May 13 and May 29, 1940. Although it was agreed in Brenner that Italy was to enter the war at some future date, Mussolini had changed his mind. The reason was not as noble as he claimed. The Germans smashed through the lines of the French Tenth Army and raced their forces toward Paris. On June 9, 1940, the Germans reached the Seine west of Paris. On June 10, Mussolini declared war on France, although Italy was not prepared for war and would not be before 1942. Easy booty in the wake of German advances made up Mussolini's mind, and under the pretext of honor and obligation toward his Axis partner, dismissed Roosevelt's overtures. He thought that Yugoslavia could be taken later anyway and on his own terms. Mario Cervi was quite right when he said that Italians entered the war to "get their share of picking." Mario Cervi, *The Hollow Legions: Mussolini's Blunder in Greece, 1940–1941*, 80.

Chapter 4. Lane's Period in the Diplomatic Wilderness

1. This was not just Russian paranoia. During the brief campaign against Denmark and Norway, for instance, the British Royal Air Force was instructed not to bomb German airfields in Norway or Denmark from fear the *Luftwaffe* might retaliate on French and British soil. When permission to attack was finally granted, the pilots were instructed to use only machine guns, not bombs. George, *The Warped Vision*, 213. Analyzing the Nazi-Soviet pact, Austrian scholar Ernst Topitsch came up with a convincing thesis—that by entering the pact with Germany, Stalin "turned the table" on the western Allies and used Hitler as his surrogate against them. In short, he paid them back in the same coin. Ernst Topitsch, *Stalin's War: A Radical New Theory of the Origins of the Second World War.*
2. Radica, *Živjeti-Nedoživjeti*, 1: 570–73.

3. Peter Barry Lane, "The United States and the Balkan Crisis," 16–19.

4. FRUS, 1939, Vol. 1, 677.

5. Ibid., 443 and 447.

6. N.A., U.S. Department of State, Doc. no. 860H.00/1127.

7. Martin Gilbert, *Finest Hour: Winston S. Churchill, 1939–1941*, 5: 103–109; Winston S. Churchill, *The Second World War: The Gathering Storm*, 561, 573.

8. DGFP, Series D, Vol. 9, Doc. no. 237.

9. Ibid., Doc. no. 100. On this occasion, Paul told von Heeren that despite the hostility between England and Germany (which he still regretted), he remained a sincere admirer of Germany and appreciated its policy toward Yugoslavia.

10. N.A., U.S. Department of State, Doc. no. 860H.00/1003.

11. Ibid., Doc. no. 860H.00/1097.

12. Ibid., Doc. no. 860H.00/1129. Actually, the transformation of Yugoslavia into a federated state was on the agenda after the elections for the *Skupština* (Parliament), which would never take place, if the political conditions afforded gradual and peaceful change. Boban, *Maček i Politika*, 2: 228–57.

13. Franz Halder, *The Halder Diaries*, 1: 311, 341.

14. N.A., U.S. War Department, Military Intelligence Branch, Report no. 4933, April 22, 1940.

15. Mark Wheeler, *Britain and the War*, 7, 244. Hitler held similar views. In his *Mein Kampf*, he called them "old impotent *Gerüempel*" (trash) and "rotten bodies." To him the region was a barbaric and inhospitable one, infested by "*Serbische Bombenschmeisser*," an uncivilized world. Taken from Van Creveld, *Hitler's Strategy*, 4–5.

16. N.A., U.S. War Department, Military Intelligence Branch, Report no. 4924, April 8, 1940.

17. Ibid.

18. Ibid. Fortier remarked sarcastically that General Weygand never even bothered to pay a visit to General Wavel, the supreme commander of the British forces in the Middle East who was headquartered in Cairo. To find out more about Britain's preoccupation with bombing the Russian oil fields in the Baku area, see Robert Cecil, "The Cambridge Comintern."

19. George, *The Warped Vision*, 213.

20. Gilbert, *Finest Hour*, 105.

21. Churchill, *Second World War*, 572.

22. N.A., U.S. Department of State, Doc. nos. 740.0011, European War 1939/3275 and 740.0011, European War 1939/3344.

23. DGFP, Series D, Vol. 10, Doc. no. 164.

24. Balfour and Mackay, *Paul of Yugoslavia*, 199–200. From an undated memorandum of that period drafted by Paul, it became evident that he was unable to stop Soviet penetration into the area. He, however, was determined to use it to his advantage in case any outside attempts against Yugoslavia's sovereignty were made. Jacob B. Hoptner, *Yugoslavia in Crisis, 1934–1941*, 175.

25. N.A., U.S. Department of State, Doc. no. 740.0011, European War 1939/3275.

26. N.A., U.S. War Department, Military Intelligence Branch, Report no. 4916, April 21, 1940.

27. Ibid. A good friend of King Alexander, the Croatian artist Ivan Meštrović, aptly described the Serbian "right" to rule Yugoslavia in his memoirs. The post–World War I Belgrade regime developed and spread the cult of "liberators" of non-Serbian peoples. Every Serbian with a šajkača (Serbian national headgear) on his

head considered himself a "liberator." In this fashion, the Serbian headgear became a royal crown on the head of every Serbian peasant. Ivan Meštrović, *Uspomene na Politčke Ljude,* 146.

28. Petrov, *Study in Diplomacy,* 134–35.

29. DGFP, Series D, Vol. 10, Doc. no. 73.

30. When Hitler heard of Mussolini's plan to attack Yugoslavia, he was anxious to convince his Italian partner why such a plan would be dangerous at the present time. Although Prince Paul was an "English slave," Hitler told Ciano, the timing was not right to finish off Yugoslavia. With England still undefeated, London might find a community of interests with Moscow. Together they could "bestir" the Balkans, which in the long run, would be costly for the Axis. Ciano agreed with Hitler's argument, as did Mussolini. He assured Hitler that the conflict should be kept out of the Balkans, but privately, he talked of attacking Yugoslavia sometime in September. DDI, Nova Series, Vol. 5, Doc. no. 101; DGFP, Series D, Vol. 10, Doc. nos. 129, 252, and 258; Ciano, entries for August 6 and 24, 1940.

31. N.A., U.S. Department of State, Doc. no. 860H.00/1102. True, communist activities coincided with that of the Croatian nationalists, but they had nothing to do with Italian support. The communists too rejected the Serbo-Croatian Agreement on the grounds that it solved nothing, and that it was an agreement between the Serbian and Croatian bourgeoisie. According to the "Theses" published by the Central Committee of the Communist Party of Yugoslavia, the struggle for democratization of the entire land should continue lest Yugoslavia become ruled by the Croatian bourgeoisie and the Serbian hegemonists, both of which were afraid of the working classes. In short, it was a marriage of convenience, which merely sharpened the contradictions within the state. Boban, *Maček i Politika,* 2: 258–61.

32. Nikola Milovanović, *Vojni Puč,* 289.

33. N.A., U.S. Department of State, Doc. nos. 860H.00/1153; 860H.00/1163; 740.0011, European War 1939/4426; and 860H.00/1186.

34. N.A., U.S. War Department, Military Intelligence Branch, Report nos. 4948, June 7, 1940, and 4954, June 7, 1940.

35. David Reynolds, *The Creation of Anglo-American Alliance,* 97–100.

36. Ibid., 100. Like Chamberlain, Churchill too was worried about American global ascendancy; having no other choice, however, he accepted it to keep Britain afloat and hoped for the best. For gradual decolonization of the British Empire see William Roger Louis, *Imperialism at Bay.*

37. Ibid., 104.

38. Peter Allen, *The Windsor Secret.*

39. Roosevelt, *Complete Presidential,* 15: 256–57.

40. When King George visited the United States the previous year on June 12, 1939, Roosevelt solemnly assured His Majesty that he himself "would lead the U.S. public opinion by defining the economic price America would have to pay, if Hitler conquered Europe." William Stevenson, *A Man Called Intrepid,* 71.

41. Roosevelt, *Complete Presidential,* 15: 570–73.

42. Adolf Berle, "Navigating the Rapids, 1918–1971," 324.

43. Stevenson, *A Man Called Intrepid,* 72.

44. The Germans engaged in the export of arms as a means of controlling Yugoslavia. Since neither Britain nor the United States could meet Yugoslavia's needs,

the Germans were the ones to fill the gap. It was a clever scheme. The German armament industry had two aims. One was to arm Germany, and the other was to export arms on credit as a means of gaining economic and political control. Germany's armament export was particularly fruitful in the Balkans. As a predominantly agricultural area, the Balkans fitted ideally into German economic space. Cvijetić, "Prodaja Naoružanja," 172–253.

45. BFPD, 1919–39, Third Series, 3: 102–103.

46. N.A., U.S. War Department, Military Intelligence Branch, Report no. 4954, June 25, 1940.

47. When Colonel General Franz Halder heard of the Italian demand for military hardware from the Germans, he laconically entered into his diaries, "What incredible nerve." Halder, entries for June 22 and August 24, 1940.

48. N.A., U.S. War Department, Military Intelligence Branch, Report no. 4966, July 26, 1940.

49. N.A., U.S. Department of State, Doc. nos. 860H.00/1196 and 860H.00/1200; U.S. War Department, Military Intelligence Branch, Report no. 496, July 26, 1940.

50. N.A., U.S. War Department, Military Intelligence Branch, Report no. 4979, September 20, 1940. According to Fortier, the document was handed to him by the Polish military attaché in Belgrade.

51. Ibid., Report no. 4981, June 7, 1940. After the fall of Poland, the Poles remained closely connected with British intelligence. It is therefore quite conceivable that the British used the Polish military attaché (as an "independent" source) to make the documents more believable.

52. Milovanović, *Draža Mihailović*, 21.

Chapter 5. The Struggle for Yugoslavia's "Neutrality"

1. Van Creveld, *Hitler's Strategy*, 15–17; MacGregor Knox, *Mussolini Unleashed, 1939–1941: Politics and Strategy of Fascist Italy's Last War*, 209.

2. Ciano, entry for October 12, 1940. When the Soviet troops moved into Bessarabia and northern Bukovina on June 26 and 28, 1939, the political map of Rumania changed. Fear of the Soviets shifted Rumania's foreign policy toward Berlin for protection. To keep Hungary quiet, Hitler forced Rumania to cede northern Transylvania to satisfy Hungarian claims. The anger was so high in the country that King Carol was forced to abdicate in favor of his son Michael. In fact, however, the country was ruled by General Ion Antonescu. Soon after Carol's abdication on September 6, 1940, the province of Dobrudja was ceded to Bulgaria (Treaty of Craiova; September 8, 1940). By mid-September, Versailles Rumania disappeared and the new Rumanian borders were guaranteed by Germany. To "protect the oil fields," German troops entered Rumania on October 8, 1940.

3. Knox, *Mussolini Unleashed*, 192–93. Actually, the real reason for Mussolini's decision to attack Greece was a mixed bag of greed, fear of German domination, and disagreement with Berlin over the Mediterranean strategy. Given the failure of the Germans to invade Britain, the war effort was shifted from England to the Mediterranean and placed, as Mussolini believed, on the Italian shoulders. The Germans, however, regarded the Mediterranean theater of war as a sideshow to their forthcoming invasion of the Soviet Union, which was why their supplies of war materials to the Italians were below those promised. Frustration, over-

confidence, to say nothing of German encroachment upon Italy's sphere of influence, led Mussolini to attack Greece. James J. Sadkovich, *The Italian Navy in World War II.* Deployment of German troops in Rumania without Italian knowledge further infuriated Mussolini, and caused him make up his mind to attack Greece. The plan of action that was to reestablish Italian dominance in their sphere of influence, however, was based on wishful thinking rather than reality. This was why it ended up so disastrously for the Italians. Tasso, *Italia e Croazia,* 2: 160–63; See Appendix in Cervi, *The Hollow Legions,* 311–44.

4. FRUS, 1940, 3: 544–45.
5. DGFP, Series D, Vol. 11, Doc. no. 110.
6. N.A., U.S. Department of State, Doc. no. FW871.00/819. According to this report, Hitler, in view of his ongoing preparation to attack the Soviet Union, was not "in the least interested in Greece provided the British did not establish themselves there." Furthermore, Hitler was displeased with Mussolini for having started a war with Greece, just before the two dictators were to meet.
7. The best book by far on the subject was written by Robin Higham, *Diary of a Disaster.*
8. N.A., U.S. War Department, Military Intelligence Branch, Report no. 4998, September 12, 1940.
9. N.A., U.S. Department of State, Doc. no. 7840.0011, European War 1939/6069.
10. Ibid., Doc. no. 7840.0011, European War 1939/6070. In a separate telegram, General Borivoje Mirković, the deputy commander of the air force, was revealed as the source of his report. The actual source, however, was Colonel Fortier. Many years after the war, Lane admitted to his biographer, Vladimir Petrov, that Fortier "managed to obtain" enough information about the coup. Petrov, *Study in Diplomacy,* 130. The document in question could not be found in the National Archives because it would have been irrefutable proof of the American connection to the putschists. The Yugoslav sources are clear on this point. Fortier, as pointed out, was connected with the conspirators since the summer of 1940. At the invitation of Colonel Žarko Popović, an intelligence officer of the Yugoslav general staff, Fortier attended the meetings of the conspirators. The meetings were presided over by Mirković, the nominal head of the conspiracy, together with the British and Colonel Draža Mihailović, the future leader of the Chetniks in wartime Yugoslavia. Milovanović, *Vojni Puč,* 21.
11. Wheeler, *Britain and the War,* 27–29. The Germans also heard of the "rumors." In his report to Berlin, von Heeren advised that Serbian dissatisfaction was directed against Paul and his conciliatory policy toward the Croatians. Such a policy, von Heeren pointed out, weakened the states. The Serbians felt that the best remedy for Yugoslavia's problems would be to replace Paul with the young king and the military dictatorship. DGFP, Series D, Vol. 11, Doc. no. 231.
12. N.A., U.S. Department of State, Doc. no. 860H.00/1218. It is true that Pavelić was on his rise in Croatia but so were the communists. The reason for Maček's dwindling authority was his close collaboration with Belgrade. The idea of an independent Croatia was gaining in the hearts and minds of the Croatian people. Enjoying the reputation of a relentless champion of Croatian independence, Pavelić's long years under Italian protection, however, made him an exponent of Mussolini's policy in Croatia. This was later reflected in his relations to Rome after the proclamation of the Croatian state on April 10, 1941. Croatia became a de facto Italian protectorate.

13. Ibid., Doc. no. 860H.00/1217.
14. N.A., U.S. War Department, Military Intelligence Branch, Report no. 4996, October 9, 1940.
15. Robin Higham, *Diary of a Disaster,* 57.
16. Ibid.
17. Richard Dunlop, *Donovan: American Master Spy,* 205–206.
18. Ibid., 222.
19. FDR Library. From Naval person to Roosevelt, December 13, 1940, M.R. Box 1. Churchill-Roosevelt, December 1939–December 1940.
20. Balfour and Mackay, *Paul of Yugoslavia,* 207–208.
21. To make sure that no "accommodation" with Germans would ever take place in Greece, the British tried a month ahead of the Italian invasion to organize a coup against the head of the Greek government, General Metaxas. As a graduate of the German military academy, Metaxas was not a British favorite, to say the least. Any negotiations with the Germans were ruled out by the British. Richard Clogg, "The Special Operation Executive in Greece," 110.
22. FDR Library, Pell to Roosevelt, May 16, 1941, P.S.F. 54, F.F. Hungary.
23. Robin Higham, *Diary of a Disaster,* 61.
24. Hewarth von Bittenfeld, *Against Two Evils,* 131, 193.
25. FRUS, 1940, Vol. 3, 400–403.
26. Ibid.
27. Stephen Clissold, *Djilas: The Progress of a Revolutionary,* 144. The difference between Churchill and Roosevelt, as Stalin saw it, was not so much in quality as quantity of greed. For Stalin, Churchill was a small-time crook, picking someone's pocket even for a kopeck, while Roosevelt would dip his hand only for bigger coins.
28. FRUS, 1940, Vol. 3, 402–403. Steinhardt correctly suspected Washington of giving tacit support to the British. No attempts were ever made to censure Sir Stafford. Ibid., 853. The Germans were concerned, but counted on the "horse sense" of the Soviet leaders to keep quiet. Halder, *Halder Diaries,* 1: 622.
29. The truth at this point was that the German troops along the Soviet borders were vastly outnumbered by the Russians. Ibid., 1: 743. Even during the war against Yugoslavia and Greece, Halder noted, the Germans were vulnerable along the Russian lines. The Russian "troop dispositions are such as to enable them to pass to the offensive on short notice." Ibid., and passim. According to German estimates, the Russian strength along the borders amounted to 171 infantry divisions, 36 cavalry divisions, 40 motor-mechanized brigades, plus the newly activated armed corps of three divisions stationed around Leningrad. Ibid., 853. The Germans were concerned, but counted on the "horse sense" of the Soviet Leaders to keep quiet. Ibid., 622.
30. Topitsch, *Stalin's War,* 68.
31. FRUS, 1940, Vol. 1, 390.
32. Ibid., Vol. 3, 430.
33. The American military attaché in London, Colonel Raymond E. Lee, eagerly warned his Soviet counterpart Colonel Skliarov that the Germans had increased the number of armored divisions, all of which were earmarked for the invasion of the Soviet Union. He intimated to Skliarov (hoping that Stalin would hear) that the United States would never allow the defeat of England. Raymond E. Lee, *London Journal of General Raymond E. Lee,* 199–200.

34. Hoptner, *Yugoslavia in Crisis,* 207.
35. Fotić, *War We Lost,* 35–36. Summing up Soviet-German relations at the end of 1940, Professor Topitsch observed correctly that although German policy was anti-Russian in southeastern Europe, the Kremlin's annoyance was moderate, which was understood by some as a sign of weakness. This apparent docility, however, was simply an element of the double game Moscow was playing. While in private, the Soviets were not afraid to challenge the Germans, in public, the Soviet leaders endeavored to avoid any semblance of antagonism and displayed their love of peace for everyone to see. Topitsch, *Stalin's War,* 92.
36. Fotić, *War We Lost,* 36.
37. Balfour and Mackay, *Paul of Yugoslavia,* 208–209.
38. "Srpski kulturni klub" (Serbian Cultural Club) was the focal point of Serbian cultural and political life. Pan-Serbian in its orientation, the club exerted powerful influence on internal and external policies of the government to bring them in line with the Serbian national interests. Some of its members were directly involved in the coup.
39. Hoptner, *Yugoslavia in Crisis,* 184–87; Balfour and Mackay, *Paul of Yugoslavia,* 208–209.
40. Milan Borković, *Milan Nedić* (Zagreb: Centar za Informacije i Publicitet, 1985), 16–18.
41. Aleksandar Cincar Marković agreed that Nedić meddled in foreign policy. He, however, believed that the putschists "framed" the general because they thought that the coup would have a better chance without Nedić in power. Dragiša Cvetković, *Dokumenti o Jugoslaviji,* 12. A Croatian physician and political emigre, Dr. Branko Jelić, was told by Göring that General Nedić was the most reliable German friend among the Serbians. Jere Jareb, *Političke Uspomene,* 137.
42. N.A., U.S. War Department, Military Intelligence Branch, Report no. 5012, November 16, 1940.
43. Francis H. Hinsley, *British Intelligence,* vol. 1, 250–53, 258–68.
44. Ibid.
45. John Wheeler-Bennett, *King George VI: His Life and Reign,* 493.
46. Halder, *Halder Diaries,* 2: 701. Halder entered in his diary that as long as Russia was not beaten, Turkey should not be attacked because it would postpone the Russian project. See also DGFP, Series D, Vol. 11, Doc. nos. 217, 295, 373, 379, 384, 438, and 606. Regarding Bulgarian claims against Yugoslavia, Hitler told Bulgarian Prime Minister Bogdan Filov that the national rights and aspiration could not be fulfilled within one generation, but by the labor of several. Ibid., Doc. no. 606.
47. Wheeler-Bennett, *King George VI,* 490–91.
48. N.A., U.S. Department of State, Doc. no. 740.0011, European War 1939/7582.
49. Wheeler, *Britain and the War,* 30. For German attempts to negotiate, see Van Creveld, *Hitler's Strategy,* 89–91.
50. Uglješa Popović, *Deseti po redu: Tajna Vojno Obavještajne Službe bivše Jugoslavenske Vojske of 1938 do Maja 1941 godine,* 71–72.
51. British Intelligence operating in the Americas often forged documents. A better example of British forgery was the case involving Italian Airline (LATI) operating in Latin America. Leslie B. Rout, Jr., and John F. Bratzel, *The Shadow War: German Espionage and United States Counterespionage in Latin America during World War II,* 111–12.
52. Ilija Jukić, *The Fall of Yugoslavia,* 30. One of the emissaries, Danilo Gregorić,

wrote a book about his mission. I used the Slovenian edition of the book, *Samomor Jugoslavije;* DGFP, Series D, Vol. II, Doc. no. 324.

53. Ciano, entry for November 16, 1940. Reflecting upon the Yugoslav proposal, he entered in his diary that "instead of gathering for ourselves a mass of uneasy Croats, I believe it is better to create a solid basis of understanding between Italy and Yugoslavia."

54. Ibid.

55. DGFP, Series D, Vol. II, Doc. no. 324.

56. Ibid., Doc. no. 324. Regarding Salonika, Hitler told the Italians that Serbian demands should be given every consideration in order to divert Russian aspirations from the Balkans and to frustrate the British consolidation in Thrace. Ibid., Doc. nos. 353, 389, and 334.

57. Ciano, entry for November 18, 1940.

58. DGFP, Series D, Vol. II, Doc. no. 417. Hitler also told the Yugoslav foreign minister that the pact would improve the Yugoslav position vis-à-vis Bulgaria, whose territorial claims had to be partially satisfied at the expense of Greece, but not at Yugoslavia's as the Russians desired. Furthermore, it would protect Yugoslavia from the Soviet Balkan policy "borrowed from the testaments of Peter the Great and Empress Catherine." Most importantly, Belgrade would secure Salonika and it would not even ask for the passage of German troops across Yugoslavia's territory.

59. Ibid., Doc. no. 467. For Stakić's version of talks with Mussolini see Vladislav D. Stakić, *Moji Razgovori sa Mussolinijem.*

60. Petrov, *Study in Diplomacy,* 134–35.

61. *New York Times,* January 5, 1941.

62. Roosevelt, *The Public Papers and Addresses of Franklin D. Roosevelt, with Special Explanatory Notes by President Roosevelt,* 9: 554–663. In his speech, Roosevelt told the world that the whole country would become an "arsenal of democracy." Radica's papers, Radica to Centralni Presbiro, Pov. br. 168, Washington, D.C., December 30, 1940.

63. N.A., U.S. Department of State, Doc. no. 740.0011, European War 1939/7589.

64. Ibid., Doc. no. 860H/1227.

65. Radica, *Živjeti-Nedoživjeti,* 2: 59.

66. While still aboard the ship crossing the Atlantic, Petrović dreamed of using his journalistic abilities against Maček and Prince Paul whom he regarded as exponents of the pro-Nazi policy. His dearest wish was to liberate Serbians from their pro-Axis chains. Among other worthy deeds, Petrović claimed that if France endured for two more weeks, he would have singlehandedly provoked an uprising in Serbia against the Yugoslav government by his broadcast from Paris. Ibid., 2: 52–56.

67. Svetislav-Sveta Petrović, *Free Yugoslavia Calling* (New York: Graystone, 1941), 46.

68. Radica's letter to the author dated October 26, 1986.

69. Fotić, *War We Lost,* 75.

Chapter 6. Mutatis Mutandis: Donovan's Balkan Mission

1. Stevenson, *A Man Called Intrepid,* 137.

2. Dunlop, *Donovan,* 230.

3. Ibid. While the American press speculated about Donovan's mission, William Stephenson communicated to Churchill that the importance of the mission could hardly be overestimated. To Sir Stewart Menzies, chief of British Intelligence, Stevenson stressed that Donovan "exercise[d] controlling influence over Knox, strong influence over Stimson, friendly and advisory influence over [the] President and Hull." Being of Irish descent, a Catholic, and a Republican, Donovan was influential with the administration in general. His service to Britain in the past was a sure guarantee that he could be trusted more than any other individual.

4. N.A., U.S. Department of State, Doc. no. 790.00118, European War 1939/20A.

5. The trip was financed by the British. Donovan's constant companion was Lieutenant Colonel Vivian Dykes of the Royal Engineers. Thomas F. Troy, *Donovan and the CIA: A History of the Establishment of the Central Intelligence Agency*, 37.

6. In the letter to this author, Mr. Bogdan Radica pointed out that he personally saw Donovan in the Yugoslav legation meeting with Fotić.

7. Dunlop, *Donovan*, 239.

8. Van Creveld, "The German Attack on the USSR," 69–88. According to the author, in August of 1940, Hitler ordered the army to be enlarged from 120 to 180 divisions, but the productive capacity of the German industry was not large enough to supply the necessary material for the newly formed units. This was why changes were made in the original plan to attack the Soviet Union in May.

9. Elisabeth Barker, *British Policy in Southeast Europe in the Second World War*, 19.

10. Wheeler, *Britain and the War*, 54. Some information strengthened British resolve. Lincoln MacVeagh, the American ambassador in Athens, reported to Washington that the Rumanians were 100 percent sure the Turks would attack Bulgaria if the latter allowed the passage of German troops, and 50 percent sure of Russian intervention to secure the Dardanelles. N.A., U.S. Department of State, Doc. no. 740.0011, European War 1939/7534.

11. Some historians have pointed out that the British decision to make a stand in the Balkans was motivated by British fear of an immediate German invasion of England. No matter what the German strategy was, the British believed it was directed exclusively against them. Hitler may have contributed more than his share to this kind of British "egocentricity," as Robin Higham calls it. After he had made his decision to leave England and attack the Soviet Union instead, Hitler would give the orders (most likely to keep the British forces in Britain) on several occasions to revive plans for the invasion of England. Basil Collier pointed out that the British were so "convinced" of an invasion that the concentration of German troops in Rumania was suspected as a "feint to draw off strength from the United Kingdom prior to an invasion attempt" of the British Isles." Basil Collier, *The Defense of the United Kingdom, History of the Second World War: United Kingdom Military Series*, 237.

12. Dunlop, *Donovan*, 239.

13. N.A., U.S. Department of State, Doc. no. 740.00116, European War 1939/153. As a response to Donovan's forthcoming trip, German Chief of Military Intelligence Wilhelm Canaris visited Greece. He promised General Metaxas to guarantee not only Greece's prewar frontiers but also the new territory conquered by the Greek army in Albania. In return, the Greeks were to cooperate in getting the British out of the Balkans. Dunlop, *Donovan*, 247–48.

14. FDR Library. MacVeagh to Roosevelt, January 19, 1941, P.S.F. Box 54. Greece 1940–42.

15. Ibid. In a somewhat more guarded language, MacVeagh communicated to the U.S. State Department that Donovan "impressed" the Greek leaders with the seriousness of America's resolve to back the democracies. Although still cautious, the Greeks in general were encouraged by Donovan and Field Marshall Wavell. As a result, General Metaxas finally allowed British reconnaissance flights north of Salonika and agreed that the British forces could land in Salonika the moment the Germans crossed the Bulgarian frontiers from Rumania. N.A., U.S. Department of State, Doc. no. 740.00118, European War 1939/88.

16. Dunlop, *Donovan*, 249.

17. N.A., U.S. Department of State. Doc. no. 740.0011, European War 1939/8742. A memorandum of the conversation with the Bulgarian leaders was attached to Earle's report.

18. Ibid.

19. Ibid. His "expertise" on the Slavs notwithstanding, one cannot say that Donovan's assessment of King Boris was very insightful. The only fault of King Boris, Donovan believed, was that the former was not only an "honest" and "shy" monarch, but an "idealistic" man who cultivated an "over-belief in the virtue of peace."

20. DGFP, Series D, Vol. 11, Doc. no. 713.

21. N.A., U.S. Department of State, Doc. no. 740.0011, European War 1939/7645.

22. N.A., U.S. Department of State, Doc. no. 740.0011, European War 1939/70. According to Sulzberger, Earle was embarrassed by this accident, but certainly not dismayed. By his own request, Earle was transferred to Istanbul as the naval attaché and married his dancing lady. Cyrus L. Sulzberger, *A Long Row of Candles: Memoirs and Diaries, 1935–1954*, 112. In view of his new position in Istanbul, one may assume that Earle knew in advance about the "theft."

23. Stevenson, *A Man Called Intrepid*, 226.

24. Ibid., N.A., U.S. Department of State, Doc. no. 7400.11, European War 1939/7936.

25. N.A., U.S. Department of State, Doc. no. 740.0011, European War 1939/7906.

26. Petrov, *Study in Diplomacy*, 142. Petrov pointed out correctly that Donovan's arrival in Belgrade was the turning point in Lane's diplomatic activities. He realized that Roosevelt stood behind the colonel, having finally decided to throw the full diplomatic weight of the United States behind Britain. When Donovan came to Belgrade, Lane handed him a personal message from President Roosevelt. The president urged Donovan to let the Yugoslav leaders know that only those who were willing to resist the Nazis would receive sympathy from the world in the future. Dunlop, *Donovan*, 256.

27. Charles E. Bohlen, *Witness to History, 1929–1969*, 155–56. Donovan's favorite story was that as the mayor of Rochester he learned how to keep the "Slavs" in line. All you had to show them a was "firm hand and consistency." He often lectured Bohlen and Averell Harriman: "You have no knowledge of how to deal with the Slavs, you people in the State Department just aren't tough enough."

28. Anthony Cave Brown, *"C", The Secret Life of Sir Stewart Graham Menzis, Spymaster to Churchill*, 355.

29. N.A., U.S. Department of State, Doc. no. 740.00118, European War 1939/152. All telegrams to the U.S. State Department were drafted by Lane.

30. Ibid. General Simović believed that Yugoslavia's role should be "active and not passive." In a separate report, Fortier pointed out that Simović was in favor of

fighting even though the Germans occupied Bulgaria." N.A., U.S. War Department, Military Intelligence Branch, Report no. 5041, January 24, 1941.

31. Maček's unequivocal answer against Yugoslavia's intervention displeased Donovan and created an ill feeling against the Croatian leader in particular and Croatians in general. Radica, Živjeti-Nedoživjeti, 2: 235. Others were more evasive than Maček and defended their views by saying that the Balkans still could be pacified, or that at this time war would not be in Germany's interest. The general feelings they managed to convey were that a premature intervention could, in fact, accelerate hostility in the Balkans.

32. N.A., U.S. Department of State, Doc. no. 740.00118, European War 1939/152.

33. N.A., U.S. War Department, Military Intelligence Branch, Report no. 5041, January 24, 1941.

34. A few days after his departure from Belgrade, Donovan told MacVeagh that he was certain the Germans would not dare to attack if they were convinced of the unified opposition of Bulgaria, Yugoslavia, and Turkey. All they needed to unify was American moral and material assistance. N.A., U.S. Department of State, Doc. no. 740.0011, European War 1939/8058. According to Lane, Aleksandar Cincar Marković delayed his meeting with Donovan for thirty-six hours, and when he finally met him, he was much less open than other Yugoslav leaders. N.A., U.S. Department of State, Doc. no. 740.0011, European War 1939/152.

35. Stevenson, A Man Called Intrepid, 228; Zoran D. Nenezić, Masoni u Jugoslaviji, 1764–1980: pregled istorije slobodnog zidarstva u Jugoslaviji: prilozi i grada.

36. Dunlop, Donovan, 259. The truth of the matter was that the Serbian army was overpowered by the Germans and only a handful of them managed to escape across Albania to freedom. On the Salonika front in 1918, there were only 60 thousand soldiers and half of them were non-Serbian Yugoslavs, prisoners of war from the Austrian army. The number of non-Serbians could have been much higher but for the fact that the Serbian government feared that such a high number of non-Serbians would deprive Serbia of its "rightful" victory.

37. Ibid. In point of fact, Peter had no idea what was occurring. Even in his biography, A King's Heritage, he denied any knowledge of the coup.

38. Popović, Deseti po redu, 143–44. Donovan entered in his journal that Britain had no strength to protect the Balkans. From Ankara, he sent a confidential messenger advising Roosevelt that only American armed intervention could prevent the Germans from taking over the entire Balkan area. Dunlop, Donovan, 263.

39. Tito passed the information to the Soviet military attaché in Belgrade. Nenezić, Masoni u Jugoslaviji, 451. Such information was hardly newsworthy to the Soviets. Apart from the fact that the British and Americans fed the Soviets with information of an imminent German invasion, the Soviets themselves had their "moles" in the center of British espionage, Bletchley Park. This was where the British decoded the Nazi enigma-machine known as "Ultra"; much was known about the German secrets. With an exceptionally strong spy network in England, the Soviets were well-informed, not only about the Germans, but about every shade of British political opinion, economic condition, and military strength. Sinclair, The Red and the Blue, 108.

40. Stevenson, A Man Called Intrepid, 228.

41. David A. T. Stafford, Camp X, 289.

42. Stevenson, Intrepid's Last Case, 180.

43. If this alleged meeting ever took place, it would have been during the Spanish

Civil War when Tito was very active in France, or after his return from the Soviet Union in March of 1940. Relying on Stevenson's allegations and suspicious of Tito's official biographers, a Croatian publicist, Professor Ivo Omrčanin, believed that Tito was a certified British agent of long standing. While his thesis is very intriguing, Professor Omrčanin offered no tangible evidence to support it. Ivo Omrčanin, *Enigma Tito*. My appeal, and those of many others, to Mr. Stevenson to elucidate this point remains unanswered. The "real evidence" still remains within the realm of "classified information."

44. Tito returned from Moscow via Istanbul in March of 1940. Phyllis Auty, *Tito*, 181. Vjenceslav Cenčić, *Enigma Kopinič* 2: 131–38.

45. Cvetković, *Dokumenti o Jugoslaviji*, 10: 13–14. The Soviets were well-informed about the coup. Dragiša Vasić, the real leader of the Serbian Cultural Club (*Srpski kulturni klub*) kept in touch with Soviet Ambassador Plotnikov at all times and apprised him as to the situation and feelings among the Serbians. To maintain Soviet-German relations, Plotnikov left Belgrade several days before the coup. Ibid.

46. Hoptner, *Yugoslavia in Crisis*, 206. According to Hoptner, Vishinsky told Gavrilović that if the British established the Balkan front, the Soviets would come in and march toward Bulgaria and the Straits, but if the Soviets remained out of the war and the western powers defeated Germany without their help, the Red Army would move into Rumania and Hungary.

47. N.A., U.S. Department of State, Doc. nos. 740.0011, European War 1939/8222; and 740.0011, European War 1939/79.

48. British hatred of Paul was so great that they branded him as a quisling and wanted to put him on trial as a war criminal at Nuremberg. Balfour and Mackay, *Paul of Yugoslavia*, 295.

49. Milovanović, *Vojni Puč*, 259.

50. After the war, one could not hear enough of the communist "patriotic" spirit. To prove their point, the communists were tirelessly citing the letter in which they called upon the people to defend Yugoslavia's integrity and independence. True, such a letter did exist, but as British publicist Nora Beloff has pointed out, it was drafted at the time of the so-called popular front line of Soviet foreign policy. Nora Beloff, *Tito's Flawed Legacy: Yugoslavia and the West, 1939–84*, 61.

51. Cvetković, *Dokumenti o Jugoslaviji*, 7: 12–14; Nenezić, *Masoni u Jugoslaviji*, 469.

52. N.A., U.S. Department of State, Doc. no. 740.0011, European War 1939/8283.

53. On the morning when the coup was executed, Tito was flown from the Zagreb military airfield to Belgrade by a group of airmen close to the Communist Party. Milovanović, *Vojni Puč*, 569. Communist sources flatly deny any connection between Simović and Tito. Jovo Popović and Darko Stuparić, in an article called "Napravit ćemo čudo" (We'll make a miracle), wrote that Tito's flight to Belgrade was a purely communist endeavor. The total blackout in Yugoslav historiography on the Donovan-Tito connection, however, makes one believe that Stevenson should not be altogether dismissed.

54. The policy was changed later during the war, at least under the surface. Both the British and the Americans became seriously concerned with regard to the Soviet incursion into central Europe. Churchill therefore gave orders to withhold the Bletchley information regarding German battle plans on the eastern front from Stalin, to slow the Soviet advances. Sinclair, *The Red and the Blue*, 108. Allen Dulles, the chief of American intelligence in Switzerland, lamented over the fail-

ure of the attempt on Hitler's life. By removing Hitler, Dulles hoped to conclude a separate peace with Germany before the Soviet troops had time to take
Berlin. R. Harris Smith, *OSS*, 221. Dulles had good reason to worry. Although
the testimony of the former Comintern master spy in Yugoslavia, Josip Kopinič,
should be taken with a grain of salt, it does seem to ring true in light of the
psychological disposition of the American people. In 1948, Donovan told Kopinič
in Istanbul that the Americans were surprised (presumably with relief) to see the
Russians content with taking only half of Europe. If Stalin had wanted to take
the rest of it he could have done so, because the Americans were not prepared
psychologically to resist the Russians who carried the main burden of the war
against the Nazis. Cenčić, *Enigma Kopinič*, 2: 128.

55. In praising Donovan's mission, Churchill in his memoirs was not very candid.
He said that the Yugoslav leaders confronting Donovan were silent and crippled
with fear to say what was on their mind. Churchill, *Second World War*, 158.

56. Robin Higham, *Diary of a Disaster*, 134.

57. N.A., U.S. Department of State, Doc. no. 740.00116, European War 1939/153.

58. Dunlop, *Donovan*, 260–61.

59. Robin Higham, *Diary of a Disaster*, 144 passim.

60. FRUS, 1941, 2: 640.

61. N.A., U.S. Department of State, Doc. no. 740.0011, European War 1939/8209,
Ω.

62. Robin Higham, *Diary of a Disaster*, 96.

63. N.A., U.S. Department of State, Doc. no. 740.0011, European War 1939/8209,
Ω.

64. Dunlop, *Donovan*, 273.

65. Radica papers. Centralnom Presbirou Predsedništva Ministarskog Saveta.
"Američka Štampa o Poseti Pukovnika Donovana," January 22, 1941.

66. Radica papers. Centralnom Presbirou Predsedništva Ministarskog Saveta. Pov.
br. 192, January 30, 1941.

67. Radica papers. Centralnom Presbirou Predsedništva Ministarskog Saveta. Pov.
br. 213, February 5, 1941.

68. Ibid.

Chapter 7. Yugoslavia between Scylla and Charybdis

1. Cvetković, *Dokumenti o Jugoslaviji*, 10: 14. The younger brother, Živan Knežević,
was in the Royal Guard, the older Radoje was King Peter's tutor and an influential member of the Serbian Cultural Club (Srpski kulturni klub). Together in
1981, they published an elephantine book, *Sloboda ili Smrt*, in which they defended their roles in the coup.

2. German representatives in Belgrade were well-informed about the putsch and
were quite skeptical that Prince Paul might survive after the accession to the
Tripartite Pact. Ibid., 17–18.

3. The 1937 treaty stipulated merely "respect for each other's territorial integrity."
There were some other stipulations regarding the Croatian and Slovenian minorities in Italy (e.g., to improve their conditions), but after the treaty was signed
the old practice of their Italianization resurfaced. From the viewpoint of Belgrade's
interests, the most valuable aspect of the treaty pertained to the liquidation of
the Ustašas camps in Italy. Tasso, *Italia e Croazia*, 1: 90–116. The Italian invasion

of Greece created additional tension in Belgrade. Italian reversals in Greece and Yugoslavia's position vis-à-vis the Axis necessitated an improvement in relations between Belgrade and Rome. To better relations on the basis of the 1937 agreement, Yugoslavia hoped to avoid the Tripartite Pact while the Italians, having Yugoslavia closer on their side, hoped to demoralize Greece and win the war without German involvement. See also Breccia, *Jugoslavia, 1939–1941*, 435–58.

4. DGFP, Series D, Vol. 12, Doc. nos. 10 and 20.
5. DGFP, Series D, Vol. 12, Doc. no. 15. Some additional clauses were to be added to the original treaty, such as demilitarization of the Adriatic coast of Yugoslavia in exchange for Italy's recognition of Yugoslavia's interest in Salonika.
6. Ibid. Doc. no. 45. In a memorandum of March 3, 1941, Ernst Wöermann, the director of the political department of the foreign ministry, noted that Mussolini accepted the German suggestion. DGFP, Series D, Vol.12, Doc. 97, note.
7. Hoptner, *Yugoslavia in Crisis*, 212.
8. N.A., U.S. Department of State. Doc. no. 740.0011, European War 1939/8209.
9. FRUS. 1941, 2: 943.
10. N.A., U.S. Department of State. Doc. no. 740.0011, European War 1939/8361.
11. FRUS, 1941, 2: 946.
12. DGFP, Series D, Vol. 12, Doc. nos. 47 and 48.
13. N.A., U.S. Department of State. Doc. no. 740.0011, European War 1939/8518.
14. Ibid., Doc. no. 740.0011, European War 1939/8520.
15. FRUS, 1941, 2: 947.
16. Ibid., 947–48.
17. N.A., U.S. Department of State. Doc. no. 740.0011, European War 1939/8574.
18. Petrov, *Study in Diplomacy*, 45.
19. Churchill, *Second World War*, 175.
20. Phyllis Auty, "Tajne četrdeset prve," *NIN*, June 25, 1972.
21. Balfour and Mackay, *Paul of Yugoslavia*, 220.
22. N.A., U.S. Department of State. Doc. no. 740.0011, European War 1939/8652.
23. Cvetković, *Dokumenti o Jugoslaviji*, 10: 54–56.
24. N.A., U.S. Department of State. Doc. no. 740.0011, European War 1939/8711. Incidentally, the Bulgarian-Turkish rapprochement received considerable publicity in the United States, reported the Yugoslav press bureau chief in Washington, Bogdan Radica. The press regarded it as a failure of British diplomacy. For that reason, the Yugoslav-German negotiations received less negative publicity. It was assumed that without the Turks and the Russians, Yugoslavia was too weak to face the Axis alone. *The Christian Science Monitor* devoted an entire editorial to the lack of Russian activity in the Balkans, and concluded that the Russians killed pan-Slavism as a political force among the Balkan Slavs. Radica papers, Balkanska situacija gledana iz Amerike. Pov. br. 243, Washington, D.C., February 22, 1941.
25. N.A., U.S. Department of State. Doc. no. 740.0011, European War 1939/8174.
26. Halder, entries for February 21 and March 13, 1941.
27. Hoptner, *Yugoslavia in Crisis*, 216–18; Balfour and Mackay, *Paul of Yugoslavia*, 226.
28. DGFP, Series D, Vol. 12, Doc. no. 130.
29. DGFP, Series D, Vol. 12, Doc. no. 130, notes 1 and 2.
30. Maček, *In the Struggle for Freedom*, 209–11; cf. Hoptner, *Yugoslavia in Crisis*, 219–

21; Balfour and Mackay, *Paul of Yugoslavia*, 227–29; Jukić, *Fall of Yugoslavia*, 212–54.

31. Ibid.
32. Ibid.
33. Ibid., Ante Smith-Pavelić, "Jugoslavija i Trojni Pakt."
34. The ministers were: Branko Čubrilović, Srdjan Budisavljević, and Mihajlo Konstantinović. All three were closely connected with the conspirators and the British. In addition, Budisavljević maintained strong relations with the Communists. Georgevich, *Na Raskrsnici*, 48–49. The Yugoslav government was informed by several independent sources that the Germans intended to invade the Soviet Union in June. The stiff timetable enabled Belgrade to extract the most favorable conditions for accession to the Tripartite Pact. Jukić, *Fall of Yugoslavia*, 52.
35. DGFP, Series D, Vol. 12, nos. 138, 145, 149, 156, 165, 192, 194, and 205.
36. Georgevich, *Na Raskrsnici*, 49.
37. Ulrich von Hassell, *Vom Andern Deutschland*, 193.
38. Jukić, *Fall of Yugoslavia*, 47.
39. Eden, *The Reckoning*, 249.
40. Sulzberger, *A Long Row of Candles*, 124.
41. Robert St. John, *The Land of Silent People*, 22.
42. Ibid.
43. Ibid. In St. John's view, the British deceptions, although not decisive, were nevertheless a strong contributing factor in the execution of the coup. Not only did the public believe in them, but more importantly the conspirators themselves did. After the coup, for instance, the people involved believed that at least fifteen British divisions and hundreds of planes would rush to Yugoslavia's aid when zero hour came.
44. Sulzberger, *A Long Row of Candles*, 124.
45. FRUS, 1941 (2): 653–54.
46. Ibid.
47. FDR Library. MacVeagh to Roosevelt, March 8, 1941, PSF, Box 54, Greece 1940–42.
48. Eden, *The Reckoning*, 249–50.
49. Ibid. Eden was referring to parts of Croatia and Slovenia given to Italy for entering World War I against the central powers.
50. Milovanović, *Vojni Puč*, 334–41.
51. DGFP, Series D, Vol. 12, Doc. nos. 138, 144, 145, and 149. Ribbentrop instructed von Heeren not to reveal outright the German decision, but to act according to the situation at hand.
52. Ivan Meštrovič, *Uspomene na Političke Ljude*, 297–99.
53. Ibid.
54. FRUS, 1941, 2: 950–51.
55. N.A., U.S. Department of State. Doc. no. 740.0011, European War 1939/8895. According to some Serbian sources, Gavrilović at his post in Moscow was more harmful than helpful to Yugoslavia. For instance, when the Soviets wanted to keep armament negotiations with Yugoslavia on the military level, Gavrilović kept interfering and finally informed his associate in the Serbian Agrarian Party (involved in the coup), Miloš Tupanjanin, that the Soviets offered an alliance with Yugoslavia. With this piece of news, Tupanjanin went straight to the parlia-

ment building shouting loudly, "You see, the Soviet Union offered us an alliance, and what are we doing?" This incident may not have been why the Soviets refused to send arms shipments to Yugoslavia, but it may have provided them, in view of the Russo-German relations, with a convenient excuse not to do anything that might have exacerbated the already strained relations with Berlin. According to the same sources, Gavrilović was a busybody who habitually invented sensational stories and passed them on to Sir Stafford Cripps as gospel truth. On the other hand, Gavrilović may have acted the way Cripps wanted him to act in order to create suspicion in Berlin between Moscow and Belgrade. Georgevich, *Na Raskrsnici*, 162–63.

56. FRUS, 1941, 2: 952–54. Lane practiced a double standard in dealing with the opposition. While, for instance, Maček was still in opposition, Lane never allowed any of his subordinates to have any connections outside of the government circle. Lane never attempted speaking to Maček on the grounds that Lane was accredited to Prince Paul and his government and not to Maček and the opposition.

57. Halifax to Roosevelt, March 10, 1941, MR. Box 1, Churchill to Roosevelt, January–June 1941, FDR Library.

58. FRUS, 1941, 2: 958.

59. N.A., U.S. Department of State, Doc. no. 740.0011, European War 1939/9257.

60. FRUS, 1941, 2: 954.

61. N.A., U.S. Department of State, Doc. no. 740.0011, European War 1939/9257.

62. Jukić, *Fall of Yugoslavia*, 37–46.

63. Graham Ross, ed., *The Foreign Office and the Kremlin: British Documents on Anglo-Soviet Relations, 1941–1955*, 69.

64. Ibid., 71.

65. Eden, *The Reckoning*, 251–60.

66. Ibid.

67. DGFP, Series D, Vol. 12, Doc. no. 113. Hitler sent a personal letter to the president of the Turkish Republic assuring the latter that Germany would not "impair . . . relationship to Turkey in any circumstances," but improve it and make it fruitful for both sides.

68. Eden, *The Reckoning*, 260.

69. Ibid.

Chapter 8. Yugoslavia Chooses the Tripartite Pact

1. Petrov, *Study in Diplomacy*, 159.

2. Ibid., 160.

3. N.A., U.S. Department of State, Doc. no. 740.0011, European War 1939/3872. Activities of American news reporters in Belgrade were best recorded by the reporters themselves. In addition to the books by St. John and Sulzberger, others are equally revealing: Leigh White, *The Long Balkan Night;* John C. Adams, *Flight in Winter.* None of these books can match Ray Brock's self-righteous arrogance expressed in his book, *Nor Any Victory.*

4. Radica papers, Radica to Press Bureau, Telegram br. 84, March 16, 1941.

5. Most of the telegrams sent to Roosevelt and the Yugoslav leaders were collectively published in the *Bulletin of the Yugoslav Courier* (Chicago) on March 15, 1941.

6. Radica papers, Radica to Press Bureau, Telegram br. 84, March 16, 1941; Roosevelt, *The Public Papers and Addresses*, 10: 60–69.

7. The erroneous view with respect to the accession to the pact is still prevalent in the historical literature. Thus, for Alex Dragnich, for instance, the case was quite black-and-white. All Croatians were for the pact, and all Serbians were against it. Alex Dragnich, *The First Yugoslavia: Search for a Viable Political System*.

8. Georgevich, *Na Raskrsnici*, 132.

9. FRUS, 1941, 2: 959.

10. Ibid. Fotić most likely was referring to the dismissal of General Milan Nedić. In point of fact, Nedić was an ardent Germanophile and no less than Dimitrije Ljotić. Both, however, were Fotić's relatives and both became Serbian quislings. Serbian propaganda in the United States, inspired and guided by Fotić, never exposed these two Nazi collaborators. The way Fotić saw it, only Croatians could be collaborators, never Serbians. If the Serbians did collaborate, then it was because they deliberately sacrificed themselves to save the Serbian people. In short, no matter whose side they were on, they were the martyrs. Radica, *Živjeti-Nedoživjeti*, 2: 124–25.

11. Radica papers. Radica to Press Bureau, Telegram br. 88, March 10, 1941.

12. Ibid., Telegram br. 98, March 22, 1941.

13. Ibid., Telegram br. 84, March 7, 1941. He sent a similar telegram to Maček with a similar request. Radica, *Živjeti-Nedoživjeti*, 2: 103.

14. *Times-Herald*, March 23, 1941.

15. St. John, *Land of Silent People*, 45. Brock's six months in Belgrade were marked with the passion of a true believer in Serbian omnipotence. Throughout his book, Brock referred to the Serbians as "my Serbians" and to Chetniks as "my Chetniks."

16. Ibid.

17. Brock, *Nor Any Victory*, 120.

18. Jozo Tomasevich, *The Chetniks: War and Revolution in Yugoslavia, 1941–1945;* Mateo J. Milazzo, *The Chetnik Movement and the Yugoslav Resistance*.

19. Milovanović, *Draža Mihajlović*, 83 and 156.

20. Radica, *Živjeti-Nedoživjeti*, 2: 106.

21. FRUS, 1941, 2: 962 and 966–967. Fortier had his doubts about Paul's sincerity. In his reports he would stress that the resistance depended on the government and that the government was Prince Paul. N.A., U.S. War Department, Military Intelligence Branch, Report no. 5088, March 16, 1941. Fortier was not far from the truth. After the war, Prince Paul confided to Sulzberger that "if he had to do it over again, he would still sign the pact with Hitler that he signed twenty years ago." Sulzberger, *Last of the Giants*, 756.

22. Radica, *Živjeti-Nedoživjeti*, 2: 109.

23. Brock, *Nor Any Victory*, 134–36.

24. Radica papers, Radica to Press Bureau, Pov. br. 258, March 21, 1941. Radica suggested that Yugoslavia should follow the same policy as Sweden. He based his recommendation on the fact that many "well-informed Americans" believed that Germany was unable to invade England, and therefore, was destined to lose the war. Moreover, they were sure that America would become belligerent by the end of 1941 or beginning of 1942.

25. N.A., U.S. Department of State, Doc. no. 740.0011, European War 1939/9172. He also reported that former Greek Prime Minister Margyropolos was sent to Belgrade to plead with Paul not to give in to German demands.

26. Eden, *The Reckoning*, 258.
27. Balfour and Mackay, *Paul of Yugoslavia*, 288. In the meantime, MacVeagh found out from a British source that the Germans had 546 aircraft in Rumania and Bulgaria with more to come, while the Italians concentrated 180 planes in the Dodocanese. The entire British air force in Greece amounted to 78 planes with no reinforcements in the future. N.A., U.S. Department of State. Doc. no. 740.0011, European War 1939/9172.
28. Churchill, *Second World War*, 160.
29. Ibid.
30. Wheeler-Bennett, *King George VI*, 497.
31. Milovanović, *Vojni Puč*, 414.
32. Ibid., 414–15.
33. Damaree Bess, "Our Frontier on the Danube," 1 ff. As an example of Donovan's behavior, Bess described the occasion of the French ambassador in Ankara suggesting that America should send food to save the French people from starvation. Donovan snapped back: "The American people are prepared to starve every Frenchman if that's what's necessary to defeat Hitler."
34. Jukić, *Fall of Yugoslavia*, 92. Apparently they were not so secret; after the third day of occupation, the Germans found the hidden arms and munitions.
35. Petrov, *Study in Diplomacy*, 161.
36. Balfour and Mackay, *Paul of Yugoslavia*, 258. The government was aware of what was going on in Belgrade, but was afraid to do anything drastic for fear that it might have an adverse effect on the citizens. Cvetković, *Dokumenti o Jugoslaviji*, 10: 16.
37. FRUS, 1941, 2: 959.
38. The evidence points out that Konstantinović changed his mind, not because of Paul, but under the influence of his Masonic friends who needed their man in the government to be informed of the current events. Nenezić, *Masoni u Jugoslaviji*, 446.
39. FRUS, 1941, 2: 963–64.
40. The accusation of his "betrayal" of Greece was deliberately spread by British agents. Mužić, *Masonstvo u Hrvata*, 371. Such accusations continued even after the coup. Brock, *Nor Any Victory*, 180.
41. FRUS, 1941, 2: 964–65.
42. Ibid. The right and left wings of the Croatian political spectrum were against it, but for entirely different reasons. To them the pact meant a continuation of German protection over Yugoslavia, which was contrary to their political aspirations. So did the Communists.
43. FDR Library, U.S. Department of State to Roosevelt, O.F. 200, Box 59, 200-1-3, March 20–30, 1941.
44. Ibid. Roosevelt to U.S. Department of State, O.F. 200.50, F.T. Sec. 1–2, March 20–30, 1941.
45. DGFP, Series D, Vol. 12, Doc. no. 201. Maček later told Meštrović that not even "four oxen would have pulled him to Vienna." Ivan Meštrović, *Uspomene na Političke Ljude*, 300.
46. FRUS, 1941, 2: 967–68.
47. DGFP, Series D, Vol. 12, Doc. no. 211.
48. N.A., U.S. Department of State, Doc. no. 740.0011, European War 1939/9321.
49. Ibid., 9312.

50. Churchill, *Second World War,* 161.

51. Eden, *The Reckoning,* 264.

52. N.A., U.S. Department of State, Doc. no. 740.0011, European War 1939/9480. The document was forwarded to Welles on March 27, 1941. R. Atherton of the Division of European Affairs, scribbled on the front page that the president received the copy "last night," which could have been before midnight. See Appendix B.

53. Ibid.

54. Milovanović, *Vojni Puč,* 426.

55. N.A., U.S. Department of State, Doc. no. 740.0011, European War 1939/948.

56. FRUS, 1941, 2: 969.

57. FDR Library. Roosevelt to Welles, O.F. 200-1-7, Box 59, Florida trip, March 28, 1941.

58. FRUS, 1941, 2: 970. Technically speaking, Welles was correct, but one can find many instances when the U.S. Government found it hard to recognize the Central American revolutionary regimes, although the continuation of a republican system of government was never in doubt. The criteria seem to have been based on U.S. national interest. Of Anastasio Somoza, Roosevelt once said, "He is a son of a bitch, but he is ours." Saul Landon, *The Dangerous Doctrine: National Security and the U.S. Foreign Policy* (Boulder, Colo.: Westview Press, 1988), 28.

59. In his telegram to Roosevelt, Welles pointed out that the coup "makes war between Serbia and Germany 95 percent." FDR Library. Welles to Roosevelt, O.F. 200-1-7, Box 59, Florida trip, March 20–30, 1941.

60. Many years after the war, Maček told Radica that he indeed joined Simović against the will of the Croatian people, because he thought such a decision was in line with the policy of the western Allies. He was also aware that because of the coup, war was inevitable and that Yugoslavia would be devastated by the slim prospect of being reestablished. Most of all, he worried that as a consequence of war, the gap between Serbia and Croatia would become unbridgeable. Radica, *Hrvatska 1945,* 333.

61. Maček, *In the Struggle for Freedom,* 222–23.

62. N.A., U.S. Department of State, Doc. no. 860.00/1278A.

Chapter 9. The American Press and the Coup

1. *Christian Science Monitor,* March 24, 1941.

2. *New York Times,* March 22, 1941.

3. *Chicago Daily News,* March 16, 1941.

4. *Washington Post,* March 26, 1941.

5. *New York Herald-Tribune,* March 22, 1941.

6. Ibid., March 26, 1941.

7. *New York Times,* March 27, 1941.

8. *Christian Science Monitor,* March 27, 1941.

9. *Washington Evening Star,* March 27, 1941.

10. *Chicago Daily News,* March 27, 1941.

11. *New York Times,* March 27, 1941.

12. *Washington Evening Star,* March 28, 1941.

13. Radica papers, an address by Constantine A. Fotitch, April 24, 1941.

14. *New York Herald-Tribune,* March 29, 1941.

15. *Chicago Daily News,* March 28, 1941.
16. *New York Times,* March 29, 1941.
17. *Washington Post,* March 29, 1941.
18. *Washington Evening Star,* March 29, 1941.
19. Ibid.
20. *New York Times,* March 29, 1941.
21. *Washington Post,* March 30, 1941.
22. *New York Times,* April 3, 1941.
23. *Washington Evening Star,* March 31, 1941.
24. *Christian Science Monitor,* April 4, 1941.
25. *New York Times,* April 2, 1941.
26. Ruth Mitchell, *The Serbs Choose War.*
27. *Saturday Review of Literature* (August, 1943), Vol. 26.
28. *Christian Science Monitor,* April 5, 1941.
29. *Washington Post,* April 7, 1941.
30. Ibid.
31. *Washington Evening Star,* April 7, 1941.
32. *New York Times,* April 8, 1941.
33. *Christian Science Monitor,* April 10, 1941.
34. *New York Times,* April 11, 1941.
35. Ibid.
36. *Christian Science Monitor,* April 21, 1941.
37. *New York Times,* April 25, 1941.
38. *Washington Post,* April 17, 1941.
39. *Life,* September 15, 1941.
40. *New York Times,* May 10, 1941.
41. The first murderous acts against Croatian civilians took place in the villages of Ilići and Mostar in the province of Herzegovina, but not the way Brock had reported. According to Monsignor Petar Čule, the Croatian bishop at Mostar who was well-known for his anti-Ustaša and anti-communist sentiments, the Yugoslav airmen bombarded the Catholic cathedral before Easter at the time when the procession was about to start. One corner of the cathedral collapsed and a small boy was killed. After the proclamation of the Croatian state on April 10, 1941, the bishop pointed out that some uneasy calm had descended upon the province which ended on June 29. Before the spring was over, the Chetniks rounded up the leading Croatians in the town of Nevesinje and their bodies were thrown into pits near the village of Bišćina. A detachment of Ustašas, mostly returnees from Italy, carried their revenge until the end of the summer when the Italians took control of Herzegovina. With Italian support and protection, the Chetniks then took charge of the killing, which carried on until the end of the war in 1945. As a result of Serbian retribution, several Croatian parishes in the area were wiped out, some others half destroyed. Many churches and villages were burned to the ground. Tens of thousands of Croatians were killed. Seventy-one Catholic priests were murdered. The fact to remember, as Monsignor Čule pointed out, was that the Serbs not only initiated the massacres but were the first to start the gruesome practice of throwing their victims into the pits. They carried out their atrocities from the end of the 1941 summer until the end of April 1945. See "Dragocjeni dokumenat pod. Biskupa Čule," *Nova Hrvatska* 9, 10, 11 (London, 1988).

Chapter 10. Coup d'Etat: Myth and Reality

1. Ben Pimlott, ed., *The Second World War Diary of Hugh Dalton, 1940–45*, 197.
2. Hugh Dalton, *The Fateful Years, 1931–1945*, 366–67; David A. T. Stafford, "SOE and British Involvement," 36: 399–419; G. N. Hugh Seton-Watson, "Afterword: Thirty Years After," 283–97; Stafford, *British and European Resistance.*
3. While McDonald dealt with Simović, Mapplebeck visited General Mirković and ordered him to carry out the coup within forty-eight hours. Mirković agreed and promised the coup would take place within that time. Tomasevich, *The Chetniks*, 45.
4. Stafford pointed out that Campbell disapproved of the SOE activities and for the most part relied on his own judgment regarding the situation in Yugoslavia. Stafford, "SOE and British Involvement," 419.
5. "Initiative came from the Yugoslavs, and only by a stretch of the imagination can the British be said to have planned or directed the coup d'etat." Ibid.
6. On the Serbian side, Dragiša N. Ristić, one of the participants in the coup, attempted to convince Professor Stafford that the coup was of Serbian origin. Concentrating exclusively on the coup's execution, Ristić merely described the mechanism of it. Dragiša N. Ristić, *Yugoslavia's Revolution of 1941.*
7. In his well-documented monograph, Milovanović demonstrated that the genesis of the coup was linked to the French and later to the British and Americans. Milovanović, *Vojni Puč,* 389–416.
8. Ibid. There is some evidence that after Donovan's departure, Simović had a clandestine meeting with an American general staff officer in Slovenia. Jukić, *Fall of Yugoslavia,* 60.
9. After twenty years in the United States, Radin returned to Belgrade. Together with a well-known historian, Charles A. Beard, he made a study of Yugoslavia's administrative system. Charles A. Beard, *The Balkan Pivot: A Study in Government and Administration.* Aside from that, not much is known about him. Radin had a reputation in Belgrade for being well-connected to the most influential circles in the United States, including President Roosevelt. He befriended General Simović and became one of his most trusted friends.
10. Milovanović, *Vojni Puč,* 406; Cvetković, *Dokumenti o Jugoslaviji,* 10: 14. Stafford's thesis is best refuted by the Yugoslav Military Intelligence. Popović in his book unequivocally stated that initiative for the putsch was given by a secret service of a friendly country. The initiative was accepted by general Simović who, inconcert with the air force officers, carried the putsch. Popović, *Deseti po redu,* 149.
11. Seton-Watson, *Eastern Europe between the Wars, 1918–1941* (Handen, Conn.: Archon Books, 1962), 407.
12. Franjo Tudjman, "Uzroci Krize Monarhističke Jugoslavije," 105. Such and similar views generally prevailed in post–World War II Yugoslavia historiography.
13. Ivan Meštrović, *Uspomene na Političke Ljude,* 249–50.
14. Jukić, *Fall of Yugoslavia,* 87.
15. Cvetković, *Dokumenti o Jugoslaviji,* 10: 20.
16. DGFP, Series D, Vol. 12, Doc. nos. 219, 221, 224, and 226.
17. FRUS, 1941, 2: 967; FDR Library, Knox to Roosevelt, O.F. 200-1-2, Box 59, March 20–30, 1941.
18. FDR Library, Roosevelt to Welles, O.F. 200-17, Box 59, March 20–30, 1941.
19. On the basis of solid research, James J. Sadkovich refuted the accepted views

attributing Axis control of the Mediterranean mostly to Germany. He demonstrated that the majority of effort in securing and controlling the sea lanes fell upon the Italian navy and air force, and that constant shortages of fuel and technical equipment (not supplied by the Germans as promised) created an erroneous picture of the Italian military performance. Sadkovich, *The Italian Navy*, 111–91.

20. Robin Higham, *Diary of a Disaster*, 207.

21. Ibid. The Yugoslav military attaché submitted to American authorities a request for 100 bombers, 100 fighters, 500 reconnaissance planes, 100 medium-sized tanks, 2,000 trucks, gas masks, helmets, and some antitank and antiaircraft guns.

22. Ibid., 199. Higham pointed out that the exaggerated numbers of the British forces in Greece could be attributed to the inaccurate reporting of the Yugoslav journalists. Undoubtedly such reporting existed, but the information was supplied by Allied sources.

23. N.A., U.S. Department of State, Doc. no. 740.0011, European War 1939/9401. The American ambassador from Bucharest, Franklin M. Gunther, reported that the Rumanian press carried stories of American guarantees to Yugoslavia for some time. Ever since the signing of the Tripartite Pact, propaganda against the United States in Rumania intensified, and American "maneuvering" in Yugoslavia was seen as a "blueprint for war." Similar accusations against Roosevelt and the United States were carried by the Italian press. N.A., U.S. Department of State, Doc. nos. 740.0011, European War 1941/9395 and 1089.

24. N.A., U.S. Department of State, Doc. no. 740.0011, European War 1941/9401.

25. N.A., U.S. Department of State, Doc. no. 740.0011, European War 1939/9449.

26. FRUS, 1941, 2: 969.

27. N.A., U.S. Department of State, Doc. no. 740.0011, European War 1939/9478.

28. Ibid., Doc. no. 740.0011, European War 1939/9449.

29. Churchill, *Second World War*, 169.

30. Having heard about the coup, Eden was so exhilarated that he "almost hugged Lady Dobbie," wife of the lieutenant general, Sir William Dobbie. Eden, *The Reckoning*, 265.

31. Churchill, *Second World War*, 169–71.

32. In his memoirs, Sir Winston conveniently forgot the fact that he wished to embroil the Germans with the Soviets, and insisted that the Balkan campaign saved the Soviet Union.

33. Eden, *The Reckoning*, 268–76. The Turks communicated to the Germans that the coup would have no effect, in spite of Belgrade's expectations regarding Ankara's foreign policy. DGFP, Series D, Vol. 12, Doc. no. 221.

34. Eden, *The Reckoning*, 124.

35. DGFP, Series D, Vol. 12, Doc. no. 219. In a separate report to Berlin, von Heeren endorsed Ninčić's views and added that the composition of the government enjoyed a broad Serbian backing. That fact in itself guaranteed support for Ninčić's foreign policy. Should his policy turn out to be unpopular among the Serbians, Berlin could always rely on Ninčić and the Croatian wing in the government for a policy of peace with Germany. Ibid., Doc. no. 221.

36. Gregorić, 145.

37. Ibid., 146. Stephen Clissold, ed., *Yugoslavia and the Soviet Union, 1939–1973* (London: Oxford University Press, 1975), 8.

38. N.A., U.S. Department of State, Doc. no. 740.0011, European War 1939/4979.

39. N.A., U.S. Department of State, Doc. no. 740.0011, European War 1939/9552.
40. Eugen Kvaternik, "Riječi i činjenice."
41. DGFP, Series D, Vol. 12, Doc. no. 252.
42. Ibid., Doc. no. 217. Göring held similar views with respect to the coup. It was much more convenient, he told a friend, to deal with it now rather than later, say during the invasion of the Soviet Union. Yugoslavia was liquidated with relative ease, for which we have General Simović to be grateful to. Cvetković, *Dokumenti o Jugoslaviji*, 10: 18.
43. DGFP, Series D, Vol. 12, Doc. nos. 215 and 216. On March 26, 1941, the Hungarian minister in Berlin, Dome Sztojay, informed the Fuehrer of Hungary's desire to extend its territorial claims on Yugoslavia, but not on Croatian territory. Hungary desired to live in peace with Croatia. As for a free port on the Adriatic, Hungary would have liked to have had it, but only with the approval of the Croatian government. Ibid., Doc. nos. 227 and 228.
44. Ibid., Doc. no. 226. In his reply to Hitler, Mussolini expressed his belief that the coup was decided upon by full cooperation of Prince Paul on the eve of the pact. "The present attitude of Yugoslavia—unprecedented in world history—was to [me] a replica of Sarajevo, acted out by the very same incorrigible elements."
45. Jukić, *Fall of Yugoslavia,* 68.
46. Hassell, *Vom Andern Deutschland,* 196; DGFP, Series D, Vol. 12, Doc. no. 259. That von Heeren was against the war may be corroborated by Ivan Meštrović. On one of his trips to Zagreb, von Heeren told Meštrović that he disagreed not only with the Nazi methods at home, but abroad as well. He agreed with Meštrović that the Communists, Fascists, and Nazis had many features in common, except that the Communists were more clever. He told Meštrović: "We Germans lack the gift of penetrating into the national psyche of other peoples, nor do we make any efforts to do so . . . We are undoubtedly one of the greatest peoples in Europe, by numbers and by our industriousness, but that gives us no right to trample upon the others. No one in his right mind could dream of dominating Europe and the World." Ivan Meštrović, *Uspomene na Političke Ljude,* 299–300.
47. Hassell, *Vom Andern Deutschland,* 201. As Hassell pointed out correctly, contradictory promises made by Hitler were designed to keep everyone dissatisfied. To keep the Italians in line, Hitler promised them whatever they asked for, but only to bring them into conflict with the "Slavs," who were expected then to ask for German arbitration. Croatians were pressured by Berlin to give in to Italian demands on Croatia. Ibid., 204. A few months after Pavelić returned to Zagreb, however, Himmler was urging Eugen Kvaternik, Pavelić's right-hand man, to get rid of Pavelić, the Italian "pawn," if the Croatians wished to be free of the Italians. Kvaternik, "Riječi i činjenice," 65–66.
48. DGFP, Series D, Vol. 12, Doc. no. 253.
49. Hoptner, *Yugoslavia in Crisis,* 276–80.
50. Ivan Krylov, *Soviet Staff Officer,* 281. Various accounts of the events are basically in agreement that the ceremony surrounding the pact with the Soviets was a comedy staged by Stalin. They were not really in agreement with respect to Stalin's behavior toward individual members of the Yugoslav delegation. Colonel Žarko Popović, the Yugoslav military attaché, claimed that Stalin paid attention only to him and disregarded Gavrilović, whom Stalin considered a fool. Popović insisted that Gavrilović was detrimental to Yugoslavia—that Gavrilović never un-

derstood the mechanism or the aims of the Soviet government, and never comprehended what the Soviets expected to gain by pushing Yugoslavia into war. Georgevich, *Na Raskrsnici,* 159–95.

51. Hoptner, *Yugoslavia in Crisis,* 281; Georgevich, *Na Raskrsnici,* 188–89.

52. Ostović, *Truth about Yugoslavia,* 217–18. The Soviets even inaugurated a separate Croatian radio broadcast from Moscow. Furthermore, at the end of the war, they contacted Pavelić promising full recognition of Croatia, provided he would tolerate the Communist Party and would never join an anti-Soviet alliance.

53. Balfour and Mackay, *Paul of Yugoslavia,* 248. According to Dr. Branko Pešelj, Maček's personal secretary, Paul rejected such a solution because of his family in Belgrade. "My wife and my children are in Belgrade. I had enough of it all. I am fed up with those irresponsible pan-Serbian elements who are pushing us all into an irreversible catastrophe." Pešelj, "Jedno Interesantno Mišljenje."

54. Ibid., 267–305. In conformity with British hostility against Paul, there appeared on March 3, 1946, an article in the *Sunday Times,* depicting Paul as a war criminal. Several articles followed the first on the same subject and Paul was expected to be tried at Nuremberg. Ibid., 295.

55. German attempts to make Maček cooperate with Berlin can be found in DGFP, Series D, Vol. 12, Doc. nos. 238, 239, 241, 243, 246, 251, 262, 263, and 270.

56. DGFP, Series D, Vol. 12, Doc. no. 262. Maček, *In the Struggle for Freedom,* 200–202.

57. Maček's decision to refuse the German offer is still debated among Croatians. In view of terrible wartime conditions in Croatia, some people believe that Maček, by assuming power, could have prevented most of them. In the above-mentioned article, Dr. Pešelj agrees, but with strong reservations. Under the circumstances, Maček would have ended up like Petain and Laval in France and Tiso in Slovakia. If, on the other hand, Maček had joined the Partizans, he would have been liquidated like other politicians who collaborated with them during the war. Pešelj, "Jedno Interesantno Mišljenje."

58. Hassell, *Vom Andern Deutschland,* 199–200.

59. N.A., U.S. Department of State, Doc. no. 740.0011, European War 1939/1247.

60. Maček, *In the Struggle for Freedom,* 222.

61. Ibid.

62. Hoptner, *Yugoslavia in Crisis,* 284–85; Maček, *In the Struggle for Freedom,* 223.

63. Hoptner, *Yugoslavia in Crisis,* 285.

64. No one really believed that peace could be maintained. Earlier in the day, Slovenian representatives Fran Kulovec and Dr. Miha Krek told Slovak Charge D'affaires Ivan Milac, that the best way out of the present situation for Slovenia would be a separate state, either with or independent of Croatia. DGFP, Series D, Vol. 12, Doc. no. 283.

65. DGFP, Series D, Vol. 12, Doc. no. 283.

Chapter 11. War and the Aftermath

1. DGFP, Series D, Vol. 12, Doc. no. 261. By the time the Italians entered, the Croatian administration was already functioning. Contrary to the Ciano-Pavelić agreement, the Italian military behaved as if they were facing the enemy.

2. Petrov, *Study in Diplomacy,* 193.

3. FRUS, 1941, 2: 976–79.

4. Petrov, *Study in Diplomacy,* 192. Lane appealed for help directly to the president, stating that Americans in general might not be aware of the gravity of the situation, but "[we] must wake up to the necessity that we must be willing to give everything we have to save the situation. This is for the sake of religion, democracy, and civilization." FRUS, 1941, 2: 978–79.

5. Petrov, *Study in Diplomacy,* 192.

6. *Washington Evening Star,* April 7, 1941.

7. *Washington Post,* April 7, 1941.

8. *Chicago Daily News,* April 8, 1941.

9. *Washington Post,* April 7, 1941; *Christian Science Monitor,* April 8, 1941.

10. *New York Times,* April 8, 1941.

11. Radica, *Živjet-Nedoživjeti,* 2: 108.

12. Ibid., 2: 118–19.

13. *Washington Evening Star,* April 9, 1941.

14. *Chicago Daily News,* April 10, 1941; *Washington Post,* April 10, 1941; *New York Times,* April 10, 1941.

15. Donald S. Detwiler et al., eds., *World War II German Military Studies,* 13: 116.

16. *New York Times,* April 11, 1941. Donovan denied the charges against him, calling them "poppycock and tripe." He even tried to turn them into a joke. "Yes, they call me no. 2 agent in Washington, but who is no. 1, I wonder?" Ibid.

17. N.A., U.S. Department of State, Doc. no. 740.0011, European War 1939/1089.

18. St. John, *Land of Silent People,* 84.

19. Detwiler et al., *World War II German Military Studies,* 116.

20. Maček, *In the Struggle for Freedom,* 226.

21. Milovanović, *Pukotine Kraljevstva,* 320–21.

22. Detwiler et al., *World War II German Military Studies,* 111–12.

23. Vice-Premier Slobodan Jovanović told Ilija Jukić that the idea involving the surrender was Simović's brainchild, conceived without the knowledge of the Yugoslav government. Jukić, *Fall of Yugoslavia,* 72.

24. Hoptner, *Yugoslavia in Crisis,* 290.

25. Milovanović, *Pukotine Kraljevstva,* 324–32; Hoptner, *Yugoslavia in Crisis,* 290.

26. *Chicago Daily News,* April 9, 1941.

27. Ibid., April 10, 1941.

28. Ante Pavelić, *Putem Hrvatskog Državnog Prava.*

29. The most accurate numbers are given by two scholars: Bogoljub Kočović, a Serbian, in *Žrtve Drugog svetskog rata u Jugoslaviji* (London: Naše delo, 1985) and Vladimir Žerjavić, a Croatian, in *Gubici stanovništva u Jugoslaviji u Drugom svjetskom ratu* (Zagreb: Jugoslavensko viktimološko društvo, 1989). Žerjavić wrote another book in English—*Yugoslavia, Manipulation with* [sic] *the Number of Second World War Victims* (Zagreb: Hrvatski Informativni Centar, 1993). For an overall exaggeration of war-related victims see Franjo Tudjman, *Horrors of War: Historical Reality and Philosophy* (New York: M. Evans, 1996).

30. Branko Bokun, *Spy in the Vatican, 1941–45,* 9–12.

31. *Washington Evening Star,* April 12, 1941.

32. Ante Starčević was the nineteenth-century Croatian political philosopher and politician. He came out of the Croatian National Revival (The Illirian Movement) as the only Croato-centric thinker and politician who concluded that salvation for Croatia resided not in supranational political structures but in the rebirth of the Croatian national state. Engulfed by a deluge of Germanism,

Magyarism, Austroslavism, and the Serbian claims (Serbs all and everywhere) based on Karadžić's quasi-linguistic theories, Starčević defended the Croatian cultural achievements and the territorial space within history. His arguments were derived from the uninterrupted existence of the Croatian state, the proof of which was based on historical sources that could not be refuted or ignored by wishful thinking. In essence, Starčević's nationalism was of a defensive nature. He rejected the romantic notion of nationalism based on "blood and soil" and, unlike Karadžić, advocated equal rights for all citizens of Croatia irrespective of their ethnic origin. In short, the body politic was to be held together by rights and responsibilities for the benefit of all. In view of Serbian claims, it is no wonder that proponents of Karadžić's linguistic dreams proclaimed him a "dangerous lunatic." American news reporters, however, appeared to be the victims of their own ignorance and were unwitting tools of Serbian propaganda. See Ante Starčević, *Politički spisi. Tomislav Ladan, Comp.* (Zagreb: Znanja, 1971).

33. *Washington Post,* April 17, 1941.
34. Radica, *Živjeti-Nedoživjeti,* 2: 120.
35. Ibid. As the main contributor to the *Srbobran,* Fotić found a former diplomat and a gifted Serbian poet, Jovan Dučić. His vitriolic tirades against the "Croatians were aptly expressed in his dictum: Croatians are the bravest people, not because they are brave, but because they are ashamed of nothing." The anti-Croatian propaganda became so poisonous that the U.S. government was forced to intervene on behalf of the Croatians.
36. *New York Times,* April 26, 1941.
37. Ibid. Simović also intimated to Mameli that the Yugoslavs desired Mussolini's intervention in Berlin on their behalf so as not to undertake an attack toward Salonika. Mussolini was hardly in a position to intervene, but the game of procrastination continued. Both sides needed time. In the meantime, the Italian intelligence broke the Yugoslav code and broadcasted to the Yugoslavs to move their divisions from the Albanian border farther inside its territory. By the time they discovered the trick, there was not very much they could do. The Germans were already in Yugoslavia. Cervi, *The Hollow Legions,* 268. Thus Italians were not afraid of an immediate Yugoslav attack against them in Albania. They hoped that an agreement with Yugoslavia, however, would demoralize Greece and precipitate its collapse without German involvement. Greccia, *Yugoslavia, 1939–1941,* 632–60.
38. Ostovic, *Truth about Yugoslavia,* 165–66; Georgevich, *Na Raskrsnici,* 52.
39. Ostovic, *Truth about Yugoslavia,* 166.
40. Charles-Drago Šporer, "Odgovor Gosp. Aćimu Kosti."
41. Borković, *Milan Nedić,* 17–19.
42. Ibid., 29–30.
43. Dragovan Šepić, *Vlada Ivana Šubašića,* 25–26. To attract as much sympathy, King Peter, without knowledge of the non-Serbian members of the cabinet, sent a telegram to President Roosevelt on June 8, 1941. In it, he described victimization of the Serbian people. Crimes against the Serbs were perpetrated by the Bulgarians, the Hungarians, and the Croatians. "Classed as an inferior race which is destined to disappear[,] Serbs are deprived by that law[,] of all rights and all means [of] existence." FDR Library. O.F. Box 59, O.F. 200-1-2, March 20–June 30, 1941.
44. Šepić, *Vlada Ivana Šubašića,* 27.

45. *New York Times,* May 10, 1941.

46. *Washington Post,* April 21, 1941.

47. Cecil B. Brown, "The Germans Are Coming,"

48. Petrov, *Study in Diplomacy,* 198.

49. Ibid., 203. The promised job never materialized. Instead of Mexico, Lane was sent to Costa Rica.

50. Arthur Bliss Lane, "Conquest of Yugoslavia."

51. Radica, *Živjeti-Nedoživjeti,* 2: 123–24.

52. Ibid., 124.

53. Radica papers, "Speech made by Arthur Bliss Lane, the United States Minister to Yugoslavia, on the Fourth of July, at Libertyville, Illinois, 1941."

54. Radica, *Živjeti-Nedoživjeti,* 2: 124.

55. N.A., U.S. Department of State, Doc. no. 860H.00/1309.

56. Ibid. The report was received in Washington on June 30. Maček's statement was induced from him by the Germans. He was careful not to give any impression that he was in agreement with Pavelić or the new regime.

57. Omrčanin, *The Pro-Allied Putsch in Croatia,* 16.

58. FRUS, 1941, 2: 979–84. Unlike the Americans, the British were unequivocal in their intent to restore Yugoslavia after the war. Šepić, *Vlada Ivana Šubašića,* 24.

59. Radica, *Živjeti-Nedoživjeti,* 2: 120 passim. Italian historian Gaetano Salvemini, then residing in the United States informed Radica that Roosevelt asked King Peter when he visited Washington in June 1941: "Peter, would you rather be the beloved King of Serbia or the hated King of Yugoslavia?" Ibid, 174.

60. For other literature relative to the future of Yugoslavia: see Welles, 136; Sherwood, *Roosevelt and Hopkins,* 711. Eden held that no better solution for either the Croatians or Slovenians could be found outside of Yugoslavia. Eden, *The Reckoning,* 433.

61. *Washington Post,* September 5, 1941.

62. *Chicago Daily News,* December 23, 1941.

63. Van Creveld, "The German Attack on the USSR."

64. H. B. Liddell Hart, *Defense of the West,* 80.

65. Trumball Higgins, *Hitler and Russia,* 10.

66. Van Creveld, *Hitler's Strategy,* 182; Detwiler et al., *World War II German Military Studies,* 118. The principal reasons for Germany's easy victory in Greece in part had to do with the early collapse of Yugoslavia. In the Yugoslav campaign, the German losses amounted to 558 men, of which 151 were listed as killed, 392 as wounded, and 15 as missing in action. Detwiler et al., *World War II German Military Studies,* 64.

67. Michael A. Barnhart, *Japan Prepares for Total War,* 265.

68. Vjekoslav Vrančić, *Postrojenje i Brojčano Stanje Hrvatskih Oružanih Snaga u Godinama 1941–1945* (Buenos Aires, 1952), 4–7. The data for this brochure was supplied by the head of the operational division of the Croatian armed forces, General Fedor Dragojlov. It might be of interest to know that the general was a Croatian Serb, a former officer of the Austro-Hungarian Army. Actually, there were many higher- and lower-ranking officers of Serbian descent who voluntarily joined the first units of the Croatian armed forces in 1941. According to Vrančić, by the end of 1941 there were 10,500 armed Ustašas in the entire state of Croatia, of whom 1,200 were guarding the railway lines.

69. Ibid. Under the pretext of fighting the Communists, Italians for "tactical" reasons made all kinds of agreements with Chetniks in Croatia. Under Italian protectorate, the Chetniks behaved more or less as they pleased. For Chetnik collaboration with Italians based mostly on Italian sources see Milazzo, *Chetnik Movement*, 42–139. For collaboration in general: Tomasevich, *The Chetniks*, 196–261. Also Milovanović, *Draža Mihailović.*

70. Jovan Marjanović, *Draža Mihailović izmedju Britanaca i Nemaca* (Belgrade: Prosveta, 1979).

71. Milovanović, *Draža Mihailović.* For a more sympathetic view of Mihailović and the Chetniks see Lucien Karchmar, *Draža Mihailović and the Rise of the Chetnik Movement, 1941–1942.*

72. Seton-Watson, *Eastern Europe,* 409.

Chapter 12. Conclusion

1. Norman Corwin, *Trivializing America,* 179.
2. Hans Kohn, *Panslavism* (Notre Dame: Notre Dame University Press, 1953), 7.
3. Ibid., 191–92.
4. For the liquidation of the Jews and collaborations with the Nazis in wartime Serbia, see Philip J. Cohen, *Serbia's Secret War.*
5. Dobrica Ćosić, *Deobe* (Belgrade: Prosveta, 1968), 91.
6. Ibid., 421.
7. For better understanding of the Serbian mind-set, one should read Stjepan G. Meštrović, *Habits of the Balkan Heart.*
8. Phyllis Auty and Richard Clogg, eds., 252.

Bibliography

Adams, John C. *Flight in Winter.* Princeton: Princeton University Press, 1942.

Albrecht-Carrie, René. *Italy at the Paris Peace Conference.* New York: Columbia University Press, 1938.

Allen, Peter. *The Windsor Secret: New Revelation of the Nazi Connection.* New York: Stein & Day, 1983.

Ambrose, Stephen E. *Rise to Globalism: American Foreign Policy since 1938.* New York: Penguin Books, 1985.

American Herald (New York City), March 22, 1941.

Andrew, Christopher, and David Dilks, eds. *The Missing Dimension: Governments and Intelligence Communities in the Twentieth Century.* London: Macmillan, 1984.

Armstrong, Hamilton Fish. "The Royal Dictatorship in Yugoslavia." *Foreign Affairs* 7(4) (July, 1929): 601–603.

——. "After the Assassination of King Alexander." *Foreign Affairs* 13(2) (January, 1935): 224–25.

Auty, Phyllis. *Tito.* New York: Ballantine Books, 1974.

Avramovski, Živko. *Balkanske Zemlje i Velike Sile 1935–1937.* Belgrade: Prosveta, 1968.

Balfour, Neil, and Sally Mackay. *Paul of Yugoslavia: Britain's Maligned Friend.* London: Hamish Hamilton, 1980.

Banac, Ivo. *The National Question in Yugoslavia: Origins, History, Politics.* Ithaca: Cornell University Press, 1984.

Barker, Elisabeth. *British Policy in Southeast Europe in the Second World War.* London: Macmillan, 1976.

Barnhart, Michael A. *Japan Prepares for Total War: The Search for Economic Security, 1919–1941.* Ithaca: Cornell University Press, 1987.

Barros, James. *The Corfu Incident of 1923: Mussolini and the League of Nations.* Princeton: Princeton University Press, 1965.

Beard, Charles A. *The Balkan Pivot: A Study in Government and Administration.* New York: Macmillan, 1927.

——. "Autobiography of Stephen Raditch." *Current History* 29(1) (October, 1928): 84.

Begić, Miron Krešimir. *Ustaški Pokret.* New York: Ustaša, 1986.

Beloff, Nora. *Tito's Flawed Legacy: Yugoslavia and the West, 1939–84.* London: Gollance, 1985.

Bennett, Edward M. *Franklin D. Roosevelt and the Search for Security, 1933–1939.* Wilmington, Del.: Scholarly Resources, Inc., 1985.

Berle, Adolf A. "Papers, 1912–1974." Franklin Delano Roosevelt Presidential Library, Hyde Park, New York.

Berle, Beatrice Bishop, and Travis Beal Jacobs, eds. *Navigating the Rapids, 1918–1971: From the Papers of Adolf A. Berle.* New York: Harcourt Brace Jovanovich, 1973.

Bess, Damaree. "Our Frontier on the Danube." *Saturday Evening Post,* May 24, 1941, pp. 1ff.

Blet, Pierre, et al. *Actes et documents du Saint Siege relatifs a la Seconde Guerre mondiale.* Vatican City: Libreria editirice vaticana, 1965.

Boban, Ljubo. *Sporazum Cvetković-Maček.* Belgrade: Institut Društvenih Nauka, 1965.

——. *Svetozar Pribičević u Opoziciji (1928–1936).* Zagreb: Institut za Hrvatsku Povijest, 1973.

——. *Maček i Politika Hrvatske Seljačke Stranke, 1928–1941.* Vol. 2. Zagreb: Liber, 1974.

——. "Britanija, Hrvatska i Hrvatska Seljačka Starnke, 1939–1945." *Časopis za Suvremenu Povijest* (Zagreb) 3 (1978): 6.

——. *Kontraverze iz Povijesti Jugoslavije.* Zagreb: Školska Knjiga, 1987.

Bohlen, Charles E. *Witness to History, 1929–1969.* New York: Norton, 1973.

Bokun, Branko. *Spy in the Vatican, 1941–45.* New York: Praeger, 1973.

Breccia, Alfredo. *Jugoslavia, 1939–1941: Diplomazia della Neutralità.* Milan: Giuffrè, 1978.

Brock, Ray. *Nor Any Victory.* New York: Reynal & Hitchcock, 1942.

Brown, Anthony Cave. *"C," the Secret Life of Sir Stewart Graham Menzis, Spymaster to Churchill.* New York: Macmillan, 1967.

——. *Bodyguard of Lies.* New York: Harper & Row, 1975.

——. *The Last Hero: Wild Bill Donovan.* New York: Times Books, 1982.

Bulletin of the Yugoslav Courier (Chicago), March 15, 1941.

Burgwyn, James H. *The Legend of the Mutilated Victory: Italy, the Great War, and the Paris Peace Conference, 1915–1919.* Westport, Conn.: Greenwood Press, 1993.

Burns, James MacGregor. *Roosevelt: The Lion and the Fox.* New York: Harcourt Brace Jovanovich, 1976.

Burrin, Philippe. *The Soldier of Freedom.* New York: Harcourt Brace Jovanovich, 1976.

——. *France under the Germans: Collaboration and Compromise.* Translated from French by Janet Lloyd. New York: New Press, 1996.

Cecil, Robert. "The Cambridge Comintern." Pp. 169–98 in *The Missing Dimension,* ed. Christopher Andrew and David Dilks. London: Macmillan, 1984.

Cencić, Vjenceslav. *Enigma Kopinič.* Belgrade: Rad, 1983.

Cerf, Bennett. *Saturday Review of Literature* 26 (August, 1943): 15.

Cervi, Mario. *The Hollow Legions: Mussolini's Blunder in Greece, 1940–1941.* Garden City, N.Y.: Doubleday, 1971.

Chicago Daily News, September 21, 1938; March 26, 27, 29, 1941; April 8–10, 12, 1941; December 23, 1941.

Christian Science Monitor, March 24, 27, 28, 1941; April 4, 5, 8, 9, 12, 21, 1941.

Churchill, Winston. *The Second World War: The Gathering Storm.* Boston: Houghton Mifflin, 1948–53.

——. *The Second World War: The Grand Alliance.* Boston: Houghton Mifflin, 1950.

Ciano, Galeazzo. *The Ciano Diaries, 1939–1943.* Garden City, N.Y.: Garden City Publishers, 1947.

——. *Ciano's Hidden Diary, 1937–1938.* New York: Dutton, 1953.

Clissold, Stephen. *Djilas: The Progress of a Revolutionary.* Hounslow, England: M. T. Smith, 1983.

Clogg, Richard. "The Special Operation Executive in Greece." P. 110 in *Greece in the 1940s: A Nation in Crisis,* ed. John O. Iatrides. Hanover, Mass.: University Press of New England, 1981.

Cohen, Philip J. *Serbia's Secret War: Propaganda and the Deceit of History.* College Station: Texas A&M University Press, 1996.

Cole, Wayne S. *Roosevelt and the Isolationists, 1932–1945.* Lincoln: University of Nebraska Press, 1983.

Collier, Basil. *The Defense of the United Kingdom, History of the Second World War: United Kingdom Military Series.* London: H. M. Stationery Office, 1957.

Cook, Cecil B. "The Germans are Coming." *Saturday Evening Post,* August 23, 1941: 18–19.

Corwin, Norman L. *Trivializing America.* Secaucus, N.J.: Lyle Stuart, 1983.

Cvetković, Dragiša. *Dokumenti o Jugoslaviji: Sovjeti Britanija i Jugoslavija 1940–1941.* Paris: Les Presses Rapides, 1958.

Cvijetić, Leposava. "Prodaja Naoružanja kao Metod Pritiska Nemačke na Jugoslaviju." *Istorija XX Veka: Zbornik Radova* Belgrade 13 (1975): 172–253.

Dallek, Robert. *Franklin D. Roosevelt and American Foreign Policy, 1931–1945.* New York: Oxford University Press, 1979.

Dalton, Hugh. *The Fateful Years, 1931–1945.* London: Muller, 1975.

———. *The Second World War Diary of Hugh Dalton.* London: Cape in association with the London School of Economics and Political Science, 1986.

Dedijer, Vladimir, ed. *Novi prilozi za biografiju Josipa Broza Tita.* Rijeka: Liburnija, 1980–84.

DePorte, Anthony W. *Europe between the Superpowers: The Enduring Balance.* New Haven: Yale University Press, 1979.

Detwiler, Donald S., Charles B. Burdick, and Jurgen Rohwer, eds. *World War II German Military Studies.* New York: Garland, 1979.

Djuretić, Veselin. *Vlada na bespuću: Internacionalizacija Jugoslavenskih Proturječnosti 1941–1944.* Belgrade: Narodna Kajiga, 1983.

———. *Saveznici i Jugoslavenska Ratna Drama, 1941–1944.* Belgrade: Narodna Kajiga, 1985.

Documents on British Foreign Policy, 1919–1939; Second and Third Series, 1930-1939 (DBFP in manuscript). Washington, D.C.: GPO, 1983.

Documents on German Foreign Policy, 1918–1945, Series C and D (DGFP in manuscript). Washington, D.C.: GPO, 1983.

Doder, Milenko. *Kopinič bez Enigme.* Zagreb: Center Informacije i Publicitet, 1986.

Doumanis, Nicholas. *Myth and Memory in the Mediterranean: Remembering Fascism's Empire.* New York: St. Martin's Press, 1997.

Dragnich, Alex. *The First Yugoslavia: Search for a Viable Political System.* Stanford, Calif.: Hoover Institute Press, 1983.

"Dragocjeni Dokumenat pok. Biskupa Čule." *Nova Hrvatska* (London) 9–11 (1988): 15–20.

Dunlop, Richard. *Donovan: American Master Spy.* Chicago: Rand McNally, 1982.

Eden, Anthony. *The Reckoning: The Memoirs of Anthony Eden.* Boston: Houghton Mifflin, 1965.

Fehrenbach, T. R. *F.D.R.'s Undeclared War, 1939–1941.* New York: David McKay, 1967.

Feiling, Keith G. *The Life of Neville Chamberlain.* London: Macmillan, 1946.

Foreign Relations of the United States, 1918–1945 (FRUS in manuscript). Washington, D.C.: GPO, 1948.

Fotitch (Fotić), Constantin. *The War We Lost: Yugoslavia Tragedy and the Failure of the West.* New York: Viking, 1948.

George, Margaret. *The Warped Vision: British Foreign Policy, 1933–1939.* Pittsburgh: University of Pittsburgh Press, 1965.

Georgevich, Dragoslav. "Two Days in Yugoslav History: March 25 and 27, 1941." Master's thesis, San Jose State College, 1967.

———. *Na Raskrsnici: Prilozi za Srpsku Istoriju Drugog Svetskog Rata.* Toronto: Brastvo, 1988.

Gilbert, Martin. *Finest Hour: Winston S. Churchill, 1939–1941.* London: Heinemann, 1983.

Good, Marie S. "International Politics and the Perception of the Croatian Problem: 1921–1941." Ph.D. diss., State University of New York at Buffalo, 1978.

Gotovac, Vlado. "Vlado Gotovac govori u Novoj Reviji." *Nova Hrvatska* 9 (May, 1988): 11.

Gregorić, Danilo. *Samomor Jugoslavije.* Ljubljana: Luč, 1945.

Grgić, Tomiša. "Frilog poznavanju Marseilleskog antentata." *Hrvatska Revija* (Munich-Barcelona: Ožujak) 37(1): 68–76.

Hagen, Walter. *Die Geheime Front: Organisation, Personen, und Aktionen des deutschen Geheimdienstes.* Zürich: Europa-Verlag, 1950.

Halder, Franz. *The Halder Diaries: The Private War Journals of Colonel General Franz Halder.* Boulder, Colo.: Westview Press, 1976.

Hart, H. B. Liddell. *Defense of the West.* New York: Morrow, 1950.

Haslam, Jonathan. *The Soviet Union and the Struggle for Collective Security in Europe, 1933–1938.* New York: St. Martin's Press, 1988.

Hassell, Ulrich von. *Vom Andern Deutschland.* Zürich: Atlantis Verlag, 1946.

———. *The von Hassell Diaries.* Garden City, N.Y.: Doubleday, 1974.

Hearden, Patrick J. *Roosevelt Confronts Hitler: America's Entry into World War II.* DeKalb: Northern Illinois University Press, 1986.

Heilbut, Anthony. *Exiled in Paradise.* New York: Viking, 1983.

Hernian, Edward S. *Manufacturing Consent: The Political Economy of the Mass Media.* New York: Pantheon Books, 1966.

Herwarth von Bittenfeld, Hans-Heinrich. *Against Two Evils.* New York: Rawson, Wade, 1981.

Higgins, Trumball. *Hitler and Russia: The Third Reich in a Two-Front War, 1939–1943.* New York: Macmillan, 1966.

Higham, Charles. *Trading with the Enemy: An Expose of the Nazi-American Money Plot, 1939–1949.* New York: Delacorte, 1983.

Higham, Robin. *Diary of a Disaster: British Aid to Greece, 1940–1941.* Lexington: University Press of Kentucky, 1986.

Hilton, Stanley E. *Hitler's Secret War in South America, 1939–1945.* Baton Rouge: Louisiana State University Press, 1981.

Hinsley, Francis H. *British Intelligence in the Second World War: Its Influence on Strategy and Operation.* Cambridge: Cambridge University Press, 1979.

Hitchens, Marilyn Giroux. "Germany, Russia, and the Balkans: Prelude to the Nazi-Soviet Non-Aggression Pact, April–August 1938." Ph.D. diss., University of Colorado, 1979.

Hoptner, Jacob B. *Yugoslavia in Crisis, 1934–1941.* New York: Columbia University Press, 1962.

Horvat, Josip. *Živjeti u Hrvatskoj: Zapisi iz Nepovrata, 1900–1941.* Zagreb: SNL Libar, 1984.

Hull, Cordell. *The Memoirs of Cordell Hull.* New York: Macmillan, 1948.

Hyde, Montgomery H. *Secret Intelligence Agent.* London: Constable, 1982.

Ickes, Harold L. *The Secret Diary of Harold L. Ickes.* New York: DaCapo Press, 1974.

I Documenti Diplomatici Italiani (DDI in manuscript). Settima series, 1922–1935; Ottava series, 1935–1939; Nova series 1939–1943. Rome: Libreria dello Stato, 1952–.

Irving, David. *The War Path: Hitler's Germany, 1933–1939.* London: Joseph, 1978.

Jareb, Jere. *Pola Stoljeća Hrvatske Politike.* Buenos Aires: Knjižnica Hrvatske Revije, 1960.

——. *Političke Uspomene i Rad Dra Branka Jelića*. Cleveland, Ohio: Mirko Šamija, 1982.

Jonas, Manfred. *The United States and Germany: A Diplomatic History*. Ithaca: Cornell University Press, 1984.

Jukic, Ilija. *The Fall of Yugoslavia*. Translated by Dorian Cooke. New York: Harcourt Brace Jovanovich, 1974.

Karchmar, Lucien. *Draža Mihailović and the Rise of the Chetnik Movement, 1941–1942*. 2 vols. New York: Garland, 1987.

Kennan, George F. *Memoirs: 1925–1950*. Boston: Little, Brown & Co., 1967.

Kennedy, Paul. *The Realities behind Diplomacy: Background Influences on British External Policy, 1865–1980*. London: Allen & Unwin, 1981.

——. *The Rise and Fall of the Great Powers: Economic Change and Military Conflict from 1500–2000*. New York: Random House, 1987.

Kerner, Robert J. "Yugoslavia and the Peace Conference." Pp. 92–103 in *Yugoslavia*, ed. Robert J. Kerner. Berkeley: University of California Press, 1949.

Kimball, Warren E., ed. *Roosevelt and Churchill: The Complete Correspondence*. Princeton: Princeton University Press, 1984.

Kneževic, Radoje. "Prince Paul, Hitler, and Salonika." *International Affairs* 27 (January, 1951): 38–44.

Knox, MacGregor. *Mussolini Unleashed, 1939–1941: Politics and Strategy of Fascist Italy's Last War*. Cambridge: Cambridge University Press, 1982.

Kovačić, Matija. *Od Radića do Pavelića*. Munich: Knjizica Hrvatske Revije, 1970.

Krizman, Bogdan. *Vanjska politika jugoslavenske države, 1918–1941 (Foreign Policy of Yugoslavia, 1918–1941)*. Zagreb: Školska Knjiga, 1975.

——. *Pavelić i Ustaše*. Zagreb: Globus, 1978.

——. *Pavelić izmedju Hitlera i Mussolinija*. Zagreb: Globus, 1980.

Krylov, Ivan. *Soviet Staff Officer*. New York: Philosophical Library, 1951.

Kulundžić, Zvonimir. *Atentat na Stjepana Radića*. Zagreb: Stvarnost, 1967.

Kvaternik, Eugen. "Ustaška Emigracija u Italiji i 10 Travnja 1941." *Hrvatska Revija* (Buenos Aires) 3 (September, 1952): 70–98.

——. "Riječi i činjenice: Prilozi povijesti Hrvatsko-Talijanskih odnosa u Drugom Svjetskom Ratu." *Hrvatska Revija* (Buenos Aires) 6 (March, 1955): 56–76.

Lane, Arthur Bliss. "Conquest of Yugoslavia." *Life* 11 (September 15, 1941): 10ff.

Lane, Peter Barry. "The United States and the Balkan Crisis of 1940–1941." Ph.D. diss., University of Washington, 1972.

Langer, William L., and S. Everett Gleason. *The Challenge to Isolation: The World Crisis of 1937–1940 and American Foreign Policy*. New York: Harper & Row, 1952.

Larson, David L. *United States Foreign Policy toward Yugoslavia*. Washington, D.C.: University Press of America, 1978.

Lederer, Ivo J. *Yugoslavia at the Paris Peace Conference: A Study in Frontiermaking*. New Haven: Yale University Press, 1963.

Lee, Lorraine Mary. "American Foreign Policy toward Yugoslavia, 1941–1949." Ph.D. diss., Pennsylvania State University, 1976.

Lee, Raymond E. *London Journal of General Raymond E. Lee*. Boston: Little, Brown & Co., 1971.

Link, Arthur S., ed. *The Papers of Woodrow Wilson*. Princeton: Princeton University Press, 1965.

——. *Woodrow Wilson: Revolution, War, and Peace*. Arlington Heights, Ill.: AHM Publishing Corporation, 1979.

Loewenheim, Francis L., et al., eds. *Roosevelt and Churchill: Their Secret Wartime Correspondence.* New York: Saturday Review Press, 1975.

Louis, William Roger. *Imperialism at Bay 1941–1945: The United States and the Decolonization of the British Empire.* Oxford: Clarendon Press, 1977.

Lukač, Dušan. *Treći Rajh i Zemlje jugoistočne Evrope.* 2 vols. Belgrade: Vojnoizdavački Zavod, 1982.

Maček, Vladimir. *In the Struggle for Freedom.* New York: Speller, 1957.

MacMillan, Harold. *War Diaries: Politics and War in the Mediterranean, January 1939 to May 1945.* London: St. Martin's Press, 1984.

Markham, Reuben. "Croats Revolt against Serbs." *Christian Century* 52 (July 3, 1935): 923.

Mastny, Wojtech. *Russia's War to Cold War: Diplomacy, Warfare, and the Politics of Communism, 1941–1945.* New York: Columbia University Press, 1979.

Matković, Hrvoje. *Svetozar Pribičević: Ideolog, Stranački Vodja, Emigrant.* Zagreb: Hrvatska Sveučilišna Naklada, 1995.

Meštrović, Ivan. *Uspomeme na Političke Ljude i Dogadjaje.* Buenos Aires: Knjižnica Hrvatske Revije, 1961.

Meštrović, Stjepan G., et al. *Habits of the Balkan Heart: Social Culture and the Fall of Communism.* College Station: Texas A&M University Press, 1993.

Middlemas, Keith. *The Strategy of Appeasement: The British Government and Germany, 1937–39.* Chicago: Quadrangle Books, 1972.

Milazzo, Matteo J. *The Chetnik Movement and the Yugoslav Resistance.* Baltimore: Johns Hopkins University Press, 1975.

Milovanović, Nikola. *Pukotine Kraljevstva.* Belgrade: Sloboda, 1978.

——. *Vojni Puč i 27, Mart 1941.* Belgrade: Sloboda, 1981.

——. *Draža Mihailovic.* Zagreb: Centar za Informacije i Publicitet, 1985.

Mitchell, Ruth. *The Serbs Choose War.* Garden City, N.Y.: Doubleday, Doran & Co., 1943.

Modisett, Edward L. "The Four-Cornered Triangle: British and American Policy toward Yugoslavia, 1939–1945." Ph.D. diss., Georgetown University, 1981.

Moraca, Pero. *Jujolsvija 1941.* Belgrade: Institut za Suvremenu Istoriju, 1971.

Mužić, Ivan. *Masonstvo u Hrvata.* Split: Crkva u Svijetu, 1984.

——. *Stjepan Radić: U Kraljevini Srba, Hrvata i Slovenaca.* Zagreb: H.K.D. Sv. Ćirila i Metoda, 1987.

Nenezić, Zoran D. *Masoni u Yugoslaviji, 1764–1980: pregled istorije slobodnog zidarstva u Jugoslaviji: prilozi i grada.* Belgrade: Narodna Knjiga, 1984.

New York Herald-Tribune, March 22, 26, 28, 29, 1941.

New York Post, June 11, 1940.

New York Times, October 4, 1938; November 22, 1940; January 5, 1941; February 15, 18, 1941; March 3, 7, 9–11, 17, 21, 22, 25–27, 29, 1941; April 2, 3, 6, 8, 10–12, 14, 25, 26, 1941; May 10, 1941.

Nisbet, Robert. *Roosevelt and Stalin: The Failed Courtship.* Washington, D.C.: Regnery Gateway, 1988.

Noel, Bernard. *Marseille-New York: Une Liaison surrealiste—a surrealist liaison.* Paris: Andre Dimanche, 1985.

Omrčanin, Ivo. *The Pro-Allied Putsch in Croatia in 1944 and the Massacre of Croatians by Tito's Communists.* Philadelphia: Dorrance, 1975.

——. *Enigma Tito.* Washington, D.C.: Samizdat, 1984.

Orlow, Dietrich. *The Nazis in the Balkans: A Case Study of Totalitarian Politics.* Pittsburgh: University of Pittsburgh Press, 1968.

Ostovic, Pavle. *The Truth about Yugoslavia*. New York: Roy, 1952.

Pavelić, Ante. *Putem Hrvatskog Državnog Prava: Članci, Govori, Izjave*. Madrid: Domovina, 1977.

Pešelj, Branko. "Serbo-Croatian Agreement of 1939 and American Policy." *Journal of Croatian Studies* 11–12 (1970–71): 15–16.

———. "Jedno Interesantno Mišljenje." *Hrvatski Dom* (Calgary) 1(5) (December, 1990): 9.

Peter, King of Yugoslavia. *A King's Heritage*. New York: Putnam, 1954.

Petrov, Vladimir. *A Study in Diplomacy: The Story of Arthur Bliss Lane*. Chicago: Regnery, 1971.

Petrović, Svatislav-Sveta. *Free Yugoslavia Calling*. New York: Graystone, 1941.

Pimlott, Ben, ed. *The Second World War Diary of Hugh Dalton 1940–45*. London: Cape in association with the London School of Economics and Political Sciences, 1986.

Popović, Jovo, and Darko Stuparić. "Napravit ćemo čudo." *Vjesnik* (Zagreb) 27(4) (1977).

Popović, Uglješa. *Deseti po redu: Tajna Vojno Obavještajne Službe bivše Jugoslavenske Vojske of 1938 do Maja 1941 godine*. Belgrade: Savo Simić, 1976.

Prpić, George J. *The Croatian Immigrants in America*. New York: Philosophical Library, 1971.

Radica, Bogdan. "Papers, 1930–1946 (Radica Archives in manuscript)." His personal library, New York City.

———. *Hrvatska 1945: Politički dnevnik*. München-Barcelona: Knjižnica Hrvatske Revije, 1974.

———. *Živjeti-Nedoživjeti*. 2 vols. München: Knjižnica Hrvatske Revije, 1984.

Radovanović, Milovan V. *Enciklopedija Jogoslavije*, 1955 ed. Vol. 7, "Srbi."

Reynolds, David. *The Creation of Anglo-American Alliance, 1937–1941: A Study in Competitive Cooperation*. London: Europe Publications, 1981.

Ristić, Dragiša N. *Yugoslavia's Revolution of 1941*. University Park: Pennsylvania State University Press, 1966.

Roosevelt, Franklin D. "Papers as President, 1933–1945." Franklin Delano Roosevelt Presidential Library, Hyde Park, New York.

———. *The Public Papers and Addresses of Franklin D. Roosevelt, with Special Explanatory Notes by President Roosevelt*. New York: Random House, 1938–50.

———. *Complete Presidential Press Conferences of Franklin D. Roosevelt*. New York: Da Capo Press, 1972.

Ross, Graham, ed. *The Foreign Office and the Kremlin: British Documents on Anglo-Soviet Relations, 1941–1955*. Cambridge: Cambridge University Press, 1984.

Rout, Leslie B., Jr., and John F. Bratzel. *The Shadow War: German Espionage and United States Counterespionage in Latin America during World War II*. Frederick, Md.: University Publications of America, 1986.

Sadkovich, James J. "Italian Support for Croatian Separatism: 1927–1937." Ph.D. diss., University of Wisconsin, 1982.

———. "The Mobilization of Croatian Immigrants: Opinion and the Croatian Press in America during World War I." *Journal of Croatian Studies* 27 (1986): 94–120.

———. "The Use of Political Trial to Repress Croatian Dissent, 1929–1934." *Journal of Croatian Studies* 28–29 (1987–88): 103–41.

———. "Terrorism in Croatia, 1929–1934." *East European Quarterly* 22(1) (March, 1988): 55–79.

———. *The Italian Navy in World War II*. Westport, Conn.: Greenwood Press, 1994.

St. John, Robert. *The Land of Silent People*. New York: Doubleday, Doran & Co., 1942.

Salvemini, Gaetano. *Prelude to World War II*. Garden City, N.Y.: Doubleday, 1954.

Schlesinger, Arthur M., Jr. *The Age of Roosevelt: The Crisis of the Old Order, 1919–1933.* Boston: Houghton Mifflin, 1957.

Schmidt, Paul. *Statist auf diplomatischer Bühne, 1923–1945 (Hitler's Interpreter).* New York: Macmillan, 1951.

Schroder, Hans-Jurgen. "Süedosteuropa als 'Informal Empire' Deutschland, Das Beispiel Jugoslawien." *Jahrbuch füer Osteuropas* (West Germany) 32 (1975): 233–66.

Šepić, Dragovan. *Vlada Ivana Šubašića.* Zagreb: Globus, 1983.

Serafis, Marion, ed. *Greece from Resistance to Civil War.* Nottingham, England: Spokesman, 1980.

Seton-Watson, G. N. Hugh. *The East European Revolution.* New York: Praeger, 1951.

———. "Afterword: Thirty Years After." Pp. 283–97 in *British Policy towards Wartime Resistance in Yugoslavia and Greece,* ed. Phyllis Auty and Richard Clogg. London: Macmillan in association with the Slavonic and East European Studies, 1975.

Sherwood, Robert E. *Roosevelt and Hopkins, an Intimate History.* New York: Harper, 1950.

Shotwell, James T. *A Balkan Mission.* New York: Columbia University Press, 1949.

Simoni, Leonard. *Berlino, Ambasciata d'Italia, 1939–1943.* Rome: Misliarese, 1946.

Sinclair, Andrew. *The Red and the Blue: Intelligence, Treason, and the Universities.* London: Weidenfeld & Nicholson, 1986.

Smith, R. Harris. *OSS: The Secret History of America's First Central Intelligence Agency.* Berkeley: University of California Press, 1971.

Šporer, Charles-Drago. "Odgovor Gosp. Aćimu-Kosti." *Amerikanski Srbobran* (September 28, 1971).

Srbija i Albanci: Pregled Politike Srbije Prema Albancima od 1944 do 1989 Godine. 3 vols. Ljubljana: Časopis za kritiko znanosti, 1989.

Stafford, David A. T. "SOE and British Involvement in the Belgrade coup d'etat of March 27, 1941." *Slavic Review* 36 (September, 1977): 399–419.

———. *British and European Resistance, 1940–1941: A Survey of Special Operation Executives, with Documents.* London: Macmillan, 1980.

———. *Camp X.* New York: Dodd, Mead, 1987.

Stakić, Vladislav D. *Moji Razgovori sa Musolinijem: Osovinske Sile i Jugoslavija.* München: published by author, 1967.

Starčević, Ante. *Izabrani Spisi.* Edited by Blaž Jurišić. Zagreb: Izdanje Hrvatskog Izdavalačkog Bibliografskog Zavoda, 1943.

Steel, Ronald. *Walter Lippmann and the American Century.* Boston: Little, Brown & Co., 1980.

Stevenson, William. *A Man Called Intrepid.* New York: Ballantine, 1980.

———. *Intrepid's Last Case.* New York: Villard, 1982.

Stojadinović, Milan. *Ni rat ni pakt: Jugoslavija izmedju dva rata.* Rijeka: Otokar Keršovani, 1972.

Sulzberger, Cyrus L. *A Long Row of Candles: Memoirs and Diaries, 1935–1954.* New York: Macmillan, 1969.

———. *Last of the Giants.* New York: Macmillan, 1970.

Tasovac, Ivo M. "Hrvati u Anglo-Američkim Enciklopedijama." *Hrvatska Revija* (Munich-Barcelona: Lipanj, 1983): 176–92.

Tasso, Antonio. *Italia e Croazia.* 3 vols. Macerata, Italy: S. Giuseppe, 1967–?.

Terzić, Velimir. *Slom Kraljevine jugoslavije 1941: Uzroci i Posljedice Poraza.* 2 vols. Belgrade: Narodna Knjiga, 1982.

Times Herald (New York City), March 23, 1941.

Tomasevich, Jozo. *The Chetniks: War and Revolution in Yugoslavia, 1941–1945.* Stanford: Stanford University Press, 1975.

Topitsch, Ernst. *Stalin's War: A Radical New Theory of the Origins of the Second World War.* New York: St. Martin's Press, 1987.

Troy, Thomas F. *Donovan and the CIA: A History of the Establishment of the Central Intelligence Agency.* Langley, Va.: Central Intelligence Agency, Center for the Study of Intelligence, 1981.

Tudjman, Franjo. "Uzroci Krize Monarhističke Jugoslavije od Ujedinjenja 1918 do Sloma 1941." *Forum* (Zagreb) 13 (January–February, 1967): 105.

———. *Stjepan Radić u Hrvatskoj Povijesti: O 60-toj obljetnici smrti.* Sudbury, Canada: Hrvatsko-kanadski Povijesni Institut, 1988.

U.S. Department of the Navy. "Naval Operations Intelligence." National Archives, Washington, D.C.

U.S. Department of State. "Commercial Division." National Archives, Washington, D.C.

———. "European War." National Archives, Washington, D.C.

———. "Military Division." National Archives, Washington, D.C.

van Creveld, Martin. "The German Attack on the USSR: The Destruction of a Legend." *European Studies Review* 2 (January, 1971): 69–88.

———. *Hitler's Strategy, 1940–1941: The Balkan Clue.* Cambridge: Cambridge University Press, 1973.

Velebit, Vladimir. *Sećanja.* Zagreb: Globus, 1983.

Vinaver, Vuk. *Jugoslavija i Madjarska, 1939–1941.* Belgrade: Institut za Suvremenu Istoriju, 1976.

Vjesnik (Zagreb), April 23, 1977; November 27, 1990.

Volkov, Fyodor. *Secrets from Whitehall and Downing Street.* Moscow: Progress Publications, 1986.

von Südland, L. *Die Südslawische Frage und der Weltkrieg: übersichtliche Darstellung des Gesamt-Problems.* Vienna: Hof-Verlag, 1918.

Washington Evening Star, March 27–29, 31, 1941; April 5, 7, 9, 12, 1941; September 5, 1941.

Washington Post, March 26, 29–31, 1941; April 7, 8, 11, 17, 21, 1941.

Watt, D. Cameron. *Succeeding John Bull: America in Britain's Place, 1900–1975.* Cambridge: Cambridge University Press, 1984.

Weber, Frank G. *The Evasive Neutral: Germany, Britain, and the Quest for a Turkish Alliance in the Second World War.* Columbia: University of Missouri Press, 1979.

Wedemeyer, Albert C. *Wedemeyer's Reports.* New York: Holt, 1958.

Welles, Sumner. *Seven Decisions That Shaped History.* New York: Harper & Row, 1951.

Wheeler, Mark. *Britain and the War for Yugoslavia, 1940–1943.* Boulder, Colo.: East European Monographs, 1980.

Wheeler-Bennett, John. *King George VI: His Life and Reign.* London: Macmillan, 1965.

White, Leigh. *The Long Balkan Night.* New York: Scribner, 1944.

Wilson, Henry M. *Eight Years Overseas.* London: Hutchison, 1948.

Winant, John G. "Papers 1916–1947." Franklin Delano Roosevelt Presidential Library, Hyde Park, New York.

Wolfe, Henry C. "Yugoslavia's Design for Democracy." *Current Affairs* (August, 1937): 46–54.

Wüscht, Johann. *Jugoslawian und das Dritte Reich: Eine dokumentierte Geschichte der deutsche-jugoslawischen Bezichungen von 1933 bis 1945.* Stuttgart: Seewald Verlag, 1969.

Zurcher, Arnold J. *The Experiment with Democracy in Central Europe.* New York: Oxford University Press, 1933.

Other periodicals consulted:

Chicago Journal of Commerce
Colliers
Hrvatski Glas
Jugoslavenski Glasnik
New Republic
Russkoe Slovo
Srbobran
Time
Washington Times Herald

Wire services consulted:
Associated Press (daily dispatches)
International News Service (daily dispatches)
United Press (daily dispatches)

These wire services reflected the American perception of Yugoslavia's accession to the Tripartite Pact and the German invasion after the coup.

Index

Bullitt, William C., 45, 47
Buria, Mirko, 142
Butterfield, Sir Herbert, 10

Campbell, Sir Ronald: and coup against Paul, 67, 117, 129; discussion with Lane about Turkish-Yugoslav relations, 97; Lane's opinion of, 96; London directives, 74, 102–103, 117; Maček meeting, 103–104; Simović discussions, 133–34; on Yugoslavia neutrality, 34, 37, 62–63, 101
Carnegie Endowment for International Peace, 169–70
Carnelutti, Amadeo, 33
Carol, King of Rumania, 67
Cassini, Oleg, 110
Catholic Church, Croatia, 58
Cerf, Bennett, 125
Chamberlain, Neville: demand of Balkan states, 31; Hitler/Mussolini meeting, 45; Italy's invasion of Albania, 31; on Roosevelt's peace strategy, 41; Scandinavian expedition, 56; Soviet Union, 36, 56
Chetniks, 110–11, 125, 153–54
Chicago Daily News, 26, 79, 121, 144, 159
Christian Science Monitor, 110, 126
Churchill, Sir Winston: accommodation with Germany, 60–61; communications with Roosevelt, 50, 60, 69, 104–105, 118; communication with Cvetković, 113; coup against Paul, 114, 117–18, 128; Donovan meeting, 80, 83, 87; on German vulnerability, 83; on Germany-Soviet conflict, 80, 152; Greece intervention strategy, 64, 66–67, 68, 159; post-coup Turkey/ Yugoslavia proposal, 133; Scandinavian expedition, 56; Soviet Union alliance efforts, 56; on U.S. alliance importance, 60; U.S. intelligence partnership, 62; on Yugoslav communism, 163; and Yugoslav neutrality, 96–97
Ciano, Galeazzo: Bombelles' report, 33; Brenner Pass meeting, 44–45; communication with Antunescu, 47;

on European approval of Mussolini ambitions, 43; on Göering's visit, 41; Hull's communication, 46; Maček proposal, 33; on Mussolini-Hitler relations, 65; on Nazi-Soviet pact, 43; Welles' visits, 44, 45; Yugoslav-Italian alliance negotiations, 75
Cincar Marković, Aleksandar: on Donovan's visit, 84; on Fortier's military plan, 55; Hitler meetings, 34, 75–76; Lane's accusation, 42; Lane's communication, 95; surrender negotiations, 144; Tripartite Pact negotiations, 94, 99–100, 116
Clarke, C. S. "Noby," 64, 129
Communist Party, Yugoslavia, 59–60, 63, 85–86, 87–89, 154
Conseils sur la conduite à suivre par la Serbie (Czartorysky), 12
Coolidge, Calvin, 156
Ćosić, Dobrica, 161–62
Cosmelli, Guiseppe, 94–95
coup against Prince Paul: British influence, 8, 67, 87, 113–14, 117–18, 128–29, 160, 179–80; Donovan's role, 85, 89, 92, 93, 159; Germany's response, 93–94, 134, 135–36; Italy's response, 134; Lane's assessment, 67, 138; Maček's response, 119, 124–25, 137; Paul's knowledge of, 114; press encouragement of, 78, 121–23, 129; Serbian Orthodox Church, 109; Simović's role, 83, 93, 118–19, 179–80; Soviet Union views, 86, 88–89; Sulzberger's awareness, 101; U.S. influence, 114, 118–19, 129–30
Cripps, Sir Stafford, 56, 71, 106
Croatia: Allied consideration of Italian interests, 47–49, 54–55; characterized, 12, 111, 127; independence declaration, 141, 144–45, 151; Italian/ German occupation of, 136, 153; Lane's assessment of Cvetković-Maček government, 37–38; response to Yugoslav ideal, 17–18. *See also* Maček, Vladimir (Vladko); news media coverage; Yugoslavia, military collapse

45; intelligence operations, 61, 62; Italy's Albania invasion, 29–30, 31; Italy's war declaration, 46; non-interference policy in Yugoslavia, 6; Paul's opinion of, 96; Paul's visit, 35, 36, 37; peace appeals to Italy, 43–44, 45–46, 47; relations with France, 156; Scandinavian expedition, 55–56; Serbians as Yugoslav policy focus, 48; Soviet Union alliance efforts, 56, 71, 87; Turkey alliance negotiations, 90–91, 97–98, 107, 133; U.S. trade/peace proposal, 45; Yugoslavia neutrality importance, 36–37, 73–74, 96–97; Yugoslavia's accession to Tripartite pact, 113, 114–15, 117. *See also* Campbell, Sir Ronald; Churchill, Sir Winston

Great Britain, intervention in Greece: Churchill's communication to Roosevelt, 104–105; Churchill's strategy, 64, 66–67, 68, 159; and Donovan's Turkish alliance efforts, 90–91; Eden's meetings, 100–103, 106–107; Metaxas' assessment, 70, 78; Pell's assessment, 69–70; *Politika* reporting, 112

Greece: on Balkan collective front, 55; Balkan Wars (1912–13), 13; Communist Party, 88; neutrality policy with Italy, 48

Greece-Axis conflict: British response, 64, 66–67, 68, 69–70, 74–75, 100–103, 104–105, 106–107, 159; Bulgarian border vulnerability, 82; German intervention, 159–60; Mussolini's attack, 65–66; *Politika* reporting, 112; U.S. intervention, 81, 89–90, 131; Yugoslavia's response, 66, 69. *See also* Salonika, Greece

Gregorić, Danilo, 75, 94
Gruber, Peter, 174
Gunther, Franklin, 52

Halder, Franz, 54
Halifax, Lord (Edward Frederick Lindley Wood), 31
Hanau, Julius, 129
Harding, Warren, 4

Hart, B. H. Liddell, 152
Hassell, Urlich von, 100
Heeren, Viktor von: and attack on Yugoslavia, 135–36; on Germany's Croatia policy, 31; Germany-Yugoslavia negotiations, 75, 76, 99, 103, 133; on Yugoslavia's appeal for German assistance, 66
Henderson, Sir Nevile, 5–6
Hess, Rudolph, 61
Higgins, Trumball, 152
Higham, Robin, 89, 91, 163
historical bias effects, 10–11
Hitler, Adolph: coup against Paul, 135, 136; Croatia plans, 136; invasion of Greece, 65, 159–160; invasion of Soviet Union, 65, 80, 152; Marković meetings, 34, 75–76; Mussolini's opinion of, 65; Paul meetings, 34–35, 98–99, 100–101; Roosevelt's communications, 41; strategy against Britain, 61, 65; Welles' visit, 44; Yugoslav-Axis alliance negotiations, 75–77, 98–99, 100–101, 116; at Yugoslavia signing of Tripartite Pact, 116. *See also* Germany
Hitler-Mussolini communications: about Yugoslavia, 59, 135; Albania invasion, 30; Brenner Pass meeting, 44; Poland campaign, 35; Yugoslavia, 59, 135
Hoover, J. Edgar, 62
Horsman, Reginald, 13
Horvat, Alexander, 170
Hull, Cordell: communications to Soviets, 57, 70; communications with Yugoslavia, 95, 96, 105; communication with Taylor, 46; coup against Paul, 119; Croatian autonomy negotiations, 23, 28; on Donovan's mission, 79–80, 82, 87, 143; Italy's invasion of Albania, 29; Kennedy's communication, 36; on Maček, 119, 138–39; Munich settlement, 26; peace strategy beliefs, 57; response to attack on Yugoslavia, 141; trade negotiations with Yugoslavia, 38; on U.S. support for British, 105

coup against Paul, 67, 138; Croatia autonomy negotiations, 29, 33, 35–36, 38–39, 53–54, 58, 158; on Cvetković-Maček government, 37–38; Donovan visit, 82–83, 84, 87, 88; election prediction, 27; on Italy-Yugoslavia relations, 66; on Kulovec, 77; on Maček, 52–53, 138; on Nazi-Soviet pact, 52; news media use, 108–109, 111; Ninčić meeting, 132–33; Paul's communications, 29, 32–33, 52, 95–96, 115, 116; on Pavelić, 60; resignation request, 59; response to Germany's attack on Yugoslavia, 141–42; Simonvić reassurance request, 132; on Soviet presence in Belgrade, 63; Stepinac's speech, 53; on Turkish-Yugoslav relations, 97; war precautions, 132; Washington's directives, 28, 29, 114, 118–19; on Yugoslav-German alliance negotiations, 76–77, 97, 104, 114–16, 161; Yugoslav gold conversion request, 105–106; Yugoslavia expertise, 27, 36, 42, 52; on Yugoslavia neutrality, 36, 42, 58, 63; on Yugoslavia war readiness, 67, 84; on Yugoslav military collapse, 127, 149–50

Lane, Margaret, 77

Laski, Harold J., 126

La Yugosavie en Peril (Pezet & Simondet), 5

League of Nations, 17, 18, 21, 145, 171–72, 176

Lebedev, Viktor Z., 133–34

Lebovich, Ivan, 172

Lend-Lease Act (1940), 69, 109

Life, 149

linguistic nationalism, 12, 15–16

Lippmann, Walter, 69, 124

Little Entente treaty, 18, 130

Ljotić, Dimitrije, 73, 122, 153, 161

Loraine, Percy, 47

Lorković, Mladen, 151

Macedonia: Alexander assassination, 18; autonomy aspirations, 145; and Bulgaria, 13, 21, 153; Serbian terrorism, 169

Maček, Vladimir (Vladko): appeals for support of Croatian autonomy, 22–23, 30, 32; Campbell meeting, 103–104; coup against Paul, 119, 124–25, 137–39; on Croatian autonomy negotiations, 28, 158; Croatian front leadership, 18; on Donovan's visit, 84; election outcome, 27–28; on German troops in Bulgaria, 84; on Germany relations, 62, 67; Italy alliance negotiations, 30, 33; negotiations with Germany, 99–100, 138–40; Paul's opinion, 32–33; post-Croatian agreement leadership, 37–38, 52–53, 60; resignation, 143; trial on "treason" charges, 167–68, 171; and Yugoslavia military collapse, 143, 151

Mackay, Sally, 37, 97

Mackensen, Georg von, 64

Mackenzie, Devitt, 124

Maclean, Fitzroy, 163

MacMurray, John V. A., 29, 82, 91, 97

MacVeagh, Lincoln, 52, 81, 87, 90, 102

Maglione, Luigi, 48

Mameli, Francesco, 133, 134, 139

Mappleback, T. G., 129

Markham, Reuben, 20, 120–21, 122, 124–25, 126–27

Massaryk, Thomas, 7

Matchek, Vladko. *See* Maček, Vladimir (Vladko)

McDonald, A. H. H., 118, 129, 179–80

media. *See* news media coverage

Meily, John, 28, 34, 58, 138, 150–51

Memminger, Robert N., 37

Menzies, Sir Stewart, 79

Messersmith, George, 22

Meštrović, Ivan, 14, 103, 131

Metaxas, Ioannis, 70, 78, 89, 101

Mihailović, Draža, 64, 111, 153–54, 161

Mihota, Anna, 172

Mikoyan, Anastas I., 137

Milanovanić, Nikola, 129

Miles (U.S. General), 48

Milićević, Todor, 147

Milichevich, ? (Serbian police attaché), 174

Mirković, Bora, 93, 129

Mitchell, Ruth, 125
Moffat, Pierrepont, 23
Montenegro, 153, 170
moral embargo, Roosevelt's, 27, 156
moral engagement, Roosevelt's
    translation, 60, 61–62
Mossner, Eugene, 55
Mowver, Edgar E., 121
Mussolini, Benito: Albanian strategies,
    30–31; alliance with Croatian
    revolutionaries, 18, 28, 43, 48, 49, 59,
    145; Balkan domination goals, 7–8,
    46; Brenner Pass meeting, 44–45;
    Croatia interests, 18, 34, 47–48, 49,
    54; early British opinion of, 156;
    Göering meeting, 32; Greece
    invasion, 65–67; on Hitler, 65; on
    Nazi-Soviet pact, 43; Paul meeting,
    32; Roosevelt's communications, 41,
    46; war declaration, 46; Welles'
    meetings, 44, 45; Yugoslav alliance
    negotiations, 75, 94–95; Yugoslav
    enmity, 18, 59. See also Hitler-
    Mussolini communications; Italy

Načartanije (Garašanin), 12
Nalich, Magda, 172
National Policy Committee, U.S., 42–
    43
National Salvation government
    (Serbia), 153, 161
Native's Return: An American
    Immigrant Visits Yugoslavia and
    Discovers His Old Country, The
    (Adamic), 6
Nazi-Soviet pact, 40, 43, 52
Nedeljković, P. (General), 146–47
Nedić, Milan: on Croatia conditions,
    67; dismissal by Paul, 72–73;
    German collaboration, 122; military
    role in Germany conflict, 148;
    National Salvation leadership, 148,
    153, 161
neutrality. See isolationism policy, U.S.;
    Yugoslavia, neutrality stance
news media coverage: Alexander's
    dictatorship, 6, 19, 20; anti-Yugoslav
    leadership slant, 77, 78, 110–11, 112–
    13, 121–23, 129; British resources for

Greece intervention, 112; Chetnik
    glorification, 125; Croatian indepen-
    dence, 144–45; Finland conflict, 55;
    German advances into Yugoslavia,
    142; Italian, 52–53, 108–109, 134;
    Lane's use, 108–109, 111; post-coup
    military expectations, 123–26; pro-
    Serbian slant, 109–11, 112–13, 120–21,
    129–30; Yugoslavia signing of
    Tripartite Pact, 116–17; Yugoslav
    military collapse, 126–27, 142–43,
    144, 146–47, 148–49
New York Herald-Tribune, 122
New York Times, 77, 110, 111, 121, 126
Nikola, King of Montenegro, 153, 170
Ninčić, Momćilo: Italian proposal for
    Yugoslav troop deployment, 139;
    Lane meeting, 132–33; negotiations
    with Germany, 133, 134–35; post-
    coup position on Tripartite Pact, 131,
    160–61; Soviet Union negotiations,
    136
Non-Aggression and Neutrality Pact
    (Italy-Yugoslavia), 43
non-interference policy, U.S. See
    isolationism policy, U.S.
North American Review, 11–12
Norway, Scandinavian expedition, 55–56

Oreski, Janja, 172

Palmer, Frederick, 124
Papas, ? (Greek journalist), 101
Partizan Movement, 154, 161
Pashich (Pasic), Nikola (Premier of
    Serbia), 170, 171
Paul, Prince of Yugoslavia: on British
    presence in Greece, 74–75; on
    Bulgaria, 83, 96, 116; on
    Chamberlain's demand, 31; commu-
    nications with Lane, 29, 32–33, 52,
    95–96, 114–15, 116; Croatian
    autonomy negotiations, 23, 28, 37,
    158; Croatia visit, 52, 53; Cvetković
    appointment, 23, 28; Eden's
    communications, 102–103, 113; exile,
    137; on French troops in Balkans, 43;
    on German troops in Bulgaria, 83;
    Germany trade policy, 19, 42, 62–63;

Great Britain alliance appeals, 35, 36, 37, 96; Greece strategy meeting, 72; Hitler meetings, 34–35, 98–99, 100–101; Italy alliance negotiations, 29, 30–31, 32, 75, 95; King George's alliance overtures, 74, 113; on Nazi-Soviet pact, 52; Nedić's dismissal, 72–73; opposition to Serbian autonomy, 54; Soviet Union relations, 57, 86; Stojadinović's dismissal, 28, 30, 109, 157–58; on U.S. neutrality over Poland, 52; Yugoslav gold conversion request, 105–106. *See also* coup against Prince Paul

Pavelić, Ante: alliance with Mussolini, 18, 28, 43, 48, 49, 145; assassination attempts, 173, 174; Bombelles' request for meeting, 33; Croatian front leadership, 18, 145; Lane's report on popularity, 60. *See also* Ustaša movement

peace strategy, U.S.: European neutrals' agreement, 45; and Italy's territorial claims, 41, 46, 47–49, 54–55, 56; motives for, 40–41, 42–43; obstacles, 51; Roosevelt's communications, 41–42, 45–46; Welles' European visit, 43, 44–45. *See also* isolationism policy, U.S.

Peal, Herbert C., 52
Pearson, Drew, 113, 122
Pećanac, Kosta, 125, 161
Pell, Herbert C., 69–70
Perchec, Gustav, 174
Perchevich (Percević), Ivo (Colonel), 174
Perich (Perić), Ninko, 171
Perišić, Milisav, 103
Pernar, Ivan (Dr.), 167
Perović, Ivo, 99
Perth, Lord (Sir James Eric Drummond), 30
Pertinax, André, 122
Pešić, Petar, 9, 72, 99–100
Pešić, Sava, 123
Peter, King of Yugoslavia, 19, 38, 137, 151
Petrov, Vladimir, 20, 26, 27, 141–42
Petrović, Svetoslav-Sveta, 78

Petrovich (Petrović), Woislav M., 14, 15, 174
Pezet, Ernest, 5
Philip of Hesse (Prince), 30
Phillips, William, 30, 46, 108, 143
Pilar, Ivo, 3
Plotnikov, V. L., 63
poetry, Slavic, as racial nationalism, 11, 12–13
Poland campaign, 35, 36, 42, 43, 52
Politika, 112, 117
Popović, Uglješa, 85
Popović, Žarko, 64
Poropat, ?, 172
Pozzi, Henri, 4, 17, 20–21
press coverage. *See* news media coverage
Pribičević, Svetozar, 4–5
Princip, Gavrilo, 170–71

Rachich, Punisha, 167, 170, 171
Radaković, Milan, 147
Radić, Stjepan, 17–18, 166, 168, 171
Radica, Bogdan: communication about U.S. neutrality, 77; on Donovan's mission, 91–92; on Fotić's radio project, 78; LaFollette conversation, 112; Smyth meeting, 150; on U.S. press coverage, 77, 109, 110
Radich, Pavle, 167
Radich, Stephan. *See* Radić, Stjepan
Radin, George, 93, 130
Radosavljevich, Paul R., 16
Rapp, Thomas G., 103, 137
refugee repatriation, German, 67
Rendell, George W., 95–96
Ribbentrop, Joachim von, 44, 76, 99, 103, 140
Ribnikar, Vladimir, 112
Ristić, Dragiša N., 129
romanticizing of Serbia, U.S., 11–13
Roosevelt, Franklin D.: arms embargo, 38; British intelligence partnership, 62; communications with Churchill, 50, 60, 69, 104–105, 118; coup against Paul, 118–19; and Croatian-Serbian tensions, 19, 22–23, 49–50, 151; Donovan's communications, 87, 91; Donovan's London trip, 68–69;

Eastern European Studies

Stjepan G. Meštrović, Series Editor

Cigar, Norman. *Genocide in Bosnia: The Policy of "Ethnic Cleansing."* 1995.

Cohen, Philip J. *Serbia's Secret War: Propaganda and the Deceit of History.* 1996.

Gachechiladze, Revaz. *The New Georgia: Space, Society, Politics.* 1996.

Gibbs, Joseph. *Gorbachev's Glasnost: The Soviet Media in the First Phase of Perestroika.* 1999.

Knezys, Stasys, and Romanas Sedlickas. *The War in Chechnya.* 1999.

Meštrović, Stjepan G., ed. *The Conceit of Innocence: Losing the Conscience of the West in the War against Bosnia.* 1997.

Polokhalo, Volodymyr, ed. *The Political Analysis of Postcommunism: Understanding Postcommunist Ukraine.* 1997.

Quinn, Frederick. *Democracy at Dawn: Notes from Poland and Points East.* 1997.

Shlapentokh, Vladimir; Christopher Vanderpool; and Boris Doktorov, eds. *The New Elite in Post-Communist Eastern Europe.* 1999.

Teglas, Csaba. *Budapest Exit: A Memoir of Fascism, Communism, and Freedom.* 1998.